Law and Theology
in the Middle Ages

Law and Theology in the Middle Ages examines the tension between ecclesiastical and secular authority in mediaeval Europe by focusing upon the relationship between legal and theological responses to concepts such as justice, mercy, fairness and sin. Central themes, such as the fundamental differences between virtue and keeping the peace, and sin and breaking the law, are used to illustrate a wide range of practical and theoretical areas of dispute in a clear and accessible way.

A unique introduction to a fascinating subject, *Law and Theology in the Middle Ages* is a thought-provoking exploration of the relationship between the academic study of law and theology in the Middle Ages.

G. R. Evans teaches mediaeval theology and intellectual history at the University of Cambridge. She is the author of *Philosophy and Theology in the Middle Ages* and *Fifty Key Medieval Thinkers*, both published by Routledge.

Law and Theology in the Middle Ages

G. R. Evans

London and New York

First published 2002
by Routledge
11 New Fetter Lane, London EC4P 4EE

Simultaneously published in the USA and Canada
by Routledge
29 West 35th Street, New York, NY 10001

Routledge is an imprint of the Taylor & Francis Group

© 2002 G. R. Evans

Typeset in Sabon by Taylor & Francis Books Ltd
Printed and bound in Great Britain by University Press, Cambridge

All rights reserved. No part of this book may be reprinted or
reproduced or utilised in any form or by any electronic,
mechanical, or other means, now known or hereafter
invented, including photocopying and recording, or in any
information storage or retrieval system, without permission in
writing from the publishers.

British Library Cataloguing in Publication Data
A catalogue record for this book is available from the British Library

Library of Congress Cataloging in Publication Data
A catalog record for this book has been requested

ISBN 0–415–25327–6 (hbk)
ISBN 0–415–25328–4 (pbk)

Contents

Preface   vii
List of abbreviations   viii

Introduction: law and theology   1

PART I
Good behaviour   5

 1 The justice of God   7
 2 Sin and breaking the law   11
 3 The public interest?   20

PART II
Theology and putting law into order   27

 4 Paradoxes   29
 5 Mapping the law   31
 6 The court system   42

PART III
Theology and the teaching of law   47

 7 Law schools   49
 8 Creating the academic discipline of law   52
 9 The professional advocate   61
 10 A moot point: disputations as academic exercises   69
 11 Legal argument and the mediaeval study of logic   76

PART IV
Law and theology in procedure   **81**

12 The theory and the practice   83

13 Equity and the mediaeval idea of fairness   85

14 The development of procedural treatises: the process   91

15 Natural justice   105

PART V
Inquiry, inquisition and summary procedure   **121**

16 Notoriety   123

17 Shortening the process   130

PART VI
Outcomes   **137**

18 Divine judgement, human judgement   139

19 Judicial discretion   144

20 Evidence   147

21 Sentencing   152

22 Appeal   159

23 Justice and mercy   162

24 Conclusion: confession, punishment and the hope of salvation   167

Notes   176
Bibliography   239
Index   252

Preface

'I am going to discuss the question why the catholic Church was not a federal state,' said Frederick William Maitland in a letter to A. V. Dicey about July 1896.[1] Mediaeval theology and the history of the study and practice of the law in the Middle Ages are both now established disciplines, each with its specialist scholars. The mediaeval student did not necessarily make the same distinctions. It was not even clear to Maitland that it was necessary to draw them, and much of the originality of his work lies in its cross-reference between the areas of study which have since been boxed artificially into compartments.

Maitland was driven partly by the perceptions, which came upon him as he explored the territory, that there were connections. He mentions in a letter to James Bradley Thayer that not much was yet known about 'our ancient modes of trial'.[2] But he was also moved by the need to persuade his readership of the importance of what was to be learned from the study of mediaeval law. 'Important conclusions are to be gained thereby.'[3] More recent work has concentrated on the implications for political theory and there is now no question of the 'importance' of the study of mediaeval law in that area. 'To sketch in outline the growth of the *Corpus Iuris Canonici* from the appearance of Gratian's *Decretum* to the outbreak of the Great Schism, is, in effect, to record the process by which the Church became a body politic, subject to one head and manifesting an external unity of organization.'[4]

Far less has been done in a systematic way on the relationship of law and theology. This is a study which thus moves perforce across disciplinary boundaries which have been more sharply drawn since Maitland's day. It does so without apology. Just as a liturgy carries a theology in every line, so canon law and law at large in the Middle Ages ride upon theology, and theology provides a rationale and underpinning and challenge to its principles. It was undeniably an uneasy relationship but it was inescapable that there should be some relationship; there was too much common ground of subject-matter for there to be any possibility of keeping the two disciplines truly distinct.[5] It is the purpose of this book to explore their relationship through the eyes of the mediaeval theorists and practitioners who wrestled with the problem.

Abbreviations

Anselm of Canterbury, *Opera Omnia*	Anselm of Canterbury, *Opera Omnia*, ed. F.S. Schmitt (Rome/Edinburgh, 1938–68)
Aquinas, *ST*	Aquinas, Thomas, *Summa Theologiae, Opera Omnia* (Parma,1852–73), 25 vols
Baldus	Baldus, *Super Decretalibus* (Lyons, 1551)
Baldus, *Digest*	Baldus de Ubaldis, *Commentarius ad Digestum vetus* (Venice, 1616)
CCCM	*Corpus Christianorum Continuatio Medievalis*
CCSL	*Corpus Christianorum Series Latina*
CSEL	*Corpus Scriptorum Ecclesiasticorum Latinorum*
Digest	*Digesta Iustiniani Augusti*, ed. T. Mommsen (Berlin, 1870), 2 vols
Gratian, *Decretum*	Gratian, *Decretum, Corpus Iuris Canonici*, ed. A. L. Richter and E. Friedberg (Leipzig, 1881)
Horn, *Aequitas*	Horn, Norbert, *Aequitas in den Lehren des Baldus* (Graz, 1968)
Irnerius, Fitting	*Summa Codicis des Irnerius*, ed. H. Fitting (Berlin, 1894)
Isidore, *Etymologiae*	Isidore, *Etymologiae*, ed. W. M. Lindsay (Oxford, 1911)
Lottin	Lottin, O., *Psychologie et morale aux xiie et xiii siècles*, V (Louvain, 1959)
Magerl, *Typologie*	Fowler-Magerl, L. *Ordines iudiciarii et libelli de ordine iudiciorum, Typologie*, Fasc. 63 (1994)
MGH	*Monumenta Germaniae Historica*
PL	*Patrologia Latina*, ed. J. P. Migne (Paris)
Quellen	*Quellen zur Geschichte des Römische-Kanonischen Prozesses im Mittelalter*, ed. L.Wahrmund (Innsbruck, 1905–31)
Summa *'Elegantius'*	Summa *'Elegantius'*, ed. G. Fransen and S. Kuttner, *Monumenta iuris canonici: Corpus Glossatorum*, 1 – (New York, 1969–)

Introduction
Law and theology

In the twelfth century Stephen of Tournai describes the embarrassment of trying to find a menu for his two dinner guests which they will both enjoy.

> I have invited the theologian and the lawyer, who have different preferences, for one delights in what is bitter, the other in what is sweet. If I write about the law the theologian will be displeased. If I write about theology, the lawyer will tear his hair. They must make allowances for one another.[1]

Law and theology were becoming 'higher degree' subjects in the developing new universities of twelfth- and thirteenth-century Europe, the period with which we shall be chiefly concerned. They attracted the ablest minds. Theology would go beyond the law in its sophistication of treatment of a topic which turned out to be of common concern, such as transubstantiation.[2] Then the law would provide a clarification from its own point of view. Or the exchange might go the other way, led by the academic lawyers with the theologians hastening in their wake.

The rivalry was unavoidable where there was so much common ground and so much of it involved vested interests. The central Middle Ages was an important period in the development of the doctrine of the Church, not merely ecclesiology itself, but also, and rather pressingly, the theory of the relation of ecclesiastical to secular authority. Stephen of Tournai comments that, 'There are two peoples in the same state and under the same king, living two lives and under two jurisdictions, clergy and laity, spiritual and carnal, *sacerdotium* and *regnum*.'[3]

One area of unavoidable competition between the two court systems, spiritual and secular, was thrown into prominence by the Becket controversy in England in the mid-twelfth century. Many offences could in principle be tried either in a secular or in an ecclesiastical court. The penalties available to a Church court, although excommunication could take one to hell in the end, were not life-threatening in this world, and so there was a good deal of incentive to get oneself tried there and not in the King's court. Henry II took exception to this. Experts were called in. The theologians and the lawyers became involved.[4] In the same period, the English master of the epistolary art and legal author Peter of Blois describes a jostling for superiority between secular law (*leges*) and ecclesiastical laws (*canones*). He says that a case is ecclesiastical only if the cause of action is one which cannot be heard except before an ecclesiastical judge.[5] Under this rule, even quite senior members of the clerical estate could be called to account in the secular courts throughout the later Middle Ages. The bishop of Worcester was put on trial in the reign of Edward I for excommunicating servants of the King's uncle because they had arrested a thief on the bishop's lands. The bishop had erred in seeking to arrogate to himself the royal jurisdiction over thieves.[6] When powerful individuals with a great deal at stake could find themselves being called to account in this way, the theoretical questions attaching to the separation of the two jurisdictions were of more than academic interest to lawyers and theologians.

There was also an area of disputed ground over the question whether a matter belonged to the spiritual or the forensic arena. The priest exercising the power of the keys was judge of the penitent sinner. The penitent confessed and if the priest judged him to be sincerely repentant and intending to lead a new amended life, he was granted absolution, and a penalty was exacted. Theologians and lawyers debated the ways in which the role of the priest in this process differed from that of a judge in a court, who makes similar judgements and also sets a penalty. Behind that question loomed the larger one of the difference between committing a sin and breaking the law, which we shall come to in a moment. The need for practical application of theological principles in areas where law also had a practical interest was urgent with the elaboration of the machinery of the penitential system from the eleventh century.

We shall watch the theologians and the lawyers argue. For it was obvious to commentators that the authoritative texts did not tell a consistent story. A major difficulty in reconciling seeming contradictions between authoritative texts in the Middle Ages was that the option of dismissing one or the other was not really available; to do that would be to treat authority with contempt. Something rather deeper than mere academic etiquette of the day ruled out that possibility. Nor did logic allow it to be said that both were true while the contradiction was allowed to remain. The task was to show that, although different, the texts in question were not in conflict.[7] Hence the use of the formula: *diversum sed non contrarium*, and its relatives.[8]

This was not by any means a new problem for the Middle Ages. Tertullian (who died early in the third century), discusses how there can be *diversitas* without contradiction in Scripture.[9] In the fourth century, Ambrose acknowledges that even if the evangelists do not seem contrary, they are diverse. How is this to be resolved unless one says that it may be possible, by some device, to take both to be true? he asks.[10] Ambrose's contemporary Augustine suggests in the *De consensus evangelistarum* that it is not a contradiction to include something which others omit.[11] Such principles were applied especially carefully to Scripture,[12] but other Christian authorities could not lightly be set aside either.

The same sort of problem began to present itself as soon as students of legal theory and practice set about creating bodies of authorities for themselves in which legal and theological texts often came confusingly together. The *De consonantia canonum*, the famous legal 'Prologue' of Ivo, Bishop of Chartres (*c*.1040–1116), travelled during the Middle Ages almost as a separate treatise on this problem of creating a unity out of disparate legal opinions.[13] Ivo says that he has made *excerptiones* from the letters of Popes, the *gesta* of Councils, treatises of the orthodox Fathers, and that he has tried to bring them together in a single corpus,[14] so that those who do not have the whole text at hand can at least have what they need.[15] He has arranged the material under titles. If the reader thinks at first that there are contradictions,[16] let him not immediately criticise: *non statim reprehendat*. Some are to be read strictly; some with a degree of flexibility; some with a view to justice: some in a spirit of mercy. This makes it possible to remove the contradictions, for justice and mercy are not in conflict,[17] and the 'merciful' reading of a given stricture will make it no longer in conflict with another, which is being read strictly.[18]

The guiding principle of interpretation, Ivo suggests, is that of *caritas*. The Christian physician adjusts the medicine to the needs of the patient. If sometimes his treatment is harsh, sometimes gentle, that is not contradictory of him.[19] This kind of thinking is borrowed from the theology and practice of penance, and yet it is being proposed for the use of lawyers.

A century later, the work of reconciling contradictions was still afoot. Peter of Blois makes a great fuss over the effort it has taken him in assiduous reading, turning over the volumes of laws and canons, catching 'canons' laying plans for rebellion,[20] so as to make a truce which will reconcile the contradictions.[21] Stephen of Tournai says that his purpose in his *Summa* on Gratian which contains the image of the mismatched dinner-party guests, was to create a unity out of his source materials and reduce contrarieties in the texts to harmony.[22] We find writers weaving together legal and theological references and assumptions. The fact that others resist this kind of thing with indignation shows how pressing was the urge to do so.

William of Pagula, one of the teachers of canon law at Oxford in the fourteenth century, made what he intended to be a comprehensive compilation of canon law and theology. His purpose was pastoral, the *regimen animarum*. He claims that it is disgraceful for lawyers not to know the law. He insists in his preface that it is equally shameful for the clergy not to have the appropriate equivalent knowledge which their calling requires. 'Therefore they ought to know the canon law and especially those things which canon law requires to be observed.'[23] But Marsilius of Padua and

Dante (in the *Monarchia*), writing as political theorists, both regarded lawyers with suspicion, fear and contempt.[24]

Our task is to explore the reasons why Stephen of Tournai's dinner guests would have been arguing as they came through the door, so as to get a picture of the extent of the common and disputed ground. For some came to realise that 'core principles' could be detected in the most confused laws and practices. In *Fleta*, a comprehensive anthology of the English system of the day written soon after 1290, the author says he has not tried to write down all the laws because there is such a confused multitude of them; the most he has been able to do is to try to draw out the ground-rules: 'there are indeed some *generalia* in the court, matters which frequently arise, which it has not seemed to me presumptuous to commit to writing'.[25]

Part I
Good behaviour

1 The justice of God

Adam and Eve handed themselves over to Satan by their own free will when they sinned. To the eyes of a feudal age, it seemed that Satan gained rights over them as their lord when they did that.[1] When God became man, it was alleged, Satan tried to extend his jurisdiction to Christ; but Christ was sinless and so Satan could have no rights over him. Had he lost his rights of dominion over the rest of humanity too by that attempted abuse of his rightful authority when he tried to make Christ his own? Would justice require that the wronged party, Christ, thus rightfully acquired the jurisdiction Satan had forfeited by his own unlawful act?[2]

It was important to make the case in this way, because otherwise God could be thought to have done Satan an injustice, or, to put it in more precise legal terms, to have committed what was technically in Roman law an 'actionable insult'[3] in taking mankind back for himself by the death of Christ.[4] For if all human flesh had been unclean, it would properly have remained subject to Satan and God would have been a thief of Satan's rightful property.[5] God would have been in the wrong in acting *contra ius diaboli*. But since Christ was free of sin, the Devil had no right (*ius*) over him.[6]

Not all contemporaries accepted this legally coloured version of the old story of the war between good and evil. In his *Cur Deus Homo*, the monastic theologian Anselm of Bec and Canterbury was insistent that the problem of human sin was a matter not involving any rights of the Devil at all; he gives an account of what was needed and what was done, in which only man and God are concerned. His explanation goes deeper than feudal categories. It assumes both mutual obligation, and ownership (in feudal terms) of one person by another. But it also understands there to be a moral duty of obedience to the supreme Justice (who is God himself). The 'court case' metaphor thus rides on profounder assumptions about divine justice.

As the jurist Baldus puts it in the fourteenth century, the justice of the creator was from eternity, before the world was made;[7] but the jurisconsult can speak of such things only as a creaturely human commentator. He and the theologian are both contemplating the same supernatural reality,

8 *The justice of God*

of God acting in the judicial process of a sinful world, with the same unavoidable limitations of understanding.

The mediaeval Christian theologian and the mediaeval Christian lawyer both have to begin from the nature of God. For such thinkers it is uncontroversial that whatever God is, he is by definition that which it is to be just and true; and more, he is substantively justice itself and truth itself.[8] It follows that his actions will reflect his justice and mercy. So in order to define or discover where 'justice' and 'mercy' lie, we need to look at the clues to be found in the divine behaviour.

Yet on the face of it, the divine behaviour is contradictory if God is not only absolute justice, but also absolute mercy. Since God cannot be at war with himself, his mercy and his justice must somehow be one. It is a paradox of this attempt to balance justice and mercy, severity and relaxation of due penalty, that justice and mercy may in fact be the same thing. It is just to help one's neighbour but it is also merciful.[9] The difference is that what is done out of obligation is just, but what is done out of compassion is merciful.[10]

Anselm of Canterbury tackles variants of this problem in the late eleventh century in the *Proslogion*, where he is concerned to demonstrate not only that God exists, but all that the faith holds about the attributes which make up his nature. These are often paradoxical. In Chapter 8 Anselm explains that God can be both merciful and incapable of suffering (*impassibilis*), even though it would seem that mercy requires fellow-feeling with sufferers. Anselm argues that this is possible because although we experience his mercy as an effect, God does not 'feel' any emotion (*tu non sentis affectum*).[11] Anselm goes on in Chapter 9 to consider the 'justice and mercy' problem directly. He asks how it can be an act of supreme justice to give eternal life to those who deserve death.[12] He argues – in line with his basic principle in the treatise that God is whatever it is better to be than not to be[13] – that it must be better for God *both* to punish and to spare than for him *only* to punish.[14] To do the first is to give sinners their deserts and that is therefore just; to do the second is in accordance with God's own goodness (*bonitati tuae condecens est*) and it is therefore also just.[15] He takes this a little further in Chapter 11, where he places side by side the two apparently contradictory texts, '*All* the ways of the Lord are mercy and truth': *universae viae domini misericordia et veritas* (Psalm 24.10) and, 'Just is the Lord in *all* his ways': *iustus dominus in omnibus viis suis* (Psalm 144.17). These he reconciles with the explanation that those whom God wishes to punish, it is just to punish and those to whom he wishes to show mercy it is just to save.[16] The justice and mercy of God are thus applied or deployed 'appropriately' for each sinner.

This Anselmian position, although it contains elements peculiarly Anselm's own, rests on assumptions set out by Augustine. Augustine argues that God condemns all men justly, for in Adam all have sinned. In the *Enchiridion*[17] Augustine says:

Would it not have been just that such a being who rebelled against God, who in the abuse of his freedom spurned and transgressed the command of his Creator when he could so easily have kept it, who defaced in himself the image of his creator by stubbornly turning away from his light, who by an evil use of his free-will broke away from his wholesome bondage to the Creator's laws – would it not have been just that such a being should have been wholly and to all eternity deserted by God and left to suffer the everlasting punishment he had so richly earned? God would certainly have done so, if he had been only just and not also merciful. He intended that his unmerited mercy should shine forth the more brightly in contrast with the unworthiness of its objects.

Mediaeval theologians are concerned with yet another contradiction arising out of this puzzle about justice and mercy. God sets a standard of justice which is beyond the attainment of fallen humanity. It is therefore one which all human beings have in fact failed to meet, and which thus involves God himself in a sort of 'litigation' with sinful men, and in its turn it prompts actual lawsuits in the ordinary world. 'As Justinian bears witness', he says, human nature is ready and prone to sin, so that daily, one after another, quarrels start and lawsuits multiply. This in itself directly generates litigation.[18] The administration of justice, in the system and the period with which we are concerned, is inseparable from the assumption of the – 'positively pullulating' – universal sinfulness of the human condition, as Bernardus Dorna the procedural theorist of a century after Anselm, puts it.[19] At this contradictory interface the problem is whether God can possibly be just if he is demanding a standard of behaviour which it is impossible for fallen human beings to attain.

There is further underlying tension here, between an immutable standard set by God in divine law, and the legitimate *variability* of human law, both in its framing in different places, and in its application to different persons. In the famous tag, the *Digest* defines justice as the constant and enduring will to give each what is proper to him. *Iustitia est constans et perpetuum voluntas ius suum cuique tribuens*.[20] Cicero had said something very similar. In the *De Inventione* he takes it that justice is a habit or disposition of mind maintained for the common good, and respecting each as he should be respected: *Iustitia est habitus animi communi utilitate conservata suam cuique tribuens dignitatem*.[21]

The principle that justice is the will to ensure that everyone always[22] gets his just deserts, with its requirement that justice should be adapted to individuals and circumstances, makes for untidiness and for inequity. Thus a twelfth-century commentator asks, knowing he is posing a crucial question, whether right itself is immutable (*ius immobile*).[23]

There is a late fourth-century story in Jerome's first *Letter* of a trial in which the possibility is canvassed of the law saying one thing, the divine requirements of justice another. At the proposed execution of an innocent woman mistakenly found guilty of adultery,[24] it proved at first impossible to get the sword to cut into the woman's flesh.[25] She who was condemned by the judge was absolved by the sword, says Jerome.[26] For the sword here was ultimately in God's hand.

So the administration of justice in the Middle Ages is expected to answer ultimately to a higher authority than the judiciary, or indeed the legislature,[27] of a given time and place. But at the same time, issues of justice and injustice have a well-defined forensic context, either literally or metaphorically, and in that forensic context particularities tend to challenge, and even sometimes seem to interfere with, justice at its purest and highest.

To the pragmatist lawyer, the law is simply 'a body of rules prescribing external conduct and considered justiciable'.[28] This recognition that the pursuit of absolute justice and the conduct of litigation are different things is a key point at which the theologian and the lawyer find themselves unable to speak the same language of expectations. The mediaeval theologian deals in absolutes. The lawyer adjusts his categories to the matter in hand. They are both doing so with an eye on a divine standard of justice which, while in principle absolute, is also complex in the face it presents to mankind, and especially to those, theologians and lawyers, whose professional task it is to make sense of it.

2 Sin and breaking the law

Sins and legal offences

Almost every baptised person in the mediaeval West would accept that all human beings are sinners who *deserve* to be punished, by a God whose justice may express itself in mercy and prove to be full of surprises, but cannot compromise the divine and ultimate standard. Nevertheless, it does not follow that the whole human race, placed as they are in a category of *iniusti* in the sight of God, ought to find themselves in court. The law is not interested in the sinful 'condition', or even in specific sins. For not all actual sin involves breaking the law. The law is interested in acts committed against the law.

The Church 'deals with' sin in different ways from those in which the law deals with offences, for reasons which arise out of essential differences between sinning and breaking the law.

In the public penance of the early Church, the murderer, adulterer or apostate was identified before the congregation. Everyone knew who he was. He wore special penitential garments and sat apart from the rest of the congregation. The bishop was his judge and excommunicated him, and he might be restored to the community if at all, only after he had 'served his sentence'. Although from Carolingian times[1] the penitential system ceased to be a public exposure of the serious sinner and could deal with secret sins (which might never be known except to God, the sinner and the confessor), an offence against the law has to be *shown* to have been committed before someone can be punished. It must be *visible*. Aquinas discusses the difference between legal and moral obligation partly in terms of a distinction between acts in the judicial arena which are *seen* to have been wrong; and offences of which only God may know.

In divine law, God is the judge and he is omnicompetent.[2] He sets the rules, and only he knows whether each person has kept them. Human law can impose penalties only about things on which the law-giver has competence to judge (*de quibus legislator habet iudicare*).[3] Those things must be tested openly in court; for it is on the basis of judgement arrived at in that way, that law punishes: *quia ex iudicio lex punit*.

Cicero's definition of justice in the *De Inventione* (II. 53) we have already touched on. It says that justice is a habit or disposition of mind maintained for the common good, and respecting each as he should be respected.[4] Abelard makes use of this Ciceronian definition in his *Dialogus*,[5] and it came to have a very general mediaeval currency. It introduces three principles. The first is that justice (which we might here translate as 'righteousness') is an attitude or stance of the person, understood as a rational and intellectual being, for it is in 'the mind'. The second is that justice is measurable against a 'common' rather than an individual good. The third is that it honours a social order in which some are more equal than others. That is, in its context, the implication of *suam cuique tribuens dignitatem*.

The Ciceronian definitional pattern naturally does not include the Christian concept of sin, but it does include the notion of virtue. There is a further Ciceronian subdivision of the law of nature into *religio, pietas, gratia, vindicatio, observantia, veritas*, which make up the six virtues issuing from it.[6] Cicero thus creates a link between law and virtue to set beside the complementarity of 'law' and 'obedience to law'. This makes obedience to law not mere submission, but, in that it is an act of virtue, a positive as well as a creditable act. In a commentary on the *Ethica Vetus* of 1230–40, probably produced by a Master in the Arts Faculty in Paris,[7] the commentator argues that if we are speaking theologically we ought to say that a good disposition (*habitus bonus*) necessarily precedes every good work. There will, in other words, be a 'tendency' or disposition to the virtue in question.[8]

The sinner under the law

A degree of ambiguity about the difference between sin and 'offence against the law' runs as a thread through the literature. For example, in the eighth-century *Penitential* of 'Theodore' there is a mixture of elements attributable to Theodore (of Tarsus and Canterbury) with material from other sources, among which we find (I. 12) a ruling which attempts to establish a boundary between the public domain and the (by now increasingly) private realm of penance.[9] Theodore includes in a penitential code topics clearly also forensic or judicial. False witnesses are to be excommunicated unless they expunge their sin (of breaking a commandment) by doing penance.[10] Especially culpable is the bearing of false witness out of anger or resentment (*odium*) towards the accused.[11] There is discussion of perjury in a forensic context, and the number of years of penance it ought to carry as a penalty, depending on whether it was done under compulsion by a superior (*compulsus a domino suo*).[12] In Bonizo's eleventh-century *Liber de Vita Christiana*,[13] which is mainly about penance, the subjects covered once more include judicial matters, and Bonizo draws a good deal on the Ps-Isidorian *Decretals*. Gratian's treatment of penance takes up a good deal of space in the definitive mid-twelfth-century *Decretum*, in a way which suggests that for him too the penitential–judicial boundary remained problematic. *Quaestio* III of the Second Part of the *Decretum*, *Causa* XXXIII, became a veritable treatise with seven *Distinctiones* of its own.

In keeping with this blurring of boundaries, the sixth-century encyclopaedist Isidore slides without comment in his *Etymologies*, from talk of 'crime', to using the word 'sin'.[14] Isidore gives a long list of *crimina*, in which he deals fairly comprehensively with *peccata* too, although he is primarily concerned with those sins which are also covered by the law.[15] He also discusses the word *malum* in this part of his discussion, and thus makes the link with evil, though he deals with *malum* under a different head from *crimen*.[16] (There are two kinds of evils, he says, those a man does and those he suffers. The evil a man does is *peccatum*, the evil he suffers is *poena*, with a long list of pains and punishments.[17] *Malum* is at its worst, *plenum*, when it is both past and present, as in grief and fear.)[18]

A term whose developing mediaeval usage explicitly straddles the sin–crime boundary is *criminalia*. The Carolingian bishop Fulgentius of Ruspe speaks of *criminalia peccata*.[19] The phrase is commonplace in twelfth- and early thirteenth-century literature. The seven *criminalia peccata* are the seven *mortal sins*.[20] Peter of Celle sets the seven *venalia* and the seven *criminalia* over against one another: *illa dicuntur capitalia et criminalia, ista minora et venalia*.[21] Peter Abelard defines *criminalia peccata* as mortal (*mortifera, id est criminalia peccata*),[22] and Bernard of Clairvaux in the twelfth century confirms that *venalia non criminalia reputantur*.[23] Venial sins are not regarded as 'criminal'.

Law: the cause or the remedy of wrongdoing?

Would there be any need for law if there were no injustice already in the world for it to discourage or put right? Conversely, it may be asked, as it is by St Paul, whether the law somehow creates sin by defining what it consists in.[24] Jerome cites an ancient proverb to a similar effect, that the more law there is the more offences there are. *Summum ius summa iniuria*.[25]

Bernard of Clairvaux is sure there would have to be law (*lex*), even if everyone were just. Even God lives according to law, he explains in a letter to Prior Guigo and the Carthusians on *caritas*.[26] *Love* is the immaculate law of the Lord, which does not seek its own good but that of many. 'The law of the Lord' is said either to be that by which God himself lives (*quod ipse ex ea vivat*), or that which no one may possess except by his gift: *quod eam nullus nisi eius dono possideat*.[27]

These definitions do not put God *under* the law, as Bernard hastens to explain. 'Let it not seem absurd that I have said that God himself lives by the law: *nec absurdum videatur quod dixi etiam Deum vivere ex lege*. This

14 *Sin and breaking the law*

law *is* simply love. For it is love which preserves the unity of the Trinity (*ineffabilem illam conservat unitatem*). Love is law and it is God's law, and it binds in the bonds of peace (*in vinculo pacis*, Ephesians 4.3).[28] Love is the eternal law, creator and governor of the universe: *Haec est lex aeterna, creatrix et gubernatrix universitatis.*[29] Everything is made according to weight and measure and number (*Sapientia*, 11. 21), and the law of love is that measure, for nothing is left outside the law, not even law itself' (*nihil sine lege relinquitur, cum ipsa quoque lex omnium sine lege non sit*),[30] says Bernard. In this way, law is irresistible but at the same time non-constrictive.

The slave and the hireling do not follow the law of the Lord, but make up their own,[31] Bernard continues. Everyone can 'invent' law, but no one can cause the law he makes to be the law of God: *et quidem suam quisque legem facere potuerunt*. The definition of such spurious 'law-making' consists in the putting of self-will before the will of God: *quando communi et aeternae legi propriam praetulit voluntatem*. Then everyone is a law unto himself: *ut sicut ipse sibi lex suique iuris est, ita is quoque seipsum regeret, et legem sibi suam faciet voluntatem*.[32] Such self-made law creates a heavy yoke, which bends down the neck. The person who does not wish to bear the light yoke of the Lord subjects himself to his own punishing régime, of his own choice casting off the sweet light burden of love in favour of an insupportable burden.[33] The result is to make someone enslaved and unhappy.[34]

Bernard develops this theme of the contrast between the ease with which God's law can be borne, and the difficulty of enduring the rule of any other. One is a law promulgated by the spirit of slavery and in fear; the other by the spirit of freedom in gentleness. We are not forced to be children of God by the one and not allowed to be his children by the other. (In I Corinthians 9.20–1 Paul explains that he is not subject to the law of Moses.[35] The law is not made for the just man: *Iustis non est lex posita* (I Timothy 1.9), but for the sinner.)[36]

It would not be true to say that the just are not under the law. But they do not embrace it willingly.[37] The willing embracing of the law would make the 'laws' of the servant and hireling light and easy to bear.[38] Love 'fulfils the law' of the slave when it pours out devotion. It keeps the law of the hireling (*mercenarius*) when it controls disorderly desire (*cupiditas*).[39] Thomas Aquinas in the mid-thirteenth century says that it is a proper attribute of law to lead those subject to it to live as they ought to.[40] So it is for their good.[41] He also believes that there is a natural inclination of all created things to the good,[42] which is in conformity with this law.

The fourteenth-century Baldus de Ubaldis *Super Decretalibus*[43] approaches the question of the relationship between sin and breaking the law from the starting-point of creation and the obligation man owes to his Creator. This is in his view both a legal and a moral obligation, so he includes sin with breaking the law. There is a *duplex ius* for the human race: *ius aut est naturale aut morale*,[44] agrees the twelfth-century *Summa 'Elegantius'*. So if not all sins are breaches of the law and not all breaches of the law are sins, there is still a great deal of overlap, and it may not be easy, or even desirable, to make them out to be the same thing. Not everything which is 'allowed' is honest,[45] comments the *Digest* in one of its *Regulae*.

While a just God is entitled to be angry with all sinners simply because they belong to the *massa peccatrix* (the 'sinful lump' of the progeny of Adam), the law makes some mechanical allowance for differences of capacity. Ignorance of the law is no excuse, says 'Irnerius'.[46] Everyone has an obligation to know and keep the law. Yet there may be reasons to forgive ignorance. Some can be excused on the grounds that they are rustics, women, soldiers,[47] and cannot be expected to know what they should do. The *Digest* recognises a difference between an act committed in anger, where the intention forms on impulse, and one done with planning aforethought.[48] It is understood, then, that motivation may affect how seriously an offence is regarded. It is commonly accepted from patristic times that it is not murder to kill by a disciplinary beating (provided, Jerome stresses, the beating is not carried out in anger).[49]

Legal theory and moral theology

In his commentary on the *Digest* (1. i. 2), Baldus de Ubaldis says that moral philosophy (*philosophia moralis*) is the mother and the door of the law (*mater et ianua*).[50] This is the *pars philosophiae* usually given in the formal academic introductions (*accessus*) to legal texts. That is to say, university lecturers would normally call law a branch of ethics.[51]

Does the law have an ultimate authority to determine choices, an authority which overrides any putative moral obligation?[52] The first problem here is that while 'legal systems are composed of hierarchies of norms',[53] there is no clear single hierarchy taking in both *moral* and *legal* obligation. The preliminary question whether theologians and lawyers would identify wrong-doing on the same or similar principles takes us at once, as we can already see, into areas of ethics which they approach from different directions.

A person acts the more unjustly the more he is drawn to act not by love of justice but by malice, says Anselm of Canterbury.[54] Anselm's tag that 'nothing is unjust in itself',[55] makes this personal choice of a good or evil purpose a defining characteristic. He thus gives us a partially 'contextual' theory of injustice.

That line of thought is more fully developed by another theologian of the next generation, Peter Abelard. Abelard comes near to Anselm's notion of what it is which makes sin 'matter' to God when he says, 'What is consent to sin but contempt of God and an offence against him?[56] He underlines, in a very Anselmian way, that it is by a kind of *lèse-majesté* that God is offended (*ex contemptu*).[57] In Abelard's view, a 'vice of the mind' is not the same thing as a sin, and a sin is not the same thing as a bad action.[58] To be irascible is a vice, because it is a potential for wrong in the soul, even when the soul is not actually moved to anger.[59] So a vice is that by which were are made 'prone to sin',[60] that is, by which we are inclined to consent to that which it is not right to consent to. Then we either commit or omit the bad act.[61] Abelard thinks we can properly call this consent sin, which he defines as a sin of the mind which deserves condemnation, or is deemed guilt by God.[62]

Abelard is better known for holding quite strongly that what counts in deciding whether an action is sinful or not is motivation, and he would say explicitly that it is not *the act in itself* which is good or evil but the *doer's reason for doing it*. In the *Summa Sententiarum* (before 1140), the same question is raised: whether bad deeds (that is, external actions) are to be called sins. The *Summa* acknowledges that some say that all acts are indifferent in themselves.[63] There are *vicia* of the body, such as *debilitas* or blindness, which are morally neutral. There are non-moral *vicia* of mind (like being stupid), which apply to the good and the wicked alike, says Abelard.[64] Among beasts there are none which are just and unjust.[65] So 'ownership' of an act as by 'choice' a known bad act is important. Not all mediaeval thinkers would go as far as Abelard but the role of the will in making a person responsible for his sins is relatively uncontroversial, and one might underline here the role of *perseverance* in a wrong intention.

It is by no means as easy to say exactly how, or how far, intention makes an act lawful (or unlawful) as it is to sketch a 'contextual' or 'intentional' theory of moral actions from a theological point of view. But that was attempted. The lawyers were presented with questions of this sort in different ways. Canon 15 of the Second Lateran Council of 1139 refers to a situation where it is contended that the Devil has persuaded someone to lay violent hands on another.[66] Did that put the commission of the act of violence beyond the control of the perpetrator? Is the assault I commit not my fault if the Devil drives? In Distinction VI Gratian turns to the cognate question of moral responsibility for actions which seem to be beyond the control of the will, such as the emission of semen in sleep. It is argued that sin in such situations consists in taking pleasure in and consenting to what one cannot help.[67] In these and other ways persons 'forced to act' (*coacti*) for good or ill may not be held culpable.[68] Similarly, a good work done willingly (with consent) is more valuable than one done unwillingly.[69]

Practical implications: the court or the confessional?

In the privacy of the 'private'[70] system of penance, no judge is 'externally appointed' to deal specifically with the matter in hand. In one of Robert Grosseteste's letters, we find the warning that the ship of the soul should not be entrusted on the choppy and rock-strewn seas of life to a fool, a child, or someone who knows nothing about sailing.[71] But in practice that could occur; the sinner confesses privately to the priest and no one else but God knows how he deals with it. Nevertheless, even here in the sacramental context of what is indubitably a penitential process, the priest is thought of as a 'judge'. As Jerome puts it in one of his letters:

> They [the clergy] judge us, in a certain measure, before the Day of Judgement, who in sober chastity guard the Lord's Bride.[72]

> Under the Old Law, whosoever was disobedient to the priests was either put outside the camp and stoned by the people, or else the sword was put to his throat and he expiated his contempt with his blood. But now the disobedient is either cut off by the sword of the Spirit or he is cast out of the Church and torn asunder by the jaws of infuriated demons.[73]

It continued to be natural to use the phrases 'by the priest's judgement' (*iudice sacerdote*)[74] and 'the judgements of penance' (*iudicia paenitentiae*).[75] There is also a tendency for penitential canons to be described as *iudicia*.[76] Gratian's Distinction VI deals with who the confession should be made to, and the kind of person the 'judge' of other men's sins ought to be.[77]

A judge cannot be impartial if he has information which would prejudice him against the accused. But in a penitential context, he will have that information, for the penitent will trustingly have told him everything. It is true that the judicial role in a penitential context is not to decide guilt but to apportion punishment, to weigh the circumstances and the character and degree of severity of the offence, but the confessor will still, in his pastoral role, know all sorts of things which may affect his judgement. Where a priest or bishop acted as judge it was easy for him to cross the pastoral–judicial boundary. The twelfth century found some tidying up in this respect with the appointment of an official who acts as the bishop's vicar in judicial matters.[78] But the fact that this difficulty is not sharply addressed in the Middle Ages may reflect the confusion which persisted over the judicial role of the priest in a pastoral situation.

There is ample precedent in the penitential codes as well as in the ancient picking out of serious offences as requiring public penance, for the view that some wrong acts are more serious than others; but even here not all the acts typically so stressed – adultery, murder, apostasy – are in breach of the law. They make up a mixture of breach of the law and sin. Fornication, homicide and avarice appear in the penitentials, but homicide would certainly also be matter for criminal trial.

The penitential manuals provide a guide to what will be appropriate by way of penance in given circumstances. This can be equated to some degree with the *talio* of Roman law, as well as with the 'eye for an eye' of the Old Testament,[79] at least in that a quantitative assessment is made of what needs to be done about an offence. The principle is that just retribution should be proportionate: *ut taliter quis patiatur ut fecit*.[80] This can, as Isidore points out, be applied equally to the rendering of kindness for kindness, benefit for benefit, for example.[81] Just as physicians prescribe different medicines for different sicknesses, so for different faults are prescribed different penances,[82] say Carolingian monastic penitentials. Ivo of Chartres cites Leo the Great on the view that the appropriate penalty can change with circumstance.[83]

Hostiensis suggests that a wise priest will decide what is the appropriate penalty not only according to the offence but also according to the kind of person he has before him.[84] Proportionality also dictates that a long period of mild penance may fairly be exchanged for a shorter period of more severe penance. So there is a good deal of leeway for the priest's judgement in setting the tariff.

Riding on all this once more are questions about rigour and mercy. Rigour cannot rightly go beyond due proportion. In other words, the priest may not at will impose a substantially more severe sentence than the circumstances deserve. On the other hand, mercy can stop a long way before due proportion for the offence is reached. Ivo of Chartres sets out the options.

> In this way, if we take examples from past and present, we find certain leaders of the Church judged more strictly, according to the rigour of the laws, many tolerated offences because of the exigencies of the times, and many concealed things for the benefit of individuals.[85]

Purging offences and starting again

It cannot necessarily be assumed that the forgiven sinner, the reconciled penitent, the criminal who has discharged his punishment, will not offend again. This possibility of repeated offending raises in another way the conception that there may be a movement across the boundary between sin and breach-of-the-law. If a second penance is needed because offences are committed again, does that mean that the sins committed the first time 'return', that is, that they have to be deemed no longer to have been wiped out? Gratian acknowledges that there is difference of opinion on this point.[86]

In *Decretum*, II, Gratian deals directly with the 'repetition' of penance itself, which had of course been an issue for the early Christian centuries. In this early period, the question was whether penance *could* be repeated, that is, whether the sinner should be given a second or third chance. The third Distinction is about another aspect of the same issue, with Gratian explicitly raising the question of the connection between sin and breach of the law. He argues that if someone who has done penance then commits a breach of the law, his penance was false and that would mean that God did not forgive him, so he would still be accountable for it; it would still be there to be dealt with.[87] The judicial and the penitential could still be found to overlap as late as the compilation of the Gregorian *Decretals* by Raymond of Peñafort, who was also the author of an important confessors' manual of the day.

It is, on one level, easy to say what the difference is between a penitential and a judicial system. One is conducted in the confessional and the other in the courts. One leads to forgiveness and salvation and the other to a punishment, with no particular thought for the salvation of the guilty. In one the penitent confesses of his own free will; in the other the accused may fight to prove his innocence. But these categories blur in the real mediaeval world; the complexities of the distinctions can already begin to be seen even in these preliminaries.

3 The public interest?

Why should society care whether an individual behaves well or badly? Roman law and early Christian thinking had much the same answers.

Justinian, the sixth-century Emperor whose codifications of the Roman law of his time were becoming texts of renewed importance for the mediaeval lawyers, begins his Code[1] with a creed, and with the requirement that everyone should publicly conform to it. He develops the point, so as to embrace a range of aspects of religious observance and conformity. Under the first heads of the Code are grouped provisions on the privileges of Churches (1.2), heretics, Manicheans, Samaritans (1.5), non-repetition of baptism (1.6), apostates (1.7), iconoclasm (1.8), Jews and sky-worshippers (1.9), sanctuary in churches (1.12), and images (1.24). Insistence on religious unity in the state is a means of keeping order, not fundamentally different in that respect from the old Roman syncretism. (For as the Romans conquered their Empire they systematically took into their pantheon the gods of the conquered peoples, all except the Jews and Christians, who would not play.) Both syncretism and the later insistence on Christian unity have the effect of making people 'feel at one', and so conduct themselves peaceably and live together as a community. Pagan Rome sought to avoid religious conflict by rolling religious beliefs into a single (if complex) system; a Christian empire eventually sought to impose a single Christian faith as a civil requirement on all.

Justinian began from the idea of God as celestial Emperor. As he sees it, Christ 'reigns' in heaven and he founds his rule on holy religion (*qui sacra religione suum fundat imperium*); the pious ruler, by derivation and analogy, governs humankind well. Good government thus seems to be strongly equated in Justinian's mind with unity of faith. Among his surviving writings is a series on theological disputes of the day in which a main thrust is again the importance of the unity of the Church. He wrote against the Acacian Schism, the Nestorians, the Monophysites, Origen, on the *tres capituli*, with the same concern in each case that unity and the concomitant consensus of the people of God should not be disrupted. He speaks of embracing *orthodoxa religio*, 'so that the churches may be united' (*ut unirentur ecclesiae*).[2] He links the peace of the Church with peace among the people: *pro ecclesiarum pace et pro plebis concordia*.[3] Even if there is some disagreement about forms of words, all may yet be well if Catholic Christians are really of one mind (*sensus inter catholicos omnes unus*).[4]

Among the sources Justinian assembles at the beginning of the Code is a text by Theodosius and Valentinus which describes the religion which the Apostle Peter brought to the Romans. It is the faith 'according to apostolic teaching and the knowledge of the Gospel', and by it we believe the Father, Son and Holy Spirit are one deity equal in majesty in the holy Trinity.[5] This is described as a law under which good citizens are good Christians (*hanc legem sequentes*). A second source in Justinian's list identifies a legal offence of failure to hold the faith as defined at Nicaea.[6] The authority of the creed is explained. It is 'authorised' by its source and by the way it has been handed down and by its conformity with true faith and the intention that it shall endure (*semper mansura*).[7] A similar pedigree is given for the creed of Chalcedon. There is the important addition of imperial ratification of what was agreed by the bishops at the Council (*per nostra praecepta statuta sunt*).[8] That makes adherence to the faith a point of law and those who do not conform can be punished under the law (*nam in contemptores huius legis poena non deerit*), including Jews and pagans as well as unfaithful Christians and heretics. The unfaithful suffer loss of legal reputation (*infamia*).[9]

Justinian's *Edict* on the true faith explains that what pleases the divine mercy is for all Christians to hold the same correct and pure faith and that there should be no dissensions in the Church: *ut omnes Christiani unum idemque sapiant in recta et immaculata fide nec sint dissensiones in sancta dei ecclesia*.[10] This is an explicitly Christian version of 'the state at work trying to make the citizen good'.[11] All good subjects of the divine Emperor will think alike. That is one meaning of the unity of faith which has always been insisted on in the Church and it carries some of the associations of the New Testament conception of *koinonia*, actively revived in recent ecumenical dialogue.[12]

A letter of Justinian uses the tag: *pro ecclesiarum pace et pro plebis concordia*. God is still the Emperor (although the Emperor is no longer God). 'Christ reigns in heaven, who founds his *imperium* on holy religion,' says Justinian.[13]

A second persistent theme underlining the link between the holding of the true faith and the protection of the common good is the idea of the *scandalum*, or stumbling-block. An offence does not only put the offender's soul at risk. He may lead others astray. This makes sin, or breach of the law, not merely a matter between the individual and God, or between the individual and the secular judiciary, but also between the individual and the community.

Augustine mediated to the Middle Ages, and within a Christian context, a significant discussion in Cicero's *De Re Publica*.[14] Cicero says that peace in the state is like harmony in music. It unites and sustains the whole. But peace cannot exist without justice.[15] Others, he knows, would take that further and argue that government cannot be sustained without *injustice*. It can even be proposed that, in a way, injustice is an advantage to the state if it makes government possible. This is tested against the following definition of the *res publica*. A people is not just a gathering of a multitude, but a 'gathering' by consent of law and for the common benefit.[16] It is, in other words, not a disorderly rabble but a community ordered for the common good. Augustine thought that if justice, a key element of the Ciceronian definition of a 'republic', were missing, the whole structure would fall apart. If there is no justice, there cannot be a community of people bound together by a mutual recognition of rights. So that means there is no 'people'; if no people, then no 'weal' of the people; so no 'commonwealth' or *res publica*.[17] In particular, if the ruler is unjust (whether, to put it in the terms of Aristotle's *Politics*, it is a monarch, an oligarchy, the people as a whole) there is no commonwealth at all. The community in question would no longer meet the definition. There would be no concern for the common good. The people, if they were unjust, would no longer be a people but simply a mob or multitude, because the common bond would disappear.[18] This is a synthesis of a Christian idea of *koinonia*, with Augustine's hypothesis that God made human beings social but the Fall made it necessary for them to be political.

Alongside this Christian–Roman thinking we must put mediaeval understandings of the *utilitas* of the state or *res publica*. All which tends to the common good is equitable, says Baldus. 'For equity is nothing other than a certain *pietas* which concerns itself especially with the public arena', as Cicero says at the beginning of *The Dream of Scipio* where he speaks of justice and piety.[19]

There was a great distance between Cicero and Baldus, more perhaps than he realised. It consisted partly in difference in the political structures and the political climate of expectation. In Italy in Baldus' day, there were still political entities which could more or less strictly be called *res publicae*. In northern Europe the concept did not sit so squarely with the political realities. *Utilitas* too acquired new colorations and dimensions in the central Middle Ages, which gave it a beneficial character which was spiritual as well as practical.

Important authority is to be found in the thinking of Augustine's *City of God*. Augustine elaborates a Christian conception of citizenship. Citizenship of the city of God makes an individual a member of a 'community of eternity'. It unites all God's people, living, dead and not yet born, in an invisible body whose members only God can identify. Over against this is set the community of the damned, also eternal, also invisible, so that a man cannot know whether his next door neighbour is his fellow-citizen or his everlasting enemy. While mediaeval Western theologians went along with Augustine, the practical reality was that membership of the Church was treated as though it were visible. Baptism was the sign of belonging and almost everyone, except the Jews, was baptised in infancy.[20] So the secular *res publica* had much the same body of citizenry as the Church's visible 'members'. This made the requirement of harmony of faith among the people relatively straightforward to frame, if not to police, and meant that Justinian's call to consistency and conformity still chimed with the politics of a later age.

The submission of some to others

It is possible to argue, on a hierarchical view of society underpinned by these principles, that the submission of some to others is for their advantage. It protects the weak against the lawless by keeping order. On the Roman view, conquered peoples are better off than they were before.[21] An analogy Augustine favours is between *this* hierarchy and that which obtains within the individual human body. In each human being the soul is submissive to God and in its turn the soul is lord of the body.[22] If an individual human being is not in due subjection to God, there is no justice in him; then an assembly of such men and women cannot live in a just environment either. Therefore there cannot be that mutual recognition of obligations which would turn a mob into a people.[23] Augustine thinks the 'common good' binding all together into a 'people', consists primarily in this mutuality of the recognition of obligations.[24] The crowd in the case of the woman accused of adultery related in Jerome's first letter, became excited and tried to rescue her. Then the official in charge of executions appealed to them. He pointed out that if the execution did not take place, he, an innocent man, would have to die. This changed the minds of the crowd. They now felt under an obligation to let her be executed.[25] Another executioner and another sword were brought, and this time the woman died, so that an innocent man need not die in her stead.[26] The context in which this sequence of reasoning was possible was one of a society of interdependent and mutually responsible elements.

So an idea of justice as something which 'looks to the common good' is based on a number of assumptions from the Roman and early Christian worlds. The first is of mutual obligation within the community. The second is of an imperative to maintain the coherence of society, and its peace and harmony. William of Conches' *Moralium dogma philosophorum* says in the Ciceronian way that justice is the virtue conserving human society and the common life.[27]

We can go a little further and explore a budding notion of public law. The concept of *publicum ius* was understood in Roman law. Ulpian says that public law is that which pertains to the Roman state (*quod ad statum rei Romanae spectat*) and private law is that which looks to the benefit of individuals (*ad singulorum utilitatem*).[28] In the Middle Ages, too, private law applies to the private individual, and public to the public good.[29]

Where the overriding consideration is the public good, there is public law.[30]

In his *De Legibus Angliae,* the pragmatic thirteenth-century English legal writer Bracton gives a helpful summary of the notion of public law with which the central Middle Ages was working. *Ius publicum* is that which pertains to the state (*quod ad statum reipublicae pertinet*). It covers sacred things (*sacra*), the clergy and magistrates. (For it is in the public interest that there should be churches.) Private law is that which looks chiefly to the good of individuals and only secondarily (*secundari*) to that of the state.[31]

Aquinas has a notion of a public interest which the law ought to protect. He concedes that since the law is designed for the whole community it must take account of the fact that not all are pillars of virtue.[32] So it is not in the public interest for the law to seek to forbid every vice but only the more serious ones, those from which it is possible for the majority to refrain; Aquinas especially has in mind those vices which hurt others (*quae sunt in nocumentum aliorum*), for unless these are prohibited, the integrity and stability of human society are at risk (*societas human conservari non posset*.)[33] That is not to say that the law could not in principle address itself to all vices and virtues. But it chooses to do so only for those which are important for the common good, says Aquinas.[34] That includes both those which have a direct effect on the common good and those which have only an indirect effect. (A case of an 'indirect' sort would be a law designed to maintain good discipline, *bona disciplina*, from which would proceed the peace and justice which are the prime need for social stability.)[35] Marsilius of Padua in the early fourteenth century takes defence of the peace as a natural theme (and title) for his book on his own version of this principle.

Parts and wholes

The theme of 'parts and wholes' is commonplace in mediaeval philosophy and theology. Aquinas says that every part stands in a relationship to the whole, and the whole is governed by order.[36] Aquinas goes so far as to hold that if a person is a citizen his personal goodness stands in a proportionate relationship to the common good.[37] In the same way, each person is a part of the complete community.[38] So it is impossible for the common good of the state to thrive unless the citizens are virtuous.[39] Aquinas goes on to argue, in elaboration of what he means by 'completeness', that the natural aptitude of human beings towards virtuous life (*aptitudo ad virtutem*) is not to be realised without the help of others – except in rare individuals: *non de facili invenitur homo sibi sufficiens*.[40] This is partly an argument for the requirement human beings have for the support of a community. But it is also an argument for the need for a law to enforce virtue in those too weak to manage it by themselves: *ut per vim et metum cohiberentur a malo*[41] (for rules to be virtuous at least in respects appropriate to their virtue). At the same time, this device protects the community from the effects of what would have been their evil actions.[42] It seems to Aquinas to follow that law should properly respect the consideration of the common good in its provisions.[43]

Loving one's neighbour

The Bible's texts support these motifs of cooperativeness, mutuality, looking beyond individual advantage. The commands to love one's neighbour as oneself and to turn the other cheek are 'social' precepts. The latter tells the injured party to accept the injustice done to him uncomplainingly, and to seek neither redress nor vengeance. Those who are persecuted for righteousness' sake and those who render to Caesar what is Caesar's are obeying similarly 'social' precepts in Scripture.

The negative implications

There is a negative side to all this. Isidore, writing still largely within Roman assumptions, discusses a number of scenarios arising within a society where it is possible to buy or bribe one's way to office – indeed where, as was the case in the late Roman period, the greasing of palms was the usual and therefore arguably the proper way, and he speaks of those who gain honours by largesse in the same breath as those who forge coins.[44] Isidore comments in this connection that theft of a public thing, *furtum rei publicae*, is not to be judged in the same way as theft of something privately owned.[45] The *res publica* has a kind of sanctity. To steal from the *res publica* is a sacrilege. That puts the state very high – and it is of course in keeping with the ideals of Roman civic religion.

Augustine is conscious of change in his own day which amounts to a loss, which has made the Roman ideal no longer accessible. Virtue was the mainstay of the old Roman state according to the poet Ennius, says Augustine. He thinks that virtue has now been lost.[46] 'Our own generation inherited the republic,' he says, but it did not restore it to its former brightness of colour, nor strive to preserve its shape, not even its bare outlines.[47] Augustine contends that since Cicero had already pointed all this out before the advent of Christianity, it can certainly not be laid at the door of the faith.[48]

Excommunication: exclusion of the individual for the common good

When a bishop in the penitential process or an ecclesiastical court imposes the sentence of excommunication, it may well be felt that the *community* needs to be protected. An accusation has to be taken seriously, if only for the sake of the example set to the community, says the *Summa 'Elegantius'*.[49] There will be no end to offences if people think they can get away with them.[50] The most characteristic way in which an individual was excluded from the mediaeval community for the public good was by excommunication. In II Thessalonians 3.14 *infamia* is linked with excommunication in the instruction not to mingle with persons of ill repute (*non commisceamini cum illo*). From this text were derived the legal consequences of excommunication.[51]

Excommunication could occur as a penalty for what was essentially contempt of court.[52] But its effect was still to bring about exclusion from the community considered as the City of God. It has been suggested that 'liturgical exclusion was ... different from social exclusion'.[53] That was not the case in the early Church, where penance was public and the excommunicates were publicly humiliated by being dressed differently and excluded from the society as well as the community of the Church.

Pope Gregory VII adopted a policy of using excommunication to control monarchs, for a Pope may depose a King. The effect will in practice depend on the willingness of the King's subjects to take the opportunity to rise up against him. But that could be made more likely by the theory that excommunication was 'catching'. *Quoniam multos* (1078) established that knowingly to associate with an excommunicated person (unless, as for a wife or child, there was no avoiding it), was to become excommunicate oneself. Excommunicated persons could not sue in civil litigation or bring accusations in criminal trials. They could not be judges, proctors, advocates, witnesses. They could not enforce contracts.[54] The civil disability was comprehensive. It has even been suggested that 'late twelfth century canonists regarded litigation versus excommunicates as a salutary harassment' (because it put pressure on them to repent so as to get back the normal rights of a litigant).[55] A peak of restriction of the legal rights of excommunicates was reached in the thirteenth century under Pope Gregory IX.[56]

A practical example

One Alicia Clement was prosecuted for apostasy in the mid-1180s. As a small child she had been placed in a convent but she had left the religious life and married. She was involved in several lawsuits over lands in Oxfordshire, resolved in the end in 1221. She was in a difficult situation. As an excommunicate she did not have the normal rights of a litigant. To accept absolution from excommunication for leaving the convent would have been to accept that she was indeed an apostate and that would have 'ratified' her profession as a nun. If she was really a nun, she would be deemed to have surrendered her inheritance of her own free will. So she could not sue to get it back.[57]

Part II
Theology and putting law into order

4 Paradoxes

The twelfth-century Placentinus begins his book on how to conduct a fair trial with a vision, which he models on the encounter of Boethius with Philosophy.[1] 'When I was at Mantua teaching large audiences the science of law, and reflecting upon points of law and the many forms of legal action, there appeared to me a woman, wonderful in "causes", knowledgeable about the law.'[2] The figure he sees has golden hair and a rosy mouth and ivory teeth and eyes like stars. She is statuesque. Her breath is sweet. She draws young men to her by the beauty of her speech. She is *Iurisprudentia*.[3]

Placentinus' vision encapsulates the difficulty we shall be in throughout this book. Everywhere we shall find a tension between the theory and the ideals – of justice and equity and fairness – and the varying and sometimes muddled realities of practice, in which even the preservation of the fundamentals of natural justice have to be looked out for vigilantly.

Antitheses and conflicts and contradictions abound, not only in the literature which provided mediaeval lawyers and theologians with their sources or 'authorities', but also in this deeper way, as between strictness and dispensation; between precept and counsel; between justice and mercy; between divine immutability and human changeableness; universal and limited legislative power; absolute and relative rule. These conflicts can be fruitful in generating edifying solutions. For example, canonical equity, *aequitas canonica*, is merciful, but it also sets a strict standard; for it aspires to something more absolute than positive law.[4] Ivo of Chartres is thinking in the context of this ultimate and spiritual law when he stresses that those charged with the administration of justice should not lose sight of the need to be true to the faith in honesty of life.[5]

There are ways of striking a balance between rigour and mercy,[6] as Ivo of Chartres explains in his *Panormia*.[7] It was Cicero's doctrine that the middle way is best: *mediocritas optima est*.[8] Baldus in the fourteenth century has no trouble with this. He too says that the justice in equity consists in seeking neither the upper nor the lower extreme, but the middle way.[9]

Alternatively, the contradictions can be 'embraced' rather than resolved by compromise, by trying to 'live out' the paradoxes. Augustine tries to suggest a way in which it may be possible *both* to suffer patiently *and* to defend oneself against injury (*patientiam tenere et iniuriam repellere*). He suggests that the precepts about patience have to do more with an attitude of mind than with actual acts. We may preserve an inward attitude of patience and good intention, while taking firm action to benefit those we wish to help.[10] This approach tries to hold together what remain to the modern reader undeniable extremes or manifest contradictions.

For the 'great contradiction', more clearly apparent to the Christian world than to that of Cicero, is the internal one of the very human condition itself. The dignity of humankind before the sin of Adam consisted in being 'just' or 'righteous'. Before the Fall Adam and Eve were able to think with unclouded clarity. Then came sin, and both their thoughts and their honesty of life were confounded.[11] From the mediaeval Christian viewpoint the lawyer's task is therefore to deal both with a lapse from truth and with a loss of righteousness. Psalm 11.5 speaks of the lover of iniquity who hates his own soul. His sin is setting him at odds with his own welfare. He evidently cannot see this clearly or he would not thus set upon himself to his own destruction.

It is instructive to set these cosmic conflicts against the familiar requirements of the 'balancing act' of the modern judge, when the two desiderata have to be weighted against one another and one chosen because, on balance, it gives the more just outcome.

5 Mapping the law

Justinian does not elaborate a theory of branches of the law.[1] But in the different intellectual and increasingly 'academic' climate of the eleventh and twelfth centuries academics and practitioners (with probably a better grasp of formal logic) made a serious effort to get to grips with the task of mapping the law's branches and aspects.

When, listing the sources he has brought together (papal letters, *gesta* of councils, treatises of the Fathers, *institutiones* of 'catholic kings'), the eleventh-century Ivo of Chartres says 'with no small labour I have tried to make a unity of these', he is speaking not only of reconciling contradictions, but of creating a systematic order.[2] Late in the twelfth century the *Summa 'Elegantius'* sees the resulting structure as overgrown and untidy, even though 'we have pruned various hanging branches from our tree'.[3]

Two kinds of difficulty faced the mediaeval *jurisperitus* who tried to do for his subject what academics in other disciplines were now trying to do for theirs.[4] The first difficulty has to do with developing a technical vocabulary for abstract ideas in and about law. The second concerns the question whether the law can usefully be seen as an organism with parts which bear a definable structural relationship to one another.

The problem of vocabulary

The difficulties with vocabulary were pervasive from the beginning. In the next few pages we shall see a sometimes bewildering lack of consistency in usage. Problems about exactitude in the use of 'legal' terms were not new to the Middle Ages. They go back to Roman law. *Digest* 50.16 takes a series of terms which may give difficulties of interpretation of their meaning in practice in actual cases. These examples reveal a preoccupation with the daily difficulties of definitional exactitude encountered in the course of actual litigation, rather than with the clarification of the abstract ideas and principles on which law and justice rest. For instance, it is explained that when a case is about physical injury *perisse* includes different kinds of physical damage and bodily interference: *scissum* and *fractum* and *vi raptum*.[5] *Mulier* includes a girl of marriageable age: *virgo viripotens*.[6] It is incorrect to use the adjective 'public' except in relation to the good of the Roman *people*. It does not apply to the city itself.[7] 'Inheritance' is nothing other than succession to all the right which the dead person had.[8]

Fresh equivocations arose in the development of the more abstract Latin technical legal vocabulary, which were of keen interest in the Middle Ages. 'Divine law', *ius divinum*, has its moral and its ritual aspects, comments the twelfth-century *Summa 'Elegantius'*. The expression 'natural law' is equivocal in three ways, for it proceeds from the supreme nature, and then it is the same as *ius divinum*[9] or (ii) it is to be taken to be the law of all nature, that is, of all created things,[10] governing such matters as the education of children, mixing of the sexes; or else, (iii) it is to be taken to be a law which applies only to *human* nature, and to cover such matters as doing good and avoiding evil.[11] We face an additional problem of vocabulary at the outset in writing about these themes in English. Both *ius* and *lex* have to be translated in English as 'law', although the mediaeval Latin tradition makes important differences between them, whereas, as we shall see in a moment, for the single Latin term *iustitia*, there are two English words. In what follows the main purpose is to illustrate the way the significance of these and related terms cluster and huddle.

Ius

In one classical sense 'the right' was an external relation to be established between persons on the basis of things.[12] 'Right' does not mean that which one can point to defend one's position on some point (as in the modern notion of 'human rights'), but rather a *rectitudo*, a sheer uprightness, which is the correct state of things.[13] This had embedded in it the germ of the mediaeval concept of *rectus ordo*, to use Anselm of Canterbury's Gregorian phrase.[14] It is about everything being in its place in a divinely ordered scheme.[15] Within that scheme persons may enter into (orderly) relationships and make arrangements with one another about the disposition of things.

Ius contains another idea too. The *Summa 'Elegantius'* quotes the *Digest*'s[16] comment that *ius* is the art of equity and good: *ius est ars equi et boni*. The *Summa* gives glosses, lining up equity, justice, good, utility and honesty: *equum iustum* and *bonum utile et honestum*.[17] *Ius* is thus demonstrably already associated in the Roman legal mind with a complex of notions of equity and beneficialness and honesty and goodness which are readily picked up in the twelfth century; but not of course with exactly the same loading as the usages of Justinian's period, when the Christian elements had a closer intimacy with the then realities of Roman legal theory and practice than they could have in a later age. The good, for example, is something more to the Christian reader than to the late Roman pagan. *Utilitas* too has changed into something primarily profitable to the

Christian soul'. One could say that for Aquinas *ius* primarily means 'the fair' or 'what's fair'; indeed, if one could use the adverb 'aright' as a noun, one could say that his primary account is of 'arights' rather than of 'rights'.[18]

Lex

If we turn from *ius* to *lex*, some would say that we move from the general to the particular, for law seems on the face of it to come lower in the hierarchy than *ius*. Strictly, divine law is *fas* (right as good) rather than *ius* (right as law), says Isidore, for the vocabulary of *ius* and *lex* might more properly be said to belong to laws written and handed down in human societies.[19] Gratian, following Isidore, set out the view that *ius* is a genus of which *lex* is a species.[20] So perhaps *lex* is a form of *ius*. To make a law is to turn *ius*, right, into a fixed rule which can be quoted, and at the same time to publish it.[21]

But more is made of *lex* by some authors, who would give to it some of the high attributes of *ius*. As so often, we are in an area of confused terminology. Augustine says that there can be no 'law' (*lex*) which is not 'just' (*iusta*).[22] In other words, an unjust law is a contradiction in terms. Can this be taken to mean that there is a spark of the divine law in all good *leges*? John of Salisbury would seem to think so, when he says that law is a gift of God, the 'form' or pattern of equity, the norm of justice, the image of divine will, guardian of safety, union and consolidation of the people, exclusion and extermination of the vices, punishment of violence and all injury.[23] The phrase *ius legitimum* would even seem to conflate *ius* and *lex*. It is in Ambrose of Milan[24] and Marius Victorinus with a sense which seems to be that of 'legitimate right'.[25] It also has a place in a legal context.[26] Rupert of Deutz, for example, uses it for the 'legitimate right' of the seed of Abraham.[27]

Iustitia

While English is short of vocabulary by means of which to distinguish *ius* and *lex*, with *iustitia* it is the other way round. *Iustitia* has two English renderings: 'justice' and 'righteousness', which are easily conflated in discussions in mediaeval Latin.

Iustitia is used throughout the Vulgate for a concept for which English affords the word 'righteousness', as well as for 'justice'. So the term 'justice' (*iustitia*) is itself equivocal in Christian usage. Divine law is a holy precept or law against sin: *in declinandis peccatis sancta preceptio*, says the author of the *Summa 'Elegantius'*.[28] A 'just man' is one who keeps God's law against sin; either because he is law-abiding (broadly, the Old Testament principle), or (in the New Testament), because although he commits sin his sin is not counted against him by God. So there is a legal coloration, but there is also, strongly, the idea of sin, conceived of as something more than a breach of law, that is, as a state or condition somehow 'not right'.

Certain ideas about *iustitia* entered the mediaeval scene from the ancient and patristic worlds. For Cicero *iustitia* is a constitution or habit of the mind, which looks to the common good and at the same time seeks to ensure that what is proper to each person is respected.[29] The *Institutes*[30] say that *iustitia* is a constant and perpetual will to give each his right.[31] Hermannus (in the Abelardian ambit of the twelfth century) borrows from Justinian this additional stress on the need for *persistence* or *constancy* in sustaining the right of the individual thus defined.[32] It is necessary to be vigilant because justice is easily overthrown. Individuals can become oppressed. Another, late twelfth-century commentator, Peter Lombard, favours the Augustinian emphasis: that what defines justice is that it helps the wretched: *iustitia est in subveniendo miseris*.[33] It is the duty of justice to do violence to no one, confirms the legal commentator Rogerius.[34]

Iustitia can also be another word for 'virtue', *virtus*. In his lecture on *De iustitia et iure* in the *Digest*, the fourteenth-century Baldus gives an expanded Ciceronian list. When someone has *iustitia*, whether it is infused or acquired, it forms in him religion, piety, severity, mercy, the grace of God, joy, love, and innocence.[35] Subdivided, this sort of *iustitia* divides into the various cardinal virtues.

There is a further, pragmatic sense of *iustitia*, as an unspoken convention designed to be of assistance to a number of people (*tacita conventio in adiutorium multorum inventa*). This definition was attributed by Paucapalea to Gregory the Great, but it is actually the work of Martin of Braga (d.579), in a treatise on the virtues which was ascribed to Seneca in the Middle Ages.[36] This emphasis on the common good has been linked with a similar definition attributed to Plato by Placentinus. On this definition, justice is the virtue which most obviously assists those least able to help themselves: *virtus que plurimum prodest ... his qui minimum possunt, nempe in personis miserabilibus evidentius clarescit iustitia*.[37]

The relationship of *ius* and *iustitia*

Is *iustitia* the mother of *ius* is it or the other way round? Either can be, and is, argued.[38] Philip the Chancellor approves a rather Anselmian notion of *iustitia* as a 'rightness' or 'uprightness', *rectitudo vitae* or *rectitudo voluntatis*.[39]

The argument for a superiority of *ius* over *iustitia* is even more conspicuous if we are talking in a Christian context about *ius divinum*. The *Summa 'Elegantius'* has it that there is a *ius humanum* in the Law and the Gospels: *est quod in lege vel in evangelio ius humanum*, and that this is a 'constitution' by which equity is preserved, injury repulsed, innocence protected, violence bridled and discord exiled.[40] In one Aristotelian type of sequence, right is the final cause of righteousness or justice, but right is formally born of righteousness, says the *Summa 'Elegantius'*.[41] *Ius* differs from *iustitia* says the *Summa 'Elegantius'*, in that man is the author of *ius* and God the author of *iustitia*:[42] *Iustitia* is thus not only higher but broader (*latius*) than *ius*. Justice is the source of law or right, agrees Baldus. He explains that *ius* derives from *iustitia* which is its essential and intrinsic cause.[43] It is possible, then, to put *ius* higher than *iustitia*, or to put it lower. There is no final agreed solution in our authors.

Divine, natural and human law

Natural law

We come now to our second question, whether the mediaeval period recognises a structural or organic or hierarchical relationship of the parts or branches of the law which come into being below the level of divine law itself, and here usages are more consistent. It is not surprising to find attempts to identify a hierarchy in the mediaeval theory of law, from the unchanging and universal down to the variable and particular, and thus to provide an overall principle of organisation for mediaeval attempts to construct *schemata* of study. Gratian depends directly upon Isidore's *Etymologiae* in setting out his initial thoughts.

In the Roman period Gaius speaks of the law 'in force equally among all men' as 'that which natural reason has appointed'. The idea seems to be that something which is of universal application is natural, such as marriage, guardianship, contract.[44] On Gratian's reading, the law of nature can itself be said to be 'divine' insofar as it is contained in Scripture, in the law and the Gospel.[45] This is the universal law which says that we should do to others what we wish them to do to us (Matthew 7.12).[46]

Natural law (*ius naturale*) can, alternatively, be defined as that to which any well-disposed person assents.[47] An example would be the principle that evil is to be avoided.[48] This notion of a need for the right disposition on the part of the knower before something can be recognised as an obviously good rule is important in theology, where the compelling force of pure reasonableness can be expected to come up against the ill disposition of the wrong-doer, who will seek to find it *un*reasonable. There is thus an inherent difficulty in attempting to use pure reason in legal argumentation. Reasonableness will tend always to be contextual. That begins to take us away from the universal and the absolute.

There is a tug in one direction towards seeing natural law as having characteristics of divine law because it is the law by which the Creator governs his creatures. There is a pull in the other direction in the recognition that there are differences between creatures which make the natural law ruling the behaviour of each different, and in some respects peculiar to the species.

The Arts Faculty in Paris at the end of the thirteenth century produced a number of accounts of the question of natural law. In a commentary by Gilles d'Orléans we find the statement that 'it should be noted that that to which man inclines by nature is called naturally just'.[49] The jurists, it is explained, reserve the term 'natural law' for the law as it governs all human 'animals', for the 'law of nations' or what we should now call 'international law', that is, *ius gentium*. Aristotle, however, includes both under 'natural law', and that discrepancy had to be accommodated.[50]

But man has a two-fold nature, one common, which is like that of other animals, and one which is unique to man.[51] So created natures vary; there are other natures apart from the human. Thus 'natural law' might be 'unchanging' with respect to a given species without being universal to all created nature. If man is an animal the duty of a son to support his destitute father would not apply. If man is a rational being, he does have that duty.[52]

This paradoxical 'universality with particularity' in the usage of the term 'natural law' is underlined in a thirteenth-century Parisian question. 'That which is not always the same everywhere is not natural; but no matter of justice is always the same everywhere'.[53]

Another way in which the question of the definition of 'natural law' can be approached is through its purpose. Here again, from the thirteenth century, a Christian 'purpose' had to be united as far as possible with the kind of purpose Aristotle envisaged. Natural law, taken universally, is that which orders what is beneficial (such as fostering friendship), and forbids what is harmful (such as killing).[54] Aquinas – writing as a theologian – believes that the order imposed by the precepts of the law of nature[55] corresponds to the order imposed by natural inclination.[56] He infers from this that natural law will be conducive to such fundamentals as the preservation of human life; he contends that certain things follow from this (a standard list normally cited in such discussions), for example, the duty to rear one's offspring.[57] Peculiar to human nature, he argues, are the inclinations which belong to a rational nature: the wish to know the truth about God and to live in society. So under natural law come the obligation to avoid ignorance,[58] and the rule of not giving offence to those one must live with, and so on.[59]

But because man is a sinful as well as a rational animal, there has to be a proviso. Natural law is that to which the understanding of a *well-disposed person* assents. A sinful intellect might not do so.[60] An example would be the principle that evil is to be avoided; the sinner in his sin is *ipso facto* presenting some resistance to that idea.[61]

Aquinas believes that there are two ways in which a rule can be derived (*derivari*) from natural law. The first is by way of the drawing of a conclusion from premises.[62] This is the syllogistic method, which was never denied to the classical orator, just not his favourite. The second is by way of *determinationes quaedam aliquorum communium*.[63] What Aquinas means by this is made clear by the example he gives. An architect begins with a common idea of a house but he 'determines' from it a particular plan for a specific house. Thus from the general rule of doing no harm to anyone derives the specific: 'thou shalt not kill'. The general rule that someone who sins should be punished becomes the basis for the specific punishment meted out in a given case.[64]

Actual law, as legislated (*ius positivum vel legale*), is not derived from natural law as a conclusion is derived from premises,[65] yet just as a necessary premiss must be followed by a necessary conclusion, so from just premisses there naturally follows by natural justice a just conclusion.[66] An example of this would be the rule that one ought not unjustly to injure another, from which it follows that one should not steal.[67] That conclusion is natural law, just like the premisses.[68] Nevertheless, *ius positivum* is not derived from natural law as a conclusion is derived from premisses, but rather by a kind of derivation, a determination and narrowing.[69] Thus *ius naturale* says that we must sacrifice to the gods, *dicit quod diis est sacrificandum*, but it is positive law to say that this or that should be sacrificed to the gods.[70]

Natural law seems to Baldus, summing up in the fourteenth century, to be a force (*vis*) with a purpose. It proceeds from the rational or sensual nature of man.[71] So it is a creaturely thing. But human nature is a rational nature, and this stands in a special relationship to the *ratio* of this highest law.[72] Natural law (*lex naturalis*) can thus be defined as the participation of eternal law in the rational creature.[73]

Human laws and customs

Alger of Liège says that 'canonical precepts should be adapted to different persons, events and times by varying procedure and varying application'.[74] *Human* laws are made up of customs (*humanae moribus constant*), says Gratian. That means that human laws differ from place to place, he points out, for different peoples have different preferences.[75] This also affects, as the *Digest* notes, the geographical limits of jurisdiction.[76] This reflects a climate of expectation in which canon law was not meant to be taken as binding 'statute' law in the modern sense. 'It required the willingness of local officials and litigants, with local interests and particular quarrels to settle, before it could be put into effect.'[77] Moreover, human laws can also change over time. This mutability is an inferiority which separates human law from divine law, but it has the advantage that human law may thus change for the better.

It is possible to divide law in yet another way, into written and unwritten. The *Summa 'Elegantius'* says that whether *ius* is 'natural' or 'moral', it is maintained either by being written down or solely by custom or usage.[78] The first is *constitutio*, the second *consuetudo*.[79]

There is a fair consensus in our authors on the need to respect custom. But there is also again a certain sense of being in the presence of a jumble of ideas about the usages of the terms involved. Some customs have the authority of antiquity.[80] Customary law is made by the people. The authority of custom is not weak but vigorous.[81] Some say a custom can in certain circumstances override the law.[82] There can be tacit approval by the legislator of what is approved by custom.[83] Law normally overrides custom,[84] but a custom of long standing is no mean authority.[85] *Lex* is a *constitutio scripta* and *mos* a *longa consuetudo*. (Law is a written text, custom something established by long usage.) Both remain 'customs' because of their 'human' origin.[86] On the other hand, custom is a law established by habit,[87] which can be taken as law *instead of a written law* when there is no actual written law (*cum deficit lex*). This would make custom inferior to law, a stop-gap to be used in its absence.[88]

Nevertheless, it can be argued that there is no difference between the two where reason supports the law or custom.[89] Gratian infers from Isidore's claim that there is no difference in such circumstances, that the difference between *lex* and *consuetudo* can be taken to lie merely in the writing down. The part which is written down is called *constitutio sive ius*. The term *consuetudo* is reserved for the unwritten part.[90] Writing at the end of the thirteenth century and for practitioners, Fleta says that 'even if laws are not written down, it is not absurd (*non absurdum*) to call them laws, for they may have their force'.[91]

Aquinas notes that in mastering a speculative science it is common for someone to gain at first only an incomplete grasp, and then to perfect it. Just so, a community may at first make imperfect laws.[92] The appropriate rules of good government are also a function of maturity in a community. If a people is orderly and serious-minded, Augustine thought, they may be entrusted with the choosing of their own *magistratus*, and that, too, would be a development or change.[93]

Law is never retrospective. When laws are made they should bind only for the future, not for the past, says the *Summa 'Elegantius'*.[94] Does it follow that later laws supersede earlier ones?[95] The principle is that whatever is 'newer' in law is likely to be clearer-sighted.[96] Laws with future reference are likely to be made on the basis of past experience of things going wrong with an earlier version.

It is, however, a problem that change in the law even if it is intended to be for the better, is somehow detrimental to the common good by virtue of the very fact that it *is* change, and mutability, to mediaeval minds, is always undesirable.[97] This is the case because custom, taken simply as sheer usualness, has a certain weightiness: *plurimum valet consuetudo*.[98] The very changing of the law diminishes its coercive power, because this customariness is lost.[99] Aquinas accepts as sensible the *Digest*'s rule that when something is newly decreed, it needs to be clear that it is *useful* to move away from that law which has seemed good for a long time.[100]

Seeming variations occur as concessions in particular human laws or in different circumstances. For example, the Old Testament lays down periods of time for cleansing before a woman who has given birth may enter the Temple. But Gregory the Great wrote to Augustine of Canterbury to tell him to allow a woman to go to Church to give thanks immediately after the birth.[101]

Human law is also inferior in that it is short-term, by comparison with the divine law. Marsilius of Padua in the *Defensor Minor* reuses his own definition of divine law from the *Defensor Pacis*.[102] God's rules are 'coercive precepts for transgressors in this world, under punishment or torment to be carried out in the future rather than the present world'. Its key points are thus that God makes his own law without consulting human beings, and that he enforces that law by means of punishments which can stretch into eternity. Marsilius contrasts this with human law, which he thinks is a precept of the community of citizens (*universitas civium*), or of its greater part (*valentior pars*). These laws ought to be made 'by immediate deliberation about any voluntary human acts committed or omitted in the present world towards the best end which any man is suited to pursue in this world'.[103] So they are strictly this-wordly.

Rites and regulations

Regulations fall into a category of law more modern than mediaeval, but with lessons for the analysis of the mediaeval scene. The essence of regulations is their localness and particularity. The same is true for theologians in the case of 'rites'. The *Digest* says that the law can be ignored with impunity outside the region where it runs.[104] The same principle is to be found in the LXXIV *tituli*.[105] Differences of rules for or 'laws' of liturgical practice from place to place are apparent from the earliest days of the Church's life.[106] The Church always countenanced variations of rite as legitimate locally.[107] This could not extend to anything which would fragment the unity of the Church, but it could legitimately respect local preferences at a number of points.[108] There are, however, limits to variability, for liturgy carries a theology within it, and there can be no local variation in matters of faith.

Times, seasons, circumstances vary, and what it is legitimate to do may vary with them. There are times when swearing, which is normally acceptable, is not allowed. This is so at certain seasons of the ecclesiastical year: *sunt quaedam tempora in quibus iuvare prohibemur*.[109] Crimes of passion are a recognised genre: *Fieri solet ut crimina etiam atrociora mente alienata committantur*.[110] So circumstances in particular cases may also affect legitimacy. The rules about the ages at which nuns may take the veil vary. There is a sense of appropriateness in setting an age, however, although that may vary from adolescence to middle age: *vel ut primum rigor, medium equitas, ultimum dispensatio sit, pro virtute et utilitate persone toleranda*.[111] This is all with the proviso that what is wrong at first does not get better merely by the passage of time: *quod initio vitiosum est, non potest tractu temporis convalescere*.[112]

Accordingly, the adverb *rite* tends to connote 'orderliness' in the context especially of worship. Augustine, for example, will speak of those who worship God in an orderly way (*qui deum rite colunt*).[113]

There is a related usage which links *rite* to the ministry of Word and sacrament. Augustine says that a new-born infant may be baptised *rite*: *mox natum rite baptizari posse*.[114] He also notes that no one who is unbaptised may *rite* receive the consecrated elements at the Eucharist: *quo nemo rite nisi baptizatus accedit*.[115] Bede, for example, says that when the sacraments are celebrated *rite* and the Word which is God's wisdom is heard and kept it is not in dispute that the angelic powers are present and that they celebrate with us in the heights of heaven.[116] Bernard of Clairvaux describes how the sacraments are celebrated *rite*, confessions take place and the people come to Church.[117]

But *rite* can also mean simply 'correctly'. 'Correctly' is certainly what Augustine seems to mean when he says that he has discussed something correctly with God's help (*rite tractavimus*),[118] and again when he says 'if I recollect correctly' (*si rite recolo*).[119] Now what is correct cannot so easily be deemed variable as what is merely customary, and therefore perhaps a custom only locally. So there is a tension between a universal rightness and a local and adaptable rightness of doing things within the late antique usage of the term *rite*, which inevitably carried over into the Middle Ages through the influence of widely read authors.

Isidore disputes this reading of the term. In his chapter on 'legal instruments' he says that in a legal context *rite* does not mean *recte* (correctly, rightly), but according to custom (*ex more*).[120] The *Summa 'Elegantius'* says that monks are not entrusted with pastoral care *rite*, which here seems to mean 'routinely' or by custom; it is a special privilege for such an office to be entrusted to a monastery: *tunc prasertim cum monasteriis hoc officium ex speciali privilegio adiectum cognoscitur*.[121]

The main mediaeval thrust of *rite* appears to be 'done in an orderly way' or 'in due order', and that would seem to include both the shading of 'correctness' and that of 'customariness'. Thus Bede has: *rite distinctis*,[122] *rite custodientes*,[123] *rite subiugatas*.[124] Those who are properly instituted and who subsequently discharge the duties of those offices in this way are happy and peaceful, says Bernard of Clairvaux: *puto bene instituti cleri mansuetos et disciplinatos mores rite que administrata officia designare*.[125]

This can be contrasted with doing something by deception or by force, both of which would be disorderly. For example, Bernard of Clairvaux describes the case of a man made a bishop *non rite et ordine, sed fraude et vi*. This man broke all the rules of right order. He was not worthy in life, honest in reputation, suitable for the task, canonically elected nor properly consecrated: *homo ille nec vita dignus, nec fama honestus, nec utilitate idoneus, nec canonice electus, nec licite consecratus.*[126] The *Summa 'Elegantius'* of the late twelfth century describes irregular houses of women in Germany who behave in ways which break canon law and are generally disruptive and disorderly.[127]

But we are once more up against definitional nicety here. *Rite* is variable. The fundamentals of faith and order are not. The person who holds the office is a variable factor, whose inevitable idiosyncrasies will make impossible the absolutely impersonal and therefore uniform discharge of the duties of office. Accordingly, there could also be differences in disciplinary practice and procedures.

It is appropriate that a chapter on making a map of mediaeval ideas about law should end with variability. Even in the area of theory there was much that was never settled in mediaeval discussion to everyone's satisfaction, especially where law abuts onto theology. We must turn now to practice, where we shall find a similar story.

So division or tabulation of different kinds of *ius* or *lex*, with variations, seems general, and within it the series of consistently recurring tensions between the universal and the particular, between the enduring and the variable, and between the written and the unwritten. But consistency of *classification* remains difficult because of the lack of consistency in the use of the technical *vocabulary*.

6 The court system

In the mediaeval centuries with which we are chiefly concerned, a regular court system was only just evolving in parts of northern Europe. The works of Bracton, in use from about 1265, and of Fleta, relying upon him in large part, are attempts to sketch the emerging provision for those using the secular court system of contemporary England. Fleta writes about 'different kinds of courts' (*De differenciis curiarum*). The King has his court in Parliament, in the presence of the bishops, earls, lords 'and other learned men' (*et aliis viris peritis*), a category which suggests that there were 'in-house lawyers'.[1] Then he has a court before the Steward of his household, the Chief Justice (*capitalis justiciarius regis*).[2] There is the King's Court of Chancery (*in cancellaria sua*).[3] There are courts especially convened for trying justices and royal ministers themselves.[4] There is a court held in various parts of England, where the judges are royal justices, lay and clerical, *tam milites quam clericos*, who hear appeals and cases involving such offences as crimes and breaches of the King's peace.[5]

There were until the twelfth or even the thirteenth century 'no church courts, at least not in the modern sense of the word "court", a separate institution staffed by professionals that resolves disputes or prosecutes crimes'.[6] The expression *curia Cantuariensis* is used in the twelfth and thirteenth centuries for various purposes, to refer to the diocesan or metropolitan jurisdiction in general rather than to a court of law.[7]

The original ecclesiastical court is the council or synod. There are two, ecclesiologically distinct, types of synod. One is the synod where bishops meet one another; the other is the diocesan synod with a single bishop meeting with this clergy. The 16th Council of Toledo, as cited by Gratian,[8] tells the bishop to call together the abbots, priest, deacons and other clergy of his diocese.[9] Council after council in the early centuries emphasise the importance of the bishops' unanimity as a sign that a decree expresses the will of the Holy Spirit. Where the bishop sits alone with his clergy the will or judgement expressed is his own. The clergy present are merely a consultative body.

Gratian is clear that each bishop has his own jurisdiction.[10] He believes that this individuated episcopal jurisdiction is derived from apostolic authority, and by that authority two *episcopatus* can be joined in one.[11] Such jurisdiction comes down a hierarchical line[12] through the archbishop to the bishop.[13]

From time to time such synods acted as courts, as at Sens, Soissons, Rheims in the mid-twelfth century. But mostly that happened in emergency circumstances such as heresy trials of high-profile academics who were feared to be leading the faithful astray. A striking example of a special-instance 'court' is the careful pursuit of due process at the Council of Constance at the beginning of the fifteenth century, in an attempt to get Benedict XIII, the third papal claimant of the day, condemned for heresy and schism. He was condemned on 26 July 1417, refused to resign and was deposed.[14]

Just as the king equipped himself with in-house lawyers, so there appears often to have been a group of lawyers in the archbishop's household, with one holding the office of chancellor. The archbishop is the judge, but he delegates that function to various persons, who may be members of the cathedral clergy, masters in the University of Oxford, local abbots, asking them either to hear the whole case or to act as examiners, to hear the evidence of the witnesses and report to the archbishop who would pronounce the sentence.[15]

The vocabulary of jurisdiction

The terminology of *ordo-jurisdictio* begins to appear in the second half of the twelfth century.[16] 'Jurisdiction' was the subject of a good deal of mediaeval reflection going wider than this specific sense. It may be useful briefly to review something of its range before we continue. 'Saying something is law' can be rendered literally as *jurisdictio* in Latin. The vocabulary of 'lawmaking' and 'law enforcement' develops, as does much other technical vocabulary in the Middle Ages, piecemeal and often confusingly. The term *jurisdictio* is quite rare in Gratian,[17] and he does not restrict it to ecclesiastical contexts.[18] An emperor can confer civil jurisdiction. Irnerius gives a straightforward definition of jurisdiction as 'the power to declare the law: *potestas iuris dicendi*.[19]

Jurisdictio also means 'authority over', in the sense of a specifically juridical authority. The direct jurisdiction of popes over monks was an important issue in the twelfth century, because it could be seen as undermining the diocesan jurisdiction of bishops. Alexander III wrote to Archbishop William of Sens on the subject.[20]

It is also quite possible at an early date to distinguish between the 'possession' of jurisdiction and the 'exercise' of jurisdiction (rather in the *potestas* and *actus* manner of Aristotle),[21] as Johannes Teutonicus does. Marsilius of Padua in the *Defensor Minor* begins squarely with the question of priestly jurisdiction.[22] Jurisdiction he derives from the pronouncement of right (*dictio iuris*).

There is a group of other terms in Gratian, covering aspects of jurisdiction and related ideas. *Amministratio* seems to refer to the carrying out of an 'office' or 'duty' which has been undertaken (*susceptum*).[23] Gratian can use *potestas* as a synonym for *auctoritas*: 'Generally, churches and ecclesiastical property are in the "power" of bishops; lay persons cannot possess tithes or churches on their own "authority" nor on that of bishops'.[24] *Potestas* can be separated into order and jurisdiction.[25] We meet *regimen*[26] and *gubernatio* in Gratian (*Iudicio et potestate episcopi res ecclesiastice gubernentur*).[27] There is *iussio*,[28] a special order or dispensation of a bishop: *Omnes presbyteri secundum iussionem episcopi ecclesiae dispensare studeant*. Gratian explains priests may reconcile for hidden sins at the bishop's *iussio*.[29] Neither clergy nor laity can travel without episcopal *iussio*.[30]

Authority to be a judge

The 'authority' vested in a court system is tested when it has to show its muscle and punish for contempt. Society has to *accept* its authority. There may have to be sanctions to ensure that what a court decrees is taken seriously.

Authority to judge is indispensable to the lawfulness of the court process.[31] A judge has to have powers, or he cannot compel the litigants to accept his resolution of the dispute; but they must be powers with limits. He cannot exceed them, acknowledges the *Digest*: *quia ultra id quod in iudicium deductum est excedere potestas iudicii non potest*.[32] The sixth *titulus* of the eleventh-century *Diversorum patrum sententie sive Collectio in LXXIV titulos digesta*, explores the rule that an offence must be dealt with within the geographical area of the jurisdiction where it was committed.[33] No judge's sentence is binding if he has gone beyond his jurisdiction.[34]

The special powers to judge of a pope and of a bishop

There is a juridical hierarchy. It is recognised – for instance in the *Summa 'Elegantius'* – that there is indeed a hierarchy of judges, and that the powers of a judge depend in some respects upon his position in that hierarchy.[35] This is an especially clearly developed principle in the Western Church. The doctrine of papal plenitude of powers emerged towards the end of the Investiture Contest, notably at the hands of Bernard of Clairvaux, who set it out in some detail in his *De Consideratione*. This mid-twelfth-century serial work became something of an 'instruction manual' for Pope Eugenius III.

Anselm of Lucca writes enthusiastically in his first book about the power and primacy of the Apostolic See. He makes the point again and again. No one should dissent from it.[36] The Apostolic See is head of all the churches: *caput omnium ecclesiarum*, and is made so by God (I. 2, p. 8).

Christ rejects everyone who grieves the pope (I. 5, p. 8). It is not fitting for anyone to break the rules of the Roman Church. *Quod a regulis Romanae ecclesiae nullatenus convenit deviare* (for members cannot deviate from their head) (1. 12, p. 12). The Roman Church has never strayed from the faith: *Quod Romana ecclesia numquam a fide erravit* (1. 12, p. 12). If there is anything injurious to the faith in the Church the Pope ought to correct and amend it: *Quod per universam ecclesiam quicquid nocivum in ea est debet papa corrigere et emendare* (1. 14, p. 13). The primary thing for salvation is to keep the faith and not to stray from the pope's commands[37] (I. 16, p. 14). The Roman Church is 'first of all' not only in the decrees of canons, but because she is the very voice of salvation (I. 17, p. 14).[38] No one may judge the 'First see' (I. 19, p. 15).[39] No one should presume to judge, or to retract the judgement of the First See (I. 21, p. 16).[40] The pope is to be judged by no one but God (I. 24, p. 16).[41] Gratian discusses legislative power in *Causa* 25 and *Distinctio* 19, mainly in connection with the authority of the papacy.[42] In *Distinctio* 19 he poses the question whether decretal letters have the force of authority, the *vis auctoritatis*, when they are not to be found in the *corpus canonum*.[43] Gratian argues that they do. In *Causa* 25 he discusses the conflict which may arise between two papal privileges, which brings him into the area of the conflict of laws. Gratian asks how papal privileges derive their authority from 'the power of the keys'.

The pope is a legislator, insofar as he is one, by virtue of (that is, 'in the power of')[44] the keys of binding and loosing entrusted to him. He can thus be said to get his legislative authority directly from Christ. On this basis, Gratian gives popes high authority. No bishop may act against pontifical decretal (XXV. i. 12).

Nevertheless, Gratian lays down a number of restrictive principles, in a series of texts which deny that the pope can change the law of his predecessors.[45] For he who does not use his power legitimately loses it: *privilegium amittit qui sua potestate non legitime utitur* (XXV. i. 23). A pope may not go against a universal Council (XXV. i. 1). He may not go against *divinae constitutiones*, or the Holy Spirit or the Gospel (XXV. 3, 4, 7). No one, not even a pope, may go against what has been decided by the holy Fathers in synod (XXV. i. 14). Indeed, it can be asked whether any privilege, that is, any law directly made by the pope, could be valid if it sought to go against existing law.[46] He who does not honour decrees fully may be deemed to act against them.[47] So even a pope may not ignore the law of the Church which has the support of authoritative texts.[48] But the pope may make new laws (*novas condere leges*) if they do not go against these higher laws.[49]

Hostiensis distils in his *Summa* the essence of what he thinks pertains to the pope. The pope establishes general laws; he makes what is not, to be, and he makes what is, not to be. He bears the pallium at all times.[50] It is his responsibility to maintain order in the Church.

Judges-delegate

This high officer of the Church stood, in theory, at the pinnacle of the judicial hierarchy. Getting the pope to be judge on appeal might be desirable – as many evidently thought it at the time of Eugenius III, when the pope was spending almost all his time hearing cases – but it was not always practicable. Bernard of Clairvaux began his *De Consideratione* to encourage this particular pope to reorder his priorities in this respect. It was frequently necessary for someone to be appointed to act as a judge-delegate to take the load from the papal shoulders. So there arises the question of delegated authority to judge. Substitute judges are already provided for in a specific and limited way in the *Digest*. These are those to whom the burdens of acting in the office of judge are transferred.[51] The *Summa 'Elegantius'* agrees that judicial authority can be delegated, but stresses that in that case the only authority the judge-delegate has is that which has been entrusted to him for the specific performance of that office.[52] The decretals often give solutions to direct questions affecting particular cases, and specify the powers of a judge-delegate in a particular case.[53]

There was a need for persons, capable of acting as judges-delegate who might be available to act 'on the ground' locally when an appellant to the Apostolic See was sent back to his locality for the case to be heard there. Alexander III felt thus, and also perceived a need for bishops clear-headed and well-intentioned enough to handle appeals from their own courts fairly.[54] Roger, Bishop of Worcester, 1164–79, who had studied theology at Paris with Robert of Melun and came young to high office, was such an individual, and Alexander's letters to him which occur throughout the *Liber Extra*, amply illustrate the way in which unforeseen problems could be referred back to the appeal judge (the pope) from his judge-delegate. A tabulation of reserved papal powers, that is, powers not automatically conferred on a legate when he is appointed, but having to be separately conferred by the pope, or carried out by him directly, is given by Figueira.[55]

This person with a limited and specific delegated office should read his mandate carefully and keep to it.[56] He cannot exceed the bounds thus set for him, and at the same time do his duty. Conversely, a judge can be punished if he does not discharge the duties of his office.[57] So there are tight constraints, exactly delineating the powers and duties of a judge in a given case.

Part III
Theology and the teaching of law

7 Law schools

After the collapse of the Roman Empire and with it the machinery of the legal system of the ancient world, 'professional lawyers' also seem to have disappeared for a time, at least in large parts of Europe. Study did not cease altogether, as we shall see, but the Corpus of Justinian was for some centuries only patchily known. The barbarian peoples had their *leges*. The Church had the beginnings of canon law, but some of it was not forged until the Carolingian period, when it was 'forged' in both senses. The Ps.-Isidorian decretals contain the Ps.-decrees of Ps.-popes. The formal, academic study of law as a discipline, and the availability of a professional training in its application, were largely a development of the central Middle Ages, of the age of the nascent universities, and of only some of those.[1]

There is a mention of the legal profession in Canon 9 of Lateran II (1139). There, monks and regular canons are actively discouraged from learning civil law. Financial reward was involved and there was a perceived danger that they would be distracted from their proper work of worship. Among those not 'banned' as professional religious, but encouraged as professional academics, 'Doctors' arose in the Bolognese law school in the twelfth century. Irnerius (?1055–1130) may even have founded the *studium* at Bologna. He is the author of a number of surviving glosses, which already assume a considerable grasp and level of knowledge in his lecture-audience, so we may take it that the need which was being met was already actively expressing itself. Irnerius has been given much of the credit for the outstanding success of Bologna as a school of law from the twelfth century.[2] Others gave notable lectures: Bulgarus, Martin Gosia, Ugo of the Ravenna Gate and James. The four Doctors left glosses on the texts, from which there arose or developed various genres of legal writing. Law became highly attractive to students as word spread that being a lawyer was as likely a way to grow rich and achieve power as seeking high preferment in the Church; a demanding crowd of 'graduate students' with the *artes* already under their belts,[3] flocked to Bologna.[4]

These students decided what was to be in their syllabus, which passages were to be read, and how the syllabus was to be covered, laying this down in detail, step by step.[5] The *doctores* who lectured to them were obliged to keep to the rules or lose their jobs.

A statute of Bologna of 1158 says that no one can be a judge or jurisconsult unless he has studied law for five years, so something like a professional qualification was evidently developing, and with it an 'academic' branch of the legal profession. Rather like modern academic experts in other disciplines, the 'decretists', as they were called, were frequently called upon to give legal opinions on the principles they were teaching. This is known to have happened to Stephen of Tournai, Simon of Bisignano, Peter of Blois, Huguccio, Sicard of Cremona, and Tancred.[6]

Soon Bologna was not the only major 'school' where law could be learned, though it remained probably the most prominent. It has been suggested that it was by way of diocesan synodal statutes that ordinary clergy got to know their canon law.[7] Law curricula became established everywhere in Europe, including cathedral schools in England.[8]

In England Roman and canon law could in due course be studied at Oxford and Cambridge, though common law could not. Master Vacarius, a Lombard, studied at Bologna, but spent most of his life teaching in England, probably at Oxford.[9] In Oxford the arrangement came to be that the decretals were to be 'read' (that is, lectured on) in the mornings. For the lawyers gave conventional mediaeval lectures, in which the lecturer read his way through the text explaining it seriatim with the aid of the standard authorities.[10] No one was to give such lectures until he had taken an oath that he was himself qualified, by having heard lectures himself for a specified number of years, and had copies of all the texts of canon and secular law with the glosses. For the would-be lecturer on the *Institutes*, for example, it was necessary to have heard lectures on the civil law for four years or to be a Master of Arts of six years' standing. (The oath need be taken only once for a lecturer to be entitled to lecture in Oxford or Cambridge.)[11]

In the universities it was possible to graduate in law by performing exercises analogous to those required of graduates in other subjects. A Bachelor took his degree by 'determining' a question. A Master or Doctor did so by 'inception' as a teacher. By the thirteenth century there seems to have been something close to a professional requirement of a stipulated *period* of training and in an approved academic context.[12] In 1295 it was a requirement of the Canterbury Court of the Arches that a professional advocate must have studied law in an academic school of law for five years, or for four years, followed by a year's attendance at court, before he was admitted as a practitioner.[13]

The Inns of Court came into being in England rather later. In 1470 Sir John Fortescue describes them as places where education in the common law took place.[14] With the Inns of Court we are in the arena of 'learning by doing'. There was a recognised 'apprenticeship' by starting off in the courts. Here proctors or advocates appear to have begun by 'learning their trade' almost as apprentices, doing odd jobs as attorneys, and learning in the process how to present and argue a case.[15]

In effect, a 'serjeant' might be said to 'graduate' by acting as an advocate in his first case. But the Inns of Court were not universities, and it became necessary to bring in a requirement that there be a formal call to prevent advocates inventing themselves by merely taking part in moots and real cases.

The *gradus* of bencher and barrister seem to be identifiable in a fifteenth-century English reference to *ipsi qui ad bancum ibidem recipiuntur*. There is no *licentia docendi*, merely domestic titles. No regulations on rights of audience can be shown before the 1540s, although Counsel practising in the late fifteenth century were readers or benchers of the Inns of Court.[16]

8 Creating the academic discipline of law

It is when we set 'vocational' alongside set 'academic' training in this way, that the interrelationships of academic law and academic theology come more clearly into play. It is important for our purposes that there is a conscious link with theology in this. For civil and canon law form a whole with theology, claims Hostiensis.[1] The first question which had to be addressed within the university law schools was whether the law constituted an academic discipline at all. For it had to gain standing as a 'higher degree' subject, like theology and medicine. It did not have a place among the liberal arts, unless it could be regarded as a branch of rhetoric.[2] It does not tend to appear by name in the wider *schemata* of study which were drawn up in the twelfth century in an endeavour to work out where such subjects as 'ethics' might fit in.[3] In reality, a new mediaeval 'discipline' of law had to make its way to acceptance, find a place alongside other disciplines and establish its relation to them in the syllabus.

Some of the earliest sources to hint at an overview of what writers on the law thought they were doing are prefaces and prologues to collections. Dionysius Exiguus, collecting conciliar canons in the late fifth century is visibly concerned about authenticity and accuracy – rightly in light of the flurry of pseudo-texts appearing in the Ps-Isidorian decretals a few centuries later. The preface to the late sixth-century Chapters of Martin of Braga shows a preoccupation with the need for clarification; the Canons of Abbo of Fleury in the late tenth century evince a defensive mood ('I have compiled many things for the defence of the monastic order').[4] These are not the confident forewords of compilers secure in their own minds about the texts. Where other disciplines could point to their textbooks, the lawyers, at least the canon lawyers, could not so easily do so, and even the civil lawyers had, as we shall see, no firm grasp of Justinian to begin with.

For textbooks are essentials of mediaeval university teaching. That was always where a lecturer began, with a formal introduction or *accessus*. Kantorowicz sees in the *accessus* to legal texts the beginning of a recognition of the parameters of a 'discipline of law'.[5] An *accessus* (or 'introduction'), covering sets of standard points, would be used routinely in the early stages of the study of any text in an academic context.[6] It may be helpful by way of illustration to give a brief review here of the ways in which this *accessus* was used in 'legal' introductions. Accordingly, we find in the *accessus* to legal texts identifications of the branch of 'philosophy' in which they fall, of their 'subject-matter', 'intention', 'purpose', 'utility', and so on. The 'branch of philosophy' (*pars philosophiae*) or subject-matter (*materia*) are commonly identified with 'ethics'. For example, Baldus holds the legal principles of 'good' and 'equity' to be the same as those of moral philosophy.[7] He argues in his commentary on the *Digest* (I. i. 2) that 'moral philosophy' is the 'mother' and the 'door' of the law.[8] Our law concerns itself entirely with moral philosophy, he explains.[9] Alternatively, the subject-matter is said to be right and divine justice (*Materia canonum dicitur de quo fiunt, idest ius et iustitia divina*).[10] The sections on *materia* usually contain discussions of the theory of the main subdivisions of the law and the concept of equity. To take a late example, Bulgarus, in his *Materia Codicis* (*c.*1125) makes a series of distinctions: between *aequitas inconstituta* or *rudis*, by which he means 'potential', as yet unformed law; *ius approbatum* or *ius fixum*, which is positive law and *voluntates*, which are actual legal acts.[11]

The 'intention' of studying this subject-matter is to give people the knowledge which will prevent them confusing right and wrong (*fas nefasque*).[12] In the section on the *modus tractandi*, commonly taken with *intentio*, come discussions of rules of interpretation and other methodological matters.

Utilitas or *finis* is treated in terms of the purpose and function of law.[13] The *utilitas* of the study of law is in the business (*consilia* and *negotia*) of the Church, says the *Summa 'Elegantius'*.[14] The *purpose* of the study of law is to instruct the ignorant, prevent and correct prevarication. The study of law runs in harness with that of theology, here leading towards the reward of eternal life; for the attainment of salvation is the ultimate reason for the study of this subject at the point where it is most clearly both theology and law. To that end, penance and punishment correct by fear; the study of right and divine justice 'invites with love'.[15]

The sources: identifying the authorities[16]

No mediaeval academic discipline could run its courses without textbooks, to each of which *accessus* such as these formed the introduction. The major theological authorities of Scripture and the Fathers stand at the head of the legal list just as they do of the theological list.

Scripture

The primary authority for mediaeval scholars is the Bible, and it was not necessary to stretch interpretation to take that to be a text with something to say to lawyers. The preoccupation of the Old Testament, and to a lesser degree the New, with 'judgements' and 'justice' is striking. Scripture is full of testing passages which raise legal principles. The association of righteousness, justice and judgement is clear in Genesis 18.19 *et faciant judicium et iustitiam*. Romans 5.20 points out that law can be said to 'create' wrongdoing by defining it: *lex autem subintravit ut abundaret delictum*. Romans 6.1 canvasses the notion that a person might be justified in sinning, so that grace might 'abound': *Quid ergo dicemus, permanibimus in peccato ut gratia abundet*.[17] 'Be ye angry and sin not,' says Psalm 4.5. Matthew, in his account of the Sermon on the Mount, equates anger which threatens murder with murder itself. So is the mere will to offend something the law ought to address? The relationship of act and intention is touched on in, 'Whoever hates his brother is a murderer' (I John 3.15). There are ideas in Scripture about the value of persons. Personal standing in the eyes of God is important in the Old Testament: Noah was a just man (Genesis 6.9). There are ideas of equity: Leviticus 9.36 speaks of just balances, just weights. Mutual obligation might be thought to go with equal treatment, as in 'Forgive us our debts as we also forgive our debtors' (Matthew 6.12). There is reflection on hierarchy and the interpersonal bonds which tie man to man. For who art thou that judgest another man's servant? Before his own lord he stands or falls (Romans 14.4). There are notes on what might in the twentieth century be called 'social justice', such as 'Bear ye one another's burdens' (Galatians 6.2). There is an eschatological dimension: *in terra sanctorum iniqua gessit, et non videbit gloriam Domini* (Isaiah 26.10). 'Judge not before the time' (I Corinthians 4.5). At the same time there is a concern with getting things put right as quickly as possible: 'Let not the sun go down upon your anger' (Ephesians 4.26).

There are also innumerable issues, for the student of law as well as the student of theology, arising from the *character* of the sacred text as an enormous living puzzle, full of seeming anomalies and contradictions, constantly posing the question whether it is telling the truth.[18] Nowhere does the theologian's task more fully overlap with that of the lawyer. The *Summa 'Elegantius'* comments that the wise man in Scripture may sometimes not be what he seems: *prudens ... simulatio vel dissimulatio in sacris litteris non prohibetur*.[19] It goes through various potentially embarrassing seeming lies in Scripture, to explain for each how it is to be excused (*qualiter excusetur*).[20]

Secular and Christian legal authorities

Among the great names of early legal scholarship, the *auctores* of the legal tradition itself, the *Summa 'Elegantius'* gives a list of those who, it says first put laws into writing: Pompey, Theodosius and Justinian, who restored them succinctly (*mira brevitate*) to order. The *Summa 'Elegantius'* also describes how Justinian composed the *Digest*,[21] then how he put together the *Novellae* from the new laws which he himself had established.[22]

The historical reality looks different. Justinian's *Code* consists of extracts from pronouncements of emperors. The earlier instances are mostly judicial, then later they become legislative; there are passages in the original Greek.[23] Justinian's *Digest*, on the other hand, is a compilation of extracts from eminent jurisconsults, again, including passages in the original Greek. The *Novels* (*Novellae*) are imperial legislation not in the *Code*, and not previously officially collected. In the Italy of the centuries immediately after Justinian, the *Institutes* and the first nine Books of the *Code* (the details of the last three Books deal with public law which did not apply after the end of the ancient Empire), and the Epitome of the *Novels* by Julian, were known. The *Digest* was not used for some centuries.

The Lombard law-books had been written in Latin and there seems to have been some formal study of these at Pavia. The need for a crib to Justinian's substantial texts was felt from an early stage. The device of making an epitome of Justinian's *Code* was tried as early as the seventh and eighth centuries.[24] MS Vaticelliano XVIII of the late ninth or early tenth century contains a collection of *capitula* covering the main points ecclesiastical lawyers are likely to need.[25] This approach of listing (and usually roughly grouping) *capitula* is repeated in other collections up to and beyond Gratian. It represents a way of approaching the task of making study materials available in a practical manner for the use of both students and practitioners.

In the 1090s Irnerius[26] began to make his own copy of the now lost Codex S[ecundus] on which the alternative text of the *Digest* later used at Bologna was based. He tried to improve the text as he did so. He also tackled the first nine books of the *Code*, here inserting material from the *Authenticum* (a larger collection of *Novels* than that of Julian) at the appropriate places. He devised a system of reference by numbers (the *Institutes*, *Digest* and *Code* already had numbers for the Titles or chapters, and Irnerius used their first words to identify the individual *leges*). The word is used for items of both legislative and juristic origin. He achieved a *corpus iuris civilis* in five books, the first three consisting of the *Digest*, the fourth of the first nine books of the *Code* and the fifth of the *Institutes* and the *Authenticum*. Irnerius omitted Greek portions. These were translated by Burgundio of Pisa (*c*.1110–93), but not included in the Bolognese texts during the Middle Ages.[27] The rediscovery of Justinian's *Digest* about 1070 provided the text without which it is doubtful whether the science of law would have been able to develop as it did in the mediaeval West.[28]

Further attempts to provide helps with the study of Justinian are to be found in later centuries. In 1149 Master Vacarius published the *Liber Pauperum*, which was a series of extracts from the *Corpus* for the use of students too poor to have access to copies of the full text. To these he added copious glosses.

But not all sources used in legal contexts began life as legal texts and not all those which purported to have done so were authentic. That is, not all were 'real' legislation or were genuinely the product of their time or presumed authors. More material was needed, and particularly in the field of canon law. Fragments of the Fathers[29] – especially of Augustine[30] – occur in legal collections but they seem not to have been derived from their sources directly, and may thus not be the fruit of a systematic search for material.[31] Such texts could certainly have moral authority, but, insofar as they represented the opinions of individuals they could contain only precepts, not laws.[32] The Ps.-Isidore compiler was eager to give a papal respectability to his texts. That is a testimony to the importance of being able to point to an *auctoritas* beyond the ultimately 'personal' (which could be provided by a patristic *auctor*), and which could be regarded as speaking in some way officially on behalf of Christ in his Church.[33]

This complex collection which is now known as the Ps.-Isidorian *Decretals* was of immense influence and significance.[34] The library and *scriptorium* of Corbie may have provided Ps.-Isidore with some of the texts he used in the *Decretals* (for example, the *Corbie ecclesiasticus*), and also been responsible itself for making early copies.[35] A great deal remains unclear about the genesis and transmission, but for our purposes it can be taken as an entity which is firmly in the tradition of texts in play in legal studies in the early attempts to treat law as a subject of study. It is not unique for its period. There are, for example, canonical compilations by Florus of Lyons, secretary to three successive bishops of Lyons in the ninth century.[36]

Before Gratian there were eleventh-century compilations which make use of Ps.-Isidore, notably that of Burchard of Worms in the early eleventh century and that of Ivo of Chartres at its end. Gregory VII actively sent searchers out to look for legal material which he could use in the battle over Investiture at the end of the eleventh century. This is one of the factors which seems to have led to the rediscovery of the *Digest*, and also to the reinstatement of the *Authenticum*.[37]

The canonists after Gregory VII were engaged in a massive task of codification, trying to tidy up and purify the tradition; trying to use the most ancient texts, trying to harmonise apparent discrepancies.[38] Yvo of Chartres was a pupil of Lanfranc and was at Bec with Anselm of Canterbury. His letters show him to have recognised a practical need for senior figures in the Church to have a knowledge of canon law. He addressed this by trying to supply them with collections of materials.[39] The existence of these collated texts raises the question what Ivo understood these materials to amount to when they had been brought together. Did they constitute an 'authority'? A canon?

Of all the compilers of the eleventh to twelfth century, Gratian proved to be the author of the definitive 'teaching text'. It did for the academic study of law much what the slightly later *Sentences* of Peter Lombard did for theology and it became a standard textbook. Gratian's achievement was to create a new orderly arrangement of the material and to intersperse commentary, so that they form a coordinated text together. He was not the first to attempt this in his generation, but he was more comprehensive than others, and his book happened to 'hit the market'.[40] It was not a unique text; like Lombard's *Sentences*, it belongs to a genre. The success of Gratian's venture may owe as much to chance timing as to its inherent quality.

Not much is known about Gratian himself, except that he was a Camaldolese monk. He is estimated to have spent a dozen years working on the compilation, and he worked from his own reading of the *corpus iuris civilis* of Justinian as well as from other existing collections. There is still no satisfactory critical edition of Gratian. Thus, a number of questions about the integrity of the text and Gratian's own intentions remain unanswered. For example, it is possible to demonstrate that the material from Roman law was added at a relatively late stage in the composition of the *Decretum*.[41] Chapter 33 q. 3 *De poenitentia* is very long, out of proportion to the treatments of other themes, and also notably digressive, and that presents problems of literary unity.[42] The impossibility in the minds of contemporary students of making a sharp separation of law and theology is plain enough.[43] There are other questions, now unanswerable, about the evolution of the text from Gratian's original conception. The 1130s were one of the most fast-moving decades in the schools of northern France and northern Italy. Anselm of Laon, Alger of Liège, Hugh of St Victor, Peter Abelard, have all been cited as possible influences and each was working in a different sort of academic or religious environment, cathedral school, monastery, house of canons, proto-university. Many scholars were entranced by the possibilities of dialectic.[44] All these influences were working on Gratian as he progressed with his work, and it seems more than likely that the *Decretum* was 'finished' not at one time but in successive redrafts.[45]

Magister Rufinus says that Gratian's intention was to unite the disparate materials he found.[46] Gregory IX was engaged in the same task in the thirteenth century in the *Decretals*. *Decretals* had force only for the situation they are addressed to. They were not laws, although sometimes they were couched in general terms.[47] The *Decretals* of Gregory IX begin with a letter of greeting to the doctors and scholars of Bologna.[48] It is explained that the various constitutions and decretal letters of Gregory's predecessors dispersed in different volumes, seem to have created confusion, because some repeat much the same points, some contradict one another, some are simply very lengthy.[49] So those who have to make judgements have been uncertain how to do it (*vacillabant*); for this reason it has been felt that it would be helpful to draw it all together in an orderly way.

The 'compilation' and the 'ordering' are hard to separate. The authors move between a conceptual tidying up, a thinking through of the subject-matter or nature of the study, to a more literal 'tidying up' of a great deal of material. Both sorts of ordering were needed if a *disciplina* was to result with textbooks which it would be practicable to teach. The *accessus* in the *Summa 'Elegantius'* recognises that some will find Gratian's wordiness tedious or incomprehensible.[50] So the *Summa* itself aims at compression and clarification of Gratian's *Decretum*. But it also introduces new material.[51] Academic study bred study-aids of its own, some of which had to be accommodated in a growing syllabus.[52]

The amassing and sorting of materials went on beyond Gratian because new law continued to be made. *Extravagantes* are legal texts falling outside the code in current use, and additional to it. The term is first used in this sense in the twelfth century after the publication of Gratian's *Decretum* to cover papal letters and conciliar decrees not in Gratian. Gregory IX's *Liber Extra* gathered these together in 1234, and thereafter material in addition to that came to be known as *extravagantes*. In 1298 the *Liber Sextus* was published, forming a new basic text, and the term *extravagantes* came to refer to still later additional material. The *Constitutiones Clementinae*, published in 1317, had the same effect of displacing the application of the term, so that it came to apply to subsequent material. By the fourteenth and fifteenth centuries the *extravagantes* are mainly papal decrees falling outside the *Constitutiones Clementinae*. Three sets of these were collected: the *Extravagantes* of Boniface VIII, three Constitutions of John XXII and the *Extravagantes* of John XXII.[53]

The early law reports

Before we come to the range of legal and theological study-aids which developed for use in the academic study of law to help students get to grips with these sources, we need to touch on one last main genre, not of great importance alongside these others in the Middle Ages, but highly significant later; these were the 'law reports', or records of the conduct and outcome of cases.[54]

It was important that a record be kept, particularly where a judgement settled a dispute about property, and indeed such decisions were not infrequently recorded in charters too. The earliest extant plea roll of the English Common Bench records the cases heard in Trinity Term 1194.[55] It is obvious that the record as it stands cannot have been made during the hearing itself, in the absence of modern aids to the making of full transcripts, and it has been suggested that notes were taken at the time and the case was then written up with the insertion of the necessary names and details. The method would have been not unlike that used by lecturers in the universities who got students to make a *reportatio* as they spoke and then polished the notes. Examples of this kind of text come in conveniently here and there throughout this study, providing examples and illustrations.

Study aids

A key element in the forming of a discipline is the consciousness on the part of those studying and teaching it that that is what they are doing. With this in mediaeval academe went an urge to write manuals and reference books and create *reportationes* of lectures and so on. In theology, *artes praedicandi* manuals, containing general directions and stock outlines and materials for sermons, were put together to assist preachers.[56] The 'friars' books' of examples for preachers provided additional resources. There were dictionaries of theological terms, such as the one put together by Alan of Lille at the end of the twelfth century. These were also designed to aid a preacher who was stuck for a cross-reference in Scripture when he was interpreting a given 'theme' or text in a sermon.[57] There were handbooks for confessors too.

In the study of law, additions and expansions also began very quickly. The additions were known as *Paleae*. There are several early glosses. The *lectura* is a *reportatio* of an actual lecture. An Apparatus was a collection of glosses without the text, but still dependent on being read with it to make sense.[58] Tancred mentions, as he sets out to write his own manual of procedure, that he knows that many people are writing this kind of book nowadays.[59] This certainly seems to have been happening, as the examples used throughout this study show.

The 'Titles' themselves gave opportunity for little essays on the rubrics, where it was possible to deal with the topics or general issues arising, such as the *nature* of 'justice' or of 'law'. For instance, Irnerius' glosses were drawn together into an *exordium* at the beginning of the *Institutes* (on the definition of justice) and another at the beginning of the *Code* (on the definition of law).

A treatise (a less common pedagogic genre among lawyers) deals with a topic but is not attached to or dependent on a particular part of the Corpus.

A *Summula* or *Summa* is a device for dealing with the subject-matter of a whole Title, with cross-referenced material taken from elsewhere in the Justinian *Corpus*. Especially important for the 'decretist' (canon law) side (as distinct from that of the 'legists' or civil lawyers, who relied in the main on Justinian) is the *Summa* of Huguccio of Pisa (1188). Between 1200 and 1265 we arrive at a definitive form of the *summa* and a more or less standard gloss. Hugolinus and Azo and Hostiensis are important names here.[60]

The *Summa 'Elegantius'* is from about 1169 and it is one of the first commentaries on Gratian from the French School, although it arranges the material in a different order from that of Gratian. Possible authors are Bertram of Metz or Godfrey of Cologne.[61] The independence of the arrangement reflects an independence of approach to the question what kind of teaching text is needed. The purpose is apparently to give those practising law or judging actual cases a grasp of principles. Although this is not one of the procedural manuals we shall be looking at a little later, it will, promises the author, instruct the *advocatus* and the *iudex* alike in the way to begin, run and conclude cases.[62]

Upon the compilations there grew up more glosses. Johannes Teutonicus wrote an *Apparatus glossarum in compilationem tertium* about 1213–18 (it was finished after the Fourth Lateran Council) while he was teaching law at Bologna.[63] His main sources were Johannes Galensis, Laurentius Hispanus and Vincentius Hispanus.

What we can glimpse of methods of teaching which made use of these study-materials shows again and again a sense that here was a subject which needed special methods of instruction, being held anxiously in balance with the deployment of the methods traditional in other fields of academic instruction. Bartolus of Saxoferrato remarks on a tendency for students to skip the difficult parts.[64] Odofredus says in his *proemium* to the *Digestum Vetus* that he was trying to move on from the old ways of teaching. But these were, inescapably, broadly speaking the 'ways of teaching' of theology too.

9 The professional advocate

It is in the records of the *litis contestatio* that the voice of the professional advocate of the Middle Ages can still sometimes be heard and the flavour of the advocacy appreciated. There are indications that the argumentation could be learned, full of references to legal authorities, civil and canonical, and clearly exemplifying adherence to rules of proof which are set out in the procedural treatises.[1]

Yet this was a different world from that of classical Rome, where education consisted of a training in rhetoric and all other aspects of learning were subordinated to the need for the citizen to be a competent public speaker, primarily for that purpose. Political or panegyric opportunities naturally came less frequently than those for the display of skills in forensic rhetoric. Tacitus describes in his *Dialogus de oratoribus* how a crowd would come to watch an advocate in court and be visibly swayed by his words: *vulgus ... adsistentium et adfluens et vagus auditor*.[2] The necessary skills had been taught in classical schools of rhetoric. They included the 'finding' of arguments and a mastery of stock illustrations, examples, or sequences of argumentation.

Cicero's *De Inventione* and *Topics*, widely accompanied by Boethius' writings on the *Topics* and the *De Differentiis Topicis*[3] were available to our mediaeval lawyers in the preliminary arts course they would have taken (those at least who were trained in the universities). From the later twelfth century Aristotle's *Topics* was added to the list of available textbooks. But teaching in rhetoric was always scanty in the Middle Ages compared with that in logic, because of a relative shortage of textbooks. The full Quintilian was not in use until the fifteenth century, nor the bulk of Cicero on rhetoric.

From Cicero's juvenile textbook the *De Inventione* the would-be mediaeval advocate could have learned how to 'find' arguments, and the art of topics would have taught him to classify them and apply them. But there is little evidence of the application of the methodology in a way which indicates that mediaeval advocates were consciously imitating their ancient counterparts, still less that there was any sense of a professional continuity with the work of those earlier generations, that a role for practical skills in a formally 'rhetorical' argumentation remained, in the arena of the courts. An exception is the *Rhetorica ecclesiastica* of the third quarter of the twelfth century. It is, it explains, its *intentio* (as in the *accessus* tradition)[4] to instruct people how to arrive at judgements, partly through a knowledge of the law and partly through the knowledge of rhetoric.[5]

The second of these promises is not really fulfilled in the treatise itself, but clearly it was felt that it ought to be fulfilled in the courts themselves. The loss of a sophisticated admiring audience may have something to do with it, though the mediaeval *vulgus* proved to be keen enough to go to watch academic disputations. The great difference lay not only in the decay of the Roman legal system with the fall of the Empire, but also the rise of Christian expectations about the advocate's role. An advocate speaks for someone who is disadvantaged in a trial because he cannot do it for himself, or not as well as the professionals,[6] but in a Christian context he has a divine 'model'.

The 'theology' of advocacy

In the Godhead there are two candidates for the role of advocate. The supreme 'advocate' for man is Christ. He speaks 'for mankind' before the Father.[7] Such an advocate acts for no reward. No lawyer, Bernard of Clairvaux describes his own *pro bono* human advocacy in which the Christian imitates Christ's selfless advocacy. 'I do not have a case, but I take the cause of these monks as mine, for they are holy men. I take it in hand as though it were mine, and I act to get justice.'[8]

The Holy Spirit is also a divine advocate; he is sent by the Father, to teach mankind and dwell with them (I John 2.1). Indeed, as Augustine points out, *advocatus* is the Latin for the Greek from which 'paraclete' derives: *paracletus … latine dicitur advocatus*, although it is Christ who is said to be our advocate with the Father in heaven.[9] It could be argued – and this possibility is raised by Ps.-Tertullian – that this advocacy of Christ's and the Holy Spirit's is a false advocacy because we are sinners and do not deserve it.[10] There is a hint here of the doctrine that an advocate is an 'officer of the court' and ought not to act against his conscience and the right.[11]

Advocacy for the poor is another matter, because that is acting for the weak and helpless, who are, in the Christian scheme of things, supremely deserving. Cyprian speaks of the advocate who takes the case of the poor to their Lord and argues on their behalf.[12] Both these forms of advocacy seem to involve a willing offering of oneself as advocate, not a hiring for money.

But normally an advocate does work for money, and it is accepted in the court systems of the Roman and mediaeval worlds that there is no shame in his doing so. He is a paid professional, he is entitled to his fee. As Augustine points out, a judge ought not to sell a just judgement, and a witness ought not to sell the truth,[13] but an advocate may be paid for his advice and his legal expertise.[14] Comments on fees and costs are common. Bernardus Dorna explains that there has been a growth in the numbers of advocates who are charging very high fees. Clients paid an advocate a salary when they retained him for a case. Annual retainers were also common.[15] If the accuser loses, he pays the costs.[16] This right to a fee could be abused. Lawyers are greedy, it is complained that they demand large fees before they will agree to represent a client.[17]

In other respects, the ground rules are broadly the same for lawyerly advocacy as for the Christian theological model. The representative conducts the action vicariously, on behalf of the party.[18] He can do so only at the party's wish and with his mandate,[19] and that requires him to be loyal once he has 'taken the case'. Advocacy requires constancy, reliability. As Ambrose points out, Christ is our advocate daily,[20] for we are always repeating our offences and our case is never finally settled.[21] The professional human advocate was not required to make such an open-ended commitment but he had to stick fast to his client for the duration of the case.

Anselm points in the *De Similitudinibus* to a likeness between a sinful monk and a layman. Let us suppose that two men are serving one master, he says. Both obtain possessions from him with the promise that they will be faithful to him: *sibi iureiurando promisso quod ei fideles existant*. But one of them makes his faithfulness a condition of the payment.[22] The other loves his master so much that be prefers to serve him as a member of his household (*familiarius*), without keeping anything for himself.[23]

It is important to the fairness of the process that those who are involved in the case are impartial unless they are acting on behalf of one side or the other, and in that case, their partiality must be unambiguous.[24] They must be clearly *identifiable* as advocates. The advocate is *meant* to be partial, and whether he acts *pro bono* or (in the usual way) for payment, he is on his client's side. It is just for advocates and jurisconsults to be allowed to be paid a fee when judges and witnesses are not, precisely because they act for only one party

It is the duty of an advocate, then, to be entirely loyal (*fidelissimus advocatus*) to the person he defends whether that person is in the right or not. In one passage Tertullian even speaks of an advocate's conceivably having a duty out of loyalty to his client to take up a case against the Holy Spirit.[25] Augustine describes the advocate's legitimately 'partial' role in one of his sermons.

> If you have a case to be tried before a judge, and you instruct an advocate, and you are accepted by the advocate as his client, he should plead your cause as well as he can; if he had not yet completed that task and you were to hear that he was going to be your judge, would you not rejoice, for he who had previously been your advocate was now going to be your judge?[26]

64 *The professional advocate*

In that situation, where of course the intended advocate turned judge is Christ, although it would be true that the rules of natural justice were being broken, it would also be apparent that this would work in the defendant's favour. Since the function of the rules of natural justice is to protect the defendant, that would make it acceptable.[27]

Professionalism and professional detachment can go only so far. The *Summa 'Elegantius'* warns the practitioner that if he has been an advocate in a case, he cannot also be a witness.[28] The advocate for one side becomes an 'enemy' to the other. And just as an enemy cannot be a witness, so a man's enemy cannot be his judge.[29] An acknowledged enemy cannot be impartial,[30] says Isidore and that applies even if he is, in a later mediaeval context, a professional advocate.

The practice

In more lowly courts, such as the manorial courts in England, there was a good deal of local variation in procedure, although many of the records surviving in manorial rolls begin with the pleading and give only the joining of issue and the resolution of the dispute, so it is hard to be sure exactly how cases were conducted.[31] The Lord's steward or bailiff presided, but he might act only as a moderator. The principle was that the work of the court was done by the whole court, *tota curia*. The suitors were usually the local villeinage, or tenants of the manor were under an obligation to be present and to take part in the proceedings as part of their *servicia debita et consueta*.[32]

Except perhaps in these humble manor courts there was scant hope of a party to litigation knowing what to do without professional help. When the parties were summoned in a civil case, the respondent could make satisfaction without further process.[33] But if the case went forward, litigants were increasingly likely, as the Middle Ages move on, to need expert help. Professional advocates came into existence to meet that need.

Roman law had addressed the question of the 'right to representation'. Ulpian says, 'if they have no advocate, I will provide one: *si non habebunt advocatum, ego dabo*.[34] Entitlement to a *professional* advocate, as distinct from the right not to have to stand trial alone, never seems to have been universally accepted as a requirement of natural justice, perhaps because it would be an expensive provision in any age. Similarly, although a defendant may mount as many defences as he can think of, litigants are forbidden to use several advocates so as to give a false opinion of the substantiveness of their defence to their adversary.[35]

In certain contexts the need for 'legal aid' in the form of the provision of an advocate was, however, accepted in the later Middle Ages. When Boniface VIII set up an inquisition, canonists argued that there must be provision for the defence of the accused. If the accused denies being a heretic, they say, he has to be given a lawyer, even if he does not ask for one.[36]

An official advocate ought to be competent to do his job, so a layman cannot be an advocate, says William de Drogheda.[37] The glossators agree that advocates must be legally qualified (*periti in legibus*).[38] This is evidence that professionalism was required. Assurance of good character was also expected, like the modern requirement of a person seeking to join an Inn of Court that he be without criminal convictions and not bankrupt. Advocates must be of good conduct (*debent moderate agere et honeste tractare*); for example, they must not attempt to bribe the witnesses.[39] Among the authors of procedural manuals, Ricardus Anglicus says that a procurator should be of good repute (*bonae famae*). An *infamis persona* cannot be a proctor.[40]

Such strictures were apparently necessary. There is evidence of advocates getting away with corruption and incompetence. Hugh Candlesby was a professional lawyer and proctor who was a leader in an attack on Corpus Christi College in Cambridge in 1381. He was a permanent functionary of the archdeacon's court, who got away with a great deal professionally. 'Candlesby illustrates splendidly how an entrenched practitioner and court functionary could not merely ignore but even openly defy the rules of professional conduct with impunity for years on end.'[41] Ralph Niger in his *Moralia* on the Second Book of Kings, describes how members of the so-called 'order of legal experts'[42] try to break down established custom to suit themselves, promising a client that they will win for a bribe (*pro lucro*) if there is a 'suitable judge' (*idoneus judex*), who will cooperate.[43]

Various types of officially approved advocate or court official were recognised. William of Drogheda discusses the office and role of *procuratores*. A proctor is someone who acts on behalf of another person at his wish, he explains.[44] He does what his principal would do if he were present.[45] It is less clear that the proctors in the ecclesiastical courts were necessarily professional lawyers though a number of them carry the academic title of Master.[46]

Such proctors had to be granted rights of audience. That is, they were formally appointed *apud acta curie* in order to be allowed to speak on behalf of the party in question (though it was also possible for someone not thus appointed to speak in the defence simply as a 'defender').[47] Proctors took precedence of mere advocates. Surviving records of speeches give the names of the proctors, even if the speech may have been made by an advocate.[48]

Who were the advocates?

In England it is possible to identify individual advocates who acted in particular cases.[49] The serjeants mentioned in the early English court records seem to be professional lawyers who could be hired as advocates (though it appears that they could also discharge other functions in the conduct of a case). About eight have been identified as acting in Common

Bench cases in the 1280s.[50] In 1295 the Statutes for the ecclesiastical Court of the Arches limit the number of advocates in a case to sixteen and stipulate that no party might have more than six advocates and two proctors.[51]

It has been possible to put together a list of 'English law officers' from the late thirteenth century. The royal writ admitting John of Cambridge on 24 June 1328 illustrates the thinking behind their appointment. The King greets his justices of the bench (*justiciariis suis de banco*). He tells them that it is his wish that John of Cambridge 'should be one of those in our service in the business (*in negotiiis*) of the aforesaid bench'.[52]

The advocate as officer of the court

William of Drogheda describes the advocate's office in the Middle Ages in terms which bear all this out, defining him as the person who is active on behalf of one of the parties in a trial.[53] But he takes us a step further by suggesting that the professional advocate is already, in a sense, an officer of the court. It is his duty to use his energies to keep things on the right lines (*lapsa erigere, fatigata reparare suae defensionis viribus*), in both public and private cases, for he who defends the life and hope of those who trust him is a warrior with words just like a soldier who fights with swords and shields, but this is a duty which extends beyond the client to the court itself.[54]

Robert Kilwardy wrote a letter to the Dean of the Arches in 1273, which includes the words of an oath to be sworn by proctors or by professional advocates who were to be given audience in the ecclesiastical court of Canterbury. The oath consisted of an undertaking of honesty and loyalty to the clients who 'retained' them as their representatives. Sometimes an advocate found himself in a position where there was conflict of interest because he had a prior commitment to others who had already retained a particular advocate.[55] According to such 'officer of the court' rules, advocates must set before them an ideal of justice. They are not to persist with an unjust cause. They are not to undermine the Church's liberties. They are not to contrive unjustified delays. (There was a tendency for advocates to use every legal subtlety available to them, even to pervert the course of justice to get a victory for their clients and that created immense delays.)[56] They are not to be paid a percentage of any damages but a straightforward salary.[57]

The advocate is to be very polite to the judge (*humiliter se gerat*) so that he is not removed for being contumacious.[58] Advocates ought to put forward rational arguments; nor should they speak ill of the other party.[59] If they fail in such restraint, they lay themselves open to being regarded as infamous, and they weaken their case.[60] In return for this courtesy, the judge ought to listen patiently to the advocate to hear him out. Indeed, if he does not there will be a ground for appeal (*locus ... appellationis*).[61]

But the advocate is not to be long-winded, for it is better to say a little well than to be wordy and take risks.[62]

Sometimes, of course, the advocate will make a mistake. If that happens, it is not to be allowed to prejudice the outcome for the defendant. The client can set the record straight, says William de Drogheda of the *Code*, up to three days after the error has been made. Sometimes an advocate may fail to say everything he should, and then the judge ought to supply what he has omitted.[63] If the error is one of fact it can be put right at any time.[64] On these stated principles there grew up a professionalism among advocates.

Counsel's opinion

There is a further dimension to the work of the professional advocate, and that is the role of jurisconsult, or source of 'expert legal opinion'. The Roman jurists were statesmen, learned in the law, not professional paid lawyers, but *hommes d'affaires* who took an interest in the subject. Paul and Ulpian are prominent examples. The number of such jurists was not large – only about seventy can be pointed to in the two and a half centuries before these great figures. A judge was expected to give weight to the *responsa* (interpretation) of a jurist, certainly by the second century.

In the late Middle Ages, in certain parts of Europe, it became, as we have seen, usual for princes to man their courts with professionally trained lawyers, holding posts as advisers. These tended to be *juristae* who had studied at Bologna or elsewhere. They maintained something of a common legal culture among themselves,[65] within a system which would otherwise have been perhaps much more legally pluriform than it was. In practice that gave some powers to advocates to influence things. The 'legal opinion' was reborn. It has even been suggested that if professionals were running the courts and the judge weighed the evidence, there might be no real point in holding an actual trial, at least not in every case. The issues could simply be discussed and the thing settled by the lawyers.[66] In due course this led to a bifurcation of function, as attorney became distinct from pleader,[67] and an evolution of the concept of a court, towards that found in the *Ancienne Coutume de Normandie* (*c.*1300), where the persons come together in 'an assembly of *wise* [emphasis added] men in a certain place at a certain day, by whom right is to be done in a dispute to those who plead'.[68]

The existence of 'standing' courts (such as can be identified in England from the twelfth century[69] and elsewhere at different stages in the evolution of local judicial systems), may not be a prerequisite for the evolution of a system of professional training for advocacy, but it is likely to encourage it, particularly in an era of conspicuous development of the academic study of law. The term *iurisperiti* occurs.[70] Aegidius de Fuscarariis describes himself in such terms in his *Ordo Iudiciarius*. He identifies himself as *doctor decretorum licet indignus* and says that he has written at the request of some of his pupils on the 'bar vocational course', for the instruction of those just setting out on the profession of advocate (*ad eruditionem novorum advocationum militantium*).[71] He promises to explain civil, spiritual and criminal law for the benefit of those who, whatever their knowledge of the law itself, may be ignorant about its practical application in actual cases.

10 A moot point
Disputations as academic exercises

In theology questions arose naturally out of the lecture on a set text, especially of the Bible. They could sometimes be dealt with in the course of the lecture itself, but increasingly as scholarship advanced and matters grew more complex, they were deferred for fuller consideration at a separate session, in the afternoon. That happened in theology as early as the mid-twelfth century, as the surviving work of Simon of Tournai shows. The academic disputation moved on from there to become a forum for debate about disputed questions. The question would be put, then the arguments on one side lined up, with the arguments against them marshalled on the other side. The Master would then 'determine' or settle the question. Of discussion of this sort of 'a question', the *quodlibet* (a question which could be on any topic), is perhaps the supreme example.

As academic law caught up with academic theology in its teaching methodologies it followed the same pattern. Johannes Bassianus describes how questions arising out of lectures in law can be dealt with either on the spot: *statim in lectione*, or if they are more difficult, they can be held over until later: *vel in vesperis pro sua difficultate prolixiori disputationi reservando, differenda.*[1] William of Drogheda describes how he has been 'lecturing day by day and frequently holding disputations about the law' (*de iure*).[2] The *distinctiones*, the *solutiones contrariorum*, the *notabilia*, the *casus*, the *summulae*, were, suggests Kuttner, 'employed to explain' the set books of the law,[3] and among these clearly fall 'disputations arising'. This 'deciding' stage gave the Master the role of 'judge' in an academic forum rather than a court. 'Disputed questions' in the academic field of law survive from the second quarter of the twelfth century for civil matters and from twenty years after that for canon law.[4]

Somewhere between the twelfth century and the end of the Middle Ages this method of teaching, common to law and theology – and incidentally to medicine as the third higher degree subject[5] – evolved into or was replaced by a device *peculiar* to the teaching of law.[6] The 'disputation' became the 'moot'. The forensic disputation potentially had an aspect which the theological disputation did not, because it was also a training for the adversarial encounter of the *litis contestatio*, and the 'academic judge' stood in for a real judge. So we need to try to sketch these legal disputations with at least two distinct forms in mind, the academic discussion, of a question arising in a teaching text, and 'practice advocacy', where the adversarial, *sic et non*, form belongs essentially to the *litis contestatio*. The paradigm as Magister Honorius puts it, is: *et videtur ... econtra tamen videtur ... solutio*.[7]

It is hard to be clear what to make of the multiple forms in which the genre survives in the mediaeval teaching of academic law, or of the precise relation of the 'academic disputation' to the 'moot'. In a pioneering pair of articles G. Fransen identifies some in which the full development of the disputation from posing of the problem to conclusion is preserved; and others in which the question has been reduced to a simple statement of the problem with the arguments for and against, on the *Sic et Non* model (that is, a version which does not 'include the answer').[8] There are several sorts of *casus*, 'problems', which may include solutions or not.[9] There may be a rubric, a preamble, a theme, for civil issues a *propositio actionis*, an argument (*pro* and *contra*), with perhaps a resolution.[10] Or we may find the posing of a problem (*casus*); the identification of a question arising from it (*quaestio*); the setting out of arguments *pro* and *contra*; and the solution (*determinatio, responsio*).[11] All this is readily intelligible on the hypothesis that what we are seeing is a natural outgrowth of a problem presented by a 'set text' which became a topic for more extended discussion; or equally, on the hypothesis that these are stock examples for practising mooting.

William of Drogheda's *Summa Aurea* (Book II)[12] is concerned with 'the method of advocating, opposing, responding, counselling, distinguishing true from false' in a context of practical advocacy. Its purpose, as he explains in the *accessus*, is to polish the skills of advocates (*quod rudes efficantur subtiles, balbutientes loquentes, subtiles subtiliores*).[13] For all skills improve with practice.[14] Fransen suggests that among the distinctive features of the lawyer's type of disputed question are, first, that it is intended to provide a practical preparation for the lawyer's profession and, second, that it must be 'disputable'.[15] That is, such questions must not be capable of resolution simply by referring the questioner to a proof-text. Such practice was manifestly available within the university syllabus.

The legacy of classical rhetoric

There is one other possible ancestry which should not pass without mention. It has already been emphasised that forensic skills developed in the Roman world as a form of oratory. Mediaeval rhetoric had three branches now generally recognised as deriving from the classical rhetorical tradition in their methodology, and all involving the exercise of live skills in composition or speaking. These are the art of letter writing; the art of poetry; and the art of preaching, reaching their definitive mediaeval development in the eleventh, twelfth and thirteenth centuries respectively.[16]

They all exploit skills of classical rhetoric in their different ways. The art of letter writing discusses the etiquette of salutation formulas and the *captatio benevolentiae*, gives the rules for the overall plan of a letter, in imitation of the scheme of a speech in classical oratory. The art of poetry explains how to deploy figures of speech for effect. The art of preaching exploits the persuasive powers of the art. For each of these branches of mediaeval rhetoric, preceptive manuals, and sets of formularies or specimens came into being.[17]

We cannot be stretching the evidence to look for a continuation of the application of classical rhetorical principles in a field which was a staple of the ancient art of oratory, and even to suggest that the disputation of the *litis contestatio* was a fourth authentic mediaeval rhetorical art. Questions edited by Fransen from three manuscripts establish that the same or similar sets of questions were in use as manuals in more than one place in the legal disputations.[18] There is also the *summa quaestionum* which brings together sets of problems under topic-headings (such as simony or excommunication, for example), much like the friars' books of materials under topic headings for use in the preaching of sermons, in theology.[19] So with the development of 'recognised' primers, one of the requirements of a mediaeval branch of rhetoric is met. Kuttner argues that the *quaestiones disputatae* were unique among mediaeval academic disputations in being *practical* exercises.[20] That is helpful to this tentative hypothesis about mediaeval rhetoric, since the art of rhetoric is an applied art and the classical tradition had been designed to make advocates of its students.

Topics

This takes us to a very difficult question, whether the classical rhetorical art of 'topics' has a place in mediaeval legal disputation.[21] It had already been adopted by students of logic in the Middle Ages. The art of topics, according to Cicero, is a systematic method of finding arguments (*inveniendorum argumentorum*).[22] He goes on to distinguish between the 'discovery' and the 'testing' of arguments (*iudicandi*), which he equates with syllogistic.[23] (It is Cicero's view that the first is the proper and supreme province of the orator and the area most developed in the art of rhetoric.)

A division of *inventio* adumbrated by Cicero, and explored well before the twelfth century,[24] thus distinguishes *schemata* of ready-made sequences of argumentation from *argumenta*, which are structurally illustrations or *exempla*.[25] We do not have to stretch the evidence to make this fit the surviving evidence about the teaching of the law. As Johannes Bassianus puts it, and also according to Baldus[26] every 'good reason' (*bona ratio*) can be called an *argumentum*. That is obvious from the definition, for an argument is (*pace* Cicero) a 'reason' which convinces.[27]

Baldus goes on to explain that he himself is using the term *argumentum* in two ways.[28] The first is for reasoning rhetoricians would call 'artificial' (that is, involving art). This is appropriate when legists want to put their case.[29] The second is argument *a ratione naturali*, from natural reason. This falls within the same broad category as the *exemplum*, or 'piece of evidence' or 'illustration'.[30]

So it is one thing for an orator to have a stock of stories (*topoi*) with which to make a point, and another thing for him to have a repository of ready-made 'frameworks' (such as syllogisms), in which to deploy sequences of argumentation (another kind of *topoi*).

This difference remained important in the academic study of the law in the Middle Ages, with the difference that the classical rhetoricians' stock of illustrative stories comes to be replaced by the circumstances of a real or hypothetical case to which *topoi* of argumentation may be applied.

Questiones disputatae can be found in the early 'mooting' literature of the fifteenth century.[31] A man has been disseised of lands which he formerly held. A statute has been passed making it possible for him to buy the land. He dies before he has made the purchase. Can a man's descendants recover their father's holdings by writ, relying on the statute, although it was not in force at the material time? Some say yes. Others say no; for this type of writ is created by the statute and it cannot be used retrospectively. Those taking this 'side' also say that there is no cause of action because the writ is designed to be used in a situation which does not exist. The first side argues against these two contentions. The second side tries to counter these points. The argument ends inconclusively: *non est certum, ideo queratur.*[32]

Some of the questions edited by Fransen in 1957 survive without the dressing of the full detail of a 'case'. Is the taint removed from a damaged reputation by baptism?[33] Can a subdeacon marry?[34] But this is unusual. A feature of examples of legal questions is the way they reflect the complexity and confusion of real-life situations. Yet as Fransen points out, 'the disputed question is always a *quaestio iuris*'.[35] It is never concerned with establishing the *facts* of a case but with the point of law it raises.[36]

Early glosses on the *Digest* contain lists of *allegationes*, in the form of references to texts which agree or disagree.[37] In Fransen's list *allegationes* are identified as the presentation by advocates of arguments which are likely to lead to victory in a case.[38] He adds *consilia*, legal 'opinions' given by jurists in connection with an actual case. These are specific and addressed either to one of the parties or to the judge.[39] That is again one way of saying that they have 'the added refinement of a "case" – a specific problem with real or hypothetical facts – upon which the question would be framed'.[40] But it is not perhaps important whether the cases taken as examples were real. In fact the statutes of universities tend to prohibit the use of real cases, just as they forbid debates on real theological controversies of the moment, so as to prevent live arguments from breaking out, in what could be a very excitable community; swords were sometimes drawn.[41] But they could still imitate 'real life', and were expected to do so.

The *Casus Placitorum*[42] and the *Brevia Placitata*[43] may fall into this category, with law teaching apparently already based on the analysis of cases even by the thirteenth century, and especially knotty fictional cases perhaps being devised for teaching purposes, just as they are in modern law courses.[44]

In the first of the series edited by Fransen in 1952, a layman commits incest with a nun. He does the necessary penance and then contracts a legitimate marriage. In due course he is accused *coram papa* of breaking the rules of consanguinity. The accuser names witnesses. But it happens that the witnesses have left the country and there is no expectation that they will return. The accuser drops his accusation. The Pope absolves the pair, believing that the accuser was motivated by malice. Unexpectedly the witnesses come back. The accuser then proceeds and proves that there is consanguinity.[45]

This confusing tale is identified as the *thema*. From it are drawn out three questions. Should the husband have married someone with whom he had formerly 'behaved wickedly'? Should he have continued to sleep with his new wife while the accusation was pending? Could the Pope (or any other judge) reverse his own former judgement, which had been arrived at not unreasonably? The argument that a judge has not exercised his discretion unreasonably works in the Middle Ages as now, as a means of preventing his decision being revisited. These are manifestly not the only questions which could have been raised on this set of facts. In other examples, as here, the choice of 'questions arising' is highly selective, and it is a reminder that the task was not (as it would have been in theology) to wrap up every point on which there is doubt (for in theology it is important that no one's faith is threatened), but to find arguments which may 'run' in court.

For instance, a bishop lapses into heresy and then ordains a number of priests. His clergy declare themselves no longer in communion with him. The accusers who say he is guilty of heresy are, respectively, themselves guilty of infamy and bigamy.[46] Three questions are derived from this *thema*. The first is whether persons ordained by heretics are to be accepted. The second is whether the bishop's clergy could separate themselves on their own authority from communion with him. The third is whether two such accusers ought to be listened to in the accusation of a bishop. Again a select list is chosen as the focus of the 'moot', and with the same apparent essentially rhetorical intention of using topos (*exemplum*, illustration) in conjunction with topos (*argumentatio*).

Another way of identifying these dualities of the abstract and the concrete, the 'practice' and the 'real' example, may lie in the contrast between *quaestiones disputatae in scholis* and *quaestiones solemnes seu publicae*. The 1552 statutes of Bologna require doctors of canon law to conduct public disputations once a year between Lent and Pentecost with due formality and with a record kept. Upon this literature was mounted another. Doctors could discuss the performance of their fellows in their own schoolrooms, holding private disputations upon the texts of the public disputations. Fransen takes the view that the bulk of the surviving questions of these types (he cites those of Pillius, Roffredus, Damasus, and Bartholomew of Brescia) are mere summaries of practice questions disputed by students. He moves on to *quaestiones reportatae* and *quaestiones redactae*. The distinction he seeks to make here is between questions which survive in the form of notes as they were taken and questions which have been edited and turned into a more formal record. Then there are *quaestiones quaternales*, which circulated as reference material and further sets of questions named after the days of the week on which they were conducted.[47]

The story, insofar as it can be traced for England, is told in outline by Thorne and Baker in the introduction to *Readings and Moots at the Inns of Court in the Fifteenth Century*.[48] A set of *Quaestiones Londinienses* survives from as early as the late twelfth century, naming Oxford masters.[49] Thorne and Baker note an Oxford and Cambridge example of the fourteenth century[50] but the main preoccupation of their introduction is with the question of the practical provision for the teaching of law in late mediaeval England. In fifteenth-century moot books (with which they are chiefly concerned) there is no 'solution' and an immense tangle of points is raised in each moot.[51]

Thorne and Baker suggest that there may be significance in the lack of a *solutio* in the fifteenth-century English moots they edit.[52] That would again take us to rhetoric, this time to a distinction between the 'potted argument' which is primarily a 'schema of argumentation', and the *argumentum*. The *argumentum* is first and foremost an example drawn from life or literature, but containing particularities rather than abstractions, and allowing ample scope for the confusion and complexity natural to the 'real case'.[53]

For example, it is postulated that an armed band of Hospitallers have forced their way into a church, attacked and beaten up the local clergy and ejected them. The local bishop has responded by denouncing the Hospitallers as excommunicate. The Hospitallers have retaliated by laying a complaint against the bishop for violating a privilege of immunity from excommunication given them by Pope Alexander III.[54] For the Hospitallers it is argued that this means that only a Pope can excommunicate them, so the bishop cannot have done so. For the bishop it is argued that he had not excommunicated them, merely 'denounced them as excommunicate'. John of Tynemouth, the Oxford scholar who contributed a 'resolution' to this, took the side of the Bishop. *Bene potuit eos denunciare*, he ends. 'He had full power to denounce them.' The Oxford series from which Brundage takes the first example for analysis has marked features of the descent of the early legal *disputatio* from *disputationes* whose unravelling depends upon the study of logic.[55] And it supports our argument that technical logical and rhetorical skills are visibly in play, for instance in the use here of the device (as much a logician's device as a lawyer's), of sidestepping by redefinition of what he did, the objection that the bishop appears to have acted *ultra vires*.

The adversarial exchange in this form came to be known as a 'brocard'.[56] The derivation of the term *brocardica* remains mysterious. It appears to be used for legal disputations. There is a possibility that it is a corruption of the name of Burchard of Worms. Peter of Blois indicates as much in saying: *Invenio tamen quosdam canones in Brocardo (Burchardo)*.[57] In the fourteenth century Azo assembled a collection of *brocardica*.[58] Pillius brought the term *brocarda* into written use.[59] After his day it is employed as a synonym for *generalia*. But it is also found linked to the device of the marshalling of contrary opinions.[60] There is, however, a definitional lack of clarity, because the conflicting arguments often took the form of axioms or propositions or *loci communes*. So these on their own and not arranged in conflicting pairs, could also be known as 'brocards'.[61] But a fourteenth-century source is clear that a brocard *in iure* is when the two sides argue against one another, for and against.[62] This setting of opposites over against one another is of the essence of the Brocard, for, as Azo explains, 'if anyone want to brocardize, he can introduce a contrary view here, for sometimes variation is admitted, as in D.5.2.8.5 and D 37.6.8.'[63] In resolving brocards, Azo proposes, the first thing to do is to decide whether the rule itself is to be held, or its contrary.[64]

It seems, then, that the moot began in the disputation on a point arising from a legal set text, but that it became something formally distinct from the disputation in several respects: in the special place it gave to the art of topics; in its use of real or pretend case materials to raise and test theory, or points of law; in its practicality as a rhetorical art with an application.

11 Legal argument and the mediaeval study of logic

Regulae and demonstrative method

The *Digest* ends with two titles: 50.16 (*De verborum significatione*) contains 246 opinions of jurists on the meanings of key terms, and 50.17 (*De diversis regulis iuris antiqui*) is made up of 211 fragments or extracts from the writings of jurists each containing a *regula* or *regulae*. Most of the latter come from the jurists Paul[1] and Ulpian,[2] writing in the early third century. A proportion are from the second-century Gaius and Pomponius.[3] Their inclusion in this position – although in some cases it is hard to justify or seems an infelicitous choice – gave them a certain standing, and later jurists tended to think them particularly important.[4] Stein lists nine classical jurists who mention or use *regulae*, Neratius Priscus, who produced fifteen books of them, Pomponius, Gaius, Cervidius Scaevola, Paul and Ulpian, Marcian, Modestinus, Licinius Rufinus.[5] There is reason, then, to think *regulae* were valued even in Justinian's time.[6] This respect for *regulae* is, however, most notable after the 'rediscovery' of the *Digest* in the mediaeval period, when scholarly legal interest was kindled by the title *De regulis*, because it was associated with the great respect felt for 'demonstrative method', which proceeds from first principles or self-evident truths, by valid reasoning, to what must be, for the logician, the securest of conclusions.[7] In Euclidean demonstrative method (and in Boethius' *De Hebdomadibus*, with its more linear and less complex structure),[8] it is clearly understood that an edifice is built on the primary self-evident truths, when further inferences are made from them. Stein discusses the link between *regula* and *canon*, which is more than etymological[9] and takes us into the cognate fields of ethics, dialectic and rhetoric.[10] 'Canon' is the Greek for 'rule', for it rules life and knowledge; that is, it affords a norm for living well, and judging rightly.[11]

Baldus, pupil of Bardolo in Perugia, believes in going back to first principles.[12] Bulgarus, in one of the earliest of the attempts to resolve contradictions (*solutiones contrariorum*), sets out *regulae iuris*, not all of which he has taken from Title 50.17 of the Digest.[13] We have to ask what is the character of these first principles in the eyes of such mediaeval authors. Strictly, for the logician, a *regula* is a 'commonplace' or *communis animi conceptio*, to use the Boethian phrase (also used in the twelfth century to render Euclid's equivalent), and that is a rule which is intuitively perceived to be correct, rather than one 'learned' by comparing examples. The *regulae* in *Digest* 50.17 often have an air of being such *communes animi conceptiones*. 'A rule,' says one, 'is that which briefly says that something is what it is; right does not derive from the rule, but the rule from right: *Regula est, quae rem quae est breviter ennarrat; non ex regula ius sumatur, sed ex iure quod est regula fiat.*[14] That is to argue that 'right' is absolute and can thus form a basis upon which general principles can be seen to rest.

The term *regula* has a weighting and an appeal in a mediaeval context which it enjoyed to only a limited extent in classical Roman law, when the demonstrative method was a less sought-after and consciously respected way of arriving at a conclusion. The ultimate security in argumentation can come only from the construction of demonstrative arguments based on 'necessary reasons' or 'axioms', and this is ultimately perhaps only possible in geometry, and even there Euclid was obliged to add to his axioms a list of definitions (which clarify the meaning of terms but do not take a position on the truth-status of the thing they define), and hypotheses, which merely take something to be the case for the purposes of argument.[15]

When classical jurists speak of a *regula*, they tend to mean a rule which carries the *authority* of precedent. The epigrammatic form of *regulae* may be secondary to this authoritativeness.[16] Thus, a matter on which judgement has been passed is taken to be a truth, says the *Digest*.[17] Several cases, brought together, can give a 'rule' to go on, as their common elements or common ground emerges.[18] 'A rule is said to be, as it were, a conjunction of "causes", that is to say, several causes conjoined make a rule.'[19] This is of interest because it seems to constitute almost a 'Euclidean rule of evidence'.

In manuscripts of the Latin translations of Euclid which became available from the twelfth century there is visual indication that there was some confusion as to the status of the theorems. They are often picked out in red as though they were simply rubrics. There seems to have been a similar muddle over the difference between a typographical convenience and a level of hierarchy of concept in the text in legal contexts. Azo comments in his Brocardica that a 'brocard' can be said to be not a general rubric but merely something 'known', for from the laws which underlie it can be drawn evidence in causes.[20] Such *generalia* may not in fact be classifiable as *regulae iuris*.[21] Nevertheless, Azo seems to want to take them as such. If that is understood, his general rule may be taken that what was valid from the start does not cease to be 'in order'.[22] The crucial point in his view is that a *regula* is something upon which other principles may rest, a solid foundation of (self-evident) truth: *Circa hoc sumenda est regula, ut si stat per eum.*[23] Nevertheless, that is not easily made to work in practice in a forensic context. Speculative reason is especially concerned with what is necessarily so, says Aquinas.[24] *Necessaria* cannot be other than they are.[25] In this way, truth is found in the conclusions as certainly as it is in the premisses.[26] The practical reasoning of the lawyer in court is concerned with contingencies, such as are human acts.[27] In the conclusions reached here there is room for flaws, for *defectus*.[28]

This is an important and perhaps inevitable differentiating principle separating the pure demonstrative method from that which will have to be used in the 'real life' of the forensic arena. It does not seem to Aquinas that this means that there are different standards of truth involved at the 'general' level, or that these standards themselves are not known equally to everyone.[29] Cicero would have backed him here, in saying that 'right' is not a matter of opinion but has a force of its very nature.[30] But he does think that at the speculative level not all the particular principles will be universally self-evident. An example is the Euclidean rule that the interior angles of a triangle add up to two right angles. This is a universal truth but not everyone knows it. In practical reasoning, some think that not only are all the rules not known to everyone, but there is in fact not even the same standard of truth for everyone in such particulars. For example, it must in general be right to repay debts. But if the repayment of a given debt were to provide money with which war would be waged, it might not in fact be right to repay it.[31]

There are examples in the *Digest*'s *Regulae* of self-evident truths which have practical application in human affairs. For instance, it seems obvious in that way that the whole contains the part:[32] *In toto et pars continetur*.[33] Likewise, particulars are always contained within the general.[34] There are also degrees of self-evidency in these Roman legal *regulae*. Some of them seem to have more the character of 'common sense'. When something is unclear, it is common sense to look for the interpretation most like the truth or most often the case.[35] That which goes against the original reason for making a law cannot be used as a basis for inference in connection with it.[36] There can be no obligation to do that which is impossible.[37]

In speculative reasoning the conclusions of different disciplines (*scientiae*) are produced naturally from principles which cannot be demonstrated. The knowledge of these is not innate in us but discovered by the working of reason, explains Aquinas.[38] So from the precepts of natural law, as though from certain common and undemonstrable principles, it is necessary for human reason to proceed to more specific dispositions.[39] And these particular dispositions which are discovered by reason, and preserve the other conditions which belong to the rational basis of law, are called 'human laws'.[40]

Cicero sets out a distinction between rhetorical and dialectical arguments in terms of the persuasiveness of the one and the (in his view) excessive attention to technical argumentational niceties of the other. This distinction persists in the underlying mediaeval assumptions. A gloss of the fourteenth century on a text of Pope Agatho (678–681) evinces a continuing suspicion of dialectic in a double *topos* where it is dangerous both in rhetorical argument and on the persuasive lips of heretics.[41] Cicero thinks topics more useful than, and prior in the order of things to, syllogisms.[42] Conscious syllogisms are found in mediaeval legal texts.[43]

Probable arguments

For our present purposes, the most important point here is that topics are regarded as involving 'probable', not 'necessary' arguments. Topics was a branch of rhetoric and also of logic, whose later mediaeval history became immensely complex.[44] But it has always furnished sources for lawyers (and also practice in legal reasoning) especially because it was, as a rhetorical area of study, primarily concerned with the 'probable arguments' which wrestle with details of human life.

In the nature of things, lawyers will usually be concerned with probability, just as they will with the contextual and contingent and particular. All definitions in civil law are unsafe, because they can be overthrown, admits the *Digest*.[45] (Similarly, as the *Summa 'Elegantius'* puts it, definitions attempting to state universal truths are dangerous in law.)[46] It is recognised to be upon the 'probable assertions' of witnesses that the advocate must build.[47] Here we even seem to be close to the notion of a balance of probability.

The logic of proving

But that poses a methodological question. *Probatio*, proving, is also supremely the logician's task in the Middle Ages. *Probatio* is understood in legal writings in a way that marks a special adaptation to the lawyer's need to prove his case. The author of the late twelfth-century *Summa 'Elegantius'* promises to collate points about *probatio* which Gratian leaves dispersed in four places in his *Decretals*.[48] He notes, for instance, that the accusation rests on the accuser's being appropriate and unassailable, and upon the bringing to bear of proofs.[49] He explains that proofs come by witnesses and instruments: *probationes per testes et instrumenta*.[50] *Instrumenta*, documentary evidence, are thus kinds of proof, *species probationis*, along with witnesses.[51] These are identified by 'Irnerius' too as *species probationum*.[52] In the manuals of legal *process* of Master Damasus the *species probationis* are again listed (*per testes, per instrumenta, per presumptiones.*).[53] These reflections emphasise that *probatio*, proving, is seen not only to be central to the theory of law,[54] but also to be part of its practice.

It was quite usual to play games with it in other subject-areas. Bernard of Clairvaux says in one of his letters that love (*caritas*) does what he (Bernard) would not be able to do: 'Love dares what I do not dare, knocks

80 Legal argument and the study of logic

trustfully (*cum omni fiducia*) on the door of a friend, confident in not being repulsed.'[55] This is a figure of thought in which, as Bernard sees it, there is a play with the categories of substance and accident. 'So love brings love, the substance brings the attribute': *Itaque caritas dat caritatem, substantiva accidentalem*. 'Where the reference is to the giver, love is the name of a substance; where it is to the gift, it is the name of a quality': *Ubi dantem significat, nomen est substantiae; ubi donum, qualitatis*.[56] Law may do what theology does in making a lively play on the technicalities and indeed, in the late antique rhetorical tradition it had an honourable background there.

Part IV
Law and theology in procedure

12 The theory and the practice

Law was studied academically in the Middle Ages primarily with a view to its being practised. It has even been suggested that it was not the theory but the practical needs which took the lead, that sometimes, or in some jurisdictions, the practice led to the refinement and even the conceptualising of the theoretical aspects.[1]

Yet that is not necessarily how lawyer authors would have wished their work to be seen. In most areas of mediaeval study there is a discomfort or uneasiness on the subject of the relative merits of the theoretical and the practical. A defensiveness about the study of practical aspects is to be found in the discussion of many subjects – music, for example, or political theory – as well as of theology. There is a predisposition to value the theory more highly than the practice. That is true above all of theology. Theology has to be *speculativa or theorica*, because it deals with God, who is the least concrete of all things, indeed, the Supreme Abstraction.[2] Yet theology as well as law is a practical science; it has as its purpose the salvation of souls and it has to be applied pastorally.

In the manuals of court procedure which were written in the late twelfth and thirteenth centuries we frequently find an author struggling in his introductory remarks with this balance between the theory and the practice of his subject. The *accessus* in Henry Bracton's *De Legibus et Consuetudinibus Angliae* is conceived as an introduction to a practical subject.[3] In the *Ordo Judiciarius* of Eibert von Bremen there is a preliminary dedication to his bishop, with the reflection that God has provided a variety of source-material, beginning with the Law of the Old Testament and the sayings of its prophets and the Gospel miracles and including the *sententiae patrum*, the *gesta* of Councils and the *decreta* of popes. Eibert has tried to put the canonical materials in order in a way which respects this tradition.[4] Eibert's *accessus* again seeks to introduce what he depicts as a practical subject. Eibert identifies four 'persons' *in iudicio, iudex, accusator, reus et testis*. These are the *materia operis*, the subject-matter of his work. The author's intention (*intentio scribentis*) is to instruct these persons in the law and in the way to present the case.[5]

In the *Liber Pauperum* of the putative early 'Oxford master' Vacarius we read a similar *apologia* for practical teaching. He says that, with God's help, and immense labour on his part, he has drawn together briefly the main points from Justinian. He has chosen – for practical reasons – what there is a daily need to know (*ad usum rerum cotidianum necessaria*).[6] There is the defensive suggestion that theory is barren unless it bears fruit in practice: *Infructuosa theorica reputatur, nisi ex practica fructus eius colligatur.*[7]

Bernardus Dorna has an opening which deliberately gives the theory of law a theological complexion, while admitting the influence, even the leading, of practical necessities. The wickedness of fallen human nature is so vigorous in people that they easily lose their grip on the faith, and faith alone can keep the frailty of human nature from going astray. He is paraphrasing for a mediaeval Christian readership Justinian's explanation of the reason why there is so much litigation. He has therefore written a manual about writs, which he has tried to make clear and accessible, so as to explain the causes of action and the way to put together and deliver a statement of claim.[8]

Rainerius Perusinus similarly dresses up in a little theological pretension what is mostly practical advice. Of all the things with which human beings busy themselves for the benefit and instruction of their fellows,[9] one of the most important concerns the resolution of disputes and the forming of judgements about them.[10] The author of the thirteenth-century *Ordo 'Invocato Christi Nomini'*, begins 'theologically', in the name of Christ, but the author admits that he has really endeavoured to do something 'very difficult but very useful', which is to compose a book on the customary and legal order (*de legali et consueto ordine*) of conducting civil cases, so that all those involved, i.e. the plaintiff and the defendant and the judge may consult it.[11]

This uneasy balancing act between the Christian ideal and the pragmatics of the practice of law is going on everywhere in the procedural texts we next discuss.

13 Equity and the mediaeval idea of fairness

The purpose of having rules of procedure is that they enable justice to be done where the parties are unequal in strength, wealth and influence. These ideas now embedded in European and British human rights legislation are present in mediaeval thinking on equity too. For *aequitas*, equity, is the mediaeval term which perhaps comes closest to modern ideas of 'fairness'. Equity has many mediaeval meanings, however, and we need to begin by sketching some of them.[1] Among them is the notion of equity as somehow broader and deeper than the law, perhaps the very source of justice. Equity ought to be respected in everything, but especially in the law, says the *Digest*.[2] 'Equity is the fount and origin of justice,'[3] says a *Summa* on the *Institutes*. God's justice is everlasting and his law is equity, stresses John of Salisbury.[4] Baldus says that justice is nothing but equity and goodness.[5]

George Conklin asks whether Stephen of Tournai saw equity

> as an intrinsic element of positive law in which case it could be used by a judge to perfect legal justice within the system of canon law; or, did he view equity as outside of the law, so that if law failed to provide justice then equity offered another means to it? In the latter case, equity would be opposed to law, or would stand above it.[6]

Equity can take us outside the law altogether in that it does not depend upon statute or on the common law (*ius commune*), but is universal, a kind of 'self-evident fairness'.[7] It is impossible to legislate for every possible occurrence, so *aequitas* has to act as a means of extending the law (*extensio legis*), in order that the law may achieve justice; in this way, too, it resembles a 'marker' for what modern usage would describe as 'fairness'.[8]

Some of these notions or their contraries are recognisable in the modern law of equity. Hostiensis classifies others in dividing up 'canonical equity' (*aequitas canonica*). He says that one kind of *aequitas canonica* is the divine positive law explicitly laid down by God to meet human needs, as when Christ proclaimed the indissolubility of marriage, the binding nature of promises, or when he outlawed lies.[9] Then there is the *aequitas sacrorum canonum*, its actual 'fairness'.[10] Finally, there is *aequitas canonica* which derives from the *spiritual character* of canon law. This is a fairness in which justice is tempered with mercy. It is balanced, equitable: *iustitia dulcore misericordiae temperata*,[11] not in the sense of getting 'the right result', but in that of doing what is best for the soul of the guilty and for the victim and fulfilling in that way the most profound underlying principles of order.

Equity may be equated with mercy. Thomas of Chobham suggests that equity is justice which mitigates the penalty according to the general circumstances – interestingly not the specific and particular. Thus: 'the justice which relaxes something from its first rigour is called equity': *iustitia que relaxat aliquid de primo rigore dicitur equitas*.[12] Equity tempers the rigour of the law, as a *temperantia legis*.[13] *Ius aequum* can be contrasted with *ius strictum* or *rigor*.[14] *Aequitas* can mean that which is *contra rigores et iuris civilis regulas*, that is, which is gentler than these. That might take us into the arena of dispensation and *oeconomia*.[15]

A further idea, that *aequitas* is 'coming to the correct decision' (*rectitudo iudicii*), is stated by Baldus in the form: 'Equity is rectitude of judgement following natural reason'.[16] Here, 'truth' can (in a limited sense) be equated with equity, if what we are really talking about is a certain 'four-squareness'. Baldus has: *nota duos lapides angulares veritatem et aequitatem* (from *Digest* 1. 18. 6. 1).[17] But no mediaeval scholar who had been trained as a logician, as all university students were, could be unaware of the difference between truth and validity. There may be an outcome which is procedurally fair (in the sense that proper procedures have been correctly followed and the evidence fairly weighed), but which is not in accordance with the truth, just as in logic a valid conclusion may follow from the premises whether or not the conclusion or premises are true.

Equity as equal treatment

Because it rests partly on self-evident principles and not only on positive law, mediaeval equity has its 'maxims' (not necessarily the same maxims as the modern law of equity).

'There is equity where there is equality', as Baldus puts it.[18] Due process should offer protection to the weaker party and seek to ensure equality of arms. That maxim is not easy to apply in an unequal society, especially one which positively sanctions and approves inequality. In the Old Testament *acceptio personae* is ruled out in 'court proceedings'. All are deemed to be equal before God in the Christian penitential process too. Yet there is a universal acceptance of the naturalness and rightness of differentiation according to rank.[19] It would not be deemed unjust to treat a serf in a particular way, although it would be so deemed if the person being thus treated was of higher social standing. In a system of thought where hierarchy is taken to be an absolute it may be deemed no injustice for some to be less equal than others.

Equity and hierarchy

There should be a level playing field in law. Anyone who expects others to obey a law should accept it as binding for himself, says the *Digest*.[20] Yet it is an important legal principle of the Middle Ages that circumstances alter cases, and we must get a sense of that wider background. What applies at one time and place may not apply at another. What I am to be blamed for in one context I may not be blamed for in another. Gratian notes that human laws differ from place to place because different things seem acceptable to different peoples.[21] Aquinas thinks that it is right that civil laws have particular applications, which fit the needs of a particular *civitas*,[22] and that these may not be the same everywhere. There are also legitimate variations of right and wrong, with time and season. Thus there are times of the ecclesiastical year when swearing is forbidden.[23] There are adjustable things which change over time in other ways, which are not fixed by eternal law, but which the care of subsequent ages discovers to be beneficial.[24] There are some things which for reasons of necessity or utility, it is right to alter or relax.[25] Even the discipline of the Church, *disciplina ecclesie* can 'sleep'.[26]

Yet, paradoxically, the maxim which determines that similar cases should be resolved in a similar way stands over against the rule that circumstances alter cases. This rule is stated by Cicero: *quae paribus in causis paria iura desiderat*.[27] The *Summa 'Iustiniani est in hoc opere'* speaks of equity as the fittingness which puts all things on the same basis (*convenientia que cuncta coequiparat*). Or it calls it the *rerum convenientia*, again, the fittingness of things, which seeks similar outcomes for similar cases.[28] Equity ensures a parity of treatment and outcome (Baldus).[29] In Azo's *Summa* too there is a development of the Ciceronian principle in the assertion that similar principles should regulate equal cases.[30] It is a principle of procedural fairness or equity that what is introduced for the safety and protection of people involved in litigation should not be interpreted in a way which oppresses them.[31] It is another maxim that no one should profit from injuring someone else.[32]

The latter are expressions of principle in the area of what we now tend to call equality of arms. There is an important tension between the notion of an equity which utilises the same rational principles for all cases, and the acceptance that there may be differences in each individual's proper rights or deserts. To each his own, *unicuique quod suum est* can be read either as implying that each person has rights (and they are all the same), or as giving to each his peculiar rights, which may vary with his position in society. The latter tends to be the mediaeval view.

For example, the laity can accuse the clergy only if what is alleged is a public crime (*in criminibus publicis*), such as heresy, simony, lèse-majesté, fraud. Otherwise equals should accuse equals, clergy clerics, laity laymen.[33]

The seventh *titulus* of the eleventh-century *Diversorum patrum sententie sive Collectio in LXXIV titulos digesta* explains that juniors may not accuse seniors, inferiors superiors. For example, a priest who wants to accuse his bishop is not lightly to be listened to.[34] Sheep may not accuse shepherds.[35] There is also no crossing of the lay-clerical boundary which places the clerical estate above the lay one. For a cleric is not subject to a secular court.[36] (Anselm of Lucca points out that the laity do not try the clergy in their own courts.)[37] A cleric cannot be thrust before a secular judge against the consent of his bishop.[38] Arguably, a cleric cannot even be accused by a lay person.[39] The reason why laity may not accuse clergy is because 'there ought always to be a separation between the life and conversation of clergy and laity'.[40]

This can be subtly rationalised, so as to see it as fitting in with a proper respect for hierarchy. Anselm of Lucca makes the remark that just as it is fitting for the clergy not to mingle in social intercourse with the laity, so it is proper for them to keep apart in litigation.[41] Just as a cleric is not subject to a secular tribunal by reason of his being in the estate he is, so for the same reason he is forbidden to engage in secular business, says the *Summa 'Elegantius'*.[42] But these prohibitions are taken to be the counsel of perfection; they do not have the necessity of the law. *Prohibitiones ... iste accipiende sunt de consilio perfectionis, non de necessitate iuris*,[43] so some negotiation is possible. If a bishop refuses to deal with a case (*vel non velit vel non possit de causa agnoscere*), it may be appropriate to get the case heard in a secular court (*apud forensem*).[44] The secular slave or servant is equally disadvantaged as accuser with the spiritual one, in that he cannot bring an accusation against his lord, though he may ask him for pardon.[45] The clerical and lay spheres are thus juridically separate in many respects, and yet they can, exceptionally, overlap in the possibility of the transfer of an individual from one to the other for the purposes of the administration of justice.[46]

Bishops seem to have been – on the basis of the argument from order – the chief beneficiaries of the protection against being called to account by their subordinates.[47] Anselm of Lucca gives more than one reason why courts should accept the principle. The first is that it is the task of bishops to teach and correct their people. It is not the responsibility of the people to teach and correct the bishops.[48] This is because the pupil is not superior to his master.[49] It is also argued that there is an issue of rite, or order, involved, in that it is a breach of order for the people to accuse the clergy.[50] In particular, the accusation of a priest amounts to an accusation of God who ordains him (*dei ordinationem*), and that is so serious that it requires (at least) most careful thought before doing it.[51]

Then there is the argument that it is, in the nature of things, proper that 'fathers' should be respected, not despised or accused.[52] Both these have to do with a sense of fittingness, which Anselm of Canterbury calls *convenientia*. This has of course a very strong sense for him and his contemporaries. It amounts to a 'belonging' to the divinely ordained harmony of the universe. So in Anselm of Lucca, too, we find the argument that it is not fitting that the worldly should pursue the spiritual in law courts, or those entangled in wickedness or fighting on the side of the world, should defame bishops, for if the apostles or their successors had allowed that, few would have remained to fight for the Lord in holy orders.[53]

When used of the condition of persons the word *proprietas* carries connotations of *potestas*. To have or hold another person in subjection is to have power over him. The *lex conditionis* covers all sorts of relationships of one person to another in which there is inequality of standing and a resulting or concomitant power of one over the other: *parentes, proximi, vicinii*.[54] In mediaeval thinking it is normal to expect a lowly person not only to be subordinate to, but also to 'belong' in some way to a higher one, to be his 'man' or, if a wife, his woman. For a person to accuse his lord is for him to accuse one of those persons of whom he himself in a sense forms part, which is a clear reason why that would not be possible. The Council of Chalcedon, 451, Canon 11, says that paupers and needy persons are to travel with the testimony (*sub probatione*) of letters of peace only to commend them. 'Letters of recommendation' are appropriate only to persons who are reputable.[55] So a cleric needs to be in good standing with whoever he belongs to, in order to retain his position.

That extends to the structure of the Church (where it is of course much more ancient), because a priest is always a *bishop's* priest, says the *Summa 'Elegantius'*.[56] There is again a system of protection here, which is also (loosely) a system of ownership. It may be asked whether a bishop can prohibit a cleric of his from entering a monastery, and what the man's position will be if he disobeys.[57] The consensus of the authorities is that a person given to the monastic life as a child by his parents cannot subsequently leave the monastic life, says the *Summa 'Elegantius'*.[58] If a girl is given to a religious house by her parents she may not leave to marry even if she is not professed.[59] These are both cases of the ownership of other human beings, in which those thus disposed of now have no, or changed and more limited, rights of their own.

A 'belonging' of a geographical sort can also be a significant element in the pattern of assumptions which governs the view that people cannot properly accuse just anyone, even if they could prove him guilty. The case of Lot is taken by Anselm of Lucca to provide a Scriptural base for this conviction. In Genesis 19.9 we find, he points out, 'You come here as a stranger; you cannot be our judge.'[60] Trial by peers goes along with trial by those who know the accused 'locally'. A foreigner may not be an accuser. The case of an accused cleric should be heard in his own province.[61]

Nothing tests the ideal of equality before the law so much as the assumption that there is no right to that equality because God created humankind unequal. Behind this presumption may lie another of tantalising interest in modern Europe: that there are no universal human rights.[62] In the mediaeval world, hierarchy may justify discrimination.

14 The development of procedural treatises
The process

Courts and their officers needed to know step by step what to do in the conduct of a case. There is an important recent attempt to put some of the manuals and treatises written on this theme in the twelfth and thirteenth century into order.[1] Linda Fowler-Magerl distinguishes writings describing the complete procedure step by step; a series of works dealing with aspects of the procedure; and formularies. Formularies are the lawyers' equivalent of the 'handbooks' of ready-made examples and outline sermons used by theologians. They provided standard versions of documents for use in litigation. They were like forms to be filled in. Only the names of accuser and accused and details specific to the case needed to be inserted.

There were various experimental variations on this kind of help in putting together the documentation. For in legal practice as in practical theology, the genres or models for all sorts of practical study aid were still in the making. For instance, Arnulphus, a Paris Master writing between 1245 and 1298, composed a *summa causarum de facto*, in which he lists ten stages of a case, and discusses the documentation needed, beginning with the period which comes before the formal citation which begins the case; the citation, when the matter comes before a judge. He deals with delays; the *litis contestatio*; the proof; the conclusion; the sentence.[2] Another collection gives materials for an appellate action between two parties, before a judge delegated by the pope in an action concerning title to a church. It includes items for use in various eventualities, such as a letter (citation) to use when the defendant does not come when summoned, which warns him at the third time of asking that the case will proceed even if he does not appear.[3]

The *Curialis* is another such guide, this time to documents to be used in evidence (*instrumenta*). It points out, for example, that it is a serious matter to falsify documents in a case, and it gives a helpful list of the ways in which it may be possible to do this, for instance, *per rasuram* (crossing out one diocese and putting in another), *per puncta, per filum, per falsam latinitatem* (using such bad Latin that the authenticity of the document will be made to look doubtful), *per veritatem suppressionem* (leaving out

92 The development of procedural treatises

key facts), *per venationem litterarum apostolicarum, per nimiam pospositionem*,[4] and so on.

For our immediate purposes the most important of these practical genres is that which sets out the components of a fair procedure, taking the student through them step by step. These are the 'preceptive manuals' of the lawyer's art. It is evident from the surviving records of cases that procedural matters were actively and consciously in play in the later Middle Ages. Professional advocates were notorious for exploiting their possibilities, causing as much delay as would serve the interests of their clients.

The phrase *ordo iudiciorum* is taken from Justinian's Code.[5] Mediaeval procedural treatises or *ordines* evolved from the middle of the twelfth century.[6] But Justinian does not set out what to do in the conduct of a case step by step. Later mediaeval teachers and practitioners of law took much further the procedural hints in Justinian, self-consciously referring what they said to Justinian as their source whenever they could. *Ordo iudiciarius* is used by Gratian (and came to be used exclusively by the canonists).

It came to be assumed that the fundamental *ordo iudicialis* will be the same whatever kind of *iudicium* is involved, civil or criminal,[7] with the important exception of summary procedures, which we shall discuss in a separate chapter. For example, it appears from the records of the Court of Canterbury that broadly the same procedures were used, whether the case was (in ecclesiastical terms), civil, criminal or 'spiritual'.[8]

The concept of the single *ordo iudicialis* implies that there are, at base, 'right ways of doing things' so as to ensure a fair trial.[9] Mediaeval cases are of various kinds, just as they were in the earlier period of Roman law. The criminal case begins with an accusation that an offence against the law has been committed.[10] A civil case is a dispute between individuals; the offence is alleged to have been committed by one of the two against the other, so that he becomes the accuser and the other the accused.[11] Ecclesiastical and secular courts both try both types of case, as the *Summa 'Elegantius'* explains.[12] A person might very well have a preference for being tried in one court rather than another, an ecclesiastical rather than a secular, for the penalty of death could not be imposed by an ecclesiastical court.[13] Then as now, only an extremely small proportion of cases in ecclesiastical courts are strictly 'spiritual' or involve clergy discipline (less than half a dozen in recent decades in the courts of the Church of England).

The late twelfth-century authors set the procedural agenda with a new thoroughness and to unprecedented standards. The consciousness of the need for handbooks of regulations had not been so apparent a generation or two earlier, and the need for clear rules of procedure can confidently be taken to be a natural outgrowth of the development of a court system. Even Gratian did not articulate in detail the need for procedural rules. He gives some account of how to handle things in specific cases but the procedural ground rules on which he is working are not yet made explicit.[14]

It is apparent from the texts that what would now be identifiable as the rules of natural justice were already at issue in the practical conduct of trials. One of the Ps-Damasus texts cited from Ps-Isidore by Anselm of Lucca has Pope Damasus writing to say, 'the Apostolic See has been informed that you are accepting written accusations without a legitimate accuser'.[15] Anselm gives detailed advice to a judge, who must listen patiently and ask questions and be thorough,[16] on the ground that no one who has not reviewed all the evidence can have conducted a fair trial. These most fundamental procedural requirements deserve a section to themselves, for it is here especially that theological considerations overlap with legal ones in matters of procedure.

Beginning the process

Johannes Bassianus at the end of the twelfth century begins with the explanation of the way to set a trial procedure in motion. If anyone wants to launch an action,[17] he should write the accusation down and take it to a judge, and when the judge has satisfied himself that there is a *prima facie* case, he must explain to the accused what he has to answer.[18] The *Ordo iudiciorum* in the *Summa Trecensis* explains the judge's duty (*officium*). He is to cite and compel litigants to come before him, show them the allegations and hear both sides (*partium audire*). After he has learned all the facts, he is to examined them closely (*subtiliter examinare*), and question the parties. The accuser has to present and prove his case until the accused confesses or the judge is convinced (*vel iudicii fidem faciat*). The accused must either confess or defend himself.

The judge's task is to put an end to litigation and settle adversarial wranglings;[19] he does this by pronouncing a definitive sentence (*sententiam diffinens*) when he has heard all he needs to hear all about the dispute (*ventilatam satis controversiam*) to enable him to form his judgement.[20] The step-by-step instructions go on, through practical guidelines resting securely on what are held to be sound procedural principles.[21]

From these beginnings came a stream of procedural manuals. Certain treatises have been picked out by modern scholars as 'milestones of thirteenth century procedural writing'.[22] The *Speculum iudiciale* of William Durantis, with its clear point-by-point explanation, seems to have been the standard textbook on procedure used in both canon and common law from the 1270s until the end of the Middle Ages.[23] ('If anyone wants to begin an action he should give the judge a statement in which he explains why he is complaining',[24] is a sample of its clarity and accessibility.) Tancred's *Ordo iudiciarius* (1209–15)[25] and William Durantis' *Speculum iudiciale* (1270, but revised by Durantis after that date and the subject of commentary by Joannes Andreae and Baldus de Ubaldis (d.1400)), were also important[26] as was Albertus Gandinus's *Tractatus de Maleficiis* (end of the thirteenth century). But to concentrate on these, influential though

Durantis in particular was to be throughout the later Middle Ages, is to miss the wider picture, for there were many more treatises than these.[27]

In the fourteenth century, with the confidence of substantial thirteenth-century work in this area behind him, Azo sets out an 'accustomed order' (*ordo solitus*) in which ensuring that there is *a proper sequence of events* is the organising principle; and that is also one of the most important insistences of the mediaeval manuals which survive from the thirteenth century. It is not just that it is easier to do things if it is clear in what order they should be done. There is also a sense of an intrinsically 'right order' in things which *require* the sequence. The judge must know the facts in the case *before* he pronounces sentence. The accused must be cited *before* he is condemned. The sentence must follow *from* the proof of the allegations. Things must come after one another like this in an orderly way.[28] Let what ought to follow follow: *et sequantur que sequi debent*. There is a recognition that this kind of orderliness helps to make the trial fair and is therefore a requirement for the validity of the sentence.

It is possible to see in England in the thirteenth century the effect of the rather rapid introduction of the rules of fair procedure which were being developed in mainland Europe, and of which we have a reasonably comprehensive picture from the surviving procedural manuals. It is not difficult to explain how the procedures reached England and were introduced there. For example, one of their authors, Ricardus Anglicus, was Dean of Salisbury in 1205, and went on to be Bishop of Chichester (1214), Bishop of Salisbury (1217) and Bishop of Durham (1228–37). His name is linked with that of Pillius at Bologna, and he had taught in Oxford in the years before he was elevated to the episcopate. He was a leading jurisconsult of his day, composing *Distinctiones* on Gratian and glosses on the Decretal collection of Bernard of Pisa,[29] and that knowledge naturally remained with him when he became a bishop and had to act as judge on his own account.

Beginning the case: the preparatory stages

A lawsuit has to have a formal beginning. Bracton says in his *De legibus* (f.112 and f.413b) that no one can begin an action without a writ (*non potest quis sine brevi agere*). The reason for this is that unless such a formal document is properly lodged with a judge no one is obliged to respond unless he wishes: *non teneatur alius sine brevi respondere nisi gratis voluerit*.[30] The procedural treatises tell us that civil cases were supposed to be begun by the plaintiff or complainant, who is called the *actor*, making a written complaint (*libellus*) to the court, asking the judge to cite the respondent or defendant (*reus*). If someone wants to begin an action (*movere quaestionem*), he has to give the judge this *libellus*, in which he explains what he is complaining of.[31] This *could* be done orally, but the normal requirement was to do it in writing.[32] Some authors said that it was not enough for the person who wishes to bring an accusation to do it orally before the judge, that there *ought* to be a written document,[33] setting out who accuses whom of what.

The *libellus* is thus the statement of the complaint. It had a standard form, or forms, such as:

> Ego G, deo et vobis R. et P. conqueror de E qui mihi centum debet. Unde vobis supplico, ut mihi plenam iustitiam faciatis.[34]

or:

> Ego B conqueror vobis de [X], qui debet mihi [Y] libras, quas sibi mutuavi vel commodavi vel apud eum deposui.[35]

in which the plaintiff makes complaint of the defendant, who owes him money, and asks the judge to give him justice.

It was emphasised that it was important for the written complaint to make it quite clear who the accused or prospective respondent was, so that there could be no confusion and no claims that the accused knew nothing of the matter.[36] The late thirteenth-century Canterbury records[37] do not usually include a description of this stage. It is evident, however, that the defendant was 'summoned', and trouble was taken to ensure that that fact was recorded, that witnesses were present when the citation was given to him, or the citation made in public in Church.

The aim here, and throughout the procedural instructions, is to ensure that things are done decently and in an orderly way, so that no one gets advantage from rushing into wild accusations.[38] Various provisions thus hedge about the task of bringing an accusation, to ensure that it is not done vexatiously, and only for a good reason. The frequency of the concern to prevent an accusation being brought hastily, casually or out of rancour throughout the literature from Rome to the Middle Ages, suggests that it was far from uncommon for this to happen. When the judge receives the written account of a complaint, the judge is to send for the accused, and he is to tell him that he has thirty days[39] to prepare his defence before the trial begins. That is in line with the provision already in place in the Roman system, that when a summons has been served (*admonitio oblata sit*) there shall be an interval of time for the accused to admit the offence or settle out of court, before the case begins and the accused shall sign to say that he has been given time. This is to prevent any trickery.[40] If someone intends to bring a case, says the *Digest*, he ought to give notice,[41] so that the accused may know whether or not to contest the case.[42]

It was a rule that he who begins the case must carry it through.[43] Indeed, he may be required to swear to his intention with someone with whom oaths may formally be sworn (*cum idoneo fideiussore*).[44] This insistence too suggests that part of the purpose of the insistence on proper procedure is to discourage trivial and vexatious litigation. He who is cited must respond.

The three persons and their assistants

There was a good deal of interest in the question who was needed to make up the necessary complement of persons for a trial. In analysing the apparently three-cornered case involving God, man and the Devil one twelfth-century text which sketches this picture takes the litigants in pairs of parties, God and the Devil, God and man, man and the Devil.[45] A *causa* is defined in the *Summa 'Elegantius'* as a controversy between two persons, with a third person empowered to adjudicate between them.[46]

Some persons, says the *Summa 'Elegantius'* are necessary in a trial, some merely useful (*utiles*). The necessary ones[47] are those without whom no *iudicium* can be completed: judge, accuser and the alleged guilty party. In the case of an inquisition or summary procedure the accuser can be dispensed with, as we shall see. Merely *utiles* are those who simply assist in the conduct of the trial, such as witnesses, advocates, scribes.[48] There will normally need to be at least two witnesses if the accused denies the accusation, because otherwise it is one man's word against another's. There may be professional advocates, and an *équipage* of clerks, and so on.[49]

Those who come together in the conduct of a trial thus have 'offices' or duties or sets of responsibilities. The phrase *officium iudicis* is common in the *Digest*[50] (*Quid ergo officium erit iudicis* ...).[51] There is a great deal to be said about judges, but that must wait for a later chapter.

Rogerius and Placentinus also give little summaries of the *officia* of accuser and accused.[52] The accuser has a 'job to do', too, but its focus is narrower. It is the 'office' of an accuser to prove his case.[53] In the particular trial which he has instigated, he is to seek to carry his point. Convincing the judge is his task, observing the proper rules of procedure. The accused has a task which he discharges for his own benefit only, that is, to escape punishment if he can, or at least get it reduced. The task of the accused is to deny to accusation or to confess or to explain the special circumstances which mitigate what he has done.[54]

The process continues

The judge, then, gives the written complaint, the *libellus*, to the respondent.[55] Although there is no universal agreement on the 'form' the *libellus* should take, we have seen that the accusation had to have a formal character, for the important reason that that is seen to be a crucial protection for the accused.[56] A preliminary fact-finding or inquiry stage followed. The judge is to be thorough in his questioning of the accused and the witnesses, and it is to be clear that the onus is on the accuser to prove his case.[57] This *interrogatio* could form a separate stage and the judge could delegate the task, which might be convenient if the witnesses lived at a distance.

Interrogations

Before the full trial the judge or his commissary thus made various interrogations,[58] to establish the facts,[59] but also having the purpose of discovering whether the accused would confess on any of the articles of claim, so that there would be no need for the *actor* to prove his case on those particular points.

The respondent evidently sometimes refused to answer or tried to escape the question with an 'I don't know' (*dubito*). Some authorities thought that acceptable. Others said that the respondent must say what he knows or believes.[60] There appears to have been no clear understanding about a right of silence, and just as the respondent has to answer the judge's questions, so does the plaintiff, when it is his turn to respond to the exceptions put forward by the respondent.[61] The inferences to be drawn from silence are another matter.

The *articuli* are the 'further and better particulars' of the later Middle Ages. A list of *articuli* of the claim might run: 'he intends to prove ...', with details of the witnesses and documents who will support the contention.[62] The party which had the burden of proof drew up a set of articles on the basis of which questions were to be put to the witnesses.[63] The opposing party could formally draw up its own list, in a form of cross-examination. It might be expensive to bring witnesses a long distance, or it might be inconvenient for the judge to question them himself. It was for this reason that examiners could be appointed to do the questioning, or even a commissary who could hear the whole case.[64]

The 'interrogatories' of Thomas de Nevill on each of the articles of one 'Master Robert' survive. They provide that first the examiners are to hear what the witnesses have to say for themselves; then they are to be asked how they know this, from seeing, hearing, knowledge, belief or public report. Then they are to be asked how they know that he was in possession as rector, and again they are to be asked how they know this, from seeing, hearing, knowledge, belief or public report. The questioning is then to move to the date of possession of the Church, with the same thorough testing of each assertion. The *bona fides* and the credibility of the witnesses themselves are also to be tested. They are to be asked whether they are of ill repute, perjured, excommunicated, accused or convicted of any crime, and what their relationship is to the person for whom they appear as witnesses; they are to be asked whether they would prefer that one side should win rather than the other. The examiners have discretion to ask further questions.[65]

98 *The development of procedural treatises*

Intimidation of witnesses was a real danger, for example by powerful relatives of the other party. The party who wanted to call them could then ask the court to make an order to compel them to come under the threat of a penalty for contempt of court.[66] The witnesses had some protection in that they were examined separately and in private. Tancred draws a parallel in his *Ordo* with the questioning of the Elders by Daniel.[67] The primary purpose of the secrecy, however, was not to protect the witnesses but to ensure that one witness was not influenced by what he heard another say.

The examiners sometimes give a clue as to their reasons for preferring one side's witnesses. For example, consistency (*constanter deponunt*), numbers (outweighing the numbers for the other side), local knowledge. 'Wherefore it seems to us examiners that greater faith is to be placed in them (*quod maior fides sit eis adhibenda*) than in the witnesses produced by the other side.'[68]

Once the witnesses had been examined, secrecy was set aside. The depositions of the witnesses were read in open court and the parties were given copies. No more testimony could be introduced after this point, for or against, on the articles on which testimony had been obtained. The exception was the contention that a witness had perjured himself.

The parties could then take exception to witnesses (although they should normally have done so at the stage when the witnesses were identified), on various grounds, seeking for example, to establish their ineligibility or bias. This was also the time to raise the main defences. One option might now be to raise an affirmative defence, that is, to concede that the plaintiff or accuser was substantially in the right and to try to mitigate the consequences. Exceptions themselves then had to be proved, and the cycle of producing and testing the evidence began again.

Instrumenta or documents could be introduced at any time before the case was concluded.[69] There was less use of documents than in a modern court because society's transactions were less generally paper-based, though in ecclesiastical cases there might well be charters or wills.

The judge would eventually set a date by which the parties must have produced all the evidence they were going to, a *terminus ad proponendum omnia in facto consistencia*, and then the case could be concluded with the adversarial hearing or *litis contestatio* itself.[70]

Delay

At the first hearing the charge would be read aloud and a seal attached to it. The defendant or his representative was given a copy and a date was set for the full hearing. Judges are instructed not only to set a date for a hearing but also to keep the parties to it. The prevention of unnecessary delay is a consistent preoccupation of the mediaeval procedural treatises. It seems to have been a commonplace for the litigants to do everything they could to obstruct the proceedings for their own advantage, in other words, to 'use' or 'abuse' the system. In the Canterbury cases we read again and again that an argument has been going on for several days about a technical point.

The record of one case, not untypical, describes a sequence in which after the two parties had been given a copy of the attestations (*attestaciones*), the defendant was given a time by which to make exception against the witnesses and their testimony. The parties then appeared in person and the defendants asked for a copy of the complete *processus*. It was agreed that they should have this by a date three weeks later, if they were willing to pay for it. One of the parties failed to appear on the day in question and was suspended by the judge from entrance to the church (that is, excommunicated for contempt of court). He said she was to be cited to appear about three more weeks later. She did appear, but she said she could not pay for her copy of the entire *processus* without her husband. Her husband was ordered to pay in two weeks. Both the married pair appeared two weeks later and asked for an adjournment until the next day. It was arranged that the clerk would write the document out during the next six weeks. But he was not able to complete the task in time. He was given several more weeks. Another three weeks was then allowed for the defendants to make their responses. Further non-appearances followed and by the time the arguments on both sides had been heard and sentence could be pronounced nearly nine months had passed.[71]

Further stages of the process

A defendant or his representative could thus make various moves once the case was under way. He could put a counter-claim (*libellus reconventionalis*). He could also propose *exceptiones*, or attempts to get parts of the accusation or claim struck out. Some were peremptory, and if these were allowed and proved that could give the defendant a judgement on the merits. Some were designed to establish that the court did not have jurisdiction (*declinatoria fori*), others to buy time by requiring delay until an imprecise charge had been restated. The dilatory exception could also seek to establish that the charge was vague or did not make sense so that the defendant could not be expected to answer it. Another exception could try to rule the *actor* out of the court with the claim that he was excommunicate and could therefore not be heard in a court of law.

Underlying all this is the presumption of mistrust of the accusation. The burden of proof is on the accuser or plaintiff throughout.[72] Ps-Isidore works on the presumption that the accused is innocent and the witnesses were suspect.[73]

Litis contestatio

The modern French system has an 'instruction' stage before the trial, resembling some of these earlier stages in the mediaeval procedure, at which questions can be asked and there may even be a preliminary confrontation between victim and accused.[74] But the core 'act' of the trial is the actual encounter of the parties. *Reus est, adversus quem contenditur.* The accused is the person *against* whom the case is conducted, says Bulgarinus.[75] This adversarial character of the courtroom arises from the fact that two opposing accounts of things necessarily come into conflict there, and normally one must triumph over the other in order to establish the guilt or innocence of the accused. So the *litis contestatio* is a 'battle' in which the defendant opposes the accusation; and the term *contestatio* is fundamental to the style of the process.

Placentinus gives an elegant description of the to and fro character of the 'contest' before the judge.[76] 'It seems thus'; 'on the contrary it seems thus', with a solution, is the disputation pattern: *et videtur ... econtra tamen videtur ... solutio*,[77] adapted to the battle in court. To give a modern parallel: 'Adversarial theory presupposes two contestants, equally matched in a struggle in which the state, which provides them with a forum for the contest and a machinery to enforce victory, takes no direct interest.'[78] In principle, this has to involve an actual debate, although in the later Middle Ages the battle normally took place between advocates, with actual litigants not necessarily present, where a professional advocate speaks for the litigant.[79]

Here the brocards[80] have their counterpart in actual debates in court. In a legal *quaestio* there may be a *titulus*; *exordium*; *casus* (*causa*; *negotium*; *materi*; *thema*); *queritur* (question); *propositio*; *argumenta*. The 'disputants' will be the advocates who argue on behalf of the accused (*reus*) and the accuser (*accusator*). They try to narrow down the issue by refining definitions so as to establish the exact point of law involved. The *quaestio* ends with 'judgment', *determinatio*; decision or definition (*determinare legem*); *iudicium*; *sententia*; *responsum*; *distinctio*.[81]

When Justinian claims that there are no contradictions in his works,[82] and Gratian calls in his *Decretum* for a harmony of discordant canons: *concordia discordantium canonum*, in a clear statement that his purpose is to harmonise contradiction,[83] they seem to be seeking something quite different in its intended outcome. Early glosses on the *Digest* contain lists of *allegationes*, in the form of references to texts which agree or disagree.[84] Peter Abelard's *Sic et non*, notorious in theology, juxtaposes apparently contradictory authorities on a number of theological issues, and poses for the student the challenge of resolving them. The common 'academic' imperative is to show that *diversa* are not necessarily *adversa*.[85] Surprisingly, we find in legal training a similar emphasis sometimes on avoiding the presumption that someone has to 'win', in favour of an attempt to find a harmony or agreement of the conflicting positions. But what goes for texts does not necessarily go for cases.

When in the fourteenth century Azo assembled a collection of *brocardica*,[86] the pattern they continue to follow is to set out opposing positions with supporting examples, and a commentary designed to resolve the differences. One of Azo's methods is reminiscent of a device used by commentators on Scripture when they were faced with the problem of a seeming contradiction.[87] This pointed out that by taking one or both halves of the contradiction figuratively, or by defining terms with exactitude, so as to avoid accidental equivocation; thus the seeming contradiction may be made to disappear. A particularly noteworthy example of this is Peter the Chanter's *De Tropis Loquendi*, in which a lecture course suggesting many such tricks of the trade to make apparent conflicts in Scripture disappear, is preserved.[88] In Azo's legal version (to take an example), things may be allowed at one time which are not permitted at another.[89] This can be read as an instance of a device which may involve 'equivocation about time' which Peter the Chanter also uses. It may be said that ignorance is an excuse and that ignorance is not an excuse. Here again the method of resolution is to look for equivocation and to proceed by making distinctions in the definition of terms: 'Ignorance is one thing, error another'. It is ignorance if I know nothing of the law or the fact, but I am suspicious. It is error when I believe something wrongly.[90] It can be argued that knowledge is beneficial (*scientia non nocet*) or that knowledge is unhelpful (*scientia nocet*).[91] The statement that judges have a duty to hear someone but not to hear him out,[92] is not always true.[93] It is stated both that the judge can interpret or correct his own sentence and that he cannot.[94] This uses the device, also familiar from Peter the Chanter's adaptation of the logicians' equivocation system for resolving conflicts in theological authorities, of taking general and particular or part and whole as sometimes requiring different understandings.[95]

As Johannes Bassianus puts it, 'arguments' can be called *loci generales vel generalia vel vulgariter brocarda*.[96] Every good reason *bona ratio* can be called an *argumentum*, says Baldus. That is obvious from the definition, for an argument is (*pace* Cicero) a reason which convinces.[97] Baldus goes on to explain that he himself is using *argumentum* in two ways.[98] The first is what rhetoricians would call 'artificial', that is, involving art, and that is *disputatio*, for that is what is appropriate when legists want to show what is proposed.[99] The second is argument *a ratione naturali*, from, natural reason. This is in the same broad category as the *exemplum*. It has its force from a general reasonableness or conviction, not by explaining why alternative positions are erroneous.[100]

But this attempt to find a middle way in the 'battle in court' is not the norm. The norm is the adversarial contest.[101] Another fourteenth-century source is clear that a brocard *in iure* is when the two sides argue against one another, for and against.[102] This setting of opposites over against one another is of the essence of the brocard, for, as Azo explains, 'If anyone wants to brocardize, he can introduce a contrary view here, for sometimes variation is admitted, as in D.5.2.8.5 and D 37.6.8.'[103]

In resolving brocards, Azo proposes, the first thing to do is to decide whether the rule itself is to be held, or its contrary.[104] In the case he is considering, although the first rule seems to be taken generally, nevertheless, its contrary is to be taken as the rule here.[105]

So legal argumentation is a sophisticated game in the Middle Ages. It is a conscious art, to whose rules the jurists were clearly giving a good deal of thought. It is above all applied argumentation, argumentation for a practical purpose, and that is perhaps its defining characteristic.

Procedural flaws and voiding

It may seem self-evident that a trial must take place in advance of its outcome. It should be obvious that the judge must not rush to judgement: *Non temere iudicandum*.[106] But this point is emphasised in text after text. What happens when the judge is unsure what to do?[107] The principle here (taken from Ambrose), is that a good judge judges according to what he hears: *sicut audit sic iudicat*.[108] The Theodosian Code says, 'Let the judge not pronounce a final sentence until either the accused himself confesses or the judge is convinced by appropriate witnesses'.[109] Do not judge on suspicion, but first prove and then pronounce sentence in a charitable spirit, Anselm of Lucca tells the judge.[110] The judge should not hurry to make his judgement, but hear the case first, says Ivo of Chartres.[111] The judge should not arrive at his judgement until he has tested all the evidence. Judges should not rush to judgement, agrees Burchard of Worms.[112] The judge should not pronounce sentence until either the guilty party has confessed or he himself is convinced by innocent witnesses, insists Gratian.[113] The *Summa 'Elegantius'* has the instruction that no judge ought to pronounce a sentence unless he is sure.[114] The rule is that nothing should be omitted.[115] The judge's failure to hear all the evidence would be a ground for appeal (*locus ... appellationis*), notes William of Drogheda,[116] so thoroughness is the watchword. The procedural sequence set out in the treatises was visibly being used in actual cases, including the technical terms we have been looking at. The emphases in the procedural manuals are clues to bad practice, to what it was feared might go wrong.

Flaws matter because they invalidate outcomes. If proper procedure is not followed, the sentence cannot hold, the *Glossa ordinaria*[117] emphasises.[118] Paucapalea discusses a principle which illustrates this rule nicely: that where goods have been despoiled in anticipation of a given outcome, there should be restitution before the trial, so that the matter is investigated on the basis on which things stood *ab initio*.[119] Rufinus is clear that if due process is not followed, the sentence is void. *Ordo si pervertitur, non valet sententia*.[120] Placentinus' *De Actionum Varietatibus* (c.1262–5) begins from the definition of Justinian, that 'an action is nothing but the right to pursue what one is owed before a judge'.[121] This used, he says, to require punctilious conformity with fair procedure: *Sollempniter omnia procedebant*.[122] If there was a single procedural slip, the whole cause was lost: *si quis a sillaba caderet causam amitteret*.

In actual cases, a variety of procedural flaws were identified. A writ could be challenged on the grounds that the court was not competent. The legal standing of the accuser could be attacked; for example, it could be alleged that he was an outlaw or a leper or a woman (unless the case was about her husband's death or her own rape, in which case she had standing as accuser). It could be alleged that the verbal accusation did not correspond with what the writ said. It could be alleged that the accusation did not take into account all relevant considerations or that it took into account irrelevant considerations. It might be alleged that the accused had already been acquitted of the charge, or that the action was out of time.[123]

In one of the Canterbury cases (C.18), Master Robert de Picheford, a member of the Chapter in the Deanery of Norwich, complains that sentence has been handed down in favour of his opponent Robert Corbet without warning (*me non vocato, non monito, non convicto, nec confeso*) and when the jurisdiction of the judge, the Prior of Bradley, a deputy of the papal legate, was in question. He therefore appeals from this sentence to the See of Rome. The Prior is, he claims, at fault in two other procedural respects. He has heard witnesses in his absence and he has published his absolution from a sentence of excommunication. These points are developed to bring out the invalidity of the sentence and the procedure. It is *iniqua*.[124]

Respect for good order is not the same thing as insistence on due process, but underlying the concerns of mediaeval authors offering guidance on the practicalities of conducting a case in an orderly way is a deeper pervasive mediaeval concern for 'order'. Gregory the Great wants to see the deposition of a bishop take place in good order (*ordinabiliter*), with care to ensure the trustworthiness of accusers and witnesses.[125] He asks whether the accused, Bishop Stephen, was present, whether testimony was given on oath, whether he was given an opportunity to reply and to defend himself. Gratian quotes this letter in his *Decretum*.[126] Gratian also insists that no one is to be condemned without due process, where again he uses the word *ordinabiliter*.[127]

A similar area of preoccupation with orderliness is to be found in Anselm of Lucca. He cites Ps-Telesporus on what may be done *rite*.[128] He notes elsewhere the principle (not of course one of natural justice, though seeming fundamental enough at this date) that those who cannot *rite* become priests may not be accusers in cases where a priest is the accused.[129] Equally, it is 'out of order' for a judge to pronounce sentence in a case where the accusation has not been made in person.[130] No one should be condemned unless confessing or legitimately convicted. Master

Rufinus echoes this insistence of Gratian just quoted.[131] All this is of interest to set beside the theologian's concern with validity. In a similar way a sacramental act of the Church as a channel of grace may be deemed invalid, or valid but not efficacious, if a constitutive element is missing.

15 Natural justice

The evolution of the rules of natural justice

'Society is so much stronger than individuals, and is capable of inflicting so much more harm on them than they as a rule can inflict on society, that it can afford to be generous.'[1] Procedural rules embody moral principles; both are needed to find fairness in judicial decisions.[2] Protecting the weak[3] was an ideal as hard to make a mediaeval reality on the uneven social playing field (sanctioned by theologians as well as by lawyers), as was that of equity or fairness at large. Canon 5 of the Council of Nicaea (325) admits that it is important to ensure that when someone is excommunicated, it is clear that the bishop has not acted under pressure or for some other unworthy reason. To deal with the consequences of unjust sentencing of this sort, provision is made for synods to be held twice a year in each province so that all the bishops of the province assembled together may decide whether the persons concerned have been 'reasonably' excommunicated (*rationabiliter excommunicati*). They may quash the decisions or decide to make the sentence more lenient, if it has been too strict. There is a recognition here that the accused is not in a strong position in litigation and that there is a need to build in protection to create a more level playing field. Justice seeks to help those who can do least for themselves. This is paraphrased by Placentinus, who tries to put the rule in a Platonic nutshell, in the form, 'Justice, according to Plato,[4] is the virtue which chiefly benefits those who are least able to help themselves; justice is most apparent in its dealing with the wretched.'[5] In modern English civil cases, 'the greater the impact on the defendant of a decision for the plaintiff, the more evidence the latter will have to find'.[6]

For the legal process to wring out of the condemned everything it is strictly entitled to is not necessarily justice,[7] as the *Digest* recognises. This theme runs as a thread of balance and compassion throughout the literature.[8] For example, Augustine remarks that justice is that which comes to the aid of the wretched.[9] It is necessary actively to *protect* the weak, emphasises Baldus.[10]

In a twelfth-century case, where there were charges of fornication, Pope

106 *Natural justice*

Alexander III sent a mandate to Archbishop Henry of Reims and Bishop Bartholomew of Beauvais to charge the chapter of Senlis to accept the cleric Johannes Poeta as a member and to protect him in the enjoyment of his benefice, while the investigation was carried out, to see if there was 'reasonable cause' to eject him.[11]

The two main rules of natural justice

Helmholz has commented on the difficulty of being sure that 'abstract principles of fairness' were consciously in play when the commentators on procedural fairness and the authors of the procedural manuals were writing.[12] The development of a set of ground-rules, not just for procedure, but for *fair* procedure, comes surprisingly late in the mediaeval story, especially considering this strong evidence that the need for it was recognised. Roman law does not provide a systematic and comprehensive treatment of the practical procedural issues which have the rules of natural justice at their heart. One twelfth-century treatise comments wryly that it seems difficult to get a grasp of Roman regulations when they are so scattered in the texts.[13] Thus such rules for the fair conduct of trials could not travel in a body into the Middle Ages as the texts of the *Code* of Justinian and the *Novels* and *Digest* variously did. In any case, needs changed with the diverse societies of the post-antique and early mediaeval worlds, and what seems a just way of going on in one context will not necessarily appear so in another. It is partly for this reason that 'actions' are such a favourite topic and the literature so vast.[14]

A few texts specifically dealing with natural justice derived from Pseudo-Isidore – a letter of Ps.-Anacletus which is a treatise in itself;[15] a letter of Ps.-Alexander.[16] These both contain the exhortation to try to settle a dispute privately and in mutual charity, which provides a foundation for, but does not strictly belong to, the instructions about the rules of natural justice which follow. There is a letter of Ps. Eleutherus;[17] a letter of Ps.-Calixtus;[18] a letter of Ps. Fabian II;[19] a letter of Ps.-Cornelius;[20] a letter of Ps.-Stephen II;[21] a letter of Ps.-Felix I;[22] and a letter of Ps.-Damasus.[23] Some of these materials or their themes are variously to be found in the group of collections with which the history of the Ps-Isidorian decretals is interfused.[24] The primitive *Vetus Gallica* touches on aspects of the rules of natural justice.[25] There is as yet no coordinated statement of principle among these scattered rules.

It is significant in this connection that the Pseudo-Isidorian texts in particular are lengthy. Some of them almost amount to short treatises. The materials taken from them by the compilers of the later collections take the form of extremely short extracts. There is, on the whole, a shrewd making of conceptual distinctions by these authors. So in this sense they were certainly 'pulling things together' into a 'theory'. The procedural rules as a whole seem to have been quite quickly understood to hang together as a group, for they tend to be found in close proximity in some of the collections from the eleventh century. Anselm of Lucca, for example, puts them all tidily in one section in a discussion of the *ordo accusandi, testificandi et iudicandi*, in Book III of his *Collectio Canonum*.

It seems likely not to be a coincidence that the drawing together of the rules occurs during the period when a more formal court system was coming into being in parts of northern Europe. Having to try cases was concentrating minds.[26] Mediaeval writers use their own wording for the rules of natural justice. Indeed, so much is that the case that the Ps-Isidorian items become absorbed and even lose their identifying labels.[27] The compiler of the *LXXIV tituli*, like others making similar collections in this period before Gratian, makes remarkably free use of his sources, in the sense that he leaves out words and phrases and sections and makes insertions, changes tenses, mood or voice of the verb. But he rarely does so in a way which materially alters the sense.[28] He is grasping the issues.

Writers of the period from the ninth to the thirteenth century have a great deal to say about natural law (*ius naturale*),[29] but they do not fall comfortably into the phrase 'natural justice' (*iustitia naturalis*). It does exist at least by the thirteenth century, but rather as an alternative for *ius naturale* than with anything like the relatively modern technical sense.[30] One commentary[31] asks whether there is any 'naturally just' thing.[32] One way of expressing the relationship of natural justice to *ius naturale*, then, may be to see it as a branch of natural law, as 'that part of natural law which relates to the administration of justice', a principle which might still hold.[33] A modern definition of natural justice as 'the natural sense of what is right and wrong' would equally cover both. That also takes it to be the case that such moral laws can be universally acceptable, somehow morally self-evident.[34]

Thus Gratian assumes *ius naturae* to be that which is contained in the law and the Gospel: *ius naturae est, quod in lege et evangelio continetur*.[35] Jesus is explicitly taken as a model in the matter of acting with natural justice in the contention that although he knew that Judas was a thief he did not cast him out because he had not been formally accused in the proper way by a person duly qualified to bring an accusation[36] (and thus not given a fair trial).[37] Other Scriptural precedents are cited. In Luke's Gospel we hear of the rich man who sends for his wastrel steward and tells him what he has heard of his conduct. He asks the steward to give an account of himself. In other words, he allows him an opportunity to defend himself (Luke 16.2). We have already touched on God's care to keep the rules of natural justice in Adam's case (Genesis 3.8).[38] In Genesis (18.21), where God conducts a fair investigation into the ill-repute of Sodom and Gomorrah, the Vulgate has *clamor*, and thus provides the necessary link by way of a technical term.[39] There are, however, some difficulties with Scripture here. God seems to break the rule of impartiality in 'I am judge and witness'.[40]

The two core principles

Natural justice insists that justice should not only be done but seen to be done. The two classic principles: *nemo iudex in re sua* (the right to an impartial judge) and *audi alteram partem* (the right to a fair hearing) are fundamental to this visible and uncontroversial *justness* of the conduct of a trial.

Nemo iudex in re sua

Should a Christian be a judge at all?

'Judge not, that ye be not judged.'[41] The first theologically important question about judges is whether a Christian, and especially a cleric, should sit in judgement on others at all. In the mid-twelfth century, Bernard of Clairvaux has a good deal to say about this. It is not, he points out, at all clear whether any of the Apostles 'sat' as a judge of men. 'I read that they stood as judges, but not that they sat.' In support of the view that Christians should not be judges he quotes Christ's example. He quotes: *Quis me constituit iudicem?* Christ himself asked, 'Who made me a judge over you?'[42]

Bernard is principally arguing here that the keys of the Kingdom of Heaven were given to deal with wrongful behaviour (*crimina*), not so that priests could have judicial authority over the control of possessions. 'Which seems to you greater power and dignity, to remit sins or to divide spoils?'[43] This passage is touched on by Robert Grosseteste in a letter on the same subject a century later.[44] He too stresses that the Apostles had no appetite for being judges. Many heretics also objected to the idea of *iudicium*. Because the ecclesiastical courts could deal with a variety of types of case, this delicacy was appropriate and the concern was real.

Becoming a judge

How did it come about that the clergy found themselves in this invidious position of being judges, perhaps despite their better judgement? Christ entrusted his disciples with 'the power of the keys', the power to bind and loose on earth as well as in heaven. The power to bind *goes with* the power to loose. In the *Digest*, too, the principle is laid down that no one who has authority to condemn lacks the authority to dismiss the accusation.[45] The bishop as judge in the penitential system and the bishop as judge in the ecclesiastical court, are not judges in the same sense, but both are 'judges' nevertheless.

The crucial matter for the clergy appears to be the need for them to keep from holding themselves out to be judges in areas where they are straying from their proper spiritual sphere. Gregory the Great as well as

Bernard, Grosseteste notes, thought it proper for clerics to keep clear of the *discussio* and *decisio* of secular cases. For them to do otherwise would be like stars falling from the sky. It is, in Grosseteste's view, a scandal for a cleric to involve himself in secular litigation.[46] At the same time, and conversely, it is inappropriate for secular judges to invade the Church's jurisdiction.[47]

Disqualification of a judge

Innocent IV produced two *novellae*: *Cum aeterni* (VI. 2. 14. 1), which required an unjust judge to pay damages to an injured party and suspended him for a year, and *Cum medicinalis* (VI. 5. 11. 1) which imposes a less heavy penalty on a judge who is negligent about writing down the reason for an excommunication and its fact. Moral as well as sacramental issues thus surround the conduct of judges.

From the theologian's point of view, Gratian (on penance) deals with to whom confession should be made; in a penitential context that partly means asking what *kind of person* the judge of other men's sins ought to be.[48] It often happens that pastors of the Church exercise their powers of binding and loosing not according to the merits of the case but on personal caprice, admits Canon 8 of the Fourth Lateran Council.[49] The judges' motives may then be contaminated by personal animosity or a wish to please.[50] This was nothing new. Indeed, it had long been taken seriously. The *Digest* underlines that the ultimate extreme of this would be being judge in one's own cause.[51] The *74 Tituli* says that this kind of behaviour ought to justify the removal even of the power of binding and loosing.[52]

It is argued in the *Summa 'Elegantius'* that it is not the judge, worthy or unworthy, who condemns, but God himself.[53] The thinking here directly concerns the problem of the unworthy minister. That had been addressed in the first Christian centuries, and it had been concluded on exactly the same principle that the grace of God can work even through unworthy ministers. That is not so clearly the case for the judge in a forensic context as it is for the 'judge' in the sacrament of penance.

No one should seek the office of judge unless he is able to attack iniquity effectively, says John of Salisbury. It is no good having a pusillanimous person as a judge.[54] In his own time he has seen nothing more wretched than judges ignorant of the law, empty of good intentions, ensnared in love of gift and reward.[55] Nor is it acceptable to have as a judge someone with a conflict of interest. Where a judge, or other senior person acting on behalf of the Church in the administration of justice, confuses his personal wishes with the duties of his office, there will be a risk of injustice. The judge should conduct the case without making any difference according to whether the accused is a lowly or a senior person, says Canon 8 of the Fourth Lateran Council,[56] interestingly in the light of the 'hierarchy' and 'equality of arms' principles we have been looking at. There is to be no special protection for the senior because he holds a high office.[57] Equally, it is the *officium judicis* to keep out evidence based on malice, for there a personal animosity on the part of an accuser or witness is likely to interfere with the discharge of the *officium* of that participant in the trial.[58] A judgement could then be contaminated (*turpis*) or even vindictive,[59] and then the judge would indeed be confusing his personal feelings with his official role. The judge ought thus to try to eliminate any 'personal' or otherwise morally compromising element in his assessment of the issues.

The rather different question is also asked in the *Summa 'Elegantius'* whether a judge guilty of a given offence can be judge of someone else accused of the same offence.[60] For that might seem to involve sentencing oneself. Master Roland asks the same question, whether someone can be a judge when he is as guilty as the accused: *cum reo par inficit malitia?* Tancred confirms that a criminal cannot be a judge.[61]

The situation is felt to be different if a judge is himself an offender but his offence is known only to God, from the way it is if he is an offender and everyone knows because he has been found guilty in a public trial. Some *crimina* of judges are hidden, others *manifesta*. If the judge's offences are known breaches of the law, the judge certainly cannot act, says Master Roland.[62]

So in the forensic arena it would seem that something like the public credibility of the judge is as important as it is in the modern world. That would seem to lie behind the insistence of the *Summa 'Elegantius'* that a judge should be of unimpeachable honesty and not disqualified by any kind of incapacity. For even if he is not himself an offender, no one can be a judge if disqualified by nature (by being deaf and dumb or habitually bad-tempered: *perpetuo furiosus*).[63] In the penitential arena the same ground-rules apply. Gratian asked whether a bishop could excommunicate if he was excommunicated himself. By the end of the twelfth century, it was accepted that he could not, and that included those who held beliefs already condemned but who had not themselves been directly excommunicated.

The human judge is of course himself a *sinner*, even if he is not a criminal himself, or biased or activated by malice. In the Gospel it is only he who is without sin who is allowed to cast the first stone.[64] The position in Roman law was that if a judge had not been removed and was allowed to sit in judgement in a properly constituted process, his judgement must stand, and that was the practical resolution of the high Middle Ages too, in a forensic context.[65]

As Hobbes puts it at the end of the Middle Ages, in his description of his 'eleventh law' of nature, what is at stake in insisting on avoidance of even the appearance of bias is not merely fairness to those subject to judgement but also the operation of the whole judicial system. Take this protection away and the parties might as well fight with their fists:

If, 'a man be trusted to judge between man and man', it is a precept of the law of nature, 'that he deal equally between them'. For without that, the controversies of men cannot be determined but by war. He therefore that is partial in judgement doth what in him lies, to deter men from the use of judges and arbitrators; and consequently, against the fundamental law of Nature, is the cause of war.[66]

Hobbes adds a rider:

> Seeing every man is presumed to do all things in order to his own benefit, no man is a fit arbitrator in his own cause and if he were never so fit; yet equity allowing to each party equal benefit, if one be admitted to be judge the other is to be admitted also.[67]

The mediaeval theory of bias

The basic rule could be cited from Scripture (Ecclesiasticus 11.7).[68] Gratian finds New Testament *auctoritas* for saying that accusers cannot also be witnesses, in the Apostles themselves.[69] But the rule is also in the *Digest* (5. 1. 17). *Iniquum est aliquem suae rei iudicem fieri*. The same rule occurs in the Theodosian Code.[70] No one can be dispassionate about the merits of his own case, and therefore he cannot be judge in it.[71]

Bribes and conflict of interest

Judges should not take bribes which could influence their judgements. There is a biblical basis for this too: '*non accipias personam nec munera*' (Deuteronomy 16.19).[72] It is recognised by Burchard of Worms that bribes blind wise men's eyes and alter the words of the just.[73] John of Salisbury calls it 'iniquity' to sell justice.[74] Accusers and judges ought to be above suspicion of vested interest not only in this way, but also in that they are seen to act out of charity, says the XXIV *tituli*.[75] They must also not be susceptible to intimidation says John of Salisbury.[76]

John of Salisbury sums up the attitude he thinks the judge ought to have by saying that in obedience to equity he should be utterly even-handed, for only thus can he be the servant of truth. He points for authority here to Cicero's remark in the *De officiis* that someone ceases to be anyone's friend when he becomes a judge.[77] Judges must look out for vested interest in other parties to the trial too, and that seems a proper extension of their responsibility. Ivo of Chartres says that judges ought to test first the spirit in which an accusation is made, before they accept it.[78] A man's enemies are not allowed to be his accusers.[79] The same principle applies to witnesses.[80] It is not right, says Burchard of Worms, for innocent lives to be damaged by malice.[81] Accusers of priests are not to be heard, says Anselm of Lucca, unless their lives and intentions are first scrutinised.[82]

Those who are known to be detractors or enemies of the accused cannot be heard as accusers, says Anselm of Lucca.[83] He says this kind of thing again and again. Those who are suspect, enemies, ready litigators, those of evil conversation, and who do not hold and teach the right faith, are not fit to be accusers.[84] The false and enemies are not to be admitted as accusers.[85] Recent enemies of the accused cannot be witnesses because they would be acting out of vengeance, notes Gratian.[86] It is an advocate's responsibility not to go beyond what the case strictly needs by way of speaking ill of the accused. He should avoid defamation, adds the *Summa 'Elegantius'*.[87] John of Salisbury concurs. The judge, he says, should first ensure that the litigants are not acting out of malice,[88] that the parties are coming to court out of a pure desire to obtain justice, that no bribes have changed hands.

Plurality of office

The judge must not only ensure that he himself is free of bias, and also all who take part in a trial over which he presides, but also that he is not himself tainted by plurality of office. There is reference to a paradox of natural justice[89] in the duplication of office in Scripture, for Christ himself is both judge and advocate. The Jews he judges, for the Christians he is advocate: *iudex plane iudaeis est, advocatus est christianis*.[90] In that there might be no breach of natural justice, for the two roles would be discharged for different individuals. But, as Augustine points out, in Christ the same person declared himself willing to be our advocate, our legal expert, our judge.[91] It is true that this might be happening at different times; the advocacy is now; the judgement is in the future.[92] It is also possible to see this multiple role as something in which God chooses his task depending on the circumstances. For example, he is our advocate, but only if we lie is he witness to that; and only if we do not mend our ways, is he our judge.[93]

But in the human arena, no one should ever presume to be judge, accuser and witness at the same time, for the proper conduct of a trial requires there to be separate persons acting as judge, accuser, defender, witnesses, say the Ps-Isidorian *Decretals*.[94] No one is to be accuser, judge and witness, for four persons are needed (the accused, of course, making the fourth), agrees Burchard of Worms.[95] Four people are needed *in iudicio* adds the *Summa 'Elegantius'*.[96] The rule of not being accuser and witness and judge is reiterated elsewhere in the *Summa 'Elegantius'*, with the same insistence on the distinction of the roles.[97]

This is because these officers and other persons needed for the proper conduct of a trial all have not only distinct but also incompatible responsibilities.[98] Judges must judge with equity; witnesses bear witness to the truth; accusers identify and expound the issue; defenders explain extenuating circumstances so as to lessen the offence.[99] This sense of a proper ordering of functions is strong. It appears again in the further reasoning that accusers and judges must not be the same person, this time on the grounds that judges, witnesses, accusers and accused are to do what is proper to them in an orderly way.[100]

In Innocent III's inquisitorial forum[101] the judge actually prefers the charges, but, as we shall shortly see, it is clearly understood that he does not do so as though he were in his own person acting both as judge and as accuser. The *fama* or notoriety about the bad behaviour is itself the denouncer or accuser, and the *clamor* is the *delator*.[102] It can, nevertheless, be a problem that if bishops are encouraged actively to pursue notorious wrongdoers, they are, in effect, making themselves into accusers as well as judges. Gregory IX's *Decretals* try to strike a balance, in prescribing that it is the bishop's duty to enquire into what he hears, but not to prejudge it.[103]

Recusatio *and the mediaeval bias rules*

That takes us conveniently to the *recusatio*, the actual challenge in a real case that the judge is disqualified by the appearance of bias.[104] To conduct a trial before a judge suspected of lack of impartiality puts the outcome in doubt.[105]

A judge could recuse *himself* at any time, before the *litis contestatio* (or even after, if the reason for him to do so should become plain at a late stage).[106] Reasons for a mediaeval judge to recuse himself in practice[107] would include financial conflict of interest; ties of kinship (*familiaris, commensalis*);[108] known enmity or partiality for accuser or defendant are all well-established reasons. William of Drogheda found sixteen reasons, extending Hostiensis' thirteen. William Durantis elaborated these to make thiry-six.[109] They can be digested down to reasons connected with existing close relations between the judge and a party (the judge might not be the lord of one of the parties or his blood-relation); some previous connection with the case, legally speaking (having earlier been an advocate for one of the parties), or with a very similar case; or where it could be shown that there had been bribery.[110]

Some prospective judges-delegate were ruled out automatically, on the basis of personal status (excommunicates, schismatics, Jews), or a status attaching to the office. Here, laymen could not serve as judges in spiritual matters (Canon of the Council of Rheims 1148), and of the clergy, only those who had held high office (such as bishops, abbots, deans, archdeacons).[111]

The relatively strong position of the parties in the choice of the judge at the appeal stage is striking to the modern eye. 'I do believe ... you are mine enemy, and make my challenge/You shall not be my judge,' says Queen Katharine in Shakespeare's *Henry VIII* (Act II, Scene iv). When an objection was made to a judge, he was normally ruled out without argument. As a rule, explains Master Damasus, it is not necessary to give a reason or to prove that there is bias (*non est necessaria causae assignatio et probatio*). It is enough for the accused (*reus*) to state that the judge is hostile to him: *quia tantum dixit reus, eos esse inimicos*.[112] To do anything else would simply extend the duration of the case still further and lead to challenges later on.

It follows that the other party will also have to be content. Among the Canterbury cases is one (D,4), in which John de Pottern's proctor protests about his 'client's' adversary asking for his own judge; both parties have to be content with the judge.[113]

On appeal, the parties could even suggest judges who would be acceptable to them.[114] Though once the matter came to trial it became impossible to object except to any judges who had not expressly been agreed to, for at the appeal stage it was usual for the canonists to set even higher standards of impartiality than at the earlier stage.[115]

There were good practical reasons for setting these high standards on appeal to the Pope would not be likely to be heard by the pope himself; he would appoint a judge-delegate. In practice, that often meant a prominent local figure, for example, a local abbot or bishop, not by any means necessarily a lawyer, who could be expected to have a preference for one side or another. By the thirteenth century, important persons and religious corporations might well have proctors in Rome who would put in a word for a preferred candidate.[116]

Although it was not considered important that the judge-delegate be legally qualified or even knowledgeable, some, such as Abbot Samson and Hugh of Lincoln, 'ignorant as I am of the law' (*quasi legum nescius*), seem conscientiously to have applied themselves to learning about the law when they were appointed.[117] It may be that cases where judges-delegate were appointed locally were sufficiently uncommon for it not to seem worthwhile to many such abbots and other prominent local figures to make the effort necessary to equip themselves to the standards of a judge 'ordinary', who was regularly hearing cases.

The effect of the raising of an objection to the proposed judge was that the case was put into suspension, because the party which had objected could not then be forced to continue with the litigation.[118] The problem then had to be referred to arbitration, but if the parties were not content with the outcome, that decision could be appealed in its turn. Attempts were made to frustrate the immense potential for delay this generated by the device of forbidding recusation (*recusatione remota*) but William of Drogheda did not think that prevented anything but recusation designed only to cause delay.[119] That would suggest that the right to object is of such importance, so universal and absolute a right, that it cannot be taken away.

There are clear practical consequences of the provision in the Ps-Isidorian *Decretals* that if someone believes that the judge in particular is hostile to him, he can make an appeal to the Apostolic See for remedy on the grounds that the proper process has not been followed: *remedio viciatam causam*, says Anselm of Lucca in a reference to the invalidation of the trial process.[120]

Audi alteram partem

The second rule which indisputably belongs today to the realm of natural justice was already proverbial in Greek texts and was included in the judicial oath of Athens.[121] Seneca makes reference to the principle that it is unjust to arrive at a judgement without a full hearing.[122] The same principle is there in the *Digest* and the *Code*.[123] So it is by no means a mediaeval discovery.

But in order to achieve a fair and open hearing of both sides, certain provisions are necessary and those had to be worked out more fully in the Middle Ages. The *audi alteram partem* rule requires that the accused be told what the accusations are. Before the late twelfth and thirteenth century, procedural treatises insist upon this,[124] it was being pointed out that prospective defendants had a right to reasonable notice.

The insistence that the accused should be *present* when the case against him is heard is very strong, from the *Digest* onwards.[125] It was uncontroversial in the early conciliar literature that proceedings could be invalidated if they took place in the absence of the accused.[126] The Ps-Isidorian *Decretals* explain that everything argued and adjudged against those who are absent, wherever it happens, is void, for no one can rightly condemn someone in his absence, nor, we are told, does any law condemn him.[127] Not having the accused present is deemed in one of the Ps.-Isidore texts to be a breach of order (*ritus*).[128] Divine and human laws both say that no one can justly be condemned in his absence, agrees Burchard of Worms at the beginning of the eleventh century.[129] Let judges of the Church beware, he continues (from Ps-Isidore), for if they pronounce sentence against someone in his absence and without hearing the case properly that will be a breach of order.[130] Anselm of Lucca says that proceedings in the absence of the accused are void.[131] Gratian stresses that an accuser who tries to carry his point in the absence of the accused is not to be believed, until there has been a 'just discussion' of both sides of the case.[132]

The *Summa 'Elegantius'* raises the question whether anyone can accuse someone or testify against him in his absence (*utrum absentem quis accusare vel in eum testificari possit*), in connection with the defaming of a notorious person we shall be looking at in a moment. For that is done 'in his absence'. Indeed, he is made 'notorious' by what people say about him behind his back.[133] The actual trial must take place in the presence of the accused,[134] says Irnerius. And after the Fourth Lateran Council, we find a gloss to the effect that even the person subject to inquisition (who may not know who his accusers are), ought to be present.[135] Vincent of Spain's commentary on Canon 8 of the Fourth Lateran Council stresses that the person against whom there is an inquisition ought to be present. He has always thought so, though others think differently.[136] The *Casus Parisienses* agree with him.[137] So do the *Casus anonymi Fudenses*.[138]

So this point is extremely well-trodden ground in our authors. They all seem to be aware of its centrality, and to find it an absolute rule, with the proviso that if the accused 'contumaciously' chooses to be absent, that removes the obligation to have him there.[139]

Because of this strong understanding the dice are loaded in favour of the parties' right to be present to the point where a great deal of delay could be occasioned by a clever advocate exploiting the possibilities. For there appears in practice to have been some difficulty in getting the parties to come to court. In a world without diaries it might be easy to miss the day. But more probably not turning up was a way of trying to avoid facing the charge. Provision was made for adjournment when that happened, but not for repeated adjournments.

For the rule about 'turning up' applied to the accuser too. Most of the earlier writers who comment on the point say that if anyone wants to make an accusation he should be prepared to do it openly, in front of the person he accuses. That was the key principle in Roman law, and a reason why defamation behind the scenes was itself regarded as an offence. There ought to be no hiding behind the scenes for the accusers. The Ps-Isidorian *Decretals* and the pre-Gratian collections derived from them insist that an accusation made behind someone's back should be discounted.[140] It is a Ps-Isidorian principle that the opinion of an absent party can carry no weight, and his testimony must not be admitted.[141] Many comments in mediaeval texts seek to sustain this rule. No one can be judged unless legitimate accusers are present, says Anselm of Lucca.[142] The accuser should make his accusation in his own voice, for just as no one can be accused in his absence, so no one can make an accusation without being present.[143] So this too is familiar territory to our earlier authors.

This 'tendency to absenteeism' on the face of the mediaeval records suggests a sometimes conscious exploitation of this 'right to be present'. For if accuser or accused fails to appear, the case would have to be adjourned. If the respondent appears but will not answer the judge's question, he is said to be contumacious.[144] (This is why it seemed fair for silence to be taken for confession.)

In ecclesiastical courts, more than one failure to appear was likely to lead to the absentee being subjected to suspension, or ultimately excommunication. There was the further possible punishment that the absentee would have to pay his opponent's costs for that day. Perhaps procedurally as important, and a better spur to compliance with the orders of the court, was the practice of depriving the absentee of rights attaching to the stage of the proceedings in question. God's presence is deemed to make up for the absence. For example, witnesses on behalf of the opponent could be admitted.[145] The Chancellor's powers to punish contumaciously absent persons were extended to twelve miles beyond the city of Oxford by a privilege granted by Henry III.

But although this looks on the face of it like a subordinate rule of natural justice, deriving from *audi alteram partem*, nevertheless it is in practice a procedural rule with room for some variation, rather than an intrinsically invariable principle of natural justice. For the rule of requiring the accuser to be present normally carries with it the result that he will be made known to the accused, and there may be objections to that in certain circumstances. Modern 'witness protection' has its mediaeval counterparts. In the time of Henry Harclay, Chancellor of the University of Oxford, it was conceded in perpetuity to the Chancellor (*concessum fuit Cancellario Universitatis in perpetuum*), that no Chancellor was bound to tell the accused the name of his accuser unless he judged it necessary to justice to do so.[146] In the *Decretals* of Gregory IX there is a long sequence of texts on the bringing of accusations, in which a number of these and related issues are aired. V. 1. 21 discusses the question of the identification of witnesses. There should be no question of proceeding against anyone on the basis of the evidence of witnesses who will not identify themselves, for witnesses who are not going to be identified cannot be called to account. On the other hand, it is recognised that to identify witnesses may in some cases be to expose them to reprisal. All this is important in connection with what we should now call 'witness protection', if it allows the identity of the informers to be kept from the accused, while insisting that someone in authority is in a position to check their story.

A decree of Boniface VIII eventually provided for anonymity for witnesses in heresy trials, expressly as a witness protection measure, when they were thought to be in danger of reprisal.[147] But the protection thus granted to one side is inevitably removed from the other, and we come up here against a classic balancing act of the requirements of natural justice. We have an uncertain area where one cannot point to absolute and universal standards.

The same uncertainty would seem to hang over another principle. Although the regular shorthand for the accused in the literature is *reus*, there is early written authority in the form of the *Digest*'s provision that the onus of proof lies on the accuser not the defender, deeming a man innocent until proved guilty.[148] The first mediaeval statement of the procedural rule about the presumption of innocence seems to be the Ps.-Jerome text *De Septem Ordinibus Ecclesiae*. This says that someone is not 'guilty' as soon as he is accused, but only after he has been proved to be an offender.[149]

Guilt is not established *merely* by accusation. The tag: *non statim qui accusatur reus est* appears in a letter of Pope Nicholas I written in 867 to Charles the Bald, forbidding the use of trial by combat as a means of purgation in a case of alleged adultery.[150] Gratian uses it (*Causa*, 15. q. 8.

118 *Natural justice*

c. 5). There was a recognition here of a need to underline the fact that something more than accusation, formal or by defamation, is needed to establish guilt, not least because the mediaeval use of the term 'guilty' (*reus*) for the accused seems to prejudge matters, and it must have been necessary to call attention to this point again and again.

In the pre-Gratian collections there are clear warnings about the need to check the credentials of accusers and witnesses, so as to discover in what spirit an accusation is being made.[151] The classical *talio* rule appears in Burchard of Worms, and had certainly not died out in mediaeval usage. (He says that a false witness should be punished for the crime of which he has falsely accused another.)[152] Burchard of Worms states the rule in the form: 'No one may be called guilty until he has been convicted'.[153] If you have accused someone and as a result of your accusation he is *occisus*, you must do penance, fasting for forty days on bread and water and doing penance for seven years, say the *Decretals* of Gregory IX.[154]

The presumption of innocence implies in its turn certain rules of procedure. The first is that, if there is any doubt, justice requires that the accused be acquitted, that it is better to let the guilty go than to condemn the innocent. That is the view of the fourteenth-century jurist Bartolus.[155] The rule is clearly very close to the natural justice principle: *audi alteram partem*, in that it insists upon an *equal* hearing of both parties, that is, without favouring the accuser at the outset by presuming that he is right.

Indicators of unease over the inequality of arms

John of Salisbury says in his *Policraticus* that it is inherently unfair if one party is of better reputation that the other, and the judge ought to make allowance for that.[156] To take a modern parallel, 'adducing evidence of the accused's good character whether or not relevant to the charge allows the jury to reach a verdict which may reflect his or her moral standing rather than the evidence adduced'.[157] It is deemed so unfair to 'try' someone who lacks the necessary capacity that a defendant can reckoned be unfit to plead; his mental capacity may make him not culpable.[158]

In the interests of not disadvantaging further someone who is already at a disadvantage, it can be asked whether an advocate ought to be allowed to use a language the accused can understand, that is the vernacular rather than Latin.[159] Some would argue that the dignity of the law is lowered by its being put unto common language.[160] The witnesses too may be unable to understand the learned language of Latin, and that would prejudice the fairness of the trial.

It can, paradoxically, be true that persons in prominent positions are also in weak positions when it comes to being the objects of accusations. The Council of Constantinople, 381, discusses in Canon 6 the problem of those who maliciously fabricate false accusations against bishops, with no other intention than to destroy their reputations and stir up the laity. It has therefore been decided not to admit accusers without prior examination.[161] If the alleged offence has done personal harm to the accuser that does not apply, because it is deemed essential that someone who alleges that he has himself been wronged should get justice,[162] even if he is not a 'member of the congregation in good standing'. But if the charge brought against the bishop is a *crimen ecclesiasticum*, then the persons who accuse must be examined. This has the intention of preventing accusations from persons themselves accused of offences, until they have been tried and cleared. Otherwise counter-accusation can be used as a means of holding off a trial. If the accusers are found to be of good standing, they are to lay the accusations before all the bishops of the province and prove them to their satisfaction.[163] If the provincial bishops cannot resolve matters, the accusers must go on to a higher synod, specially convened to hear the case. But before they put their case there they must give a written promise to submit to the penalty of *talio* (*aequale periculum sibi statuant*) if they are found to be making a false accusation.

It is clear from these provisions that the concept of a 'weak' position is not without its difficulties. It must be qualified. The accuser and accused cannot be seen simply as having an active and a passive role respectively. As the *Digest* explains, when he mounts his defence the accused is actually an *actor*; for to make a defence is to present a case.[164] In the *Digest* it is allowed that a person may bring a variety of defences, even if they have different thrusts.[165] Out of this complex set of expectations evolved the rules of natural justice at the hands of a mediaeval court system which took them much further than Roman law had done.

Part V
Inquiry, inquisition and summary procedure

16 Notoriety

The 8th Canon of the Fourth Lateran Council begins with the guidance to be found in Scripture on how to deal with someone 'defamed as notorious'. Upon this was to be built an attempt to find a shorter way to decide a case, a summary procedure, which was not 'adversarial', but closer to a modern inquiry.

Damaging someone's reputation: offence or public-spirited action?

Scripture refers to an 'informer', in the story of the rich man who had a steward, and who was told that his steward was mismanaging his master's resources.[1] The Vulgate has *hic diffamatus est apud illum*. We hear nothing more about the informer in this parable, or what became of him. He is not reproached for his action.[2]

The Roman legal system linked *existimatio*, the way someone was 'thought of', with dignity or standing in the community.[3] In the centuries immediately before and after the birth of Christ the idea emerged that individuals whose *existimatio*, or reputation had been formally lost could not bring a suit because that would lower the *dignitas* of the court itself.[4]

There were other terms for this sort of loss or lack of a good name. The earlier legal term *ignominia* (used several times in the Vulgate)[5] was giving way by the fifth century to *infamia* as the preferred word in Christian legal usage, although Isidore still uses *ignominia* for the loss of good name when someone is convicted of a crime.[6] The Council of Carthage (419) says that infamous persons may not be witnesses in ecclesiastical cases.[7] The Council of Tours (567) included incest in the offences leading to infamy and that of Mâcon (583) added perjury.[8] So there were several ways in which one's good name could be lost.

There is also a developing vocabulary. *Iniuria* is mostly discussed in terms of reputation in Roman law.[9] There is material in Salic law on the possibility of injuring, defaming and falsely accusing and thus causing injuries by words, with lists of possible insults which might have such an effect.[10] In his *Etymologies*, Isidore discusses loss of reputation in connection with the loss of standing a person experiences when he is found out in a crime. 'Ignominy is that by which he who is caught committing a crime loses his name for honesty. It is called ignominy because it means "without a name".'[11] What is lost here is specifically the 'name for honesty'. This is the association of the individual with certain attributes or characteristics which made him respected. It is a strong idea in Roman society.[12]

Fama is in itself a neutral term for reputation.[13] It can be qualified by 'bad'.[14] Or it can be qualified by 'good' and then one might call it 'praise'.[15] But *fama* can also mean 'rumour', and then it is an uncertain thing: *fama nomen incerti, locum non habet ubi certum est*, says Tertullian.[16] Moreover, in its capacity as rumour, *fama* is likely to spread: *et exiit fama haec per universam terram illam*, as Chromatius of Aquileia puts it.[17] Augustine speaks of widespread fame: *late patens fama*.[18]

This linking of rumour and reputation is central to the problem we are trying to address here. *Fama* is people's good opinion: *bona hominum opinio*. That can be lost or diminished.[19] Loss of reputation is frequently mentioned in the Theodosian Code as a just penalty of certain actions.[20] Thus infamy is a legally defined state or condition of someone who has been condemned by a court. The twelfth-century *Summa 'Elegantius'* says that no one ought to be removed from office (*deiectus*) solely for *infamia*, and what is understood there is the technical status of one convicted in a court.[21] Infamy is created by the sentence of a judge (*sententia iudicis*), as it is by the declaration that someone has broken the law and the imposition of a penalty.[22] *Infamia* thus both destroys reputation and makes that state of affairs public knowledge.

In the late classical period *clamor* is often mere noise. This seems to be so in the *Code* of Justinian (6. 35. 12. 1; 1.3. 32. 8; 9. 30. 2). It is commonly no more than that in Jerome's Vulgate version. 'Their cry goes up to God': *Ascenditque clamor eorum ad Deum* (Exodus 2.23). But *clamor* comes to mean an outcry related to moral indignation. The *clamor* surrounding Sodom and Gomorrah in Genesis is a key case in point in the Vulgate (Genesis 18.20).[23] There are also hints of this notion in 'and I expected him to do justice and behold iniquity, and I expected righteousness and behold an outcry'.[24] The notion of malice as an outcry rising to the ears of God is in: *quia ascendit malitia eius coram me* (Jonah 1.2). In the New Testament Ephesians 4.31 is important in its linking of *clamor* and *malitia*: 'Let all bitterness and anger and indignation and outcry and blasphemy be removed from among you with all malice.'[25] *Clamor* can be itself a testimony, as it is already in Augustine: *Clamor tuus testis sit contra te*.[26] Gregory the Great, commenting on Genesis 18.20, has a usage of *clamor* which links it with sin: *peccatum quippe cum voce, est culpa in actione; peccato vero etiam cum clamore, est culpa cum libertate*.[27]

Yet in Roman law of the early Christian period it is held to be profoundly reprehensible to damage someone else's reputation; indeed to take someone's good reputation away is a serious offence in itself. The Theodosian Code contains numerous references to *delatores* or informers, in terms of the strongest disapproval. It recognises that good reputation is a valuable possession, easily destroyed. Anonymous defamatory writings should be burned at once.[28] If anyone accidentally finds such a writing he ought to destroy it and not repeat what it says, and if he does repeat it he himself will be guilty of defamation.[29] There must be no investigation of the accusations such writings contain, for he who brings someone else's life into question ought to do so by an open charge in court.[30] Authors of defamatory writings must be prepared to prove what they say, and even if they are able to do so they must expect to be punished because they chose to defame rather than to make a formal accusation through the courts in the proper way.[31] A defamed person who lacks an accuser prepared to do that must be considered innocent, even though he conspicuously does not lack an enemy.[32]

The Theodosian Code makes an exception to the rule that an informer is himself committing a serious offence, in the case of informers who tell about a practitioner of the magic arts who goes to a secret meeting in someone's house.[33] The presumption here is clearly that clandestine magical practices are worse than the crime of damaging reputation. Similarly, if someone informs on a person who rapes a consecrated virgin he does not deserve punishment.[34] So there are exceptions to the general rule that 'informing' is a discreditable activity. But in most cases informers are to be punished severely, by deportation (to prevent their repeating the calumny).[35] It is not the Emperor's wish that the innocent should be ruined by the attacks of devious men, says the Theodosian Code.[36] Informers may even deserve capital punishment, because that is proportionate to an offence which essentially consists in attacking a man's *caput* (his head figuratively taken to mean his status).[37]

In the period between Gratian and the Fourth Lateran Council there seems to have been a radical shift away from these assumptions of late Roman society, with the arrival of a vocabulary of 'notoriety' and a concomitant change in the legal procedures required for dealing with cases which fall into that category.[38]

In classical legal usage a *notoria* is a written statement 'notifying' the authorities about a crime.[39] *Falsis necne notoriis* may be closer to the mediaeval *notorius*. Gratian has *notorius* twice, but of the offence not the person.[40] Neither *notorius* nor *notorietas*[41] seems to come into common legal usage until well on into the mediaeval period.

Yet there were certainly notorious persons before there was a word for them. Three-quarters of a century before Lateran IV Bernard of Clairvaux refers to the notion in one of his letters with a casualness which strongly implies that he could expect his correspondents to pick up the implications at once. Indeed, as he reports it, it is they who are saying to him, 'How shall we condemn those who are not convicted and have not confessed?[42]

Condemnation on mere gossip?

In the pre-Gratian collections there is an insistence that no one can be condemned unless proved guilty, nor excommunicated without the evidence being considered and the accused allowed to speak up for himself.[43] But these ground rules would seem to be set at risk by subsequent developments in the handling of cases of notorious wrongdoing.

The starting-point is the arrival of a rumour to the ears of a person in authority.[44] There is clear Biblical guidance for such an official. The right thing to do is to check the accuracy of the story. In Luke's Gospel (16.2) Jesus describes how the rich man asks his steward about whom he has been told a rumour (*qui diffamatus erat apud dominum suum*) 'What is this I hear about you?' (*Quid hoc audio de te?*). And in Genesis, God says that he will go down and see for himself whether the rumour which has reached him about Sodom and Gomorrah is true (*descendam, et videbo utrum clamorem, qui venit ad me, opere compleverunt*) (Genesis 18.21). The next task is to ensure that no malice is involved: *non quidem a malevolis et maledici sed a providis et honestis*. If *clamor et fama* come to the ears of someone who holds a responsible office, he has a duty to check that the sources of the story are not motivated by ill-will or malice, but honest people. He should also not rely upon a single witness, but ensure that the story is being widely told. The next task is to check how far this story is widespread: *nec semel tantum sed saepe*. Even then, there must be careful investigation of its truth. This means that the investigator will have looked carefully into the evidence before deciding it is true, and acting upon it (Canon 8). There is to be no secret proceeding on the basis of allegations.[45] That would imply that the investigator or judge at least ought to know who the accusers are.

Three sorts of 'accuser' are possible where notoriety is involved. It may be by calumny that a crime comes to public notice.[46] It may be that something which is a secret is claimed not to be a secret (*secretum non secreto arguitur*) (and of course the moment such a claim is made it ceases to be a secret). Someone's crime may be published by a person acting not out of zeal for justice but from motives of malice.[47] Calumny ought to carry the penalty of *talio*.[48] The proven *calumniator* is to suffer penalties of demotion and deprivation.[49]

Apart from calumniators there are two other categories, of those who may make unjust accusations, or accusations which may have the result of giving rise to unjust condemnation. Prevaricators pretend to be on one side but in fact they are on the other.[50] Someone who behaves in this way should be banned from testifying or accusing again.

A turncoat may act for money, or under undue influence.[51]

> *Tergiversator est qui prece vel pretio corruptus in universum ab accusatione desistit*
>
> (*Digest* 48. 16.1. 1 and 48. 16. 13 pr.)

Hoc vitium cum sua causa quidam satis urbane notavit dicens:
   Cum mihi sudanti manus ungitur ere deorsum
   vertre non verero tunc pro cataplasmate dorsum.

It is an indication of malice – like the rule that you can tell heresy by its persistence – that it presses on and on with an accusation even after it has been dismissed in a fair trial.[52] Burchard of Worms, who is concerned about malice, says that a person should not be tried twice for the same offence.[53] Gregory IX has: *absolutus de certo crimine, de eodem iterum accusari non potest*.[54]

There is a recognition that some cases may be so outrageous and blatant that it becomes impossible to 'do nothing about them'; for fear of causing scandal to the people, something has to be done.[55] The Scriptural principle adduced here is that the steward ought to be removed from his stewardship if he cannot give a satisfactory account of it (Luke 16.2). (There are parallels with the 'stumbling-block' principle in Church of England ecclesiastical law of the nineteenth and twentieth centuries, which recognises circumstances in which scandal may in itself be a reason for removing or disciplining a cleric even if he has not been shown to be guilty of the offence with which he is charged.)

Thomas of Piperata, a late thirteenth-century Bolognese jurist, defined ill repute (*fama*) as 'something that the people of any city, town, camp, village, or district commonly believe (*communiter opinantur*), asserting it in words or speech, but that they do not hold as certain and true or manifest'.[56] By 'the people', Thomas means the majority, not the entirety of the local population.

There are some protections. He says that there has to be an appropriate relationship between the thing alleged to be 'known' and the group of people alleged to 'know' it (a local rumour has to be about a local person, and so on). But these are slippery requirements and they can be circular. In the end Thomas comes back to the familiar requirement of proof by the testimony of two witnesses or the judge's 'knowledge' that the story is notorious (*nisi judici constet de dicta fama, quia sit nota sibi ut notoria*). The *sibi* here is crucial, for the method by which the judge 'gets to know' requires there to be rules of evidence. So the great problem is to know when it is safe to proceed to conviction of the individual about whom something is 'known'. It therefore became clear that *fama* was a sufficient ground for beginning an inquisitorial process but that it could not be enough to found a conviction.[57]

Fama was not the only type of imperfect or incomplete proof. *Indicia* are merely 'circumstantial' evidences. They may, taken together, point in a certain direction. In one of Thomas de Piperata's examples, it is alleged that S. has arranged the killing of T. There is no witness to this conspiracy. But there is proof that S. is T.'s enemy, that S. was near the scene of the crime when T. was killed and that after the murder he gave the killer shelter; that the murderer was a member of S's household. that S. had sworn that he would have T. killed and that there was old bad blood between S. and T. These are alleged to be enough to amount to *indicia indubitata*.[58] On this a judge had discretion to condemn, if it was his judgement (*arbitrium*) that that was right.

Sufficiently strong *indicia* create presumptions. Presumptions are things 'more likely than not', and again a judge had discretion to convict on presumptions. It was accepted, indeed well established, that a more serious matter required a higher standard of proof.[59] So a criminal conviction on mere *fama* or *indicia* was perhaps inherently unsafe.

Suing for defamation

The converse of making notorious a manifest sin or an offence against the law by 'reporting' it, is defamation in something closer to the modern sense, the destruction of someone's good name by false report out of malice.

Peter the Chanter at the end of the twelfth century was not entirely happy about the assumptions which lay behind the 'gossips' charter' development of his day. 'The just man not only avoids the opportunity to behave with levity but also roots out rash judgements, that is suspicion'.[60] (Peter the Chanter here cites Augustine on the view that a person who suspects someone else is revealing a fault in himself not in the other person.) People of a suspicious disposition are also often gossips.[61] He who hears and relays vile talk is a dishonest man.[62] Such a dubious witness will not remain unpunished.[63] It is dangerous to spread an opinion which damages someone's reputation.[64] This vice of rumour-mongering goes with inconstancy.[65]

Among the *Decretals* is a recognition that there is such a thing as 'verbal injury'. It is insisted that, as with other injuries, someone guilty of injuring another ought to make reparation.[66] Canonists discussed whether plenitude of papal power could extend to the restoration of someone's good name when the just sentence of a secular court had rendered him *infames*.[67] But more important for our purposes was the attempt to define defamation. It must impute an *offence* to someone (not merely criticise his personal qualities); it is not essential that the accusation be false; but it is essential to defamation that it be malicious. If someone lost his temper and committed a defamation and then apologised, he might be forgiven, as might someone who could show he had been provoked. The defamed person's reputation must have been attacked in the ears of good men, or he must have been made to undergo purgation or to suffer in some other way.[68]

England took something of an early lead, surprisingly quickly after the developments of the late twelfth century. Gratian is unlikely to have been the principal source, since he does not deal with the topic in a coordinated way.[69] In 1222 the Council of Oxford promulgated a provincial constitution on defamation, which Helmholz argues had no link with Lateran IV's *Auctoritate Dei Patris*.[70] However, it made its way into English ecclesiastical court formularies and was glossed by William Lyndwood. The Constitution excommunicates all those who *gracia odii, lucri vel favoris*, or for any other reason of malice, destroy someone's reputation among decent people. The person defamed can then seek canonical punishment and a remedy for himself (although there was dispute according to the *Decretals* as to whether he could do so if the issue was secular).[71]

In one defamation case the complaint is that John has falsely accused Henry of being a thief and of being involved in various other crimes (*et aliis diversis criminibus irretitum*) and has thus defamed him so that Henry's reputation is injured. Moreover, John has taken no notice of a sentence of excommunication imposed on him and has gone on exercising his priestly ministry.[72]

17 Shortening the process

Mediaeval trials could become immensely long, as lawyers took advantage of every available provision for the benefit of their clients. The advantage of the device of deeming someone 'notorious' was that it made it possible to consider shortening the process of establishing guilt.

In certain situations a judge himself could make the accusation by virtue of his office (*ex officio*).[1] The urge to shorten the process was particularly strong in such cases, for the protections of the adversarial system which had a way of proliferating and greatly extending the time it all took, were not needed to keep a balance between the parties when there was no 'accuser'.

The *ex officio* power to initiate a case[2] did not merely shift the launching of litigation from the private individual to the public official; it also set up a model in which the old adversarial pattern was fundamentally altered. When one private individual accused another before a judge, the judge acted as a referee. When the judge himself initiated the case and also conducted his own investigation, he acted, in effect, as prosecutor as well as judge. It is true that he did that even in full adversarial hearings, where he could to some extent conduct an inquiry through the *interrogationes*, but the rights and role of the accuser were crucial in limiting the scope of the judge's investigatory powers. Properly conducted, the adversarial method has an advantage as a mechanism for getting at the truth. South Africa's Truth and Reconciliation Committee has suffered from the lack of such a mechanism.

The problem created by the judge's role in the inquisition was recognised without the restraining factor of the rights of the accuser as a party. The 'senior person' authorised *ex officio* to take action was assumed to act not as if he himself were both *actor* and *iudex*, but as though the rumour itself made the accusation and the outcry did the denouncing: *sed quasi deferente fama vel denunciante clamore*. Thus the rules of natural justice are deemed to be preserved even within a truncated process.

Even in adversarial processes, the judge has sole responsibility for dealing with the evidence, deciding what to reject and what to accept and which witnesses are to attend and be examined.[3] The judge can on his own authority (it is part of his *officium*) produce witnesses so that he can find out the truth.[4] (Though, as noted already, the judge cannot be a witness in the same trial as the one where he is judge.)[5] Because it is the judge's responsibility to decide what evidence to admit, it is he who must make the decision about the state of mind and intention of the witness which is everywhere held to be so important.[6]

When these generally accepted powers of a judge are used in a process which he has initiated, he is in the driving seat. There are similar well-known modern dangers in the inquiry model, and a parallel problem of lack of protection for those who may have no proper chance to defend themselves.[7]

Innocent III and the Inquisition

In Innocent III's pontificate trial by ordeal was abandoned and the inquisitorial method of initiating and carrying through a case was begun. The consequences were profound because two of the load-bearing columns of mediaeval jurisprudence were thus shifted.

Fraher[8] groups the abandonment of trial by ordeal, the move to *ex officio* and summary procedure and the proliferation of treatises forming a literature on procedure. Much of this literature was written after 1215 and can therefore be considered to show us how far contemporaries understood the implications which now seem, with hindsight, to have followed. But that assumes that mediaeval academic and practising lawyers were able to see the field of their endeavours laid out, with the lie of the land clear before them. There is no evidence that they did. These major changes were made in response to practical requirements rather than on policy grounds and their knock-on effects do not appear even to have been considered until they began to make themselves uncomfortably apparent.

Gregory IX deals in Book V of his *Decretals* with the three modes of conducting legal proceedings known to the ecclesiastical world at the turn of the twelfth to thirteenth century. The first is based on the form used in the late Roman world, where an accuser must be found who is willing to bring a formal charge, and to take the risk of suffering the penalty for the same crime (designed to put off an accuser motivated by malice),[9] if his accusation is found unproved (*sub pena talionis*).

The second method of instigating a trial is by *denunciatio*. Here the accuser brings the formal charge against the alleged culprit only after he has tried and failed to persuade him to repent and give up his wrongdoing. So an ideal of charity or reconciliation underlies this way of doing things, and it is closer to the modern 'alternative dispute resolution', in ways we shall come to later.[10]

Innocent III took a much greater step beyond the old *accusatio* pattern in his provisions for *inquisitio*, and it was this third mode of proceeding which came to dominate the late mediaeval scene in all ecclesiastical

132 *Shortening the process*

courts.[11] The initial inspiration was the situation where evil-doing was so blatant that there really seemed no need to go through all the usual procedures. Among the rubrics to Canon 8 of the Fourth Lateran Council is one which says that bishops can proceed to inquisition when the outcry about an offence cannot be tolerated without scandal.[12]

First moves in the three modes differ, but are in each case laid down as appropriate for the form of proceeding in question. In the case of an accusation, there should first be a *legitima inscriptio*, that is, a lawful charge. In the case of denunciation, there should first be a *caritativa adhibitio*, a loving broaching of the matter. In the case of the inquisition all that is needed is public scandal. An adroit gossip can easily start that. Here something which would have been discreditable in the days of the Theodosian Code becomes a legitimate practice. The informer becomes a responsible citizen.

Paucapalea and Rufinus, writing on Gratian's *Decretum*, discuss the question of the abbreviation of due process, where the offence is publicly known.[13] The *Summa* of Master Roland asks whether an *ordo* is required *in manifestis*. Yes, he says, except when the accused publicly confesses the crime: *excepto eo, ubi reus crimen publice confitetur*. There are also crimes known beyond question to the judge and all the people, in which only a minimal process is needed.[14]

Due process for cases involving *inquisitio* is set out in Canon 8 of the Fourth Lateran Council:

1 The person concerned ought to be present, unless he absents himself *per contumaciam*.
2 He should be given the accusations against him (*exponenda ei sunt capitula, de quibus fuerit inquirendum*).
3 He should be allowed to defend himself (*et facultatem habeat defendendi seipsum*).
4 With the reservations already mentioned, he should be told not only what witnesses have said but also who they are (*non solum dicta sed etiam nomina ipsa testium sunt ei ... publicanda*). The intention of this is to prevent people bringing false accusations for which they cannot be called to account (*ne per suppressionem nominum infamandi ... falsum audacia praebeatur*). But Canon 8 makes a potentially dangerous exception of notorious cases (*ut de notoriis excessibus taceatur*), and in the nature of things if the foundation of the case is gossip, 'common knowledge', it may be impossible to say who is the author of the story.

For every notorious criminal there have to have been persons to whom his crime seems blatant and who are prepared to say so. Being public property does not make a story true. So the legal concept of notoriety cannot be considered apart from those of calumny and defamation and the making of accusations by those who are ill disposed to the accused in general. The texts are very conscious of this. If a criminal can be defined as 'notorious' because a great many people know of his offence, the defining factor is the effectiveness with which the gossip has been disseminated. This test of 'the numbers who know' is discussed in the *Summa 'Elegantius'*, in a passage in which it is suggested that there are three kinds of manifest or notorious crimes. Some are known to the judge but to no one else. Some are known to the judge and to a few others. Some are known to the judge and many others. The basis for declaring something notorious would thus seem in part to depend on how many people know about it.[15] But it is realised that even if two or more witnesses swear that they actually saw the accused commit the crime there can still be a possibility that they were *all* moved by malice (Gregory IX, *Decretals*, V. 1. 21).

What everyone thus 'knows' may not be something for which objective proof can easily be found. There may be a general view that a priest is a fornicator, even though no one has ever seen him in bed with his mistress. The *Summa 'Elegantius'* makes the point that no one can see into another person's conscience and so although it may be possible to judge others where the offence is manifest, it is not possible to judge *in occultis*.[16] This 'secrecy' problem can be partly addressed by dealing with things tactfully and quietly.

Despite this problem with the secrets of the heart, and perhaps paradoxically, *notorii* are deemed to be offenders whose crime is so publicly or certainly known that it seems there can be no doubt about it. That was the justification for making special rules for them. And because this is so, it could be argued, there is no need for them to be tried according to the rules which would be necessary to protect someone whose guilt is in any doubt. The key point in processes against the *notorius* is that notoriety is deemed to remove the need for a formal accusation.[17]

But the justice of taking a short-cut to punishment depended on the security of the information laid, and here we come back to the central paradox of this move to create short-cuts. The authority most commonly cited in this connection came to be a letter of 866 from Pope Nicholas I to the Bulgars. He instructed them to go on receiving the sacraments from a priest publicly known to be an adulterer, until he has been properly convicted and deposed.[18] Gratian, who includes a reference to this letter,[19] errs on the safe side. He says that due process would be required even in these circumstances unless the crime or misbehaviour is so obvious that it actually constitutes a confession of guilt.[20] At the same time Gratian is already raising the question whether *in manifestis*, in 'obvious' crimes, it is necessary to observe due process.[21] *Manifesta* are a different matter, because there is no need for proof. The truth is known. He gives a series of patristic *allegationes* to support this view (*Causa* II. q. 1). Does Gratian's exacting procedural standard hold even for a case apparently needing no proof? The tension is there, between the obvious and gossiped-about; and the secret but suspected.

The problem is that the truth may not be 'manifest' to everyone; if only the judge knows it in that way, or only the public but not the judge, then there must be a fair trial to bring everything publicly to the test in an orderly manner. And the *Summa 'Elegantius'* says that even if the judge has seen, for example, a murder, with his own eyes, there would still have to be a trial if the murderer denied that he had done it.[22] There could thus in reality be some difficulty in proving even something of which the accused seems manifestly guilty.[23] The same line is pursued by the *Summa 'Elegantius'*, with a reference to Gratian. The author reminds the student that even *in notoriis* Gratian expects proof.[24] The *Summa 'Elegantius'* says that if the judge himself does not have direct knowledge that the alleged offender is guilty, he should not pronounce sentence on suspicion.[25] For one reason why a proper procedure is needed is that it would be unjust for an accused person to be found guilty on a basis of untested malicious rumour.[26]

Canon 8 of the Fourth Lateran Council[27] presses for a sense of proportion, to avoid great damage being done for a very small benefit: *ne forte per leve compendium ad grave dispendium veniatur*.

The Canon goes on to set out further rules of proper procedure in line with these principles. The prelate responsible is to behave in the same way whether the story is about a subordinate or a senior person: *non solum cum subditis verum etiam cum praelatus excedit*. There is to be no special protection for the senior official. On the other hand, careful adherence to fair process is seen to be especially important in the case of senior prelates, because they will inevitably make enemies, since they must *ex officio* condemn and discipline others.[28]

There is wider recognition after Lateran IV that there might be circumstances in which it would be desirable to shorten the process of trial. But this pragmatic reason apart, subsequent developments seem to take things outside the category of the *notorii* while still being to some degree attributable to the Innocent III codification of earlier developments concerning the handling of notorious cases.

The reason for wanting to cut things short might be simply that there appeared to be an open and shut case.[29] The example of a case where short-cuts are appropriate, to which Johannes Fagelli de Pisis repeatedly recurs, is that of the son who petitions for sustenance (*alimenta*) from his father. But if this was to happen it needed, in the interests of justice, to be very strictly regulated. Johannes Fagelli sets out in his *Tractatus brevis de summariis cognitionibus* an account of the ground-rules as he sees them.[30] He suggests that there are two possibilities: to abbreviate procedure and deal with things summarily (*summatim*) or to go outside ordinary procedure altogether (*in eis extra ordinem procedere*).[31] But he sees that the grounds on which either route might be taken require careful thought. There are difficult problems of definition: *nam huiusmodi rei difficilis est diffinitio*, for some cases need not be dealt with by adversarial trial while other cases require full process, and it is important to be clear which is which.[32]

The minimum essentials

If proceedings are to be abbreviated (*semiplena sive summaria*), what are the elements which it is essential to retain?[33] A judge may be able to deal rapidly with objections such as that a witness is old or ill or a calumniator, but they must still be considered.[34] It might be open to question whether a formal written accusation is required in a summary process (*in summariis*).[35] But Johannes Fagelli de Pisis stresses that no one can be justly condemned without a hearing.[36] It is also important that what happens should be transparent, 'brighter than the noonday sun'.[37] Some degree of due form must be preserved before a sentence is pronounced.[38] In the *Summa 'Elegantius'* and elsewhere it states that there must at least *be* a sentence (*sententia*).[39] Even if someone can be tried in his absence when he refuses to come, he ought to be present to be sentenced.[40]

Innocent III's rules set out his own view of the minimum essentials of a fair trial. He insists that the *infamatus* is to be present before the judge unless he chooses contumaciously to be absent. The specific points of inquiry or *capitula* are to be explained to him, so that he may have a chance to defend himself. He is to be given the name and details of the testimony of each witness against him so that he can object or comment. This is once more explicitly designed to prevent cowardly and malicious attacks succeeding.[41] But the accused may not be told what his rights are,[42] and, as we shall see in a moment, there were dangers in the *inquisitio* that the justice done would be rough justice.

There are perhaps three *genera causarum* in which it may be possible to shorten the process or eliminate elements of the *ordo judiciarius*, in the view of Johannes Fagelli de Pisis. The first is that in which it is possible to proceed *summatim* because only a limited standard of proof is needed: *semiplena probatio sufficit*. (This might be the equivalent of the 'balance of probabilities' required in a civil case in modern English law.)

There are, second, cases which are in some degree *extraordinariae*, such as grave-robbing. The notion here is that the judge may proceed on his own sole authority.[43] But that does not mean that such cases do not require *plena probatio* (*immo plena requiritur*). 'For in every case, civil and criminal the accused is found not guilty if the accuser does not prove his case.'[44]

The third type of special case is our old friend, the one in which the matter is obvious.[45] An example of this would be flagrant adultery.[46] But again here full proofs are required, not *semiplenae*.[47] Everywhere the judge ought to place great weight on being able to pronounce a sentence with certainty, and not merely give his opinion.[48]

In Johannes de Lignano's *Super Clementina 'Saepe'*[49], there is a further discussion of the circumstances in which procedure may be abbreviated. 'It often happens that no one is clear how to proceed,' he says. In those circumstances, the judge can take short cuts but not in such a way as to exclude legitimate defences and the necessary proofs. The question is again which elements are indispensable to fairness.

Theology is useful here. Johannes de Lignano asks in his treatise *Super Clementina* what can be left out without breaking the rules of natural or divine justice: *nec videtur remissa, nam est de iure naturali et divino*.[50] Is a citation necessary? God visibly keeps the rule that no one may be tried in his absence by asking 'Adam where are you?' when he comes to investigate the episode of the eating of the forbidden fruit (Genesis 3.8).[51] So that must be essential. Is a written accusation (*libellus*) necessary? The woman who appeared before Solomon had only to say *filius meus vivit*, 'my son is living'. Can adjournments be granted so that everything the parties wish to produce can be brought before the judge? Should the witnesses take oaths?

He perceives that a number of technical issues are raised by the text of *Saepe contingit* itself. 'It often happens that we instruct that in certain causes the matter should be handled straightforwardly and without adversarial conflict,' says Clement V.[52] He acknowledges that this gives rise to confusion about how to proceed,[53] explains the text. The rules are accordingly set out. The judge before whom such a case comes is not to insist on a written accusation (*libellus*). He does not have to require the actual adversarial setting out of the case: *litis contestationem non postulat*. He can cut short the treatment of the subject-matter (*amputet dilationum materiam*). He can ensure that the whole process is kept to the minimum and prevent the calling of innumerable witnesses. But matters such as making sure that there is no malice in the accusation and that the truth is being told, are not to be skimped.[54] The overriding purpose is to ensure that nothing is done in a disorderly way (*irritus*) because of being simplified.[55]

The question of the standard of proof required is clarified by Lignano. He defies *plena probatio* as that which makes the judge quite sure (*plena fides*).[56] He also accepts that there are grades of proof, from the point where the judge merely begins to suspect something to his having absolutely no doubt about it.[57]

It is worth pausing for a moment and asking whether what is developing here is something akin to a recognition that it is sometimes best to handle things informally. If that is what these changes point to, it is important that it is so clearly recognised that there are ground rules which apply even to the most informal procedure.

So there are changes in the direction of speed and efficiency, and of rapid but not intentionally rough justice, in the case of notorious offenders. But there is a continuing awareness of the danger that natural justice's rules may be betrayed where short-cuts are taken, and it is to the credit of our writers that they see that very clearly, and draw back from the brink. The informers now get away unpunished, though not entirely without disapproval, unless it can be shown that they are acting out of malice. The protection of reputation is no longer seen as a high good in itself.

Part VI
Outcomes

18 Divine judgement, human judgement

Where God is judge there can be no doubt that he gets it right. In the courts a human substitute acts for him, and his decisions about guilt or innocence may be less reliable. It may be asked why, in that case, God leaves judgement to human judges. Agobard of Lyons comments that if the omnipotent Lord had wished the secrets of human hearts to be revealed in any other way he would not have ordered that judges and magistrates should be established in each city or that witnesses should be called to give evidence (Esdras 7.25; Leviticus 6.3–4: Hebrews 6.16).[1]

God could declare his will in a Council of the Church. 'Conciliar theology' historically assumes that the Holy Spirit is present at such a council, and guides its deliberations so that the Council does not err. The theme recurs in the literature of the early Councils and it was a major debating point again at the Reformation as to whether this was the case. Thus, this could be a way of finding out whether God had condemned an accused person.

There are two ecclesiologically distinct types of council or synod. One is the synod of bishops; the other is the diocesan synod. In the first there is a presumption of collegiality. The decisions of such a body are tested by the agreement of the bishops present. Council after council in the early centuries emphasise the importance of the bishops' unanimity as a sign that a decree expresses with will of the Holy Spirit. In the second, the bishop sits with his clergy and not with fellow-bishops and the will or judgement expressed is that of the bishop. The 16th Council of Toledo, as cited by Gratian,[2] tells the bishop to call together 'all' the abbots, priests, deacons and other clergy of the diocese, and also its people. The clergy present are merely a consultative body.[3] Synods could impose canonical penalties. They could employ *purgatio canonica* or ordeal could be used to establish guilt.[4] But though there are examples of councils and synods behaving as courts, it was far more usual to rely upon a human judge, a secular judge or bishop.

Proof by ordeal as test of the divine will

The contrast between divine and human judgement was less stark in the centuries up to the Fourth Lateran Council, when proof by ordeal was allowed, than it became later. Proof by ordeal was a method of finding out what God wished to say about the guilt or innocence of the accused, to get God to test the facts (since man cannot), and reveal his decisions through the outcome of the ordeal.

Such *purgatio canonica* is seen with some disquiet to put God himself on trial, since it is he who must determine the outcome.[5] Reluctance to use it showed itself in various ways. It was always clear that ordeal is a last resort. If any other form of proof was available, purgation was deemed inappropriate. *Si delictum est probabile, non indicitur purgatio.*[6] An accused person can be forced to undergo an ordeal where there is no one to bring the accusation.[7] This too was controversial. Master Roland would say that where there is no common gossip (*communis infamia*) in such a case, there is no place for ordeal (*non est iniungenda purgatio*). But if there is danger to the people, there remains a remedy in the ordeal.[8] So that might be the determining factor in deciding whether or not to go on to 'trial by ordeal', when other forms of proof fail.

Theological notions are particularly important here. *Purgatio* is an equivocal term; it can be theological or legal. In Hebrews 1.3 *purgatio* refers to purification from guilt. In Ambrose, too, that is the sense of *plena purgatio*.[9] The literal sense of the term in classical usage is 'cleansing'. From this derive various figurative meanings. On the secular side, Cicero preserves a technical forensic sense. *Purgatio* in legal usage of his day takes place when the deed is admitted but the guilt for it denied.[10] Again in Cicero, purgation takes place when someone defends himself against the accusation not that he did the deed but that he had a culpable intention in doing it.[11] So *purgatio* also has the 'sense of clearing from the responsibility' for something about which an accusation has been made. The difference is that the first involves actually discharging an existing guilt or making right an acknowledged wrong; the second declares that the guilt for the wrong perpetrated was not there in the first place, or the wrong itself was not done. From the first descends the usage of the mediaeval penitential tradition. From the second comes the usage which takes *purgatio* as the technical term for the ordeal, as employed to establish guilt or innocence in a judicial context where the accused denies responsibility for the wrong.

What is the difference between absolution and purgation, *absolutio* and *purgatio*? Augustine says that to absolve someone is to judge him innocent. But that does not mean that the absolution can be immediate, or that there is not some guilt to be purged before the absolution. *Absolutio* is thus a process determining a status of guilt or innocence, either by some action or by declaration: *absolvere est innocentem iudicare.*[12]

Mediaeval forensic *purgatio* before 1215 is by physical ordeal. Here two sorts of ordeal were normal. The test could involve only the accused, who would be tested by hot iron or hot and cold water.[13] Or it could involve the accuser and the accused, who fight a judicial duel, on the principle that God will ensure that whoever is in the right will win.[14]

Ninth-century popes had already stated their disapproval of such ordeals as a method of proof.[15] Gratian is clear that *purgatio vulgaris*, the use of hot and cold water or any other popular invention of that sort, rests on no canonical authority, and is indeed forbidden on the apostolic authority of popes.[16] Lucius III (1184–5) speaks in a text which was used in the *Decretals* of Gregory IX,[17] of the unacceptability of such judgments. He objects to them because they lie outside the proper boundaries of the system of administration of justice. They are *peregrina iudicia*. They are, he says, not to be used (*inhibita*). The thrust of the phrase *peregrina iudicia* is that such proofs are outside the law of the Church.

And yet they depend on miraculous intervention, and thus in a profound sense they must be seen as *God's* way. Peter the Chanter discusses this question of miraculous proof in his *Verbum Abbreviatum*. One should not *expect* heat and water to change their properties in the ordeal. That is, one should not take miracle for granted. This is a philosophically interesting point, because Peter the Chanter has put his finger on the paradoxicality of expecting the extraordinary to be ordinary. He takes the line that the Church does not now proceed by the taking of lots in appointing bishops and popes. It has a procedure of an orderly and non-miraculous kind. It is improper to expect God to be at the disposal of the legal process.[18]

Purgatio vulgaris, the form of purgation which consisted in a test by duel, is also prohibited because often it is unreliable, and it causes an innocent person to be condemned, and again, paradoxically, because God seems to be being tested, when two people engage in a duel to establish who is telling the truth or who is in the right.[19]

Ordeal was officially abolished by and after the Fourth Lateran Council of 1215.[20] But it had met a primitive need which persisted because of the continuing need for a means of proof when confession, or witness to the fact, or other 'human' indications, were not to be had. It has been suggested that the method of extracting confessions by torture in some degree replaced the ordeal.[21] There was, however, a less violent alternative, and that was compurgation.

Compurgation makes a different use of the oath from that which lent authority to an individual witness's testimony. Gratian explains that the corollary of confession is the denial of the accusation, which is done, in the case of a priest, on oath.[22] A priest may strengthen his own oath by getting others to come and swear 'with him' (*com-purgatio*). Thus, as Gratian puts it:

If legitimate accusers cannot prove the crimes of the priest, and he himself denies it, then he with seven fellow-priests may purge his crime if he can. A deacon can purge himself, with the aid of three fellow-deacons, if he is accused of the same crime.[23]

The principle is that he who is accused should be prepared to confirm his innocence on oath, and fellow-oath-takers who believe him to have sworn truthfully, ought to support him.[24] Gratian says this more than once. The accused, against whom the crime cannot be proved, ought to purge the accusation by swearing an oath and his supporters who believe him swear too.[25]

For their oath to be worth having, those who support the accused ought themselves to be known as honest men, who are acquainted with the person 'with whom' and on whose behalf they swear;[26] and neither the judge nor anyone else ought to stand in their way.[27] A person who fails in this is to be punished as though he had been convicted,[28] for he has aligned himself with the guilty.

The accused's oath is his testimony to the truth. The oath others swear is a testimony to his credibility. So this is certainly proof by testimony, but not as to the fact. Rather, it is testimony to *character*. It says, 'this is not the kind of person who would do this'.[29] The notion that this is the only way to prove a negative seems quite well developed: '*Chescune ley gage est proprement en le negative de la demaunde au de la querele.*'[30]

The possession of a clear conscience is demonstrated by a 'good oath'. The oath-takers risk their own reputations if they support someone unworthy of their trust. The defendant risks being condemned to hell if he perjures himself. So there is a sense that here, too, is a form of ordeal, in that the judgement is still in God's hands, and that is underlined by the practice of keeping a hand upon the Gospel book while the oath is being taken.[31]

Principles on purgation of this sort, assembled in the *Decretals* of Gregory IX, include the notion that someone against whom an accusation is made may purge *himself* on oath, if his word is deemed trustworthy.[32] (The kind of thing which would make him unsuitable to be trusted is having previous convictions.)[33] There is some indication in the procedural treatises that jurists were having to rethink a good deal about proof in the period between 1215 and 1270, when the *Speculum iudiciale* of William Durant was published.[34] The problem was that if a confession could not be obtained and two eye-witnesses could not be found, so that there might be no secure proof, and the various 'ordeal' options were ruled out, it was necessary to consider whether the required elements in proof might not have to be modified. In the *Tractatus de Fama* of the thirteenth-century Bolognese Thomas de Piperata a concept of *arbitrium* (judicial discretion) is explored, and a notion of circumstantial evidence, which falls short of the foundation principle of mediaeval witnessing as to fact, that the witnesses should be eye-witnesses.[35]

Some of the ideas to be met about a judge's function and his powers strongly suggest that the Divine Judge's reliability in arriving at the right decision was an advantage not easily lost sight of. Asking God what to do through the ordeal and its like was a crude request for a sign. What was needed was machinery to assist the human judge in exercising his own discretion, preferably with divine guidance.

Thought-crime

Stephen of Tournai asks whether anyone should be punished merely for his wrong intention or mistaken private opinions. Imperial rescript in Roman law asserts that the treasonous will deserves punishment as much as the treasonous deed. The New Testament, too, identifies as an offence merely lusting after a woman. Stephen begins from the stray thought, and moves with it to the will actually to do the deed, defining a stage of *studiosa voluntas*, in which the intention becomes firm, and at which, as he thinks, it may be appropriate to speak of imposing a penalty.[36]

The question of 'trying' heretics became more straightforward when the thought-crimes became public, repeated, obstinate assertions. That led to 'trial by synod' (Peter Abelard at Soissons and Sens and Gilbert of Poitiers at the Council of Rheims, all in the first half of the twelfth century). Or, in the later Middle Ages, it led to the use by the inquisitions of lists of standard heretical opinions and attempts to make individuals confess, under pressure, to holding them.

The important point for our immediate purposes here is that a human judge needed something out in the open (however oppressively obtained), before he could exercise his discretion. He could not, like God, see into men's hearts, know exactly what they were thinking and judge fairly accordingly.

19 Judicial discretion

In the judicial process there may be an invocation of the name of the divine judge: 'In the name of God, Amen' (*In dei nomine, Amen*). In a higher court, the Holy Spirit may be invoked. For added authority, reference may be made to counsel (*the iuris periti*) sitting with the judge. But otherwise the judge is on his own in making a finding of guilt and deciding on the appropriate sentence. 'How justly, how mercifully, how discreetly (*discrete*) [he behaved] towards his subjects, himself in a time of peace the author and lover of peace,' says Fleta, wishing to flatter his own king.[1]

An uncertain opinion cannot be the ground of a secure conclusion.[2] Julian of Eclanum makes this comment in another connection, but it is nevertheless germane to the question what kind of a foundation must be laid before a human judge can pronounce a sentence with confidence. For the judge has to be convinced of the justice of a charge.[3]

An attempt is made in a trial to establish facts[4] which are in dispute.[5] But it will rarely be possible to reach absolute certainty about the actual events at issue.[6] The principle is explicitly stated in the *Digest* (with reference to the forensic context), that a matter in doubt cannot be the ground of a secure sentence.[7]

The prior requirement is that of assessing whether there is anything in it, getting that 'feel' for a case on which a modern judge founds his reasons for finding one way or the other. The judge can do this by looking for a general 'reasonableness' or consistency. The lying plaintiff either asserts a falsehood or he suppresses what he knows to be the truth.[8] 'The only genuine characteristics of truthful stories pertain to their contents, and include such factors as internal consistency and accordance with other known facts,'[9] says a modern legal commentator. On this reading, it is possible to see justice as being satisfactorily done on a basis of ensuring that the pattern of considerations within a case hangs together.

Rogerius says that when those who write on law want to establish what is justice and equity, they sometimes point to the dictate of reason. He has in mind here the sorts of themes which are commonly taken in the Middle Ages to be dictates of natural law. So, we revere God; parents feed their children, and so on.[10] But when princes and others write about equity and justice, they only sometimes refer to this 'reasonable' kind of justice; 'often they look to that second part in which justice is defined by comparison with injustice'.[11] What Rogerius means here is that justice is relative. An example is striking back when someone hits you: *ut percussum repercutere*.[12] To strike the first blow might be unjust. To strike a blow in return might be just. For it is the duty of justice to do violence to no one unless one has been injured oneself: *nisi lacessitus iniuria*.[13] So justice in one context or situation may not be justice in another.

Despite this rather primitive 'theory' of what was in fact a sophisticated practice, the rules determining whether or not there was to be a finding of guilt became quite mechanical. Common law (*ius commune*) required a judge to acquit a suspect if two witnesses could not be produced, with no one to contradict them; or else if there was a confession from the accused. This was not a matter for his discretion.[14] The purpose of this rule was to ensure that even if the guilty sometimes went unpunished there was no risk of convicting the innocent (*Digest*, 48. 19. 5). A single witness will do where, for example, a cleric has been beaten in front of witnesses, and no one is prepared to testify that it did *not* happen.[15]

Nevertheless, despite these rather mechanical methods of arriving at a result, under Roman law, and Italian statutory law of the Middle Ages,[16] a judge had a discretion (*arbitrium*).[17] If the judge *thought* the *indicia* were strong enough, he could convict.[18] This was expressly said to be not an 'inherent' power, such as the sacerdotal power to bind and loose, but a personal discretion granted to an individual magistrate (*podestà*) when he entered office; he lost it when he left office.[19] The mediaeval priest, on the other hand, retains the power to bind and loose all his life because his orders are deemed to be indelible.

It is dangerous to allow too much judicial discretion unless there are effective protections against partiality and prejudice. That recognition also lies behind the setting of a low threshold of bias we looked at earlier.[20] Yet, inescapably, it is in the end 'up to the judge' to decide whom to believe.[21] Thus, as Irnerius puts it, with a Ciceronian echo, a proof is the creation of an opinion in a judge about something in doubt, by means of arguments.[22]

The author of the late twelfth-century *Summa 'Elegantius'* promises to collate points about *probatio*[23] which Gratian leaves dispersed in four places in his *Decretals*.[24] He notes, for instance, that the accusation rests on the accuser's being appropriate and unassailable, and upon the bringing to bear of proofs.[25] He explains that proofs come by way of witnesses and instruments: *probationes per testes et instrumenta*.[26] *Instrumenta*, documentary evidence, are thus kinds of proof, *species probationis*, along with witnesses. [27] The same things are identified by 'Irnerius' too as *species probationum*.[28] In the manuals of legal *process* of Master Damasus the *species probationis* are again listed (*per testes, per instrumenta, per presumptiones*).[29]

In exercising his discretion, the judge was expected to take account of the 'likelihood' of what was being claimed. If it went against a presumption, a proof had to be strong. When it is a presumption of fact it stands unless the contrary is proved, explains Ricardus Anglicus, and when it is a presumption of law, it stands unless there is any actual law to counter it.[30] If it went against probability, it had to be stronger still.[31] This rule comes into play when, for example, witnesses disagree. Then the judge should follow those whose testimony he considers to fit the events best: *sequetur iudex illa dicta, quae rei aptiora esse intellexerit.*[32]

The requirements about the standard of proof will vary according to what is at issue. Fourteenth-century jurists require more detailed evidence in criminal trials than in civil proceedings, because more is at stake for the accused.[33] It is something of a stock principle in fourteenth-century lectures that proofs therefore need to be 'clearer' in criminal trials.[34] According to the fourteenth-century jurist Baldus, pupil of Bardolo in Perugia, proving a case (*probatio*) requires that guilt be established beyond reasonable doubt. He himself would hold to that as much in civil as in criminal cases.[35] So what in modern English usage is a distinction between the tests of reasonable doubt (in criminal cases) and a balance of probabilities (in civil cases) is adumbrated in the Middle Ages.

The intrinsic uncertainty of the facts and the state of mind of the judge as the holder of an opinion about those facts are not necessarily related in the texts as clear-headedly as might be hoped. The judge is a 'public person in an intermediary position',[36] whom it is the task of accuser and accused to convince.[37] It was accepted that the task in a trial was to reach a stage where the judge was able to place credence (*credulitas*) on a particular view. That is thought of as 'a mental state of being convinced that a fact is proved'. This involves the progressive removal of any doubt there may be in the judge's mind.[38] But this does not in itself alter or establish the truth-status of the matter in question. It is for this reason that the state of *credulitas* is deemed to fall in the area between knowing and not knowing (*scientia* and *nescientia*)[39] where we should normally speak of 'opinion' or 'belief'.

20 Evidence

A mediaeval judge gave little in the way of reasons as to how he had arrived at his decision. The judge may merely say that he has heard and understood the arguments on the merits. (*Auditis et intellectis meritis cause*). There may follow a summary of the main stages in the proceedings, with a terse statement that the judge has found the plaintiff has (or has not) sufficiently proved his claim (*quia invenimus actorem intencionem suam sufficienter probasse*).[1]

A few fixed rules governing the use and testing of evidence lay behind this, and they take us further than the sketch in the previous chapter of the way the judge exercised his discretion.

Witnesses

The concept of 'bearing witness' contains a number of elements for our Christian legal authors. In Scripture to bear witness is to give testimony to the faith. In the same context, to speak or swear 'by God' is to call on *him* to be witness (*hoc est testem exhibere Deum*), as the Apostle did when he said 'God is my witness' (*testis est mihi Deus*) (Romans 1.9).[2] This sets the 'bearing of witness' in a context where its role is above all to support the truth. It is proof at a high level of conviction. In this frame of reference, swearing an oath can be looked on favourably as an act of loyalty to God: *ius Deo reddere*.

In the field of logic, mediaeval 'proving' normally looked to 'reasoning' and 'authorities' as grounds for accepting a conclusion. This was not an entirely tidy separation. In Aquinas, for example, syllogisms are composed of premisses which may either be deemed true in the light of reason, or will be considered reliable because they come on good authority. But 'good authority' *is* essentially testimony. Its authoritativeness depends upon the identity and standing of the 'author'. It will, preferably, be divine (for Scripture's author is God) or failing that, it will ideally have the weight of a leading figure of the early Church (Augustine, Jerome, Gregory for instance), or, *faute de mieux*, that of a respected secular authority such as Cicero or Aristotle. A trial relies on something much inferior, in its dependence on the testimony of living human witnesses who are not 'authorities' in the same way, but whose credibility and reliability are still important considerations. The oath may be taken on the Gospels or a statue of Christ or a saint. That can be taken to be a way of supporting what the witness says with a higher authority.[3] The witness remains in himself a person of essentially only limited authority, but his trustworthiness is heightened by his willingness to swear on something holy.

Testimony should not be a *'nuda assertio'* (bare assertion), but given on oath, says the *Summa 'Elegantius'*.[4] There are also hierarchical questions about this taking of oaths. A lowlier person, or one who is in any way an 'outsider', may not exact an oath from his superior. Jews ought to swear to Christians; Christians ought never to swear to Jews.[5] A heretic cannot accuse a Christian or testify against him: *Hereticus christianum accusare vel in eum testificari non potest.*[6]

The degree to which the oath binds can be quite precisely delimited. An oath need not be binding in perpetuity. The judge can set a time-limit or confine it in some other way, says the *Digest*:[7] A typical 'limited' oath is 'I swear to tell only the truth and the whole truth for both sides on those matters on which I am called and on which I shall be questioned.'[8] It is significant that the oath contains the expectation that the witness will be cross-examined, which extends the commitment he makes in the oath, because he must not only tell the truth when he gives his account, but also answer truthfully what may prove to be awkward ensuing questions.

'Swearing' is a subject of active interest to commentators on Gratian, from the twelfth century.[9] It was seen to raise all sorts of questions, about the very use of language in so strong a way, about the appropriateness and bindingness of various kinds of oath taken by different sorts of people. It is also importantly linked to the practical and theoretical issues which surround witnessing, for it will commonly be upon the reliability of a witness that probability will be assessed.

Is all false swearing perjury? To some it seems not, for it is possible to speak what is not the truth without lying, and equally to swear what is not true without perjury.[10] Paul spoke falsely perhaps when he said that he was going to Corinth; but he intended to go. The tongue, Augustine says, is not guilty unless the mind which governs it is guilty.[11] Augustine includes *periuria* things which are done without deceit: *sine fraude*. An example would be when someone swears falsely out of ignorance.[12] It is perjury to swear falsehood with the intention to deceive, or to swear the truth with the intention to deceive. To swear truth or falsehood without intention to deceive is perjury if done *temere*, rashly, but it may be done responsibly (*circumspecte*).[13]

To bear *false* witness is an offence against truth. To cavil, for example, can be defined, as it is in the *Digest*, as moving by imperceptible steps from what is clearly true to what is evidently false.[14] The testimony of a witness who is known to have lied cannot be accepted in court; nor can that of a witness who has been bribed, because neither can be relied on to tell the truth.[15] Bernard of Clairvaux underlines that it is wicked to try to tempt someone away from the path of justice by persuasion or bribery (*vel prece vel pretio*).[16] The *Summa 'Elegantius'* stresses that those whose testimony has been suborned are to be rejected as witnesses if it appears that that has led to falsehood.[17] Calumny and lying for gain both come under this general heading.[18] On the same theme that the witness has a duty to support the truth we meet the view that to tell a lie is also to bear false witness against oneself.[19]

The credibility of an ordinary person, whose very name on its own is not sufficient to compel loyalty, can be strengthened if the hearers know that he feels constrained to tell the truth by a higher authority or a sanction. That can be achieved to some degree by the taking of an oath.

The mediaeval witness has two functions, as a furnisher of testimony about the facts and as a guarantor of character. In the later connection, the witness's own character and standing are important. The *Digest* insists that the credibility of witnesses shall be enquired into.[20] 'That is why only those witnesses are to be accepted 'whose integrity is beyond dispute'.[21] Witnesses may, accordingly, be open to cross-examination about their own bad character.[22]

Gratian outlines the rules which determine who may and who may not be a witness.[23] These can be summed up under the heads of (i) inherent or generic incapacity; and (ii) bias. (i) Children below the age when they could reason about what they had seen or heard were not admitted as witnesses. The elderly were disqualified not by age alone, but if they seemed to be suffering from a senile failure of their mental powers.[24] Women could be banned as witnesses because of the frailty of their sex (*propter fragilitatem sexus*) especially because that implied unreliability (whether instability or a tendency to tell lies).[25]

(ii) A witness who has a personal or vested interest is unacceptable.[26] This extends to someone known to hate, as well as to someone known to favour, the accused. Some witnesses are useless because they have a bad reputation (*propter infamie maculam*), others because, for example, family loyalty or piety prevents a father and son testifying against one another.[27] The independence of the witness is thus important. One reason for not allowing cases to go forward where there is known bad feeling on the part of the accuser towards the accused is that it leads to unseemly wrangles, which are at all costs to be avoided, says Anselm of Lucca.[28]

The forensic weighing of evidence in the Middle Ages takes account of the source of the witness's knowledge (*causa scientiae*). This seeks to rely not upon his character or sincerity or personal authority (although, if these are in doubt his testimony will be inadmissible or disregarded), but on something altogether more objective lying behind these. The question is whether he has sufficient cause for saying what he does.[29] It should be possible for the witness to be able to say that he saw something with his

150   *Evidence*

own eyes, or heard it with his own ears or otherwise perceived it directly with his own senses.[30] We meet this insistence again and again. A witness should speak on a basis of certain knowledge and not on opinion.[31] Witnesses must speak from what they have seen for themselves.[32] An expert witness seems already to be an accepted sort of special witness in a medieval context,[33] and eye-witness is in itself a form of expertise, for it certainly provides 'expert knowledge' of the events in question.

How many witnesses?

It was a commonplace of legal procedure that one witness is not enough to convince: *non facit fidem*. That would merely produce a conflict of one man's word against another, with the accused denying what the accuser accuses him of. One witness is not sufficient, agrees the *Summa 'Elegantius'*. One witness is as bad as no witnesses, even if he is a very important person.[34] Two witnesses will be enough unless the sheer scale of the matter (*magnitudo negotii*) demands more.[35] It is not thought acceptable to allow the accuser to 'outweigh' the accused, even by the device of taking the accused's silence for a confession.[36] The *Digest* lays down the rule that 'he who is silent should not be taken to admit the accusation because he does not deny it'.[37]

Are two witnesses enough? As a rule, yes, because then it is not just one man's word against another's.[38] The law is not specific, but two or at the most three will suffice, says a thirteenth-century procedural treatise.[39] But if the person accused is important or if, for example, he is a priest or a bishop, more are needed (because it is, as we have seen, acknowledged that such persons must especially be protected against malicious attacks).[40]

Instrumenta: documents

Sometimes proof is by witnesses and sometimes by documents (*instrumenta*), sometimes by both. That by witnesses is *dignior* than that by documents.[41] Despite the high respect given to written authority in theology, in the courts documentary and witness-evidence do not carry the same weight. A person prepared to come and give evidence with his own voice, outweighs a written *testimonium* read out, which lacks that immediacy.[42] 'The living voice of the witness strikes the judge's ear with more force.'[43] On the other hand, it is admitted that in the case of testimony against the defendant it may be very helpful to have it in writing so that it can be examined closely.[44]

There are various ways in which the truth of documentary, that is, *written*, evidence can be tested. The *Summa 'Elegantius'* gives advice about this. If *prima facie* the documentary evidence seems *vitiosum*, test its truth by witnesses.[45] If there are no witnesses, test it against other written evidence.[46] The authenticity of the document is important. There should be a check as to whether it came from a public archive (*ex archivo publico*) and whether and by whom it is witnessed.[47] Some have argued that a public written document ought to be preferred to live testimony and that in its turn is to be preferred to a private written document, but not all would agree. Anselm of Lucca argues that the reason why written evidence is not to be admitted on its own is not that there is anything wrong with written evidence, but that a person must be prepared to stand by his accusation and to make it in person.[48]

Lack of agreement among witnesses harms the case (*diversitates noceant in testimonio*).[49] When there are contradictions in documents, they detract from one another.[50] The rule is that if there is conflict within the testimony that in itself refutes it.[51] The side whose account best fits the circumstances and is clearly not influenced by enmity is to be preferred.[52]

Reasonableness

Roman law has the concept of 'reasonable cause': *iusta et rationabilis causa*.[53] The Council of Chalcedon, 452, Canon 29, says that if a bishop has been degraded without reasonable cause (*rationabili causa*) and is seen to be innocent, he should be restored. In the texts which use the phrase during the Middle Ages the emphasis appears to be upon being able to justify an action by giving reasons for it.[54] Although rhetoric rightly appeals to emotion as well as reason, persuading as well as convincing, there is a consistent emphasis on 'reasonableness' in the legal texts. It is an important principle, from the Roman period, that legal formulations 'should not be given an absolute meaning but should be subject to interpretation according to the standard of reasonableness'.[55] In the twelfth century, Gratian asserts the principle that custom cannot stand up in opposition to reason.[56] In the fourteenth century, Baldus puts the task of proving not only in terms of an absence of doubt but also in terms of the reasonableness of that absence of doubt in a given case.

Clarity is important for our authors alongside this legal style of 'reasonableness'. The two come together in a notion of 'elegance' which is certainly a conscious presence in mediaeval legal texts. The *Summa 'Elegantius'* begins in this way with a call for elegance[57] in legal reasoning.[58] This is seen as involving an avoidance of the faults of *style* of Gratian's work. Although it was already becoming the basic textbook, it is castigated as prolix, tedious and inexplicable. Elegance is also mentioned in connection with the simplicity and force of legal maxims or *regulae*.[59] Their elegance is a recognised attraction of the *regula*.[60] A rule says crisply 'what something is'.[61] This notion of elegance again has its roots for our authors in classical rhetoric.[62]

21 Sentencing

There can be no just punishment until guilt is established.[1] One Sentence of the Laon School describes a class of truths which 'although they are true' (*quamvis vera sint*) are not to be believed unless they are proved on solid evidence.[2] A confession freely made may prompt the judge to mercy, says Victricius of Rouen.[3] Where there is no confession, a sentence is a judicial ruling based on the evidence before the judge. Gratian refers to the 'pronunciation' of guilt or innocence: *et alios quidem innocentem eum pronunciare, alios reum*,[4] and *pronunciare* is also used for the sentence: *pronuntiare sententiam*.[5]

By pronouncing a judgement a judge brings a controversy to an end. *Diffinitiva sententia omnibus controversiis finem imponit*.[6] The matter is then said to be *res iudicata*. So a sentence cannot be merely provisional says the *Summa 'Elegantius'*.[7] It ought to contain an outright absolution or condemnation.[8] And it appears to be logically impossible to have a judgement of which part is valid, part not.[9] Once a judge has pronounced sentence he ceases to be the judge and he himself cannot make any changes.[10] Once sentence has finally been passed so that something becomes *res iudicata*, that sentence stands even if the same issue is raised again.[11] It is often asked whether a confession made to one judge stands when the matter comes up in another court before another judge. The answer is yes.[12]

On the other hand, if there is merely agreement between the litigants that does not predetermine the outcome in other cases.[13]

The next task is to determine the 'sentence', in the sense of the 'penalty'. This is a separate task and does not have to be performed by the judge who made the finding of guilt.

The law and theology of *sententia*

For the mediaeval theologian, a *sententia* is a thought expressed in words. The term carries three senses in classical Latin, which roughly correspond to 'opinion', 'maxim' and the determination of a disputed matter of the sort a judge makes when he pronounces a 'sentence'. The first two present an interesting contradiction, for, in logic, an opinion is precisely *not* a maxim. A maxim is a self-evident or necessary truth. An opinion remains uncertain, or it would not be necessary to regard it as a mere opinion. We need to make a map of these notions about 'sentences' so as to see where the legal species of sentence fits in.

Sentence as opinion

The usage which regards a 'sentence' as an 'opinion' is found in the Vulgate, in the Old Testament rather than the New: Joel 9.2: *uno animo eademque sententia*; Job 22.18: *quorum sententia procul sit a me*; Daniel 4.21: *Haec est interpretatio sententiae Altissimi.*

Peter Lombard's mid-twelfth-century *Sentences*, which became, after a fitful start, a staple textbook for theologians throughout the Middle Ages takes its title from the *sententiae* or 'opinions' of the Fathers it brings helpfully together under topic headings. This was already an established 'school' usage from the end of the eleventh century. Peter Abelard uses *sententia* in a similar way with reference to the *Sentences* of Sextus, citing Jerome *Contra Jovinianum*: '*Sextus in Sententiis: "Adulter est," inquit, in suam uxorum amator ardentior.*'[14]

The same notion of 'sentence' as opinion runs through the *sententiae* of the school of Anselm of Laon and his brother at the end of the eleventh and the beginning of the twelfth century. There is a frequent conjunction of *sententie vel questiones* in the manuscripts of the *Sentences* of Anselm of Laon and his school.[15] The conjunction underlines the uncertainty of mere *sententiae*. In the Prose Salernitan Questions it is explained that there are two opinions on the origin of thunder, according to one of which the mystery can be solved (*due super hoc sunt sententie*).[16]

It is of the essence of a *sententia* in this frequent eleventh- to twelfth-century usage that it is open to question and that some will hold one *sententia* and some another. So among the questions to be answered about a *sententia* is whether it is true or right. It must be possible that it may be wrong.

If the reasoning a *sententia* relies on is secure, there is no reason to reject it, says Anselm of Canterbury. 'I do not deny anyone's opinion if it can be proved to be right: *Nullius respuo sententiam, si vera probari poterit*.[17] But it may be difficult to establish the truth of a *sententia* by such straightforward means as looking at evidence and at whether it stands to reason. It may be necessary to live with difference of opinion.

For, although one of two contradictories must logically be wrong and the other right, it may not be important to establish which, a difference of opinion may concern something intrinsically unimportant. The Middle Ages as well as the sixteenth century thus recognise the existence of *adiaphora*. In a letter of Fulbert of Chartres we find the reflection that there are different observances in the Churches of the East and the West as well as many which are the same.[18] These are the familiar differences of rite, which had never historically been a bar to unity in the Church.[19] 'Diversity of observation is not a stumbling-block to us where the unity of the faith is not divided', said Fulbert of Chartres.[20]

It is a concomitant of the possibility that one may hold different opinions that there can be *change* of opinion, especially where God leads the holder of an opinion to alter it: *ille qui praefata, protulit sententiam, deo corrigente.*[21] Anselm of Canterbury thinks that on the matter of faith which is dividing East and West over the question of the procession of the Holy Spirit, there is a situation where the Greeks either ought to change the opinion: *debent cessare ab hac sua sententia*, or at least not set themselves up in opposition to the Latins.[22]

Easier to negotiate without a sense of being in danger of departing from the truth may be change of *sententia* leading to change of the manner of life. A woman who has been a sinner may begin meekly to obey God's commandments. Peter Damian gives that illustration: *Iusto quippe Dei iudicio mulier quae olim illum in hac vita subsannando despexerat, iam mutata sententia, eius praecepta humiliter observabat.*[23]

One expects to find talk of 'authority' alongside talk of 'reason' in eleventh- to twelfth-century texts. For authors of the eleventh and early twelfth centuries, authority is not inferior to reason as a ground for holding an opinion. It may be a better ground if the authority is God himself speaking in Scripture. So, as a means of judging whether a given opinion is likely to be reliable, it would simply be asked whose *sententia* an opinion is. 'Is a *sententia* authoritative?' is a different question from whether it is right or true. But either may be a route for the establishing of conviction, *facere fidem.*[24]

One method of deriving confidence in a *sententia* merely from the fact that someone holds it may be to see whether *many* hold it. Is a *sententia* confirmed by being shared? Yes, says Anselm of Canterbury. *Non parum suffragatur illi sententiae.*[25] Anselm thinks that may even be important where the opinion is God's own, if it is expressed more than once in the Sacred Page: *Divina dicta, ut diversis sententiis favere videantur.*[26] That might make it somehow more certain than God's saying it only once. Peter Damian says something similar in his *Sermones*. 'See how Truth itself agrees with this *sententia*,' he cries.[27]

Authoritative opinion is of two sorts. *Sententiae* of Scripture or the Fathers have a high authority in that the first cannot be wrong and the second ought not readily to be presumed to be wrong. 'That *sententia* of Scripture is true', says Peter Damian: *vera est illa Scripturae sententia.*[28] A 'prophetic' sententia is authoritative too.[29] An 'apostolic opinion' is so secure that it is scarcely to be regarded as a mere 'opinion' at all.[30]

There are three 'ways of thinking' about the divine law, *Lex divina tripliciter sentienda est*, says a sentence of the school of Laon. One is to take it historically and believe what it says literally. Another is to interpret it morally. The third is to understand it spiritually. One should seek to do all three.[31] But they are somehow all 'right' and can all to be taken in conjunction because of their innate harmoniousness.

Because they are so reliable the opinions of the highest authorities thus begin to constitute a form of knowledge. Abelard speaks of a certain 'learnedness' in those who have so much *doctrina* and know so many *sententiae* of the philosophers that they can sprinkle their books with them, and one does not know whether to admire more their learning or their knowledge of the texts.[32]

The second sort of 'authoritative' opinion is the one which primarily concerns us here. This is the *judicialis sententia*, the sentence of a judge in a forensic context. If it is the judge's opinion (*sententia*) that the accused is guilty a punishment is appropriate. The term is equivocal, for fixing an appropriate punishment also requires an exercise of opinion, a further 'sentence'. We shall look at this further in a moment.

Anselm of Canterbury explores a distinction between the way something is expressed or put (*prolatio*) and the meaning intended to be conveyed (*sententia*).[33] In considering a matter of opinion, one must examine the force of the words so as to determine where the truth lies, says Peter Abelard.[34] For example, the difference between *ex fide* and *per fidem* is a difference of expression not of meaning, Abelard argues.[35]

As Abelard comments, comparing the creeds, there are differences in wording there which may not reflect differences of opinion or belief.[36] Indeed, we must presume that they do not, for it could certainly not be held that the creeds differ on points of faith. And the question what the philosophers taught about the origin of the soul and whether it is born or created or made may be unnecessarily complicated by looking at the terminology rather than the sense. To create or to become implies a beginning but the birth (*nasci*) of Christ from the Father is without beginning.[37]

There is a difference in definition when opinions cannot be contained in the same definition, when the definition of one does not 'require' the definition of the other, even when the same thing can be described as either, as 'substance' and 'body' or 'white' and 'hard'.[38]

A single expression may carry two meanings, as when it is said that there was nothing before the Supreme Being. One meaning is that there was a time before the Supreme Being when there was nothing. The other is that there was nothing – not even a time – before the Supreme Being.[39]

The governing principle is that there are different ways of putting the same thing and the same way of putting things may convey more than one understanding. We need not therefore necessarily infer from what appear to be differences that there really are differences of opinion.[40]

Sententia as 'maxim'

Word-forms derived from or linked with *sententia* take us into an area where *sententia* is clearly close to 'maxim' in its meaning. *Sententialiter* (post-classical, but as early as Tertullian and Cassiodorus) can be rendered by 'in the form of maxims', but the main connotation is of a weightiness attaching to the security or obviousness or the magisterial quality of what is being said. Tertullian has: *vel quia ipse dominus sententialiter et definitive pronuntiat: quod in carne natum est, caro est, quia ex carne natum est*.[41]

In Cassiodorus we find this same hint of 'solidity' in *sententialiter*: To speak of the Lord and Saviour is to speak weightily: *quando de domine salvatore sententialiter sunt locuti*.[42] 'This is their path': *Haec via eorum*. According to Cassiodorus, that is said weightily in Ps.48.4: *sententialiter enuntiatur*.[43]

Sententiosus, full of meaning, is Ciceronian. Salimbene de Adam, *Chronica*, gives us: *Dictator nobilissimus fuit de stilo polito et sententiosus valde, quando voluit, in suis epistolis*.[44] Here again, it is the authoritativeness that is important, but this time perhaps deriving from a richness or density, a sheer meaningfulness, rather than from the weightiness of the *author* of the subject matter.

Sententiola appears less rarely than *sententialiter* and *sententiosus*. It is quite frequent in Jerome. Augustine uses it in the *De moribus ecclesiae catholicae et manichaeorum*, I, to make the point that even a very brief saying may have great force: *ita ut una sententiola duobusque verbis propheta et vim et fructum charitatis ostendat*.[45] The word remains rare in mediaeval usage. Bede uses *sententiola*[46] and Rupert of Deutz has it.[47]

The equivocation which diminishes the security of *sententia* itself by making it so often mere opinion, even if well-founded or authoritative opinion, is largely absent here in these derivatives.

The sentence of a judge

Our third sense of *sententia* also has strong Vulgate backing (cf. Exodus 18.15; 21.31; 23.2). The sentence of a judge may declare guilt or innocence. Then it is an opinion, as it were 'ratified'. Or it may impose a punishment. Then it is an opinion upon which reliance is being placed – perhaps great reliance, for there can be severity in such a sentence.[48]

The School of Anselm of Laon is much concerned with the forensic arena: *Cum ex auctoritate Dei in ore duorum vel trium testium stare debeat omne verbum* (Deuteronomy 19.15), *propter nequitiam nominum multiplicatus et numerus testium*.

If two or three can be found who agree and have no reason to lie, that is enough. Factors affecting the certainty of testimony are the *qualitas* of the accused and accuser; and the past record.[49]

But contemporaries of the late eleventh and twelfth centuries see the Scriptural terminology in this area broadly. In Hildegard of Bingen we have: *Deinde caeli laudes suas interim in silentio continent, cum Filius Dei iudicialem sententiam et ad iustos et ad iniustos profert*.[50]

Rupert of Deutz speaks of the *iudicialis sententia* in his book on the Trinity: *ut iudicialem sub illo accipiat sententiam*.[51]

This association with 'sentence' is to do with the usage by which the sentence which declares a man guilty leads on to the 'sentence' of punishment. In this context it may be appropriate to speak of a 'harsh sentence': *iusti iudicis districtam sententiam*.[52] That is a secondary or transferred meaning, for the primary meaning must be that of a judicial opinion or determination. It is only as a consequence of the making of that determination that a sentence of punishment can be handed down.

Anselm of Laon and his school have a number of comments on the *sententia iudicialis*, the form of 'sentence' pronounced in the law-courts. A sentence will be 'pronounced' in a different way if it is judicial; once it is pronounced, it is no longer treated as a mere opinion, but as, from that moment of pronouncement, an established truth. God pronounces sentence on the damned, and once the sentence is pronounced the condemned man is tormented.[53]

The running theme is that such a judicial opinion must come as close to certainty as it can. Why would Scripture speak of the naming of a brother as a fornicator or idolator if this possibility of uncertainty were not a problem (I Corinthians 5.11: *si quis frater nominatur fornicator aut idolis serviens*)?

The Anselm of Laon 'sentence' which makes this point says that such a sentence must be arrived at by 'due process': *ordine iudiciario atque ecclesiastica integritate profertur*. No one is to be judged on mere suspicion or outside due process, but according to the law of God within the order of the Church: *nemo iudicandus ex arbitrio suspicionis vel extra ordinem usurpate iudicio, sed ex lege Dei secundum ordinem ecclesie*.[54] If it were enough merely to 'name' someone, to point to him and declare him guilty, many innocent people would be condemned. It is not uncommon for false allegations to be made by ill-disposed persons.[55] Even if a judge thinks he 'knows for sure' that someone is guilty he ought not to name him as an offender, publicly or privately, without due process. This is in line with Augustine's stricture that people must not be excommunicated on a whim but by a proper judicial process.[56] The authority for this requirement is Christ's own conduct in relation to Judas. Christ nowhere named Judas as his betrayer. He said only: 'One of you will betray me.'[57]

If the matter remains uncertain, the individual must remain in the community like the husk with the grain, until it is winnowed, and the inedible fish is jumbled with the edible in the net until all are brought to shore.[58] There are circumstances in which that means, among other things, that even obvious wrongdoing must be tolerated, to see if the miscreant will repent; and only if he will not and proves incorrigible, should he be removed from the community: *denique tollant*.[59]

Semiplena

At best a *sententia* is a judgement in the sense of 'opinion'. It is particularly clear that it is only an opinion when it is linked with *semiplena*. *Semiplena* is a technical expression of the later Middle Ages, which we have seen being used in the context of summary process. but it has earlier antecedents. Julian of Eclanum says: *videtur semiplena esse sententia: post dubitationem enim non est illata confirmatio, ut quod intulerat merito conveniret*.[60]

But even where he is giving no more than his opinion, a judge must have a *reason* for his judgement, says the *Digest*.[61] If the judge condemns, the condemnation ought to be certain argues the *Summa 'Elegantius'*.[62] If it is arrived at on the basis of certain knowledge and secure proof, *ex certa cognitione et competenti probatione*, then certainly the sentence ought to be unambiguous. But there may be no more than suggestion or opinion to go on,[63] and then, at least, the sentence ought to be, as far as possible, true and honest (*et vera et sincera*), and also public, that is, pronounced in the presence of the parties (unless they are contumaciously absent),[64] so that everyone can hear it, and that is in itself arguably a way of testing its reasonableness. If there is any question about it, it is better for the judge to let off someone who is guilty than to condemn the innocent. It is a lesser offence to be wrong on the side of mercy than on that of cruelty.[65]

22 Appeal

Why should someone found guilty be allowed to appeal? The *Summa 'Elegantius'* has two answers. First, an innocent man may have been found guilty; and, second, there is a need to preserve the Church from the harm which might follow from allowing a wrong judgement to stand.[1]

It was impossible for the ecclesiastical authorities not to be aware that injustices occurred. 'We know that many have been unjustly deposed by wicked machinations', says Anselm of Lucca from a Ps.-Damasus text.[2] Anselm of Lucca accordingly gives the second book of his collection to the question of appeal, with an emphasis on speedy and effective protection of the innocent.[3] Those to whom injustices happen need help, and they need it at a senior level, he stresses. 'For we carry the burdens which weigh people down,' continues the same text.[4]

The principle is that anyone involved in a case (whose interests are affected) can make an appeal.[5] But 'anyone' may have to be qualified. The appeal of a manifest thief should not be admitted when it is clear that his intention is simply to avoid punishment.[6] With a similar concern to keep things under control, Lateran III (1179), Canon 6, addresses the practice of passing a sentence of excommunication or suspension (*suspensio*) without previous admonition on those thought likely to lodge an appeal without grounds just because they fear a sentence of canonical discipline.[7]

Appeal should be allowed once. It does not follow that appeal should be allowed again and again.[8] Three times against the sentence seems to be the conventional limit, but appeal based on the substance of the matter, that is, where fresh evidence is adduced to show that the facts of the case were not as thought, might be brought as often as necessary.[9]

It takes a higher court to override the sentence of the lower. *Appellatio est ab inferiore ad superiorem iudicem*.[10] Appeals should go through the proper channels, that is systematically upwards through the hierarchy, but Vincent of Spain notes the provision that if an intermediate officer (here the bishop) is suspect (*medium ... suspectum*), there may be appeal directly to a higher officer (here the archbishop).[11]

Appealing to Rome

A divine warrant is claimed for the highest court of appeal, on the basis of Christ's word's to Peter: *tu es Petrus*, etc.[12] The Petrine office is the *apex* and the 'head' from whom judgement may be obtained with apostolic finality: *caput, ut apostolico terminentur iudicio*.[13] Mother Church is protectress of her children.[14] This motif of motherhood reappears linked with the idea of *magistra*.[15]

The judgement of the Apostolic See is final because it cannot err. *Negotia ... iuste ibi terminentur*, claims Anselm of Lucca;[16] we see in the eleventh and twelfth centuries an assumption that this one judge at least has never been wrong: *quod numquam erravit*.[17] The Roman See has authority, without acting in a synod, to free those who are unjustly condemned and to condemn those who ought to be condemned, says Anselm of Lucca[18] This is deemed to derive from the *potestas ligandi et solvendi* given by Christ and, importantly, it is held to be passed on by him to his successors: *in suos transponit successores*.[19] The Pope is at the end of the line in another sense; he cannot be judged by anyone but he himself can judge all.[20] No one is *iudex* of the Pope, unless he falls into heresy or schism.[21] The Pope has judicial immunity.[22]

Dealing with undue delay is a central preoccupation of litigants. It was not allowable, however, for a cleric frustrated by delay in the delivery of a judgement to go to the Apostolic See for that reason alone.[23] Yet paradoxically appeal had to be made quickly. There should be no more than ten days' delay in making an appeal, says the *Ordo 'Invocato Christi Nomini'*.[24]

A good reason to appeal to Rome would be the *difficulty* or the *scale* of the issues (*difficiliores causae et maiora negocia*), for higher courts are the proper place for serious matters.[25] On the other hand, the *seriousness* (*atrocitas*) of the crime might work the other way. Serious offenders are robbers, those who encourage sedition, leaders of factions, rapists of virgins, homicides, adulterers (*latrones, seditionum concitatores, duces factionum, raptores virginum; similiter homicida, ... adulter*), and so on. The perpetrators of these could be denied a right of appeal because of the sheer heinousness of what they had done.[26]

There is a question whether appeal may be made from church to secular authority or vice versa. For instance, it is asked whether in a case with a financial element (*in causis pecunariis*) there can be appeal from a secular tribunal to the Pope. (For it can be argued that the Pope is the true Emperor.)[27] Some held that there can be no appeal 'sideways', for example, from one bishop to another.[28] But the appeal *may* go sideways between ecclesiastical and secular courts.

Appeal 161

Review?

'No man is concluded by the first judgement, but if he apprehends himself to be aggrieved he has another court to which he can resort for relief.'[29] The underlying principle that there must be provision for appeal was thus stated in the Bentley case in the early eighteenth century. The Bentley case led on to the development of a system of 'judicial review' in England, eventually drawing together into a group as remedies the prerogative writs. These were not so much appeal as 'review'. 'Prohibition' developed in the thirteenth century from cases where ecclesiastical courts were trying to interfere in temporal matters. 'Mandamus' (a mandatory order) developed early in the seventeenth century where it became necessary to control city and borough authorities. *Certiorari* (a quashing order) was originally a means by which a superior court would discover what had happened in an inferior one.[30] These are post-mediaeval refinements of the simpler mediaeval understanding that no one should be condemned without hope of reprieve, that mercy requires a right of appeal.

23 Justice and mercy

It is possible to contrast the mercy a father will show with the strictness of a judge, says Valerius Maximus.[1] Scripture exhorts those in dispute to try to achieve reconciliation. Agreeing with one's adversary is Scriptural (Matthew 5.25). The Ps-Isidorian Decretals try to find 'canon law' backing for this principle. A letter of Ps.-Anacletus[2] and a letter of Ps.-Alexander[3] both contain the exhortation to try to settle a dispute privately and in mutual charity. *Denunciatio* made formal provision for that according to Canon 8 of the Fourth Lateran Council. The difference is already crisply set out in V.1.6 of Gratian's *Decretum*. The *accusator* has punishment in mind, the *denunciator* correction.[4]

The duty to complete a case once it has begun is often emphasised in the procedural manuals.[5] Once the case had been properly initiated, not only the defendant was bound by the authority of the court to appear; the plaintiff, too, was under an obligation, and sometimes judgement might be passed in favour of the defendant when the plaintiff defaulted.[6] Nevertheless, in the later Middle Ages most disputes ended in compromise.[7] Much as often happens today, going to court is a move designed to trigger an effort to settle. There could also, as today, be a formal decision to attempt 'alternative dispute resolution'.[8]

Dramatic circumstances could arise which were able to prevent a case from running its course. In litigation between Bishop Herfast of Theford and the abbey of Bury St. Edmunds in the reign of William I of England, the bishop appears to have had a breakdown. He admitted that he had 'sinned in word' and declared himself 'guilty of all these undertakings'. He excommunicated his advisers and promised 'utterly to repudiate them'. When he had thus made public confession he moved 'weeping abundantly' to the main altar and placed his bishop's staff upon it, then prostrated himself. That was not the end of the matter, for later the bishop went back to his old ways and recanted his confession, 'breathing flames of wrath', and biting venomously when Archbishop Lanfranc tried to resolve the matter.[9]

Even where no confession, capitulation and self-abasement was forthcoming, it could not be sensible to prevent the parties coming to informal settlement and force them to go through with a case, if there was a shorter route to a conclusion. It is recognised that consent between the accused, and the complainant or accuser, can settle a case directly, saving costs and the time of the court. Because of the strict rules about completing a case once it had been begun it was necessary to obtain permission to seek a settlement, a *licentia concordandi*, and to pay a fee. Alternatively, a court could grant a *dies amoris* at the request of the suitor or plaintiff to 'allow time' for the parties to try to reach a settlement.[10]

Agreement was the key. Justinian describes the reaching of a 'friendly agreement' (*amicabilis conventus*),[11] if there is a rapprochement between the litigants: *Si convenit inter ligatores*.[12] The *Digest* explains that controversies are decided either by the agreement of the litigants or by the authority of the judge.[13] If agreement cannot be reached, the judge has to reach a decision before the case can be ended, and because, by definition, that will be necessary only where there *is* no agreement, he must disappoint one party in order to be fair to the other.

Arbitration and mediation

Is there is a role for arbitration in the mediaeval legal scene, as there had been in the Roman one, and as there is beginning to be again in the modern world? The job of the arbitrator is to call the parties together and hear them either in person or through a notary, explains a procedural manual of the third quarter of the thirteenth century by Egidius de Fuscariis.[14] (It is not easy to agree whether lay persons can act as *arbitrii*, says this text. Egidius himself says not.) In the Middle Ages *judges* (*arbitrii*) can force litigants to accept a resolution, even if they do not wish to. The *arbiter* is not given his jurisdiction by the parties' agreement; his jurisdiction comes from the law itself.[15] Arbiters, according to Ulpian, have the role of adjudicators in bringing a trial to an end.[16] There is a distinction between this *arbiter* and an *arbitrator*.[17]

Johannes Bassianus gives a late twelfth-century account of something closer to mediation or conciliation in that the arbitrator may ask the litigants' permission to make a compromise in their presences, so as to avoid the expense of a trial. This amounts to a transaction (*arbitratus*), in which, because the consent of the parties is involved, there is the element of amicable agreement. This resembles modern mediation. There is the further Roman model in which the parties submit themselves to the arbitrator's judgement, once they had entered into the agreement to do so.[18] But even this is clearly different from a judgement (*arbitrium*) which the judge imposes on *unwilling* litigants.[19]

Despite the consensus it involves, which in many contexts would be a desirable way of proceeding among Christians, the notion of a 'transaction' is suspect in canon law, because of its associations with the long struggle to outlaw simony. True consensus does not involve a 'deal' of this sort. There is a third question as to what is to be done if there is a lack of good faith in the acceptance of arbitration, that is, if the parties do not keep the bargain.[20]

Practical examples

In a late eleventh-century case in which Bishop Wulfstan of Worcester and Abbot Walter of Evesham were disputing over some land, in the hundred of Oswaldstow, the case was proceeding adversarially until the abbot realised that he was going to lose. Then 'he accepted his friends' counsel and renounced the oath in favour of the bishop, recognising the whole complaint and everything which the bishop had claimed and agreed to conclude a concord with the bishop'.[21]

In a dispute about a dowry in 1274, Beatrix, wife of the Earl of Cornwall, was also running on with witnesses and *instrumenta* to hand when 'by licence' the parties were given leave to settle (*et concordati sunt*), and the agreement is recorded (*Et est concordia talis*).[22]

Making allowances: dispensation and *oeconomia*

If someone breaks the Church's law, it can sometimes be possible for a decision to be taken retrospectively to change the law for that occasion, and to dispose of the 'charge' in that way. That takes us conveniently to the theology of dispensation.[23] A dispensation can be defined as the relaxation of the rigour of the law by someone with authority to do it, and in an appropriate situation.[24] There can be various reasons for making a dispensation. It may be needed for the particular place or time or person, or for religious reasons, for necessity, for utility or in a specific circumstance.[25] The *Summa 'Elegantius'* says some such reason should be identified for the granting of any dispensation.[26]

The factor of 'place' is relevant because of the rule that there may always be local variation in rites and customs in the Church.[27] The idea of variation because of *time* is linked to the recognition that emergency situations may arise. For example, if it happens that some province is short of priests, even monks may baptise.[28] But this is a limited concession because it breaks no fundamental rules. A dispensation may be made *pro persona,* if, for example, a subdeacon or a simple clerk (*simplex clericus*), or even a layman of good life and reputation, is chosen to be a bishop: *honeste fame vel vite laicum in episcopum elegi*.[29] There can be a dispensation *pro causa*. For example, if someone becomes besmirched with heresy there is a question whether he can go on functioning as a priest because he will be a stumbling-block to the people.[30]

Dispensation tends to be retrospective.[31] It can then deal with an anomaly as an emergency, which is a very different thing from deliberately creating an anomaly by bending the rules in advance.[32] There are ground rules about when a dispensation should be given, and when the normal rule should be kept to.[33] The key consideration is whether the dispensation will injure anyone or 'discolour' (cause *decoloratio* to) the Church,[34] and here it is clearly important not deliberately to allow something inappropriate to happen. If not, so long as the spirit of the rule is honoured, the 'letter' can be waived.[35] A layman, for example, cannot be elected a bishop because his previous mode of life would not have fitted him for the office. It would not have given him the necessary learning or taught him to set an example to others in the right way.[36] But if a given layman did fulfil those conditions, it would be perfectly appropriate for him to be elected.[37] Similarly, a pope does not have powers to change laws or remove privileges granted before his time.[38] Yet he does have full powers to make new canons and privileges and to revoke those he has given,[39] so long as there is nothing in what he does which is contrary to the faith or in which they offend the universal Church.[40]

So part of what is happening in granting a dispensation is the recognition that laws have to match specific needs and requirements. The *Digest* lays down the rule that law should not be interpreted so rigidly that it is damaging to the community.[41] It is a commonplace that law is framed to meet a general need and is consequently always needing to be adjusted to particular cases.[42]

Aquinas argues that the decision to waive or adapt a rule cannot be taken by 'just anyone'; there must be authority to dispense from the law: *auctoritas in legibus dispensandi*.[43] And then there may be different grounds for so acting. *Permissio* can be divided into *concessio, tolerantia, dispensatio*. The first would apply, in the case of things which are in any case allowable (*de licitis*). 'Tolerance' would apply to things not normally, but sometimes allowable.[44] Various circumstances may make *permissio* appropriate. The rule here is that because of 'the hardness of their hearts', people may need concessions. This happened in the past, in the Old Testament context, although it would not be necessary now, for the law is now more perfect and the people more kindly: *quia et lex perfectior et populus benignior est*.[45] The exception to *permissio* would be where there is *perplexio*. That would happen where it was the case that whichever way someone turned, he would do harm: *ut quodcumque se vertat offensum incurrat*.[46] For instance, let us put it that someone swears a solemn oath that he will kill someone, believing that oath to be binding. He is then caught between the guilt he will incur if he commits murder and the guilt of perjuring himself by not keeping his oath.[47] In case of *perplexio* difference of circumstances, times, places, persons, does not apply. There can be no propriety in an agreement which allows us to let small concessions turn into large ones: *nullo enim pacto convenit nos minora admittere ne lii in gravioribus delinquant*, for that way lies damnation.[48]

Talio: an eye for an eye

In stark contrast to the theme of mercy, reasonableness, reconciliation, changing the rules retrospectively, stands the *talio* rule. This arises from the Roman law's insistence that people do not get away with knowingly making unfounded accusations. In a way, the accuser is also on trial. That is to say, the instigator of a case may be just or unjust, for it is perfectly possible for someone to make an unjust accusation. In the case involving God, man and the Devil, God's intervention is supremely just, the Devil's supremely unjust, it was argued in the twelfth-century debate.[49]

The old *talio* rule survived into the Middle Ages. *Talio* is seen by Isidore in terms of revenge (*similitudo vindictae*).[50] This is seen as a natural law and also as demonstrably Biblical.[51] Isidore cites '*an eye for an eye, a tooth for a tooth*'.[52] The *talio* rule appears in Burchard of Worms. He says that a false witness should be punished for the crime of which he has falsely accused someone else.[53] There is also a provision that no one shall find the same accusation being brought against him again after he has been acquitted. A person should not be tried twice for the same offence, says Burchard of Worms.[54] The accuser cannot simply try again. So there is protection against a vindictiveness which might seek to manifest itself in either way. Also Gratian asks what penalty should be suffered by someone whose accusation is shown to be unfounded.[55] Rufinus argued in his commentary on this portion of Gratian that those who turn out to have brought a false accusation, but who did it as a result of a mistake, or even without checking the facts first (*temeritate*), should be excused. But knowingly to make a false accusation is culpable.

Stephen of Tournai takes a slightly different view, distinguishing between written and spoken accusations. He argues that if someone brings an accusation in writing and fails to prove his case, he should suffer *talio*, unless he can show that he was deceived by fraudulent witnesses, that is, that he acted in good faith. If his accusation is spoken not written he will be guilty of slander, and then he can be made to pay damages.[56] So not only is intention important; so is form, and for the false accuser there should be justice, not mercy.

24 Conclusion
Confession, punishment and the hope of salvation

Admitting fault: confession in theology and law

A marginal note contains what appears to be a warning for the Chancellor of the University of Oxford from the scribe.

> I have known people who have sworn a great oath that they are not guilty of the charge against them, and yet in private they say that they are really guilty. Note this, Chancellor, that among the purgations admitted there are perjuries.

He says he knows this from long experience.[1] Nevertheless, confession is normally the most secure way of establishing who committed an offence.

The best proof that the offence has been committed is for the accused to admit it, says the *Digest*.[2] To confess is to be convicted by oneself.[3] Yet it is possible for a confession to be false and to admit liability does not necessarily lead to condemnation; it has to be established whether the thing admitted really happened.[4] False confession may even be deemed an aspect of false witness.[5]

Confession, however, is a penitential act, and it can be impossible to classify offences straightforwardly into those properly dealt with judicially, and those which ought to be dealt with in the penitential process. One might confess *within* the penitential process either a breach of the law, or an offence against one's neighbour which was not a breach of the law. Both might require repentance and be dealt with by penitential sanctions. The breach of the law might require punishment by the secular authorities, but confessing it in penance would not bring that retribution directly. From the Carolingian period penitential confession would not be made publicly, and a court would have to start from the beginning in establishing guilt, for the penitent would not necessarily have to confess in court as he had to his priest.

The obvious difference between penitential and forensic confession lies in the consequences. To confess to a priest is to obtain absolution and a punishment. To confess to a judge is to lay oneself open to punishment without the 'reward' of forgiveness. It does not put one right with God, who knows the truth. The alleged perpetrator of an offence against the law may say one thing in court and another in the confessional. Or he may be found not guilty in court but still want to set things right with God, who knows the truth. In the *Invocato Christi Nomini*, one of the authors of the procedural manuals of the thirteenth century raises the question of confession after the trial in court has taken place. He asks whether this is a *locus penitentiae*, a place for penance.[6] It is recognised to be of no small importance that if the accused had confessed to an earthly judge he would have been condemned whereas if he confesses (through a priest) to the heavenly judge he will be forgiven.[7] Indeed, a confession in one forum may often 'prejudge' a confession in another.[8] This contrast is not wholly sharp, however. Once the punishment imposed by an earthly court is discharged, the guilty party is cleared, in that he cannot be held liable for punishment for that offence again. So there is an end of the matter. And although God forgives the sinner the Church will impose a temporal penalty for the sin. So forgiveness in the penitential process is not in practice wholly divorced from punishment.

In his *De Sacramentis Ecclesiae*, Hugh of St Victor distinguishes four kinds of judgement. The first is according to divine foreknowledge, for God judges each person before birth. The second is according to the cause we have given for him to judge us since we were born. Both these are hidden judgements. The third is a judgement based on the outward fruits which reveal our inner natures, and the fourth is the judgement which brings eternal reward or condemnation. These last two are open and visible judgements.[9] The pronouncing of sentence upon the soul, says Hugh of St Victor, is the work of the Trinity, although it is Christ alone as Judge who makes that judgement known.[10] Yet God judges mysteriously in this life. Some go out from the 'court' of life unavenged; some are condemned oppressively by the iniquity of a human judge; some are destroyed by false testimonies. Bad men prosper.[11] The apparent outcome of the divine judging process as we see it now[12] may be puzzling and contradictory. In this discussion Hugh moves between the partly secret and penitential and the open and visible judicial processes, until it is not clear which is a metaphor for which. In doing so, he takes us to the question of the benefit to the offender of his confession or his discharge of any penalty imposed on him.

Questions about boundaries in this area are questions about jurisdiction. Is there a juridical dimension in the Church which is irreducible to a purely sacramental reality? The Church regarded penance as a sacrament,[13] but not the administration of ecclesiastical law, which takes place outside the penitential context. The *claves ecclesiae* are functions of judicial power, as well as penitential instruments. They are concerned with the tasks of binding and loosing in both spheres, and thus not only with the imposition and removal of excommunication and penitential obligations, but also with the Church's authority to pass judgement in an ecclesiastical court.[14] So both responsibilities ultimately derive from the power of the keys, but they are exercised by different routes, and on different assumptions. Yet this is a very important matter, because the keys bind and loose in heaven as well as on earth. Salvation may be at stake.

A key issue in distinguishing the penitential and judicial arenas here[15] was whether the priest's absolution was merely a 'declaration' of a state of forgiveness which already existed because God had responded to the sinner's repentance, or an act which brought that state of things about.[16] Jerome's comment on Matthew 16.18 is relevant. He takes a minimal view of the actual powers of those who hold the keys. He says priests do not make people into lepers or unclean, but they have the knowledge to see who is leprous and unclean and who is not.[17] Thus the lepers whom Jesus told to go and show themselves to the priests were cleansed of their leprosy on the way, not when they were before the priests.[18] The priests merely declared a change which had already occurred. If that is the position, the sinner is cleansed not by the action of the priest but by the grace of God.

For Gratian the change of 'heart' of the penitent is what makes the difference.[19] If our heart turns from evil to God, he says, it quickly deserves the reward of God's turning from his anger to mercy and forgiving the sin for which formerly he intended to be avenged.[20] (It should never be forgotten that *cor* in the Vulgate is the sea of thought rather than feeling.) A penitent still offers sacrifice under the law when he discharges the penalty of satisfaction imposed on him by the Church.[21] But Gratian would argue that the purgative force of satisfaction consists in the willingness of the person accused to make it, not in the judge's will that he should.[22] He finds this as a consensus in his sources, which generally seem to him to imply that the key element is the willingness of the sinner to accept the punishment, not the authority of the Church to impose it on him.[23]

Indeed, the willingness of the sinner to repent may even remove the Church's right to exercise the power of the keys to 'bind' by condemnation. It is unjust to bind someone who is ready to make satisfaction and begging for an ear in order to confess.[24] To condemn such a one is to condemn oneself, says Beno at the end of the eleventh century.[25] The act of will which is repentance thus sets up a direct transaction of the penitent with God, which partly sets aside the judicial element in the process of penance.

Behind the *willingness* to admit it stands the *acknowledgement* of having done wrong. In the penitential system the sinner makes for himself the acknowledgement that there has been an offence. In the judicial system he is taxed with it by being brought to trial. But penitential theory recognises that even if he makes the acknowledgement freely, by confessing his guilt and accepting his punishment and thus not resisting the condemnation, the sinner may not do so in a spirit which constitutes true repentance.

An act of will is not in itself a means of setting up the direct transaction with grace which diminished the judicial part of penance, precisely because it may be merely mechanical.

True repentance arises from hatred of what one has done and desire for absolution; shame at looking bad and the hope and ambition to be honoured as someone who has thus confessed create a merely simulated penance, says the *Summa 'Elegantius'*.[26] The motivation or intention of the sinner in acknowledging that he has done wrong and ought to be punished is of central concern in this passage, and it underlines for the author of the *Summa 'Elegantius'* the inadequacy of the criterion of spontaneous confession as an indicator that what is happening is taking place within a penitential rather than a judicial process. The *Summa* points out that people confess for different reasons. Some are afraid that proof will shortly be provided (*aut est metu imminentium probationum extorta*). Some fear that the truth will be extracted from them by questions or by force (*aut questionibus aut tormentis eruta*). Only some of those who confess do so voluntarily (*aut spontanea*).[27]

These are texts which suggest that the secret places of the penitential process are very important in giving it its distinctive character in comparison with the court of law. It has, then to be asked – and of course it was insistently asked by the reformers of the sixteenth century – whether it can be enough to repent in the heart and make satisfaction secretly, without confessing aloud? Is this a sufficient acknowledgement of the offence if it is really only important what happens between the sinner and God ? Gratian stresses the importance of 'showing' repentance as an indication of experiencing real contrition, and that in itself would bring the offence out of the realm of thought into an external arena, where it can be judicially addressed.[28]

From this, it is clear that sin is not remitted without confession of the mouth and satisfaction by deeds.[29] But if no one can be justified unless he has already confessed his sin, and if only that confession is *utilis* which is made *cum paenitentia*, it may begin to look as though the power of the keys is nugatory.[30] Gratian is obliged to wrestle at some length with the question whether a person can be freed of the consequences of sin by any means other than the full penitential process discharged, not secretly in his heart, but through the Church's procedure. There remained a sharp difference between penitential and judicial treatments of what is 'visible'. Jesus condemned the man who only thought adulterous thoughts, as if he had been an actual adulterer (Matthew 5.28). But the law does not punish someone who thinks of murder but does not commit it.[31]

Excommunication

Excommunication, the ultimate sanction of the penitential process, cuts the condemned offender off from the community at the point where his belonging is most evident, that is in his participation in the celebration of the Eucharist. We have already looked at the shift from the early public penance to the private penance of the Middle Ages. Penance in the early Church was public because it was deemed important to deal publicly with known serious offences which would otherwise be potential stumbling-blocks to the community. In Ps.-Isidore the second letter of Calixtus is on the theme that public sins require public penance.[32] There was no question that this was a punishment within a penitential context, for the excommunicated who wished to be restored to communion *ipso facto* became penitents, and dressed and acted accordingly. But it is also important that it was public, because being public is always a definitive feature of a judicial process (justice must be seen to be done). When someone is accused and after the third warning he does not mend his ways, he is to be suspended from his office until he has been 'purged'.[33] The principle here is again that he should not constitute a stumbling-block to the faithful, so they need to see that satisfaction has been made (*condignam satisfactionem*).

All this has to do less with a Ciceronian notion of the 'common good' than with concern for the risk to others' souls of seeing bad examples unchecked. Nevertheless, embedded in the public and community context in which these processes take place is an acknowledgement that society, whether it is the society of the Church or that of the secular world, has a proper interest in seeing that serious offences are dealt with and offenders brought to account, and that is a judicial as well as, if perhaps not more than, a penitential concept.

Satisfaction and vicarious satisfaction

The account of things we have been looking at, especially perhaps in the provision for tinkering with it, assumes that there is a deserved penalty of either sin or breach of the law, which is a social or group punishment as well as the punishment of an individual. God threatened man with the punishment of death if he should sin, explains Augustine. He put him in Eden with the intention that he should ascend to heaven if he preserved his righteousness.[34] The sinful mass of fallen man (*massa peccatrix*) joins the fallen angels in suffering the punishment their rebellion deserved.[35]

Something has to be done to 'enforce' punishment. Magistrates can enforce their *iurisdictio* by a penal judgement (*poenali iudicio*),[36] and even if the condemned person does not consent to the sentence it can be carried out regardless. Moreover, it is intended according the *Digest* that this enforcement shall extend to making the condemned man discharge every detail of the sentence imposed on him.[37]

There is a strong theme of 'making satisfaction' here. Must the guilty make satisfaction personally? The principle of vicarious satisfaction is Biblical, and the supreme example of willing submission to a punishment which others ought to be suffering is the sacrifice of Christ. In the later Middle Ages the indulgence system provides for someone else to act on my behalf in such a way that something which previously was my responsibility becomes not my responsibility. (Though this does not apply to the guilt but only to the liability for the penalty.)

The wrong and its righting: repairing the damage: compensating the victim

In the forensic or the penitential arena, the task is to put right the specific wrong done by the sinner. This is thought of almost entirely in terms of its reference to the sinner and not the person sinned against, the miscreant not the victim. Nevertheless, there does seem to be some sense that it is appropriate to look for a fittingness in the outcome when seeking to put sin right. Is a rapist allowed to marry the woman he has raped? No, say many authorities.[38] Jerome says yes; if her father is willing and the husband pays him the value of her lost virginity (*dabit pretium pudicitie eius*), she can be married to him.[39] The temporal penalties for forgiven sin imposed by the Church in the system of penance do not, characteristically, primarily have to do with any direct repairing of the damage experienced by any individual against whom the sin has been committed. But in this example there is an attempt to get back as far as possible to the *status quo*. The lost virginity cannot be restored. But the situation can be made more or less as it would have been if the loss of virginity had taken place within a marriage between the two parties. The brief analysis on this point in the *Summa 'Elegantius'* stresses the importance of putting right a wrong which has been done.

The purposes of punishment

To the mediaeval mind, punishment has a purpose, which is adumbrated in what has just been said, broadly, to make good the ill. The principle that reparation should be made for fault is widespread. Roman law and barbarian laws contain numerous insistences on this point, as do Tertullian, Ambrose, Augustine, local councils of the early Church and the early penitential codes, especially those on the Celtic tradition.[40] The daily prayer of the believer makes satisfaction for the trivial sins that daily stain his life, says Augustine.[41] Alan of Lille in his *Liber Poenitentialis* begins by berating the contemporary clergy for their inadequacy. If indeed the guilty person seems to the priest to be sufficiently repentant, let him enjoin a penance appropriate to the sin: *si vero reus, prout sacerdoti videbitur, sufficienter poeniteat, prout sacerdoti videbitur, sufficienter poeniteat, juxta peccati statum satisfactionem injungat.*[42]

In the penitential system the primary offence is clearly understood to be against God and the repentance and reparation is directed towards him.

That does not rule out an element of reparation to the community or to the victim. But in any case there is an assumption that the penitential acts are acts both of reparation and of satisfaction. This is less explicit and less well thought out in the forensic arena, but there, too, there must be the assumption that there is a place for punishment and that punishment does some good; the offender must discharge the penalty imposed upon him. This requirement assumes that in so doing he will alter his position and make it possible for him to be restored to the community as a forgiven man.

The carrying out of a punishment might in principle 'work' in various ways.[43] It might count because of being done sincerely and with a real intention not to offend again, so that its force is that of an *indication* of a change of heart. That would make it primarily a sign. The payment of the penalty goes with a requirement of amendment of life, says Augustine. Even if they give alms, those who live in gross wickedness and do not try to reform their lives and manners are not thus made clean.[44]

The 'sign' would have a reverse side, in that it is also a manifestation of the shame and distress of the penitent. *Infamia* is an important issue in the judicial process, especially after the Fourth Lateran Council. Yet because the matter is private there is no question of loss of reputation in mediaeval penance.[45] But that does not mean that damage to reputation is not felt. The sanction of the shame applies even in the small 'court' held by the solitary priest as judge. 'It is better to blush now before one man than to do so at the Judgement to come before all the nations.'[46] This eighth-century sentiment became familiar in succeeding centuries in this form[47] and that found in a Ps.-Augustinian *De vera et falsa penitentia*, which teaches that shame has its place in the remission of sins. 'He who blushes for Christ is worthy of mercy': *qui erubescit pro Christo, fit dignus misericordia*.[48] The principle here seems to be that someone who is sincerely undergoing a change of heart will see his former self in a new light and not like what he sees. A criminal undergoing punishment may not be sorry at all. He may feel no shame, at least not a healing shame. The effect of his punishment is simply to counterbalance his breach of the law, in some *quid pro quo* way.

Willing submission to punishment might 'count' as an act of obedience to God. It might 'count' as an act of obedience to the Church, by whose authority it was imposed. But in a Christian context this discharging of the penalty is surely above all an act of reconciliation, and here it is most signally distinct from the judicial punishment. It is a fundamental of the Christian system that Christians should be at one. Jerome wrote a letter to his mother's sister Castorina, seeking reconciliation. He begins by reminding her of a series of Scriptural texts. He cites, 'Whoever hates his brother is a murderer' (I John 3.15); 'Be ye angry and sin not' (Psalm 4.5); 'Let not the sun go down upon your anger' (Ephesians 4.26). He points out that neither he nor she is able to pray 'Forgive us our debts as we also forgive our debtors' (Matthew 6.12) as long as the estrangement continues. He warns that at the day of judgement their reconciliation will receive its reward or their discord its penalty. For his part, he would mend things. But reconciliation takes two. 'Yet if you are unwilling ... I shall be blameless. This letter when read shall absolve me.'[49] The Christian ideal for which Jerome is reaching here is to mend wrongdoing peaceably, by mutual agreement, in the spirit of Matthew 5.25–6, if possible bringing the miscreant to repent of his own free will, so that there can be both healing and amendment of life, without the need to use force, that is, without the need to subject him to punishment against his will. We have already seen how the same fundamental principle applies in the penitential system, where the penitent comes of his own free will to confess his sins and gladly accepts his punishment.[50] Just as the essence of confession is the willingness of the sinner to make it, so it is of the essence of reconciliation that it should be entered into freely.[51]

The subject-matter of Theodore of Canterbury is chiefly the elements which may have a place in a ministry of reconciliation: baptism, the love for which many sins are forgiven, almsgiving, the tears which are tokens of sincere repentance, the confession of sins, affliction of heart and body, amendment of life, the intercession of the saints, the merit of having faith, and so on.

Again, an aspect of penitential restoration and reconciliation is the strong mediaeval 'medical' theme of the healing of the individual. In the *Paenitentiale Ambrosianum*, for example, there is a discussion in the Preface of the medicinal intention of penance, its healing powers, and such imagery pervades the penitential literature.[52] Theodore of Canterbury speaks in the language of healing. Those who supervise the penitential system are *spirituales medici* curing the wounds and the sickness of souls.[53]

Bringing good out of ill

A similar accommodation of the fact that something irreparably wrong has been done may be glimpsed in the discussion as to whether it is just to give alms from ill-gotten gains (for example, from money got by simony or usury?). It is possible to argue in terms of the principle that good should if possible be brought out of evil, that ill-gotten gains ought to be made good by turning them into alms.[54]

Redress and retaliation

Redress differs from revenge. Both involve 'getting even'. But redress has a benevolent intention towards the person harmed, whereas revenge has a hostile intention towards the cause of the harm. A given action is unjust on the part of the one who strikes the blow. It may be just on the part of the person who is struck to strike back, because the person who struck a blow unjustly justly deserved to be struck himself: *ex parte percutientis est iniusta quia non debuit se vindicare; ex parte vero percussi iusta, quia iniuste percutiens iuste percuti meruit*. On another understanding, that of the just and the unjust is the same action, which can be judged just in one case and unjust in the other, says Anselm of Canterbury. *Diverso igitur intuitu iusta et iniusta est eadem actio, quam contingere potes ab alio iudicari iustam tantum, ab alio iniustam*.[55]

Anselm speaks of balancing, a wrong with a wrong, or a wrong with a right. It is possible to go further as he would himself want to do – and to require not merely an act of reparation for each particular offence, but a new consistency of life in good behaviour. Those who live in gross wickedness and do not try to reform their lives and manners, but give alms, are not thus made clean[56] because the act of almsgiving is not coherent with the rest of the individual's life. It is anomalous, and therefore to be considered insincere.

Salvation

The *accessus* in the *Summa 'Elegantius'* says that the 'subject-matter' of canon law is *ius et iustitia divina*. The 'purpose' of studying it is to exhort people to observance, for he who neglects the law confounds good and evil (*fas nefasque confundit*). The end in view is salvation, by educating the ignorant in the law, curbing and correcting the prevaricators, so those who keep the law may be rewarded with eternal life.[57] That is what all this comes to. It is our conclusion, for lawyer and theologian alike were working in a 'Christian' society where the destiny of the soul was always the most important question. But there remained the great Church-dividing dilemma of the Reformation. Is obedience to the law the way to heaven? Or does salvation come by grace even to some of those conspicuous among the law-breakers?

Notes

Preface

1 *Letter* 116, *Letters of F. W. Maitland*, ed. N. N. R. Zutschi (London, 1995), vol. II, p. 105.
2 *Letter* 22, *Letters of F. W. Maitland*, ed. N. N. R. Zutschi (London, 1995), vol. II, p. 24.
3 Letter 49, to Paul Vinogradoff, *Letters of F. W. Maitland*, ed. N. N. R. Zutschi (London, 1995), vol. II, p. 48.
4 B. Tierney, *Foundations of the Conciliar Theory* (Cambridge, 1955), pp. 13–14.
5 G.H.M. Posthumus Meyjes, 'Exponents of sovereignty: canonists as seen by theologians in the late Middle Ages', *The Church and Sovereignty: Essays in Honour of Michael Wilks*, ed. D. Wood, *Studies in Church History, Subsidia*, 9 (Oxford, 1991), pp. 299–312.

Introduction

1 *Die Summa des Stephanus Tornacensis über das Decretum Gratiani*, ed. J. F. von Schulte (Geissen, 1891), pp. 1, 5. He continues: 'Just as the Latin embraces unleavened bread, the Greek, leavened bread, but when they come to the altar, neither ought to despise the other's sacrament.' This was an unfortunate analogy since there was in fact a profound mistrust of the other's sacrament on both sides, which lingers into the twentieth century.
2 This is noticeable in the comparison of work of theologians on the subject of transubstantiation, with legal glosses on the same theme in the aftermath of the Fourth Lateran Council of 1215.
3 Herbert Kalb, *Studien zur Summa Stephans von Tournai* (Innsbruck, 1983).
4 Beryl Smalley, *The Becket Conflict and the Schools: A Study of Intellectuals in Politics* (Oxford, 1973).
5 *Que coram iudice ecclesiastico tantum tractandum est*. Petri Blesensis, *De Distinctionibus in Canonum Interpretatione Adhibendis sive Speculum Iuris Canonici*, XVI, ed. T. A. Reimarus (Berlin, 1837), p. 40.
6 *Select Cases in the Court of the King's Bench under Edward I*, ed. G. O. Sayles, Selden Society, 57 (London, 1938), II, p. lii.
7 Kuttner finds various patterns of antithesis: between strictness and dispensation; between precept and counsel; between justice and mercy; between divine immutability and human changeableness; universal and limited legislative power; absolute and relative rule. The question is whether these need be regarded as in conflict. The answer, for our authors is no, because circum-

stances alter cases. See S. Kuttner, 'Harmony from dissonance: an interpretation of mediaeval canon law', *The History of Ideas and Doctrines of Canon Law in the Middle Ages* (London, 1980), p. 8.
8 H. de Lubac, 'A propos de la formule: "diversi sed non adversi"', *Mélanges Lebreton, Recherches de science réligieuse*, 39–40 (1951-2), II., p. 27 and Tertullian, *Adversus Marcionem*, IV. 11.
9 Tertullian, *Adversus Marcionem*, IV. p. xi.
10 *Magna oritur hoc loco plerisque dubitatio; nam etsi non videntur evangelistae dixisse contraria, tamen diversa dixerunt. … Quomodo solvendum, nisi quatuor evangelistas de diversis quatuor putes dixisse temporibus. Et ideo verum utrumque putamus. Non sententiarum varietate, nec personarum diversitate distinctum.* PL, 15. 1841, on Luke X (24.1–4).
11 Augustine, *De Consensu Evangelistarum*, II. v. 14; II. xii. 27; II. xlvi. 98.
12 Cf. Tertullian, *Liber Quaestionum ex Novo Testamento*, q.1, PL, 35. 2391 and q.10, PL, 35. 2223 and q. 66, PL, 35. 2261. Ambrose, *Expositio* on Luke X, 147, 148, 171, has *non … contraria, … tamen diversa.*
13 See S. Kuttner, 'Harmony from dissonance: an interpretation of mediaeval canon law', *The History of Ideas and Doctrines of Canon Law in the Middle Ages* (London, 1980), and cf. H. de Lubac, 'A propos de la formule: "diversi sed non adversi"', *Mélanges Lebreton, Recherches de science réligieuse*, 39–40 (1951–2), II. 27–40.
14 *In unum corpus adunare curavi.*
15 *Quod ad commodum causae suae valere perspexerit.* PL, 161. 47.
16 *Vel sibi invicem adversari existimaverit.*
17 Psalm 100; Psalm 24.
18 PL, 161. 47. See also Norman Doe, *Fundamental Authority in Late Mediaeval English Law* (Cambridge, 1990), on rigour and justice.
19 *Doctores videlicet sanctae Ecclesiae, nec a se, nec inter se dissentiunt, cum illicita prohibent, necessaria iubent, summa suadent, venalia indulgent.* PL, 161. 48.
20 *Inter canones rebellionum insidias apprehendi.*
21 *Que coram iudice ecclesiastico tantum tractandum est.* Petri Blesensis, *De Distinctionibus in Canonum Interpretatione Adhibendis sive Speculum Iuris Canonici*, Preface, ed. T. A. Reimarus (Berlin, 1837), p. 1.
22 *Diversas diversorum patrum regulas, quae canones dicuntur, in unum colligere, et contrarietates … in concordiam revocare. Die Summa des Stephanus Tornacensis über das Decretum Gratiani*, ed. J. F. von Schulte (Geissen, 1891), p. 5.
23 L. Boyle, 'The "Summa summarum": and some other English works of Canon Law', *Monumenta Iuris Canonici*, Ser. C, 1 (1965), pp. 440–2. The text is in Bodleian Library MS 293 fol.1r.
24 Takashi Shogimen, 'The relationship between theology and canon law: another context of political thought in the early fourteenth century', *Journal of the History of Ideas*, 60 (1999), p. 419.
25 *Fleta*, ed. and tran. H. G. Richardson and G. Sayles, Selden Society, 72 (1955), p. 3.

1 The justice of God

1 The assumptions here are feudal.
2 A sentence from the *Liber Pancrisis* associated with the 'school' of Laon at the end of the eleventh and the beginning of the twelfth century uses the paradigm just sketched. Cf. R. W. Southern, *St. Anselm* (Cambridge, 1990), pp. 207ff. on this theory, R. W. Southern, *St. Anselm and his Biographer* (Cambridge, 1963).

3 *Iniuria.*
4 *Aliter enim facere illi iniuriam Deus videtur.*
5 *Et per hoc diabolo subiecta.*
6 Lottin, V, p. 46.
7 Baldus de Ubaldis, *Commentarius ad Digestum vetus*, D. 1. 1. 2, no. 3 (Venice, 1616), p. 389.
8 It was a mediaeval commonplace, following Augustine and Boethius, that in the Godhead all the Aristotelian *Categories* are 'substantial', with the exception of relation, for Father, Son and Holy Spirit stand in relationship to one another. But in God goodness is not merely a quality or accident; it is substance, and so on.
9 *Item subvenire proximo non potest dici proprius actus iustitie, quia eque convenit misericordie.* O. Lottin, 'Le concept de justice chez les théologiens du moyen âge avant l'introduction d'Aristote', *Revue thomiste*, 44 (1938), p. 516, edited from Brussels Bib. roy.1801–03 (1551), f. 144va–144vb and Paris, nat lat. 16387, f.125rb–125va.
10 *Set differt in modo, quia iustite est secundum quod fit ex debito, misericordie secundum quod est ex compassione*, O. Lottin, 'Le concept de justice chez les théologiens du moyen âge avant l'introduction d'Aristote', *Revue thomiste*, 44 (1938), p. 516, edited from Brussels Bib. roy.1801–03 (1551), f. 144va–144vb and Paris, nat lat. 16387, f.125rb–125va.
11 *Opera Omnia*, 1. 106. 12.
12 *Opera Omnia*, 1. 107. 1.
13 Chapter 5, *Opera Omnia*, 1. 104.
14 *Opera Omnia*, 1. 107. 9–11.
15 *Opera Omnia*, 1. 109. 28–9.
16 *Opera Omnia*, 1. 109. 16–18.
17 *Enchiridion*, 27, and cf. the final books of the *De Civitate Dei* on this theme.
18 *Nam, ut testatur Justinanus. humana natura prona et labilis est ad delicta, unde cotidie et successive discordiae suscitantur et litigia multiplicantur. Ideo advocatorum numerus ampliatus est et eorum subtilitas adeo convaluit, quod semper ab adversariis actionum editionem et libellorum exigunt dationem, in qua re plures nostri advocati temporis hactenus titubaverunt.*
19 That is put rather well by Bernardus Dorna: *Quoniam nefanda subdolaque hominum calliditas adeo pullulavit, quod quasi penitus fides recta ab eorum mentibus transmigravit, unde nihil secundum bonam fidem, nihil secundum credulitatem potest inter homines expediri, alveum fragilitatis naturae sequentes.*
20 *Digest*, 1. 1. 10 (Ulpian).
21 Cicero, *De Inventione*, II. 53.
22 S. Kuttner, 'A forgotten definition of justice', reprinted in *The History of Ideas and Doctrines of Canon Law in the Middle Ages* (London, 1980), pp. 75–6 discusses the relationship of this principle to Ciceronian thinking about virtue as a *habitus*, that is, a constant of a given mind.
23 *Summa 'Elegantius'*, Part I (31), p. 8.
24 Jerome, *Epistulae*, ed. I. Hilberg, *CSEL*, 54 (Vienna, 1910). *The Letters of St. Jerome*, tr. C. C. Mierow and T. C. Lawlor, Ancient Christian Writers (London, 1963).
25 Jerome, *Letters*, 1. vii–8.
26 *Haec a iudice damnata absoluta per gladium est.* Jerome, *Letters* 1. ix.
27 For the human legislative process can get out of touch with justice too.
28 H. Kantorowicz, *The Definition of Law*, ed. A. H. Campbell (Cambridge, 1958), p. 21.

2 Sin and breaking the law

1. B. Poschmann, *Penance and the Anointing of the Sick* (London, 1963) traces this change.
2. Aquinas, *ST*, II i q. c a.9.
3. Aquinas, *ST*, II i q. c a. 9.
4. *Iustitia est habitus animi communi utilitate conservata suam cuique tribuens dignitatem.*
5. *PL*, 178. 1653A.
6. Cicero, *De Inventione*, II. 53. 161.
7. Lottin, pp. 225–35.
8. Right reason (*ratio recta*) is the foundation of every good work and this it is which theologians say is infused by God, suggests our commentator, as the *prima intelligentia* to illuminate the human intellect. But it can be argued that we are ourselves the source of any virtue we display (*quod nos sumus principium virtutis tantum*), Lottin, p. 227.
9. *Reconciliatio in hac provincia publice statuta non est, quia et publica paenitentia non est.* See B. Poschmann, *Penance and the Anointing of the Sick* (London, 1963), p. 126 for discussion of this passage.
10. *Falsos testes a communione aecclesiastica summovent, nisi poenitentiae satisfactione crimina admissa deleverint.* Theodore of Canterbury, *Die Lateinischen Pönitentialbücher*, ed. F. Kunstmann (Mainz, 1844), XXII, p. 68.
11. Theodore of Canterbury, *Die Lateinischen Pönitentialbücher*, ed. F. Kunstmann (Mainz, 1844), XXII, p. 69.
12. Theodore of Canterbury, *Die Lateinischen Pönitentialbücher*, ed. F. Kunstmann (Mainz, 1844), XXIV, pp. 71–2.
13. Bonizo, *Liber de Vita Christiana*, ed. E. Perels (Berlin, 1930).
14. Isidore, *Etymologiae*, V. 26.
15. Isidore, *Etymologiae*, V. 26. Including points on the use of force dealt with below.
16. Isidore, *Etymologiae*, V. 27.
17. Isidore, *Etymologiae*, V. 27.
18. Isidore, *Etymologiae*, V. 27.
19. Fulgentius Ruspensis, *De Trinitate*, XII, line 466.
20. Bernard of Clairvaux, *Sententiae 110*, *Opera Omnia*, VI ii, p. 187, cf. Thomas of Chobham, *Sermons*, 5, line 119 and Robert Grosseteste, *Statutes of Lincoln*, in *Council and Synods, II (1205–1313)*, ed. F. M. Powicke and C. R. Cheney (Oxford, 1964), p. 276.
21. Peter of Celle, *Commentaria in Ruth*, 2, line 2428.
22. Peter Abelard, *Commentary on Romans* I.3, CCCM, XI, line 386.
23. Bernard of Clairvaux, *De praecepto et dispensatione*, 26, *Opera Omnia*, III, p. 272.
24. Romans 5.20.
25. Jerome, *Letters* 1.xiv, Cf. the proverb *Summum ius summa iniuria*.
26. Bernard of Clairvaux, Letter 11, 1, *Opera Omnia*, V. 52.
27. Bernard of Clairvaux, Letter 11, 4, *Opera Omnia*, V. 55.
28. Bernard of Clairvaux, Letter 11, 4, *Opera Omnia*, V. 55.
29. Bernard of Clairvaux, Letter 11, 4, *Opera Omnia*, V. 55.
30. Bernard of Clairvaux, Letter 11, 4, *Opera Omnia*, V. 55.
31. Bernard of Clairvaux, Letter 11, 5, *Opera Omnia*, V. 56.
32. Bernard of Clairvaux, Letter 11, 5, *Opera Omnia*, V. 56.
33. Bernard of Clairvaux, Letter 11, 5, *Opera Omnia*, V. 56.
34. Bernard of Clairvaux, Letter 11, 6, *Opera Omnia*, V. 56–7.
35. Bernard of Clairvaux, Letter 11, 6, *Opera Omnia*, V. 57.

180 *Notes*

36 Bernard of Clairvaux, Letter 11, 6, *Opera Omnia*, V. 57.
37 Bernard of Clairvaux, Letter 11, 6, *Opera Omnia*, V. 57.
38 Bernard of Clairvaux, Letter 11, 7, *Opera Omnia*, V. 57.
39 Bernard of Clairvaux, Letter 11, 7, *Opera Omnia*, V. 57.
40 *Inducere subiectos ad propriam ipsorum virtutem*, Aquinas, *ST*, IIi q. xcii a. 1.
41 *Sequitur quod proprius effectus legis sit bonos facere eos quibus datur*, Aquinas, *ST*, IIi q. xcii a. 1.
42 Aquinas, *ST*, IIi q. xciv a. 2.
43 (Lyons,1551).
44 *Summa 'Elegantius'*, Part I, (8), p. 3.
45 *Non omne quod licet honestum est. Digest*, 50. 17, no. 144.
46 *Sacrarum legum precepta ab omnibus sunt intelligenda atque observanda*, Irnerius, Fitting, *Titulus* I. 16. p. 18.
47 Irnerius, Fitting,*Titulus* I. 16. p. 19.
48 *Quidquid in calore iracundiae vel fit vel dicitur, non prius ratum est, quam si perseverantia apparuit iudicium animi fuisse, Digest*, 50. 17, no. 48.
49 *Eum qui propter disciplinam verberant occidit homicida non est, Summa 'Elegantius'*, Part IX (79), p. 87.
50 Baldus de Ubaldis, *De iustitia et iure*, 6, *Commentaries ad Digestum Vetus* (Venice, 1616) and see Walter Ullmann, 'Baldus's conception of law', *Law Quarterly Review*, lvii (1942), p. 387.
51 Though it also had claims to be a branch of rhetoric, as we shall see.
52 Kent Greenawalt, *Conflicts of Law and Morality* (Oxford, 1987), p. 18.
53 Kent Greenawalt, *Conflicts of Law and Morality* (Oxford, 1987), p. 7.
54 *Immo tanto hoc faciebat iniustius, quanto non ad hoc amore iustitiae trahebatur, sed instincti malitiae impellebatur, Cur Deus Homo*, I. 7, Anselm, *Opera Omnia*, I. 57. 11.
55 *Nulla essentia est iniusta per se, De Conceptu Virginali* 4, Anselm, *Opera Omnia*, II. 145. 31.
56 *Quid est enim iste consensus* [to sin] *nisi Dei contemptus et offensa ipsius*, Peter Abelard, *Ethics*, ed. D. Luscombe (Oxford, 1971), p. 4.
57 Peter Abelard, *Ethics*, ed. D. Luscombe (Oxford, 1971), p. 4. *Non est autem huiusmodi animi vicium idem quod peccatum, nec peccatum idem quod actio mala.*
58 Peter Abelard, *Ethics*, ed. D. Luscombe (Oxford, 1971), p. 3.
59 *Facilis sit ad irascendum, etiam cum non movetur ad iram*, Peter Abelard, *Ethics*, ed. D. Luscombe (Oxford, 1971), p. 3.
60 *Ad peccandum proni efficimur.*
61 *Hoc est, inclinamur ad consentiendum ei quod non convenit, ut illud scilicet faciamus aut dimittamus*, Peter Abelard, *Ethics*, ed. D. Luscombe (Oxford, 1971), p. 4.
62 *Culpa animae qua dampnationem meretur vel apud deum rea statuitur*, Peter Abelard, *Ethics*, ed. D. Luscombe (Oxford, 1971), p. 4.
63 Lottin, IV i, p. 315.
64 Peter Abelard, *Ethics*, ed. D. Luscombe (Oxford, 1971), p. 2.
65 *In brutis ... animalibus non sunt mali vel iniusti, De Concordia*, 13, Anselm, *Opera Omnia*, II. 287. 21.
66 *Si quis suadente diabolo huius sacrilegii vicium incurrerit, quod in clericum vel monachum violenta manus iniecerit.* And Gratian, *Decretum*, C 17. q. 4. c. 29.
67 Gratian, *Decretum*, I, Dist. VI. 2.
68 *Summa 'Elegantius'*, Part XII (1), p. 213.
69 Cf. Ps.-Anselm, *De similitudinibus*, 84, *omne opus bonum factum cum voto plus valet quam factum sine voto, PL*, 159. 655–7.

Notes 181

70 The most useful study of this change is still B. Poschmann, *Penance and the Anointing of the Sick* (London, 1963). This seems to have happened in response to pastoral need and not to have been the result of any attempt to impose change from above.
71 *Nam qui navem hominibus plenam in mari scopuloso et procelloso regendam tradit imbecilli, puero, ... seu artis navalis penitus ignaro.* Grosseteste, *Epistola*, 72, *Epistolae*, ed. H. R. Luard, Rolls Series (London, 1861).
72 Jerome, *Letter*, 14. viii. 1.
73 Jerome, *Letter*, 14. viii. 3.
74 B. Poschmann, *Penance and the Anointing of the Sick* (London, 1963), p. 147, as recurring in ancient Celtic penitentials. He cites Finnian 9.23; Cummean III. 3, 12; IV. 3, 12; IV. 4; V. 2; VIII. 2, 3, 20.
75 B. Poschmann, *Penance and the Anointing of the Sick* (London, 1963), p. 147.
76 Frankish penitentials of the second half of the eighth century speak in this way of the *iudicia canonica, iudicia Cummenai, iudicia Theodori*. See B. Poschmann, *Penance and the Anointing of the Sick* (London, 1963), p. 133.
77 Gratian, *Decretum*, II, *Causa* XXXIII q. iii, Dist. VI. c. 1.
78 C. Lefebvre, 'Juges et Savants en Europe, xiiie–xvie siècle', *Ephemerides Iuris Canonici* 22 (1966), p. 100.
79 See pp. 118 and 166.
80 Isidore, *Etymologiae*, V. 27.
81 *Talio autem non solum ad iniuriam referendam, sed etiam pro beneficio reddendo ponitur. Est enim communis sermo et iniuriae et beneficiae,* Isidore, *Etymologiae*, V. 27.
82 *Règles et pénitentiels monastiques de Saint Colomban,* (14B), ed. A. de Vogüé (Bégrolles-en-Mauges, 1989), p. 164.
83 *Multa sunt quae aut pro consideratione aetatum aut pro necessitate rerum oporteat temperari, illa semper conditione servata ut in his quae vel dubia fuerint vel obscura, id noverimus sequendum quod nec praeceptis evangelicis contrarium nec decretis sanctorum patrum **inveniatur** adversum.* Leo the Great, *Epistulae*, 167, ed. Ballerini I. 1419, Quoted in Ivo of Chartres, Prologue, *PL*, 161. 52 and others including Gratian, *Decretum*, I, Dist. xiv, c. 2. And see S. Kuttner, 'Urban II and the doctrine of interpretation: a turning point?', *Studia Gratiana*, 16 (Rome, 1972), p. 63. And circumstance may make a great deal of difference. Is there such a thing as a context in which murder is not murder? Just war may arguably be possible, says Master Roland, *Causa*, XXIII, q. 2, p. 88.
84 *Discretus sacerdos secundum quod qualitas persone et verborum exigit, eliget quod sibi necessarium videbitur et utile.* Hostiensis, *Summa Aurea* (Lyons, 1556), V. 62.
85 *In hunc quoque modum, si velimus praeteriti et praesenti temporis exempla colligere, invenimus principes ecclesiarum quaedam pro rigore canonum districtius iudicasse, multa pro temporum necessitates tolerasse, multa pro personarum utilitate dissimulasse.* PL 162.67.
86 Gratian, *Decretum*, II, *Causa* XXXIII q. iii, Dist. IV, c. 1.
87 *Si vero criminalis culpa [paenitentiam] aliquando sequitur, vera paenitentia non fuit, nec veniam unquam a Domine impetravit.* Gratian, *Decretum*, II, *Causa* XXXIII q. iii, Dist. III, c. 24.

3 The public interest?

1 A revision of the fourth-century Theodosian Code.

182   Notes

2. *Letter* 1, *CSEL* 35, 614, n.162. and *Scritti teologici ed ecclesiastici di Giustiniano*, ed. M. Amelotti and L. M. Zingale, *Legum iustiniani imperatoris vocabularium, Subsidia*, III (Milan, 1977).
3. *Letter* 2, *CSEL*, 35, 655 nr.196 and *Scritti teologici ed ecclesiastici di Giustiniano*, ed. M. Amelotti and L. M. Zingale, *Legum iustiniani imperatoris vocabularium, Subsidia*, III (Milan, 1977).
4. *Letter* 5, *CSEL*, 35, 645, nr.188 and *Scritti teologici ed ecclesiastici di Giustiniano*, ed. M. Amelotti and L. M. Zingale, *Legum iustiniani imperatoris vocabularium, Subsidia*, III (Milan, 1977).
5. Code 1.1.
6. Code 1.2.
7. Code 1.2.
8. Code 1.4.
9. Code 1.1.
10. *Justinians Edict über den Rechten Glauben*, ed. E. Schwartz, *In legum Iustiniani Imperatoris Vocabularium, Subsidia*, II (Milan, 1973), p. 131.
11. O.F. Robertson, 'Public law and Justinian's Institutes', *Studies in Justinian's Institutes in Memory of J.A.C. Thomas*, ed. P. G. Stein and A. D. E. Lewis (London, 1983), p. 126.
12. *Letter* 6, *CSEL*, 35, 655 nr.196 and *Scritti teologici ed ecclesiastici di Giustiniano*, ed. M. Amelotti and L. M. Zingale, *Legum iustiniani imperatoris vocabularium, Subsidia*, III (Milan, 1977). See my *The Church and the Churches* (Cambridge, 1994).
13. *Letter* 2, *CSEL*, 35, 614 nr.162 and *Scritti teologici ed ecclesiastici di Giustiniano*, ed. M. Amelotti and L. M. Zingale, *Legum iustiniani imperatoris vocabularium, Subsidia*, III (Milan, 1977).
14. *De Civitate Dei*, II. 21.
15. Cicero, *De Re Publica*, 2. 42.
16. *Populum autem non omnem coetum multitudinis, sed coetum iuris consensu et utilitatis communione sociatum esse determinat*. Cicero, *De Re Publica*, 1. 25.
17. Augustine, *De Civitate Dei*, XIX. 21.
18. Augustine, *De Civitate Dei*, II. 21.
19. *Omne enim quod in public[o] utile est id equum est. Equitas enim nihil aliud est nisi quedam pietas quae maxime debet esse circa rem publicam, ut ait author in principio de Somnio Scipionis ibi dum dicit iustitiam sole et pietatem*. Baldus, on *Digest*, 1. 14.3, n.6, Norbert Horn, *Aequitas*, p. 109.
20. W. Ullmann, *Mediaeval Foundations of Renaissance Humanism* (London, 1977), explores this theme.
21. Augustine, *De Civitate Dei*, XIX. 21.
22. Augustine, *De Civitate Dei*, XIX. 21.
23. Augustine, *De Civitate Dei*, XIX. 21.
24. Augustine, *De Civitate Dei*, XIX. 21.
25. Jerome, *Letter*, 1 (x).
26. Jerome, *Letter*, 1 (xi).
27. *Iustitia est virtus conservatrix humanae societatis et vite communitatis*, William of Conches' *Moralium dogma philosophorum*, ed. J. Holmberg (Uppsala, 1929), p. 12.
28. *Digest*, 1. 1. 1. 2.
29. Walter Ullmann, 'Baldus's conception of law', *Law Quarterly Review*, lviii (London, 1942), p. 396.
30. *Nota quod illud est publicum (ius), quod continet publicum bonum principaliter*. On *Digest*, 1. 1. 4 (Ulpian).
31. Bracton, *De legibus Angliae*, V, ed. T. Twiss, Rolls Series (1978–80), 3 vols, I, p. 20.

Notes 183

32 *In qua maior pars est hominum non perfectorum virtute*. Aquinas, *ST*, II i q. 96 a. 2.
33 Aquinas, *ST*, II i q. 96 a. 2.
34 *Sed solum de illis qui sunt ordinabiles ad bonum commune.*
35 Aquinas, *ST*, II i q. 96 a. 3.
36 *Cum omnis pars ordinetur ad totum sicut imperfectum ad perfectum; unus autem homo est pars communitatis perfectae: necesse est quod lex proprie respiciat ordinem ad felicitatem communem*, Aquinas, *ST*, II i q. xc a. 2.
37 *Cum igitur quilibet homo sit pars civitatis, impossibile est quod aliquis homo sit bonus, nisi sit bene proportionatus bono communi; nec totum potest bene consistere nisi ex partibus sibi proportionatis*. Aquinas, *ST*, II i q. xcii a. 1 to 3.
38 *Cum omnis pars ordinetur ad totum sicut imperfectum as perfectum; unus autem homo est past communitatis perfectae*. Aquinas, *ST*, II i q. xc a. 2.
39 *Unde impossibile est quod bonum commune civitatis bene se habeat, nisi cives sint virtuosi, ad minus illi quibus convenit principari*, Aquinas, *ST*, II i q. xcii a. 1 to 3.
40 Aquinas, *ST*, II i q. xcv a. 1.
41 Aquinas, *ST*, II i q. xcv a. 1.
42 Aquinas, *ST*, II i q. xcv a. 1.
43 Aquinas, *ST*, II i q. xc a. 2.
44 Isidore, *Etymologiae*, V. 26.
45 *Nam ille sic iudicatur ut sacrilegus, quia fur est sacrorum*. Isidore, *Etymologiae*, V. 26.
46 Augustine, *De Civitate Dei*, II. 21.
47 Augustine, *De Civitate Dei*, II. 21.
48 Augustine, *De Civitate Dei*, II. 21.
49 *Ex predictis illud innotescere potest quod ratione clam peracte penitentie nullus accusationem effugere valet, cum publice intersit maleficia punire, ut delinquentes corrigantur et ceteri deterreantur et sic omnius peccandi ausus adimatur. Summa 'Elegantius'*, Part VI (26a), p. 115.
50 *Nullus autem delictorum finis erit, si sub pretextus implete penitentie ceperint homines a criminibus excusari et penas legibus insertas evitare. Summa 'Elegantius'*, Part VI (26a), p. 115.
51 A. H. J. Grenidge, *Infamia: Its Place in Roman Public and Private Law* (Oxford, 1984).
52 See pp. 26, 74, 105.
53 Elisabeth Vodola, *Excommunication in the Middle Ages* (Berkeley, 1986), p. 8.
54 Elisabeth Vodola, *Excommunication in the Middle Ages* (Berkeley, 1986), p. 70.
55 Elisabeth Vodola, *Excommunication in the Middle Ages* (Berkeley, 1986), p. 112.
56 Elisabeth Vodola, *Excommunication in the Middle Ages* (Berkeley, 1986), p. 85.
57 Case described in Elisabeth Vodola, *Excommunication in the Middle Ages* (Berkeley, 1986), p. 102ff.

4 Paradoxes

1 Cf. Boethius, *De Consolatione Philosophiae* I, pr. 1.
2 *Cum essem Mantuae ubique iuris scientiae praecepta pluribus auditoribus traderem et attentius diu quadam de iuris apicibus actionumque multiplicitatibus cogitarem, astitit michi mulier in causis mirifica, legibus imbuta.*
3 Placentinus, *Die Summa 'De actionum varietatibus' des Placentinus*, ed. Wahrmund, *Quellen*, IV. iii, p. 1.
4 Gabriel le Bras, *Histoire du Droit et les Institutions de l'Église en Occident* (Paris, 1965), VII, p. 406ff. C. Lefebvre, 'La doctrine de l'Hostensis sur la

184 *Notes*

préférence à assurer en droit aux intérêts spirituels', *Ephemerides Iuris Canonici*, 8 (1952), p. 24. Cf. C.J. Hering, 'Die Aequitas bei Gratian', *Studia Gratiana*, 2 (1954), 95–114.
5 *Aedificationem Dei fidei veritate et morum honestate constantem construere*, PL, 141. 47.
6 P. G. Caron, '"Aequitas et interpretatio" dans la doctrine canonique aux xiiie et xive siècles', *Proceedings of the Third International Congress on Medieval Canon Law* (1971), p. 133.
7 *Quid secundum rigorem, quid secundum moderationem, quid secundum dicatur, diligenter attendat*. George Conklin, 'Stephen of Tournai and the Development of *aequitas canonica*. The theory and practice of law after Gratian', *Proceedings of the Eighth International Congress on Medieval Canon Law* (1990), p. 370. On this passage, see C. Lefebvre, 'Natural equity and canonical equity', *Natural Law Forum*, 8 (1963), p. 123. Lefebvre argues that Roman law was the decisive shaping force on the doctrine of canonical equity.
8 Cicero, *De officiis*, I. 36. 130.
9 *Illa enim est iustitia aequitatis, quae ned summum petit, nec infimum, sed mediocre*. Baldus on C 8.53. Baldus adds: *rigor in specie vincit aequitatem*. Cf. *Digest*, 12. 6. 13.
10 *Summa 'Elegantius'*, Part XII (2), p. 214.
11 Die *Summa Decretorum des Magister Rufinus*, ed. H. Singer (Paderborn, 1902), Preface, p. 4.

5 Mapping the law

1 Walter Ullmann, 'Baldus's conception of law', *Law Quarterly Review*, lviii (London, 1942), p. 392. Ullmann argues that it is only the post-glossators who explore this.
2 *Nonnullo labore in unum ... adunare curavi*, PL, 161, 47.
3 *Summa 'Elegantius'*, Part I (42), p. 12.
4 On *schemata* of the *artes* and philosophy, see my *Old Arts and New Theology* (Oxford, 1980). It is striking that while ethics has a place in such schemes, law does not.
5 *Digest*, 50. 16, no. 9, from Ulpian.
6 *Digest*, 50. 16, no. 13, from Ulpian.
7 *Bona civitatis abusive 'publica' dicta sunt: sola enim ea publica sunt, quae populi Romani sunt. Digest*, 50. 16, no. 15, from Ulpian.
8 *Nihil est aliud 'hereditas' quam successio in universum ius quod defunctus habuit*. 'Openly' is 'before many'. *Palam est coram pluribus. Digest*, 50. 16, no. 33, from Ulpian.
9 *Equivocatur, sic iuris naturalis appellatio triplicatur. Quia vel ius divinum a summa natura, que Deus est, per legem et prophetas et evangelium humane cognitionis oblatum, Summa 'Elegantius'*, Part I (38), p. 10.
10 *Vel quod ab ipsa natura non in hominibus tantum vel etiam in omnibus animalibus plantatum*.
11 *Vel quo hominibus solis a natura est inditum ad faciendum bonum et vitandum contrarium sic dicitur*. This last is found in mandates, prohibitions and demonstrations. *Mandatis, prohibitionibus et demonstrationibus. Summa 'Elegantius'*, Part I (38), p. 10.
12 Ralph McInerny, 'Natural law and natural rights', in his *Aquinas in Human Action* (Washington, 1992), p. 217.
13 'Both the classical common law and the classical Roman law were action-oriented rather than right-oriented', Peter Stein, *The Character and Influence of the Roman Civil Law* (London, 1988), p. 38.

Notes   185

14 The term has of course much more subtlety in Anselm than in Gregory the Great.
15 *Naturae ius est quod non opinio genuit, sed quaedam in natura vis.* Cicero, *De Inventione*, II. liii. 161.
16 *Digest*, I. i. 1.
17 *Summa 'Elegantius'*, Part I (2), p. 1.
18 Paul John Finnis, *Natural Law and Natural Rights* (Oxford, 1982), p. 206.
19 Isidore, *Etymologiae*, V. 3, Gratian, *Decretum*, I, Dist. I. i.
20 Isidore, *Etymologiae*, V. 3, Gratian, *Decretum*, I, Dist. I. i.
21 Peter Stein, *Regulae Iuris* (Edinburgh, 1966), p. 13.
22 *Non videtur esse lex, quae iusta non fuerit,* Augustine, *De Libero Arbitrio* I. v.
23 *Porro lex donum Dei est, aequitatis forma, norma iustitiae, divinae voluntatis imago. salutis custodia, unio et consolidatio populorum, regula officiorum, exclusio et exterminatio vitiorum, violentiae et totius iniuriae pena.* John of Salisbury, *Policraticus*, ed. C. C. J. Webb (Oxford, 1909), vol. 2, p. 345.
24 Ambrose, *De apologia David ad Teodosium Augustum*, CSEL, iii. 14, p. 308.
25 Marius Victorinus, *Explanationes in Ciceronis rhetoricam*, II. 22, p. 280.
26 *Ius legitimum* appears in a legal context in Gaius, *Institutiones*, 3. 27. 5 and 4. 111. 2, and in the *Digest*, 37. 1. 6. 1. In 585 it may mean simply 'just title'. It is found with *legitimi diei, legitimae horae*, Joseph Balon, *Ius medii aevi, ii, Lex Jurisdictio* (Namur, 1960), p. 175.
27 Rupert of Deutz, *De Sancta Trinitate*, VI, on Genesis 6, CCCM, 21–2, p. 414.
28 *Summa 'Elegantius'*, Part 1 (19), p. 5.
29 *Habitus animi, communi utilitate conservata, suam suique tribuens dignitatem,* Cicero, *De Inventione*, II. 53.
30 *Institutes*, I. 1, pr. 1.
31 *Iustitia est constans et perpetua voluntas ius suum inicuique tribuens.*
32 *Epitome theologicae Christianae*, 32, PL, 178.1750.
33 Augustine, *De Trinitate*, XIV. 9, Peter Lombard, *Sentences*, IV. 3 dist. 33. c. 1.3.
34 *Quia hoc est in officio iustitie ne alium violes, nisi lacessitus iniuria, aut referunt se ad eam artem iuris que circa ius contentionum expediendarum regendarum versatur, aut referunt se ad illam partem que vertitur circa ius interpretandum, condendum, observandum,* Rogerius, *Summa Codicis, Biblioteca juridica medii aevi* (1888), I, p. 50.
35 *Iustitia in subiecto infusa vel acquisita informat ad religionem, pietatem, severitatem, vindictam, misericordiam, gratiam Dei, laetitiam, charitatem et innocentiam.* Baldus, on the *Digest, De iustitia et iure, Lex iustitia* no. 2.
36 S. Kuttner, 'A forgotten definition of canon law', *Studia Gratiana*, 20 (1977), p. 80.
37 S. Kuttner, 'A forgotten definition of canon law', *Studia Gratiana*, 20 (1977), p. 80.
38 Norbert Horn, *Aequitas*, p. 16.
39 O. Lottin, 'Le concept de justice chez les théologiens du moyen âge avant l'introduction d'Aristote', *Revue thomiste*, 44 (1938), p. 515.
40 *Humanum constitutio qua equitas servatur, iniuria propellitur, custoditur innocentia, frenatur violentia et exulat discordia. Summa 'Elegantius'*, Part I (4), p. 2.
41 *Ius causale finis est iustitie sed ius formale nascitur ex iustitia.* Norbert Horn, *Aequitas*, p. 16, citing D. 1. 1. 1 pr. n.4.
42 *Eo quod auctor iuris homo, auctor iustitie Deus, Summa 'Elegantius'*, Part I (3), p. 1.
43 *Ius descendit, id est, nascitur a iustitia ... ius nascitur ex sua causa praesertim essentiali et intrinseca. Iustitia est causa instrinseca iuris ... ius sine causa nasci*

186 *Notes*

non potest, Baldus de Ubaldis, *Commentarius ad Digestum* (Venice, 1616), *De iustitia et iure*, no. 7.
44 J. A. C. Thomas, *Textbook of Roman Law* (New York, 1976).
45 *Humanum genus duobus regitur, naturali videlicet iure et moribus. Ius naturae sit, quod in lege et evangelio continetur.*
46 *Quo quisque iubetur alii facere, quod sibi vult fieri et prohibetur alii inferre quod sibi nolit fieri.* For a useful discussion of this passage, see M. Villey, 'Le droit naturel chez Gratian', *Studia Gratiana*, III (Bologna, 1955), p. 85.
47 *Ius naturale [est] ad quod intellectus cuiuslibet bene dispositus assentit.*
48 Ms. Vat. lat. 832, s.xiiiex, from the Arts Faculty in Paris, Lottin, IVii, p. 543.
49 *Notandum tamen quod naturale iustum dicitur id ad quod inclinat natura hominis.*
50 Lottin, IV. ii, p. 540.
51 *In homine autem est duplex natura: una communis que sibi debetur in quantum animal, et alia specialis que sibi debetur in quantum homo.* In MS Paris nat. lat. 16089, Lottin, IV. ii, p. 542.
52 Walter Ullmann, 'Baldus's conception of law', *Law Quarterly Review*, lviii (London, 1942), pp. 394–5.
53 *Illud non est naturale quod non manet idem apud omnes; sed nullum iustum manet idem apud omnes*, Ms. Vat. lat. 832, s. xiiiex, from the Arts Faculty in Paris, Lottin, IV. ii, p. 543.
54 *Mandat, quod prosit, ut amicitiam collere; prohibet quod ledit, ut occidere.* Summa 'Elegantius', Part I (38), p. 11.
55 *Ordo praeceptorum legis naturae.*
56 *Ordo inclinationum naturalium*, Aquinas, *ST*, II i q. xciv a. 2.
57 *Pertinent ad legem naturalem.*
58 *Quod homo ignorantiam vitet.*
59 *Quod alios non offendat cum quibus debet conversari*, Aquinas, *ST*, II i q. xciv a. 2.
60 *Ius naturale [est] ad quod intellectus cuiuslibet bene dispositus assentit.*
61 Ms. Vat. lat. 832, s. xiiiex, from the Arts Faculty in Paris, Lottin, IV. ii, p. 543.
62 *Sicut conclusiones ex principiis.*
63 Aquinas, *ST*, II i q. xcv a. 2.
64 Aquinas, *ST*, II i q. xcv a. 2.
65 *Derivatum a iure naturali non sicut conclusio derivatur a premissis.*
66 *Sicut ex premissis necessariis non sequitur nisi conclusio necessaria, ita ex premissis que sunt iuste iustitia naturali sequitur conclusio iusta naturaliter.*
67 *Non est nocendum iniuste alteri, sed furari est iniuste nocere alteri, ergo non est furandum.*
68 *Ista conclusio est ius naturale, sicut premisse.*
69 *Sed magis per modum cuiusdam determinationis et contractionis.*
70 Ms. Vat. lat. 832, s. xiiiex, from the Arts Faculty in Paris, Lottin, IV ii, p. 543.
71 Walter Ullmann, 'Baldus's conception of law', *Law Quarterly Review*, lviii (London, 1942), p. 392.
72 *Unde et ipsa participatur ratio aeterna.* Aquinas, *ST*, II i q. xci a. 2.
73 *Participatio legis aeternae in rationali creatura.* Aquinas, *ST*, II i q. xci a. 2.
74 Alger of Liège, *On mercy and justice*, Preface, ed. Robert Krezschman, *Quellen und Forschungen zum Recht im Mittelalters*, 2 (Sigmaringen, 1985), pp. 187–9.
75 *Quoniam aliae aliis gentibus placent.* Isidore, *Etymologiae*, V. 2, Gratian, *Concordia Discordantium Canonum*, Dist. I. i, *PL*, 187. 29.
76 *Extra territorium ius dicenti impune non paretur. Idem est, et si supra jurisdictionem suam velit ius dicere. Digest*, II. i. 20 (Paulus).
77 *Select Cases on Defamation to 1600*, ed. R. Helmholz, Selden Society, 101 (London, 1985), pp. xxiv–xxv.

Notes 187

78 *Ius ergo, sit naturale sit morale, aut scriptura aut usu solo perpetuatur.*
79 *Summa 'Elegantius'*, Part I (10), p. 3.
80 *Mosis consuetudo antiquitate venerabilis. Summa 'Elegantius'*, Part I (11), p. 3.
81 *Consuetudinis auctoritas is non vilis sed vigens. Summa 'Elegantius'*, Part I (16), p. 4.
82 *Summa 'Elegantius'*, Part I (14), p. 4.
83 Aquinas, *ST*, II i q. xcvii a. 3 ad 3.
84 *Lex tollat consuetudinem.*
85 *Non vilis est auctoritas.*
86 Isidore, *Etymologiae*, V. 3 and II. 10, Gratian, *Decretum*, I, Dist. I, I.V.
87 *Ius quoddam moribus institutum.*
88 Isidore, *Etymologiae*, V. 3 and II. 10, Gratian, *Decretum*, I, Dist. I. i.
89 *An scriptura, an ratione consistat, quando et legem ratio commendat. Porro si ratione lex constat, let erit omne iam, quod rationi constiterit, dumtaxat quod religioni conveniat quod disciplinae congruat, quod saluti proficiat.* Isidore, *Etymologiae*, V. 3 and II. 10, Gratian, *Decretum*, I, Dist I. i.
90 Gratian, *Decretum*, I, Dist. I. i.
91 *Fleta*, ed. and tr. H. G. Richardson and G. O. Sayles, Selden Society, 72 (1955), II, p. 2.
92 Aquinas, *ST*, II i q. xcvii a. 1.
93 Augustine, *De Libero Arbitrio*, I. 6, CCSL, 29.
94 *Cum leges instituuntur, de futuris dari tantum debent, non de preteritis. Summa 'Elegantius'*, Part I (26), p. 7.
95 *An ... per canones posteriores prioribus derogetur.*
96 *Quanto iuniores tanto perspicaciores in iure.*
97 *Ipsa legis mutatio, quantum in se est, detrimentum quoddam communis salutis.*
98 Aquinas, *ST*, II i q. xcvii a. 2.
99 *Unde quandoque mutatur lex, diminuitur vis constrictiva legis, inquantum tollitur consuetudo.* Aquinas, *ST*, II i q. xcvii a. 2.
100 *In rebus novis constituendis, evidens debet esse utilitas, ut recedatur ab eo iure quod diu aequum visum est.* Aquinas, *ST*, II i q. xcvii a. 2.
101 Gratian, *Concordia Discordantium Canonum*, Dist. V. 2, *PL*, 187. 37–8.
102 Marsilius of Padua, *Defensor Minor*, ed. Cary J. Nederman (Cambridge, 1993).
103 'Divine law is the immediate precept of God without human deliberation regarding voluntary acts committed or omitted in the present world towards the best end or condition in the future world which human beings are suited to pursue'. Disc. I. 10. Marsilius of Padua, *Defensor Minor*, I. ii, ed. Cary J. Nederman (Cambridge, 1993), p. 1, tr. Nederman.
104 *Extra territorium ius dicenti impune non paretur. Digest*, II. 1. 20.
105 LXXIV *tituli*, p. 52 ff.
106 See my *The Church and the Churches* (Cambridge, 1994).
107 See my *The Church and the Churches* (Cambridge, 1994).
108 See my *The Church and the Churches* (Cambridge, 1994), pp. 199–212.
109 *Summa 'Elegantius'*, Part XII (90), p. 212.
110 *Summa 'Elegantius'*, Part IX (78), p. 86.
111 *Summa 'Elegantius'*, Part XI (102), p. 167.
112 *Digest*, 50. 17, no. 29,
113 Augustine, *Epistulae*, 138. 1, *CSEL*, 44, p. 130.
114 Augustine, *Epistulae*, 166. 8, *CSEL*, 44, p. 579.
115 Augustine, *De peccatorum meritis*, I. 20.xxvi, *CSEL*, 60, p. 25.
116 *At cum rite in ecclesia Christi sacramenta celebrantur Christi uerbum auditur et conseruatur, qui est sapientia Dei, constat quod angelicae uirtutes ibi sint et*

188 Notes

in excelsis caelorum conuiuae fidelium, Bede, *In prouerbia Salomonis*, 1. 9, CCSL, 119B.

117 *Sacramentorum rite sollemnia celebrantur, confessiones fiunt, ad ecclesiam conveniunt plebes.* Bernard of Clairvaux, *Vita sancti Malachiae*, 17, *Opera Omnia*, III, p. 326.
118 Augustine, *Epistulae*, 187. 13, CSEL, 57, p. 118.
119 Augustine, *Epistulae*, 233, CSEL, 57, p. 517.
120 Isidore, *Etymologiae*, V. 24.
121 *Summa 'Elegantius'*, Part XI (12), p. 130.
122 Bede, *In Ezram et Neemiam*, 1. 444, CCSL, 119A.
123 Bede, *In Ezram et Neemiam*, 1. 1458, CCSL, 119A.
124 Bede, *In Ezram et Neemiam*, 3. 618, CCSL, 119A.
125 Bernard of Clairvaux, *Sermones super Cantica Canticorum*, 46, 2, *Opera Omnia*, I, p. 57.
126 Bernard of Clairvaux, *Epistulae*, *Opera Omnia*, VIII, p. 458.
127 *Inveniuntur in Germania mulierum irregulares conventus, que, albis indute, propria habere et privata receptacula facere contra sacros canones permittuntur, cum periculose sint in lubrico sexu libertas et familiaritas.* Summa *'Elegantius'*, Part XI (79), p. 155.

6 The court system

1 *Fleta*, II. 2, ed. and tr. H. G. Richardson and G. Sayles, Selden Society, 72 (1955), II, p. 109.
2 *Fleta*, II. 2, ed. and tr. H. G. Richardson and G. Sayles, Selden Society, 72 (1955), II, p. 109.
3 *Fleta*, II. 2, ed. and tr. H. G. Richardson and G. Sayles, Selden Society, 72 (1955), II, p. 109.
4 *Fleta*, II. 2, ed. and tr. H. G. Richardson and G. Sayles, Selden Society, 72 (1955), II, p. 109.
5 *Fleta*, II. 2, ed. and tr. H.G. Richardson and G. Sayles, Selden Society, 72 (1955), II, p. 109.
6 Charles Donahue, 'The monastic judge: social practice, formal rule and the mediaeval canon law of incest', *Studia Gratiana*, xxvii (1996), pp. 49–69.
7 *Select Cases from the Ecclesiastical Courts of the Province of Canterbury*, p. 7.
8 Gratian, *Decretum*, I, Dist. 1, xviii.17.
9 C. R. Cheney, *English Synodalia of the Thirteenth Century* (Oxford, 1941), 2nd. edn (1968), p. 3.
10 *Nam si sua unicuique episcopo iurisdictio non servatur quid aliud agitur, nisi ut per nos, per quos ecclesiasticus custodiri debet ordo, confundatur.* Gratian, *Decretum*, *Causa* XI. 1. 39.
11 Gratian, *Decretum*, II, *Causa* XVI. 1. 47.
12 *Qui iurisdictioni preest.* Gratian, *Decretum*, *Causa* III. 7. 2, from *Digest*.
13 *Apostolica auctoritas a iurisdictione archiepiscopi episcopos valet eximere.* Gratian, *Decretum*, II, *Causa* XVI. 1. 52.
14 'More easily and more securely': legal procedure and due process at the Council of Constance'. *Popes, Teachers and Canon Law in the Middle Ages*, ed. James Ross Sweeney and Stanley Chodorow (Ithaca and London, 1989), pp. 234–47.
15 *Select Cases from …Canterbury*, p. 8.
16 D.E. Heintschel, *The Mediaeval Concept of an Ecclesiastical Office* (Washington, 1956) and A. C. Rouco, *Le primat de l'Évêque de Rome* (Fribourg, 1990), p. 117 and see p. 112, note 302 for bibliography.

17 Occurring only ten times.
18 Gratian, *Decretum*, II, *Causa* XXIII. 1. 1.
19 Fitting, Irnerius, *Titulus* II. 6, p. 51.
20 *In patrimonio siquidem beati Petri sunt eiusdem ordinis monasteria in quibus, licet spiritualiter et temporaliter ad dispositionem nostram pertineant, nil tamen per nos ipso corrigimus, sed si quid inibi fuerit corrigendum, per patres abbates corrigitur emendatur.* Decretales ineditae s. xii, *Monumenta Iuris Canonici*, Series B: *Corpus Collectioneum*, 4 (Vatican, 1982) 5, p. 10.
21 *De Rescriptis: habet ergo iurisdictionem, licet non habeat exercitium, unde non potest mandare alii jurisdictionem.* Johannes Teutonicus, *Apparatus glossarum in compilationem tertium*, ed. K. Pennington (Vatican, 1981), I. i, p. 11.
22 Marsilius of Padua, *Defensor Minor*, I. i, ed. Cary J. Nederman (Cambridge, 1993), p. 1.
23 *Qui susceptum offficium non administrat, non est episcopus, sed canis impudicus.* Gratian, *Decretum, Causa* II, 7. 32.
24 *Generaliter enim tam ecclesiae quam res ecclesiarum in episcoporum potestate consistunt. Laici autem nec sua, nec episcoporum auctoritate decimas vel ecclesias possidere possunt.* Gratian, *Decretum, Causa* XVI. 7. pr.
25 A.C.Rouco, *Le primat de l'Évêque de Rome* (Fribourg, 1990), pp. 121–2.
26 Gratian, *Decretum*, II, *Causa* VII. 1. 16.
27 Gratian, *Decretum*, II, *Causa* X. 1. 5.
28 Gratian, *Decretum*, II, *Causa* XII. 2. 32.
29 *Presbyteri de occultis peccatis iussione episcopi penitentes reconcilient.* Gratian, *Decretum*, II, *Causa* XXVI. 6. 4
30 *Clericus vel laicus sine iussione episcopi non peregrinetur.* Gratian, *De Consecratione*, rubric, 5.37.
31 *Potestas iudicandi requiritur. Pilii, Tancredi, Gratiae Libri de Iudiciorum Ordine*, ed. F. Bergmann (Göttingen, 1842), p. 320.
32 *Digest* 10. 3. 18. The decretals often give solutions to direct questions and specify the powers of a judge-delegate in a particular case. C. Lefebvre, 'Juges et savants en Europe, xiiie–xvie siècle', *Ephemerides Iuris Canonici*, 22 (1966), p. 81.
33 *Diversorum patrum sententie sive Collectio in LXXIV titulos digesta*, ed. J. T. Gilchrist, *Monumenta Iuris Canonici*, 1 (Vatican, 1973), p. 52ff.
34 *Et nulla sententia a quolibet iudicium vim firmitatis obteneat, quae modum legis adque aequitatis excedit.* Dated about 560, Cap. 1.8, in J. Balon, *Grand dictionnaire de droit du moyen âge, Ius Medii Aevi*, 5 (Belgium, 1972), Aequitas.
35 *Summa 'Elegantius in iure divino'*, Part V (68 and 69), p. 86.
36 *Ut nemo dissentiat a Romanae ecclesiae, quae est caput omnium ecclesiarum* (1. 11), p. 11.
37 *Quod prima salus est regulae rectae fide custodire et a statutis patrum non deviare.*
38 *Quod Romana ecclesia omnibus est prelata non tantum canonum decretis sed voce ipsius salvatoris.*
39 *Ut prima sedes a nullo iudicetur.*
40 *Ut nemo presumat iudicium primae sedis retractare aut iudicare.*
41 *Quod papa a nullo nisi a Deo erit iudicandus.*
42 S. Chodorow, 'Ideology and Canon Law in the Crisis of 1111', *Proceedings of the Fourth Congress on Mediaeval Canon Law* (1976), 55–80 is useful here.
43 S. Chodorow, 'Ideology and Canon Law in the Crisis of 1111', *Proceedings of the Fourth Congress on Mediaeval Canon Law* (1976), p. 59.
44 Virtue here is 'power'.

190 Notes

45 S. Chodorow, 'Ideology and Canon Law in the Crisis of 1111', *Proceedings of the Fourth Congress on Mediaeval Canon Law* (1976), p. 63.
46 S. Chodorow, 'Ideology and Canon Law in the Crisis of 1111', *Proceedings of the Fourth Congress on Mediaeval Canon Law* (1976), p. 62.
47 *Contra statuta sanctorum Patrum agit qui ea non servat intacta* (XXV. i. 16). What is reasonably prescribed ought not to be violated (XXV. ii. 9).
48 *Non licet Pontifici ab ecclesiae iure discedere, quod documentorum auctoritate firmatur* (XXV. i. 21).
49 XXV. i. i. 6.
50 *Sibi specialiter reservavit ... legem condit generalem. Ens non esse facit, non ens fore pallia semper. portat. Concedit, legi nec subditus ulli... iudiciumque? Est pro lege suum*. Robert C. Figueira, 'Papal reserved powers and the limitations on legatine authority', *Popes, Teachers and Canon Law in the Middle Ages*, ed. James Ross Sweeney and Stanley Chodorow (Ithaca and London, 1989), p. 199.
51 *In quos onera actionis officio iudicis translata sunt* (*Digest* 10. 2. 3).
52 *Delegatus nisi ex delegantis auctoritate nichil habet in lite*.
53 C. Lefebvre, 'Juges et savants en Europe, xiiie–xvie siècle', *Ephemerides Iuris Canonici* 22 (1966), p. 81.
54 See Mary Cheney, 'Pope Alexander III and Roger, Bishop of Worcester, 1164–1179: the exchange of ideas', 'Fourth International Conference on Mediaeval Canon Law', *Monumenta Iuris Canonici Subsidia*, 5 (1976), p. 209.
55 Robert C. Figueira, 'Papal reserved powers and the limitations on legatine authority', *Popes, Teachers and Canon Law in the Middle Ages*, ed. James Ross Sweeney and Stanley Chodorow (Ithaca and London, 1989), pp. 191–211, pp. 206–11.
56 *Interest ergo ipsius mandatum inspicere et formam tenere. Summa 'Elegantius'*, Part VII (1), p. 151.
57 *Sed et si iudex constitutiones principum neglexerit, punitur*, *Digest* 48. 10. 1. 3.

7 Law schools

1 Manlio Bellomo, *The Common Legal Past of Europe, 1000–1800*, tr. L. G. Cochrane (1988, tr. Washington, 1995), p. 34 ff.
2 *Popes, Teachers and Canon Law in the Middle Ages*, ed. J. R. Sweeney and Stanley Chodorow (Ithaca, 1989).
3 Magister Arnulfus speaks of *nos minores*, raising the question whether he means Masters of Arts rather than those engaged in the higher study of law. Magister Arnulphus, *Summa Minorum, Quellen*, I. ii (1905), p. xvi.
4 Manlio Bellomo, *The Common Legal Past of Europe, 1000–1800*, tr. L. G. Cochrane (1988, tr. Washington, 1995), p. 124.
5 Manlio Bellomo, *The Common Legal Past of Europe, 1000–18000*, tr. L. G.Cochrane (1988, tr. Washington, 1995), p. 136.
6 C. Lefebvre, 'Juges et savants en Europe, xiiie–xvie siècle', *Ephemerides Iuris Canonici* 22 (1966), p. 82.
7 A. Artonne, 'L'influence du décret de Gratien sur les statuts synodaux', *Studia Gratiana*, 2 (1956), 645–56.
8 P. Brand, 'Courtroom and schoolroom: the education of lawyers in England prior to 1400', *Bulletin of the Institute of Historical Research* (1987), 147–65.
9 On the unresolved debate about Vacarius and Oxford, see Vacarius, *Liber Paurerum*, ed. F. de Zulueta, Selden Society, 44 (1927), introduction, p. xvii and F. de Zulueta and Peter Stein, *The Teaching of Roman Law in England around 1200*, p. xxii ff.

10 *Sic leget cum glossis et expositione textus, secundum quod auditoribus magis videbitur expedire. Munimenta Academica*, ed. H. Anstey, Rolls Series (1857), 2 vols, vol. 2, p. 404.
11 *Munimenta Academica*, ed. H. Anstey, Rolls Series (1857), 2 vols, vol. 2, pp. 398–402.
12 *Select Cases from ... Canterbury*, p. 22.
13 Wilkins, *Concilia*, ii, 27.
14 P. Brand, 'Courtroom and schoolroom: the education of lawyers in England prior to 1400', *Bulletin of the Institute of Historical Research* (1987), p. 151.
15 *The Earliest English Law Reports*, ed. Paul A. Brand, Selden Society (1996), p. cxxxv.
16 *Readings and Moots*, Selden Society, 105, pp. liv–lvi.

8 Creating the academic discipline of law

1 C. Gallagher, 'Canon law and the Christian community: the role of law in the Church according to the Summa Aurea of Cardinal Hostiensis', *Analecta Gregoriana* (Rome, 1978).
2 See pp. 61ff. and 70ff.
3 On *schemata* of study in the twelfth century which included tabulations of various sorts, see R. W. Southern, *Mediaeval Humanism* (Oxford, 1970) and G. R. Evans, *Old Arts and New Theology* (Oxford, 1980).
4 For convenience, see Robert Somerville and Bruce Brasington, *Prefaces to Canon Law Books in Latin Christianity: Selected Translations, 500–1245* (Yale, 1998), pp. 46–7, 54, 98.
5 H. Kantorowicz, *Studies in the Glossators of the Roman Law* (Cambridge, 1938), p. 38.
6 See R.B. C. Huygens, *Accessus ad Auctores* (Leiden, 1970).
7 *Bonum et malum et voluntates hominum sunt materia huius scientiae*. Baldus de Ubaldis, *Commentaries ad Digestum Vetus* (Venice, 1616), *De iustitia et iure*, 5. Walter Ullmann, 'Baldus's conception of law', *Law Quarterly Review*, lviii (London, 1942), p. 388.
8 *Philosophia moralis est legum mater et ianua.*
9 *Ius nostrum applicat sibi totam moralem philosophiam*, Baldus de Ubaldis, *Commentaries ad Digestum Vetus* (Venice, 1616), *De iustitia et iure*, 6. Walter Ullmann,'Baldus's conception of law', *Law Quarterly Review*, lviii (London, 1942), p. 387.
10 *Summa 'Elegantius'*, Part 1 (46), p. 13.
11 H. Kantorowicz, *Studies in the Glossators of the Roman Law* (Cambridge, 1938), p. 42.
12 *Intentio est horum observationem monere quia qui iura negligit fasque nefasque confundit*, *Summa 'Elegantius'*, 1, Part 1 (46), p. 13.
13 H.Kantorowicz, *Studies in the Glossators of the Roman Law* (Cambridge, 1938), p. 37.
14 *Proinde ad consilia et negotia ecclesiastica valet, et ad hoc dupliciter ut presentium lector iuris questiones per rationes et auctoritate instituere et eventilatas iudici terminare paratior habeatur*, *Summa 'Elegantius'*, Part I (1), p. 1.
15 *Finis est ut ignari erudiantur, prevaricatores arceantur et corrigantur, conservatores eterne vita premio remunerentur. Sicque pro causa duplici probitati studeatur: comminatione pene et glorie promissione, ut hinc timor pungat, inde amore invitet*, *Summa 'Elegantius'*, Part 1 (48), p. 14.

16 *Auctoritas apostolorum, auctoritas canonica* are cited in J. Balon, *Grand dictionnaire*. *Auctoritas legalis* and *auctoritas legitima* are found from 873, though their exact sense is unclear, J. Balon, *Grand dictionnaire*.
17 See pp. 11ff.
18 I have looked at these themes in *The Language and Logic of the Bible* (Cambridge, 1984–5), 2 vols.
19 *Summa 'Elegantius'*, Part XII, (59), pp. 195.
20 *Summa 'Elegantius'*, Part XII, pp. 193ff.
21 *Nam leges principum que multorum erant voluminum in xii libros redegit, consuetudines que in tribus codicibus erant conscripte, Gregoriano, Hermogeniano et Theodosiano et novellarum libro, in uno componens codice, suo enim felici nomine decoravit, et leges magistratuum.* Summa 'Elegantius', I, Part 1 (23), p. 6.
22 *Demum novas leges quas ipse condiderat in unum volumen redigens, codicem novellarum appellavit,* Summa 'Elegantius', I, Part 1 (23), p. 6.
23 J. A. Clarence Smith, *Medieval Law Teachers and Writers* (Ottawa, 1975).
24 A group of three manuscripts is cited by F. Patetta, *Studi sulle fonti giuridiche medievali* (Turin, 1967), p. 219, and see the facsimile in F. Chiappelli, *La glossa Pistoiese al Codice Giustinianeo* (Turin, 1885).
25 F. Patetta, *Studi sulle fonti giuridiche medievali* (Turin, 1967), p. 1 ff.
26 Kantorowicz, *Studies in the Glossators* (Cambridge, 1938), p. 33, discusses problems with the attribution to Irnerius of the texts published as his by Fitting.
27 John of Salisbury uses the *Digest* in *Policraticus* V, ed. C. C. J. Webb (Oxford, 1909), CCCM, 118, even though there is much else he could have drawn on. Does he do so because he wants to show off his knowledge of the *Roman* material?
28 The *Digest* seems to have come back into use at the end of the eleventh century, when Ivo cites it: S. Kuttner, 'The revival of jurisprudence', *Studies in the History of Mediaeval Canon Law* (London, 1990), p. 299.
29 C. Munier, 'Les sources patristiques du droit de l'Église du viii au xiiie siécle', *Revue du droit canonique*, 4 (Strasbourg, 1954), p. 185.
30 Augustine is as much used as all the others put together. C. Munier, 'Les sources patristiques du droit de l'Église du viii au xiiie siècle', *Revue du droit canonique*, 4 (Strasbourg, 1954), p. 186.
31 C. Munier, 'Les sources patristiques du droit de l'Église du viii au xiiie siècle', *Revue du droit canonique*, 4 (Strasbourg, 1954), p. 185.
32 C. Munier, 'Les sources patristiques du droit de l'Église du viii au xiiie siècle', *Revue du droit canonique*, 4 (Strasbourg, 1954), p. 187.
33 C. Munier, 'Les sources patristiques du droit de l'Église du viii au xiiie siècle', *Revue du droit canonique*, 4 (Strasbourg, 1954), p. 185.
34 Hubert Mordek, *Kirchenrecht und Reform im Frankenreich* (Berlin/New York, 1975).
35 Richard H. Rouse and Mary A. Rouse, 'Ennodius in the Middle Ages: Adonics, Pseudo-Isidore, Cistercians and the Schools', in *Popes, Teachers and Canon Law in the Middle Ages*, ed. James Ross Sweeney and Stanley Chodorow (Ithaca and London, 1989), p. 100. (Vat. lat 630 and Leipzig Universitätsbibliothek II. 7).
36 B. Blumenkranz, 'Deux compilations canoniques de Florus de Lyon et l'Action Antijuive d'Agobard', *Revue historique de droit français et étranger*, 4, xxxiii (1955), 227–54 and 560–82.
37 The rediscovered *Digest* represented a substantially different recension from that which had been preserved from the late sixth century in a single manuscript which was (by the twelfth century) at Pisa. This conspicuous differ-

ence made it necessary for the school at Bologna eventually to distinguish the *Littera Pisana* from the *Littera Bononiensis*. This came to be known as the Florentina because it was carried off to Florence in 1406.
38 S. Kuttner, 'Harmony from dissonance: an interpretation of mediaeval canon law', *The History of Ideas and Doctrines of Canon Law in the Middle Ages* (London, 1980), p. 7.
39 Paul Fournier, *Yves de Chartres et le droit canonique* (Paris, 1898), p. 2 ff. Yvo of Chartres' *Panormia* is unquestionably his; the *Decretum* probably so, the *Tripartita* probably not. Fournier seeks to show that the *Tripartita* is the source of the *Decretum*, the *Decretum* of the *Panormia*. Paul Fournier, *Les collections canoniques attribués à Yves de Chartres* (Paris, 1897), pp. 1–2.
40 Robert Somerville and Bruce Brasington, *Prefaces to Canon Law Books in Katin Christianity: Selected Translations, 500–1245* (Yale, 1998), p. 170.
41 S. Kuttner, 'New studies on Roman Law in Gratian's Decretum', *Seminar: An Annual Extraordinary Number of the Jurist*, 11 (Washington, 1953), p. 17ff.
42 See S. Kuttner, 'New studies on Roman Law in Gratian's Decretum', *Seminar: An Annual Extraordinary Number of the Jurist*, 11 (Washington, 1953), p. 17.
43 S. Kuttner, 'Zur Frage der theologischen Vorlagen Gratians', reprinted in S. Kuttner, *Gratian and the Schools of Law* (London, 1983), p. 245.
44 Johannes Teutonicus seems to have found a 'Sic et Non' approach the only realistic possibility, leaving a number of matters hypothetical.
45 A.Vetulani, *Sur Gratien et les Décrétales* (Variorum, Aldershot, 1990). See, too, R. Metz, 'La contribution de la France à l'étude du décret de Gratien depuis le xvie siècle jusqu'à nos jours', *Studia Gratiana*, 2 (1956), 496–518. Johannes Teutonicus, *Glosses to the Compilatio Tertia*, ed. K. Pennington, *Monumenta Iuris Canonici*, Series A: *Corpus Glossatorum*, 3, 1981, p. xi.
46 *Canones in quam pluribus locis vage passimque dispersos ordinata quidem dispositione componere et eorum contrarietates interiectis distinctionibus unire. Die Summa Decretorum des Magister Rufinus*, ed. H. Singer (Paderborn, 1902), Preface, p. 5.
47 G.Fransen, *Les Décrétales et les collections de Décrétales, Les collections canoniques*, Fasc.2 *Typologie*, 10 (1972), p. 34.
48 Gregory IX, *Decretalium Collectiones, Corpus Iuris Canonici*, ed. A. L. Richter and E. Friedberg (Leipzig, 1881), vol. 2, p. 2.
49 *Sane diversas constitutiones et decretales epistolas praedecessorum nostrorum, in diversa dispersas volumina, quarum aliquae propter nimiam similitudinem, et quaedam propter contrarietatem, nonnullae etiam propter sui prolixitatem, confusionem inducere videbantur.*
50 *Prolixitas Gratiani aut tediosa aut inexplicabilis.*
51 *Summa 'Elegantius'*, Part I (1), p. 1.
52 The *Decretals* of 1234 show a great deal of the influence of Alexander III. But there is no real indication of a grand plan of development. See Mary Cheney, 'Pope Alexander III and Roger, Bishop of Worcester, 1164–1179: the exchange of ideas', Fourth International Conference on Mediaeval Canon Law, *Monumenta Iuris Canonici Subsidia*, 5 (1976), p. 207.
53 *Extravagantes Johannes XXII*, ed. J. Tarrant, *Monumenta Iuris Canonici*, Series B: *Corpus Collectionum*, 6 (Rome, 1983), p. 1. with the commentary of Jesselinus (completed 1325).
54 *The Earliest English Law Reports*, ed. Paul A. Brand, Selden Society III (1996).
55 *Select Cases in the Court of Kings Bench under Edward I*, ed. G. O. Sales, Selden Society, 57 (1938), pp. xv–xix.
56 David d'Avray, *The Preaching of Friars* (Oxford, 1985).
57 *PL*, 210.

194   *Notes*

58 Bulgarus was born before 1100; Martinus (fl. mid-twelfth century). Bulgarus d.1166; Martinus, Hugo, Jacobus (d.1178); Johannes Azo (d.1220); Placentinus (d.1192); Pillius. On all these see H. Kantorowicz, 'The *Quaestiones Disputatae* of the Glossators', *La revue d'histoire du droit*, xvi. 1 (1937/8), 1–67. Various French schools of Roman law grew up as offshoots of Bologna. Rogerius is a contemporary of the Four Doctors. See H. Kantorowicz, *Studies in the Glossators of the Roman Law* (Cambridge, 1938), pp. 87, 112.
59 *Pilii, Tancredi, Gratiae Libri de Iudiciorum Ordine*, ed. F. Bergmann (Göttingen, 1842), p. 319.
60 On the influence of theologians on Hostiensis, see C. Lefebvre, 'Hostiensis, maître de l'equité canonique', *Ephemerides Iuris Canonici* 28 (1972), p. 13.
61 See introductory remarks to the edition of G. Franken and S. Kuttner, *Monumenta iuris Canonici: Corpus Glossatorum*, I (New York, 1969), I.
62 *In causis inchoandis exercendis et iudicio terminandis. Summa 'Elegantius'*, Part I (1), p. 1.
63 Johannes Teutonicus, *Apparatus glossarum in compilationem tertium*, ed. K. Pennington (Vatican, 1981), p. xi. He is also the author of a Gloss on Gratian's *Decretum*, which is less coherent and original.
64 See *Commentaria in Digestum* (Venice, 1615), fol. 90va and Manlio Bellomo, *The Common Legal Past of Europe, 1000–1800*, tr. L. G. Cochrane (1988, tr. Washington, 1995), p. 135.

9 The professional advocate

1 *Select Cases from ... Canterbury*, pp. 53–4, discusses an example, but points out that such records are unusual.
2 Tacitus, *Dialogus de oratoribus*, 20.3, ed. W. Peterson and M. Winterbottom (London, 1970), p. 235.
3 Eleanor Stump, *Boethius, De topicis differentiis* (Ithaca/London, 1978).
4 On this, see R. B. C. Huygens, *Accessus ad Auctores* (Leiden, 1970).
5 *Intentio ... instruere personas in iudici constituendas, partim secundum artificiosam doctrinam rhetorum. Die Rhetorica ecclesiastica, Quellen*, I iv, p. 2.
6 *Advocatum habemus apud Patrem Jesum Christum iustum.* 1 John 2. 1.
7 Ambrose of Milan, *De Jacob et Vita Beata*, I. vi. 21, CSEL, 32 ii. p. 18.
8 *Ego causam non habeo; causam tamen Divionensium monachorum, quia viri religiosi sunt, meam. Manu tenete eam ut meam, sic tamen mean, ut et iustitiae sit. facio.* Letter 16, *Bernardi Opera Omnia*, 7. 64.
9 Augustine, *In Iohannis evangelium tractatus*, 74. 4, line 2.
10 Ps.-Tertullian, *Adversus omnes haereses*.
11 See p. 66.
12 Cyprian, *De opere et eleemosynis*, 6.123.
13 *Non ... debet iudex vendere iustum iudicium aut testis verum testimonium.*
14 Augustine, *Epistulae* 153. 6, CSEL, 44, p. 423.
15 *The Earliest English Law Reports*, ed. Paul A. Brand, Selden Society (1996), p. cxxxvi.
16 Ricardus Anglicus, *Die Summa de ordine iudiciario* (XVI), *Quellen*, II. iii, p. 13.
17 R. Helmholz, 'Ethical standards for advocates and proctors in theory and practice', *Canon Law and the Law of England*, p. 43.
18 *Et quia socius non tantum suum sed et alienum quasi ex mandato tacito gerit negotium.* Placentinus, *Die Summa 'De actionum varietatibus' des Placentinus*, XLIV, ed. Wahrmund, *Quellen* IV. iii, p. 70.
19 *Qui vero alieno nominem agit vel convenitur, aut certum est, eum habere mandatum aut non habere aut dubitatio de mandato.* Ricardus Anglicus, *Die Summa de ordine iudiciario*, XVIII, *Quellen*, p. 19.

20 *Cotidie advocatus pro nobis est apud patrem.*
21 Ambrose, *Expositio Psalmorum cxviii*, 21. xiv, p. 481.
22 *Si quid in eum quandoque delinquat, de proprio suo prout fuerit iustum sibi emendet.*
23 *Memorials of St. Anselm*, ed. R. W. Southern and F. S. Schmitt (London, 1969), pp. 72–3.
24 *Qui iurisdictioni piae est, neque sibi ius dicere debet neque uxori vel liberis suis Seque libertis vel ceteris, quos secum habet. Digest*, II. 1. 10 (Ulpian).
25 Tertullian, *De Pudicitia*, CCSL, 16.
26 Augustine, *Sermo* 213.
27 *Nemo iudex* and *audi alteram partem* both have this prupose.
28 *Item si [iudex aut] executor vel advocatus in aliqua causa fuisti, in eadem non es exaudiendus ut testis.* Summa 'Elegantius', II, Part VI (73), p. 136. The principle that the same person cannot be judge and witness is repeated by the Summa 'Elegantius'. Summa 'Elegantius', Part VII (3), p. 154.
29 *Sicut autem non potest idem esse testis et hostis, sic qui hostis est iudex esse non debet.*
30 *Internecivum iudicium in eum dabatur qui falsum testamentum fecerat et ob id hominem occiderat. Accusatorem eius possessio bonorum sequebatur. Internecivi autem significatio est, quasi quaedam hominis enectio. Nam praepositionem inter pro e ponebant,* Isidore, *Etymologiae*, V. 26.
31 *Select Cases in Manorial Courts 1250–1550*, ed. L. R. Poos and Lloyd Bonfied, Selden Society, (1998), p. xxxiv.
32 John S. Beckerman, 'Procedural innovation and institutional change in mediaeval English manorial courts', *Law and History Review*, 10 (1992), pp. 198–201.
33 Ricardus Anglicus, *Die Summa de ordine iudiciario* (XI), p. 8.
34 *Digest*, 3. 1.1.4.
35 William de Drogheda, *Quellen*, xlviii, p. 48.
36 *Tunc ei dandus est, etiam non petenti.* W. Ullmann, 'The defence of the accused in the medieval inquisition', *The Irish Ecclesiastical Record*, lxxiii (Dublin, 1950), 481–9, p. 482.
37 William de Drogheda, xxv, xcviii, p. 91.
38 *Roffredi Beneventani Libelli Iuris Civilis, Corpus Glossatorum Iuris Civilis* (1968) Part I, vol. 6, p. 7, col. 1.
39 *Roffredi Beneventani Libelli Iuris Civilis, Corpus Glossatorum Iuris Civilis* (1968) Part I, vol. 6, p. 7, col. 1.
40 Ricardus Anglicus, *Die Summa de ordine iudiciario* (XIX), *Quellen*, II. iii. p. 22.
41 James A. Brundage, 'Professional discipline in the mediaeval courts Christian: the Candlesby case', *Studia Gratiana*, xxvii (1996), p. 48.
42 *Ordo legis peritorum vel potius legis picatorum.* E. Rathbone, 'Roman Law in the Anglo-Norman Realm', *Studia Gratiana XI, Collectanea S. Kuttner*, 1 (Bologna, 1967), p. 256.
43 E. Rathbone, 'Roman Law in the Anglo-Norman Realm', *Studia Gratiana XI, Collectanea S. Kuttner*, 1 (Bologna, 1967), pp. 256–7.
44 William of Drogheda's *Summa Aurea*, *Quellen*, II. ii, p. 94.
45 William of Drogheda's *Summa Aurea*, *Quellen*, II. ii, p. 95.
46 *Select Cases from ... Canterbury*, p. 23.
47 *Select Cases from ... Canterbury*, p. 24.
48 Some names of advocates are given in *Select Cases from ... Canterbury*, p. 22.
49 *The Earliest English Law Reports*, ed. Paul A. Brand, Selden Society (1996), p. cxix.

196 Notes

50 *The Earliest English Law Reports*, ed. Paul A. Brand, Selden Society (1996), p. cxxxi, and Paul A. Brand, *Origins of the English Legal Profession* (Oxford, 1992), p. vii.
51 Wilkins, *Concilia*, ii, 27.
52 *A List of English Law Officers. King's Counsel and Holders of Patents of Precedence*, Selden Society, Supplementary Series, 7 (1987), p. 285.
53 *Qui quoquo studio causis agendis operatur*, William de Drogheda, xviii, p. 36.
54 *Quia non solum militant, qui gladiis et thoracibus et clipeis nituntur, sed etiam patronis causarum, qui gloriosae vocis confisi munimine laborantium spem vitamque defendunt .... Postulare is: desiderium suum vel amicis sui apud eum, qui iurisdictionis praeest, exponere agendo, respondendo, voluntati rei contradicendo*, William de Drogheda, xxxiv, p. 37.
55 *The Earliest English Law Reports*, ed. Paul A. Brand, Selden Society 111, (1996), p. cxxxvi.
56 R. Helmholz, 'Ethical standards for advocates and proctors', *Canon Law and the Law of England*, p. 43.
57 *Select Cases from ... Canterbury*, p. 22, note 5 for a list of similar oaths required to be taken elsewhere.
58 William de Drogheda, xxxvi, p. 39.
59 *Prohibentur advocati, ne iudicibus atrocitatem verborum inferant...rationibus contendant. Non prorumpant ad temeritatem conviciandi vel maledicendi, neque contra partem neque contra iudicem agant*, William de Drogheda, xlvi, p. 45.
60 *Infames efficientur et diminutionem opinionis patientur*, William de Drogheda, xlvii, p. 47.
61 William de Drogheda, xlix, p. 48.
62 *Non verbosus, quia pauca bene agere melius est, quam multis interesses periculose*, William de Drogheda, xxxvi, p. 39.
63 *Ideo iudex supplere eius defectum*, William de Drogheda, liii, p. 53.
64 William de Drogheda, lii, p. 52.
65 Peter Stein, *The Character and Influence of the Roman Civil Law* (London, 1988), p. 133.
66 Peter Stein, *The Character and Influence of the Roman Civil Law* (London, 1988), p. 137.
67 J. H. Baker, *The Legal Profession and the Common Law* (London, 1986), p. 99.
68 J. H. Baker, *The Legal Profession and the Common Law* (London, 1986), p. 160.
69 Charles Donahue, 'The monastic judge: social practice, formal rule and the mediaeval canon law of incest', *Studia Gratiana*, xxvii (1996), pp. 49–69.
70 For example, *Select Cases from ... Canterbury*, B. 3ii, p. 93.
71 Aegidius de Fuscarariis, *Der Ordo Iudiciarius*, *Quellen*, III. i, p. 1.

10 A moot point: disputations as academic exercises

1 Joannes Bassianus, *Materia ad Pandectum*, post Azo, *Summa* (Pavia, 1506, repr., Turin, 1966), p. 384.
2 *Cum in singulis diebus legendo et saepissime disputando dixerim de iure*.
3 S. Kuttner, 'Réflexions sur les Brocards des Glossateurs', reprinted in S. Kuttner, *Gratian and the Schools of Law* (London, 1983), p. 777.
4 *Les questions disputées*, ed. G. Fransen et al., *Typologie*, Fasc. 44–5 (1985), p. 231.
5 *Prose Salternitan Questions*, C 6, ed. B. Lawn (London, 1979).
6 For a bibliography, see *Les questions disputées*, ed. G. Fransen et al., *Typologie*, Fasc. 44–5 (1985).
7 *Die Ehelehre des Magister Honorius*, ed. B. Grimm, *Studia Gratiana*, XXIV (Rome, 1989), pp. 316–17.

8 'Les "Quaestiones" des canonistes: Essai de dépouillement et de classement', (1) *Traditio*, 12 (1956), p. 568.
9 *Les questions disputées*, ed. G. Fransen et al., *Typologie*, Fasc.44–5 (1985), p. 240.
10 *Les questions disputées*, ed. G. Fransen et al., *Typologie*, Fasc.44–5 (1985), p. 233.
11 *Readings and Moots at the Inns of Court in the Fifteenth Century*, ed. S. E. Thorne and J. H. Baker, Selden Society, 105 (London, 1990), p. xvii.
12 William of Drogheda's *Summa Aurea*, *Quellen*, II. ii.
13 William of Drogheda's *Summa Aurea*, *Quellen*, II. ii, p. 2.
14 William of Drogheda's *Summa Aurea*, *Quellen*, II. ii, p. 3.
15 *Les questions disputées*, ed. G. Fransen et al., *Typologie*, Fasc.44–5 (1985), p. 231.
16 For a bibliography, see J. J. Murphy, *A Bibliography of Mediaeval Rhetoric* (Toronto, 1971).
17 For convenient examples, see J. J. Murphy, *Three Mediaeval Rhetorical Arts* (Berkeley, 1971),
18 G.Fransen, 'Les "Quaestiones" des canonistes: Essai de dépouillement et de classement' (II) *Traditio*, 13 (1957), p. 482.
19 *Les questions disputées*, ed. G. Fransen et al., *Typologie*, Fasc.44–5 (1985), p. 240.
20 S. Kuttner, 'Réflexions sur les Brocards des Glossateurs', reprinted in S. Kuttner, *Gratian and the Schools of Law* (London, 1983),
21 It is striking that there is no mention of the topics in the forensic context in N. J. Green-Pedersen, *The Tradition of the Topics on the Middle Ages* (Vienna, 1984).
22 Cicero, *Topica*, I.2.
23 Cicero, *Topica*, II.6.
24 The mediaeval development of the theory of topics is a complex story. The debt of the early centuries is to Cicero and Boethius. The Latin version of Aristotle's *Topics* arrived in the West comparatively late, in the twelfth century.
25 See my *Old Arts and New Theology* (Oxford, 1980).
26 *Argumenta ad causas de facto annotamus, que loci generales vel generalia vel vulgariter brocarda*. Quoted in Peter Weimar, 'Argumenta Brocardica', *Studia Gratiana* XIV (Bologna, 1967), p. 95, from his *Materia pandectarum*.
27 *Quod patet ex diffinitione, nam argumentum est ratio rei dubie faciens fidem.*
28 *Tractabo autem de argumentis dupliciter.*
29 *Convenit legistis pro proposito ostendendo.*
30 Baldus ad C 1.3.15 (Lyons 1545 and 1561), cited in Weimar, 'Argumenta Brocardica', pp. 97–8.
31 *Readings and Moots in the Inns of Court in the Fifteenth Century*, ed. S. E. Thorne and J. H. Baker, Selden Society, 105 (1990), p. xxi.
32 *Readings and Moots in the Inns of Court*, vol. 1, Selden Society, 105(1989), p. cxxxiv-vi.
33 *Utrum infamia per baptismum aboleatur.* G. Fransen, 'Les "Quaestiones" des canonistes: Essai de dépouillement et de classement' (II) *Traditio*, 13 (1957), p. 482.
34 *An et ubinam subdiaconus possit ducere uxorem.* G. Fransen, 'Les "Quaestiones" des canonistes: Essai de dépouillement et de classement' (II) *Traditio*, 13 (1957), p. 482.
35 *Les questions disputées*, ed. G. Fransen et al., *Typologie*, Fasc.44–5 (1985), p. 241.
36 *Les questions disputées*, ed. G. Fransen et al., *Typologie*, Fasc.44–5 (1985), p. 241.
37 S. Kuttner, 'The revival of jurisprudence', *Studies in the History of Mediaeval Canon Law* (London, 1990), p. 310.
38 See *Allegationes Phalempinianae*, *Tijdschrift voor Rechsgeschiedenis*, 49 (1981), pp. 251–85 and G. Fransen, *Colligite Fragmenta*, *Studia Gratiana*, 13 (1967), 83–5.
39 *Les questions disputées*, ed. G. Fransen et al., *Typologie*, Fasc.44–5 (1985), p. 242. Unlike a theological question, a legal *quaestio* could be finally resolved.

198   Notes

Hodie non est quaestio appears in Bamberg, Staatsbibl. Can. 45, cited by Fransen.
40 *Readings and Moots at the Inns of Court in the Fifteenth Century*, ed. S. E. Thorne and J. H. Baker, Selden Society, 105 (London, 1990), p. xvi.
41 Cf. M. Bellomo, 'Le questiones disputatae', *Aspetti dell'insegnamento giuridico nelle Università medievali* (Reggio Calabria: Parallelo, 1974), vol. 1 38.
42 *The Casus Placitorum and the Reports of Cases in the King's Courts 1272–1278*, ed. William Huse Dunham, Selden Society, 69 (1952).
43 *Brevia Placitata*, ed. G. J. Turner and Theodore F. T. Plucknett, Selden Society (1951).
44 *Readings and Moots in the Inns of Court in the Fifteenth Century*, ed. S. E. Thorne and J. H. Baker, Selden Society, 105 (1990), p. xv, p. xviii.
45 'Les "Quaestiones" des canonistes: Essai de dépouillement et de classement' (1) *Traditio*, 12 (1956), p. 569.
46 'Les "Quaestiones" des canonistes: Essai de dépouillement et de classement' (II) *Traditio*, 13 (1957), pp. 481–501.
47 *Les questions disputées*, ed. G. Fransen *et al.*, *Typologie*, Fasc.44–5 (1985), pp. 234–7.
48 *Readings and Moots at the Inns of Court in the Fifteenth Century*, ed. S. E. Thorne and J. H. Baker, Selden Society, 105 (London, 1990).
49 London, British Library, MS Royal 9 E VII contains fifty-seven disputations. One *quaestio* is edited and discussed by James A. Brundage, 'A twelfth century Oxford Disputation Concerning the privileges of the Knights Hospitallers', *Medieval Studies*, 24 (1962), 153–60.
50 *Readings and Moots at the Inns of Court in the Fifteenth Century*, ed. S. E. Thorne and J. H. Baker, Selden Society, 105 (London, 1990), p. xvii.
51 *Readings and Moots at the Inns of Court in the Fifteenth Century*, ed. S. E. Thorne and J. H. Baker, Selden Society, 105 (London, 1990), pp. xlv–xlvi.
52 *Readings and Moots at the Inns of Court in the Fifteenth Century*, ed. S. E. Thorne and J. H. Baker, Selden Society, 105 (London, 1990), pp. xlv–xlvi.
53 The *argumentatio* is a condensed sequence of argumentation.
54 The *quaestio* discussed by Brundage is from British Library MS 9 E VII f.191ra, where it is the first of fifty-seven disputations. James A. Brundage, 'A twelfth century Oxford Disputation Concerning the privileges of the Knights Hospitallers', *Medieval Studies*, 24 (1962), p. 157.
55 *Infirmum est argumentum ... nam cui conceditur maius et minus non eum cui tollitur maius et minus ....*, James A. Brundage, 'A twelfth century Oxford Disputation Concerning the privileges of the Knights Hospitallers', *Medieval Studies*, 24 (1962), p. 159.
56 Peter Weimar, 'Argumenta Brocardica', *Studia Gratiana* XIV (Bologna, 1967), 91–123.
57 Peter of Blois, *De Distinctionibus in Canonum Interpretatione Adhibendis sive Speculum Iuris Canonici*, XVI, ed. T. A. Reimarus (Berlin, 1837), p. 40.
58 *Brocardica Aurea* (Naples, 1568), *Corpus glossatorum iuris civilis*, IV (Turin, 1967).
59 U.Nicolini, *Pillii Medicinensis Quaestiones sabbatinae, Introduzione all'edizione critica* (Modena, 1933), p. 25.
60 S. Kuttner, 'Réflexions sur les Brocards des Glossateurs', reprinted in S. Kuttner, *Gratian and the Schools of Law* (London, 1983), p. 769.
61 Robert C. Figuiera, 'Ricardus de Mores and his *Casus Decretalium*: the birth of a canonistic genre', *Proceedings of the Eighth International Congress of Mediaeval Canon Law, Monumenta iuris Canonici, Subsidia 9* (1992), p. 170.

Notes 199

62 *Brocardicum in iure dicitur, quando ex utraque parte racionibus fortibus pro et contra argumentatur,* Vocabularius Lipsiensis, ed. E. Seckel, *Beiträge zur Geschichte beider Rechte im Mittelalter* (Tübingen, 1898), pp. 306–22.
63 Azo, *Lectura Codicis* 4.30. 13 (Paris, 1577).
64 *Illud est diligenter considerandum. utrum primum sit pro regula tenendum, an eius contrarium* .... *Hic enim, licet primum velut generale videatur assignari, tamen eius contrarium pro regula tenendum est.* Azo, *Brocardica* (Basle, 1567), Tit. 1, p. 9. *Hoc generale licet multas videatur recipere contrarietates, tamen si singula individua referantur ad suum genus, potius diversitates dicentur.* Azo, *Brocardica* (Basle, 1567), tit. 1, p. 5.

11 Legal argument and the mediaeval study of logic

1 69 fragments.
2 62 fragments.
3 17 fragments each. Peter Stein, *The Character and Influence of the Roman Civil Law* (London, 1988), p. 56.
4 Peter Stein, *The Character and Influence of the Roman Civil Law* (London, 1988), p. 53.
5 Peter Stein, *Regulae Iuris* (Edinburgh, 1966), p. 50.
6 Stein argues that Justinian saw the *regulae* in *Digest* 50 as, far from being an afterthought, the culmination of the whole work. Peter Stein, *Regulae Iuris* (Edinburgh, 1966), pp. 114–15.
7 See my *Alan of Lille* (Cambridge, 1983). See, too, the *Cambridge History of Later Mediaeval Philosophy*, ed. N. Kretzmann, A. Kenny, J. Pinborg (Cambridge, 1982), *passim* for discussions.
8 *Regula*, 2.
9 See Isidore, *Etymologiae*, VI. xvi. 1.
10 Peter Stein, *Regulae Iuris* (Edinburgh, 1966), p. 52.
11 *Canon in greco sonat regula eo quod et vitam et scientiam regat, idest et bene vivendi et recte iudicandi normam prebeat.* Summa 'Elegantius', I, Part I (48), p. 14.
12 *Iurisconsultus...quasi proemialiter incipit ab origine iuris ab investigatione principiorum. Digest,* 1. 1. 1, pr. Add. Norbert Horn, *Aequitas in den Lehren des Baldus* (Graz, 1968), p. 7.
13 S. Kuttner, 'Réflexions sur les Brocards des Glossateurs', reprinted in S. Kuttner, *Gratian and the Schools of Law* (London, 1983), p. 789.
14 *Digest*, 50.17, no.1. The text continues: *per regulam igitur brevis rerum narratio traditur, et, ut ait Sabinus, quasi causae coniectio est, quae simul cum in aliquo vitiata est, perdit officium suum.*
15 Analogy finds a number of similar features in two things compared, but does not seek to make them match at every point. A *regula* has universal application. Peter Stein, *Regulae Iuris* (Edinburgh, 1966), p. 60.
16 Peter Stein, *Regulae Iuris* (Edinburgh, 1966), pp. 49–50 on the modern scholarly debate on this point.
17 *Res iudicata pro veritate accipitur. Digest,* 50. 17, no. 207.
18 *Plures cause simul coniuncte regulam constituunt.* Erich Genzmer, 'Gli apparati di azzone al digestum novum 50.17.1', *Annali di storia del diritto*, 1 (1957), pp. 10–11.
19 *Dicitur autem regula quasi cause coniunctio,* Erich Genzmer, 'Gli apparati di azzone al digestum novum 50.17.1', *Annali di storia del diretto*, 1 (1957), pp. 10–11.

200 Notes

20 *Hec rubrica non generale, sed nota dici potest, quia ex legibus sub ea positis elici possunt argumenta ad causas.* Azo, *Brocardica* (Basle, 1567), Tit.32.
21 Weimar argues thus, Peter Weimar, 'Argumenta Brocardica', *Studia Gratiana* XIV (Bologna, 1967), p. 101, citing this passage from Azo for this rather different purpose.
22 *His ... precognitis sumenda est regula huius generalis, ut quod valuit a principio ... non irritatur.* Azo, *Brocardica* (Basle, 1567), Tit. 1, p. 14.
23 Azo, *Brocardica* (Basle, 1567), Tit. 10.
24 *Praecipue negotiatur circa necessaria*, On Aquinas and the law, see Vincent McNabb, 'St. Thomas Aquinas and Law', *Blackfriars* (1929), 1047–67.
25 *Quae impossibile est aliter se habere.*
26 *Invenitur veritas in conclusionibus propriis, sicut et in principiis communibus.*
27 *Contingentia, in quibus sunt operationes humanae.*
28 Aquinas, *ST*, IIi q. xci a. 2.
29 *Est eadem veritas seu rectituto apud omnes, et aequaliter nota.* Aquinas, *ST*, IIi q. xciv a. 4.
30 *Naturae ius est quod non opinio genuit, sed quaedam in natura vis.* Cicero, *De Inventione*, II. liii. 161.
31 Aquinas, *ST*, IIi q. xciv a. 4.
32 *In eo, quod plus sit, semper inest et minus. Digest*, 50. 17, no. 110.
33 *Digest*, 50. 17, no. 113.
34 *Semper specialia generalibus insunt. Digest*, 50. 17, no. 147.
35 *In obscuris inspici solere, quod verisimilius est aut quod plerumque fieri solet. Digest*, 50. 17, no. 114.
36 *Quod contra rationem iuris receptum est, non est producendum ad consequentia. Digest*, 50. 17, no. 141.
37 *Impossibilium nulla obligatio est. Digest*, 50. 17, no. 185.
38 *In ratione speculativa ex principiis indemonstrabilibus naturaliter cognitis producuntur conclusiones diversarum scientiarum, quarum cognitio non est nobis naturaliter indita, sed per industriam rationis inventa.*
39 *Ita etiam ex praeceptis legis naturalis, quasi ex quibusdam principiis communibus et indemonstrabilibus, necesse est quod ratio humana procedat ad aliqua magis particulariter disponenda.*
40 *Et istae particulares dispositiones adinventae secundum rationem humanam, dicuntur leges humanae, servatis aliis conditionibus quae pertinent ad rationem legis*, Aquinas, *ST*, II i q. xci a.3.
41 *Nota admonitionem principis orthodoxi et quae scripturae in disputationibus fidei inducantur. Sciebat enim quod omnem vim inventorum suorum in dialectica disputatione ponunt haeretici.* Pietro Bohier, Bishop of Orvieto, *Liber Pontificalis Glossato*, III, ed. U. Prerovsky, *Studia Gratiana*, XXIII (Rome, 1978), p. 243.
42 Cicero, *Topica*, II. 6.
43 In Vatican lat. 832: *iustum habet in communicatione hominum; sed nulla communicatio hominum est naturalis; quare etc. Major patet, quia omne minor de se patet; quia omnis communicatio humana est ex voluntate et contritione humana.* Lottin, IV ii, p. 543.
44 *The Cambridge History of Later Mediaeval Philosophy*, ed. N. Kretzmann, A. Kenny and J. Pinborg (Cambridge, 1982) has a convenient bibliography.
45 *Omnis definitio in iure civili periculosa est: parum est enim, ut non subverti posset, Digest*, 50. 17, no. 202.
46 *Periculose in iure sunt sicut diffinitiones ... universales enunciationes.* Summa 'Elegantius', I, Part Prima (76), p. 26.

47 *Testium probabili astipulatione, advocatorum legali executione fuerit servata aequitas et auctoritas.Vita Meinwerci, episcopi patherbunensis*, ed. G.H. Pertz, *MGHSS*, XI (Hanover, 1854), vol. 1, p. 132.
48 *Summa 'Elegantius'*, Part VI (70), p. 135.
49 *Quia ergo, per accusationem ydoneum et irreprobabilem fundata accusatione, superest probationes inducere. Summa 'Elegantius'*, Part VI (70), p. 135.
50 *Summa 'Elegantius'*, Part VI (70), p. 135.
51 *Instrumentum vero non omne quod instruit mentem nunc dicitur, sed id specialiter quod scriptura continetur.* They can be either public or private documents, *Summa 'Elegantius'*, Part VI (98a), p. 149, cf. *Summa codicis des Irnerius*, ed. H. Fitting (Berlin, 1894), IV. 20, p. 91.
52 *Summa codicis des Irnerius*, ed. H. Fitting (Berlin, 1894), IV.20, p. 91. H. Kantorowicz, *Studies in the Glossators of the Roman Law* (Cambridge, 1938), discusses the attribution to Irnerius of the text published as his by Fitting, p. 33.
53 Magister Damasus, *Summa de ordine iudiciario*, ed. L. Wahrmund, *Quellen zur Geschichte des Römisch-Kanonischen Processes im Mittelalter* (Innsbruck, 1926), IV i, p. 42.
54 On aspects of this theme, see Gerhard Otte, *Dialektik und Jurisprudenz, Ius commune, Monographien* 1, (Frankfurt, 1971) and Alejandro Guzmán, Ratio Scripta, *Ius commune, Mongraphien*14 (Frankfurt-am-Main, 1981).
55 Bernard of Clairvaux, Letter 11, 2, *Opera Omnia*, V. 53.
56 Bernard of Clairvaux, Letter 11, 4, *Opera Omnia*, V. 55.

12 The theory and the practice

1 F. W. Maitland, *The Forms of Action at Common Law* (Cambridge, 1936).
2 Boethius, *De Trinitate*, II.
3 Henry Bracton's *De Legibus et Consuetudinibus Angliae*, ed. T. Twiss, Rolls Series (London, 1857), vol. II. 1–6.
4 Eibert von Bremen, *Ordo Judiciarius, Quellen* (1906), p. 1. Eibert's treatise is unusual in another respect. He writes in verse.
5 *Partim secundum normam canonum, partim secundum artificiosam rhetorum doctrinam.* Eibert von Bremen, *Ordo Judiciarius, Quellen* (1906), p. 1.
6 Vacarius, *Liber Pauperum*, ed. F. de Zulueta, Selden Society, 44 (1927), Prologue, p. 1.
7 *Ordo judiciarius 'scientiam', Quellen*, II. i, p. 1.
8 *Die Summa Libellorum des Bernardus Dorna, Quellen* (1905), p. 1.
9 *Pro utili et compediosa sociorum honorabilium eruditione sive doctrina.*
10 Rainerius Perusinus, *Ars Norarie, Quellen*, III, ii, p. 1.
11 *Der Ordo 'Invocato Christi Nomine', Quellen*, III, ii, p. 1.

13 Equity and the mediaeval idea of fairness

1 See C. Lefebvre, 'Récents développements des recherches sur l'équité canonique', *Proceedings of the Sixth International Congress of Medieval Canon Law*, ed. S. Kuttner and K. Pennington, *Monumenta Iuris Canonici*, Series 6: *Subsidia*, 7 (Vatican, 1985), 369–87.
2 *In omnibus quidem, maxime tamen in iure aequitas spectanda est. Digest*, 50. 17, no. 90,
3 'La Summa Institutionum "Iustiniani est in hoc opere"', IV.i. 1, ed. P. Legendre, *Ius Commune*, Sonderhefte, 2 (1973), p. 23.

4 *Iustitia in evum est, et lex eius aequitas*, John of Salisbury, *Policraticus*, IV. 2, CCCM, 118, p. 234. Cf. *Porro lex donum Dei est, aequitatis forma, norma iustitiae, divinae voluntatis imago. Salutis custodia, unio et consolidatio populorum, regula officiorum, exclusio et exterminatio vitiorum, violentiae et totius iniuria pena.* John of Salisbury, *Policraticus*, VIII, 17, ed. C. C. J. Webb (Oxford, 1909), vol. 2, p. 345. Cf. Cicero, *Topica* IV.23 and *De Amicitia* 27. 100.
5 *Iustitia non est aliud quam aequitas et bonitas.* Baldus, *Digest*, 1. 1. 1, pr. n. 4.
6 George Conklin, 'Stephen of Tournai and the *aequitas canonica*: the theory and practice of the law after Gratian', *Proceedings of the Eighth International Congress of Medieval Canon Law*, ed. S. Chodorow, *Monumenta Iuris Canonici, Series 6, Subsidia*, 9 (Vatican, 1992), p. 370.
7 G. Boyer, 'La notion d'équité et son rôle dans la jurisprudence des Parlements', *Mélanges Maury* II (Paris, 1960); P.G. Caron, '"Aequitas romana", "Misericordia patristica" et "epicheia" aristotelica nella doctrina dell "aequitas canonica"' (Milan, 1968).
8 Baldus on *Digest* 1. 3. 10, Norbert Horn, *Aequitas*, p. 30.
9 C. Lefebvre, 'Hostiensis, maître de l'équité canonique', 28 (1972), pp. 15–16.
10 C. Lefebvre, 'Hostiensis, maître de l'équité canonique', 28 (1972), pp. 15–16.
11 Attributed to Cyprian. C. Lefebvre, 'Hostiensis, maître de l'équité canonique', 28 (1972), pp. 15–16.
12 Thomas of Chobham, *Summa de arte praedicandi*, 5, CCCM, 82, p. 222. Cf. George Conklin, 'Stephen of Tournai and the aequitas canonica: the theory and practice of the law after Gratian', *Proceedings of the Eighth International Congress of Medieval Canon Law*, ed. S. Chodorow, *Monumenta Iuris Canonici, Series 6, Subsidia*, 9 (Vatican, 1992), pp. 369–70.
13 About the year 560, Cap. 1.8, in J. Balon, *Grand dictionnaire de droit du moyen âge, Ius Medii Aevi*, 5 (Belgium, 1972), *Aequitas*.
14 Norbert Horn, *Aequitas*, p. 22.
15 See p. 164.
16 *Equitas vero est rectitudo iudicii naturalem sequens rationem.* I.c.n.20, Norbert Horn, *Aequitas in den Lehren des Baldus* (Graz, 1968), p. 9.
17 *Porro aequitas, ut iuris periti asserunt, rerum convenientia est, quae cuncta coaequiparat ratione et imparibus rebus paria iura desiderat, in omnes aequabilis, tribuens unicuique quod suum est.* John of Salisbury, *Policraticus*, IV. 2, CCCM, 118, p. 237. Cf. Code 6.55. 9, n.8. See, also, Norbert Horn, *Aequitas*, p. 11.
18 *Ibi est aequitas ubi est aequalitas.* Baldus, in Code 4.64, no. 3. Norbert Horn, *Aequitas*, p. 95.
19 Cf. J. M. Kelly, *A Short History of Western Legal Theory* (Oxford, 1992), pp. 70 ff. Richard M. Fraher, 'Ut nullus describatur reus prius quam convincatur. Presumption of innocence in medieval canon law,' *Proceedings of the Sixth International Congress, Monumenta Iuris Canonici*, Series C: *Subsidia*, 7 (1985), p. 493.
20 *Quod quisque iuris in alterum statuerit, ut ipse eodem iure utatur. Digest*, II. 2.
21 *Quoniam aliae aliis gentibus placent.* Isidore, *Etymologiae*, V. 2, Gratian, *Decretum*, I, Dist. I. i.
22 Aquinas, *ST*, IIi, q. xcv a. 4.
23 *Sunt quaedam tempora in quibus iurare prohibemur. Summa 'Elegantius'*, Part III (90), p. 212.
24 *Mobiles sunt quas lex eterna non sanxit set posteriorum diligentia ratione utilitatis invenit, non ad salutem principaliter obtinendam set ad eam tutius muniendam.*

25 *Pro necessitate vel utilitate mutilare vel laxare fas est.* Summa 'Elegantius', Part 1 (8), p. 27.
26 *Dormitet.* Summa 'Elegantius', Part 1 (8), p. 27.
27 Cicero, *Topica*, IV. ii. 3. Cf. Marius Victorinus, *De Definitionibus*, ed. C. Halm, *Rhetores Latini Minores* (Leipzig, 1863), p. 9.
28 'La Summa Institutionum "Iustiniani est in hoc opere"', IV. i. 1, ed. P. Legendre, *Ius Commune*, Sonderhefte, 2 (1973), p. 23.
29 *Inter cetera est paritas aequitatis: quae similia iura in diversis terminis creditur suadere.* Baldus D.1.1.9, no. 20, Norbert Horn, *Aequitas*, p. 96.
30 *Dicitur enim aequitas rerum convenientia, quae in paribus causis paria iura desiderat, et bona omnia aequiparat.* Azo, Inst. I.i.n.7 and Norbert Horn, *Aequitas*, p. 11.
31 *Nulla iuris ratio aut aequitatis benignia patitur, ut quae salubriter pro utilitate hominum introducuntur, ea nos duriore interpretatione contra ipsorum commodum producamus ad severitatem.* D 1.3.25. Norbert Horn, *Aequitas*, p. 27. All this is in keeping with the notion of *rectus ordo*.
32 *Iure naturae aequum est neminem cum alterius detrimento et iniuria fieri locupletiorem. Digest,* 50. 17. 206.
33 *Summa 'Elegantius',* II, Part V (90), p. 94.
34 *Clericus qui episcopum suum accusaverit ... non est recipiendus, quia infamis effectus est et a gradu debet recedere ac curie tradi serviendus. Diversorum patrum sententie sive Collectio in LXXIV titulos digesta,* ed. J. T. Gilchrist, *Monumenta Iuris Canonici,* 1 (Vatican, 1973), Titulus 8, p. 54ff.
35 *Diversorum patrum sententie sive Collectio in LXXIV titulos digesta,* ed. J. T. Gilchrist, *Monumenta Iuris Canonici,* 1 (Vatican, 1973), Titulus 9, p. 58 ff.
36 *Sicut ergo clericus ratione persone seculari tribunali non subicitur, sic et secularium negotiorum cogitur fieri prohibetur ... Prohibitiones ... iste accipiende sunt de consilio perfectionis, non de necessitate iuris.* Summa 'Elegantius', Part IX (8), p. 55.
37 *Laici et seculares homines nolunt clericos recipere in accusationibus ... suis.* Anselm of Lucca, *Collectio canonum,* ed. F. Thaner (Oeniponte, 1906), III. 29, p. 131.
38 *Summa 'Elegantius',* Part IX (3), p. 50.
39 Gratian, *Decretum,* II, *Causa* II. ii. q. 7, *Summa 'Elegantius',* Part IX (1), p. 50.
40 *Sicut layci et seculares homines nolunt clericos recipere in accusationibus et infamationibus suis, ita nec clerici debent eos recipere in infamationibus suis, quoniam in omnibus discreta debet semper esse et segregata vita et conversatio clericorum ac secularium laycorum,* Ps-Telesporus, Ep. 1, *Decretales Pseudo-Isidorianae et Capitula Angilramni,* ed. P. Hinschius (Leipzig, 1863), 110, *Diversorum patrum sententie sive Collectio in LXXIV titulos digesta,* ed. J. T. Gilchrist, *Monumenta Iuris Canonici,* 1 (Vatican, 1973), Titulus 5, (46), p. 45.
41 *Sicut Domini sacerdotum segregata debet esse conversatione, ita et litigatio, quia servum Dei non oportet litigare.* Anselm of Lucca, *Collectio canonum,* ed. F. Thaner (Oeniponte, 1906), III. 15, p. 125.
42 *Sicut ergo clericus ratione persone seculari tribunali non subicitur, sic et secularium negotiorum cognitur fieri prohibetur.*
43 *Summa 'Elegantius',* Part IX (8), p. 55.
44 *Summa 'Elegantius',* Part IX (3), p. 50.
45 *Servi atque liberi, qui et si in casibus accusationes instituere permittantur, ob patronatus tamen et dominii reverentiam contra patronos vel dominos nisi venia edicti impetrata non recipiuntur.* Summa 'Elegantius', Part IV, II (8), p. 4.
46 *Fieri etiam solet ut clericus propter graviora delicta a castris dominicis eiciatur et honore privatus seculari tribunali exponatur.* Summa 'Elegantius', Part IX (4), p. 52.

47 *Quod episcopi a populis non sunt corrigendi.* Anselm of Lucca, *Collectio canonum*, ed. F. Thaner (Oeniponte, 1906), III. 13, p. 123.
48 *Populus enim ab eis docendus est et corripiendus, non ipsi ab eo.* Anselm of Lucca, *Collectio canonum*, ed. F. Thaner (Oeniponte, 1906), III. 13, p. 123.
49 *Quia non est discipulus super magistrum.* Anselm of Lucca, *Collectio canonum*, ed. F. Thaner (Oeniponte, 1906), III. 13, p. 123.
50 Anselm of Lucca, *Collectio canonum*, ed. F. Thaner (Oeniponte, 1906), III. 13, p. 123.
51 Anselm of Lucca, *Collectio canonum*, ed. F. Thaner (Oeniponte, 1906), III. 13, p. 123.
52 *Patres enim omnes venerandi sunt, non respuendi au insinuandi.* Anselm of Lucca, *Collectio canonum*, ed. F. Thaner (Oeniponte, 1906), III. 13, p. 123.
53 *Non enim oportet, ut permittantur carnales spirituales persequi nec sceleribus irretitos vel saeculo militantes episcopos infamare vel lacerare aut crimen opponere. Nam si hoc apostolici aut successores eorum permitterent, perpauci remansissent, qui Domino in sacerdotali ordine militassent.* Anselm of Lucca, *Collectio canonum*, ed. F. Thaner (Oeniponte, 1906), III. 26, p. 129.
54 Joseph Balon, *Ius medii aevi,ii, Lex Jurisdictio* (Namur, 1960), p. 89.
55 *Personis honoratioribus solummodo conceduntur.*
56 *Clerici ratione persone sue episcopi subiecti. Summa 'Elegantius'*, Tome III, Part IX (2), p. 50.
57 *Summa 'Elegantius'*, Part XI (83), pp. 156–7.
58 *Summa 'Elegantius'*, Part XI (92), p. 161.
59 *Summa 'Elegantius'*, Part XI (93), p. 162.
60 *Ingressus es ut advena, numquid ut iudices?*, Genesis 19.9, Anselm of Lucca, *Collectio canonum*, ed. F. Thaner (Oeniponte, 1906), III. 18, p. 125.
61 Anselm of Lucca, *Collectio canonum*, ed. F. Thaner (Oeniponte, 1906), III. 28, p. 130.
62 Some would argue that there is an inchoate theory of human rights in the Middle Ages. Cf. Jacques Maritain, *Scholasticism and Politics*, ed. Mortimer Adler (London, 1954), p. 88, and A. P. D'Entrèves, *Natural Law* (London, 1970), p. 48.

14 The development of procedural treatises: the process

1 L. Fowler-Magerl, *Ordo iudiciorum vel ordo iudiciarius* (Frankfurt, 1984).
2 Magister Arnulphus, *Summa Minorum, Quellen* (1905).
3 F. Donald Logan, 'An early thirteenth century papal judge-delegate formulary of English origin', *Studia Gratiana*, XIV, *Collectanea S. Kuttner*, IV (Bologna, 1967), 73–87, and especially p. 81, 4, *Forma Tertie citationis et secundi premporii*.
4 *Der 'Curialis'*, VI, *Quellen*, I. iii, p. 3.
5 Code, 3.8 takes it as the rubric. Code, 7. 45.4. 3 is the main source.
6 Fowler-Magerl, *Ordines iudiciarii et libelli de ordine iudiciorum*, *Typologie*, Fasc. 63 (1994). See pp. 8 ff for bibliography. On pp. 14–15 Fowler-Magerl describes the *status quaestionis* on the description and edition by modern scholars of the literature on judicial procedure based on Roman and canon law and written before 1234.
7 Knut Wolfgang Nörr, '*Ordo iudiciorum* und *Ordo iudiciarius*', *Studia Gratiana*, XI, *Collectanea Kuttneriana*, 1 (Bologna, 1967), p. 341.
8 A number of the examples in what follows are taken from these materials.
9 Cf. Thomas E. Morissey, '"More easily and more securely": legal procedure and due process at the Council of Constance', in *Popes, Teachers and Canon*

Law in the Middle Ages, ed. James Ross Sweeney and Stanley Chodorow (Ithaca and London, 1989).
10 *Per accusationem instituitur. Summa 'Elegantius'*, Part IV (3), pp. 2–3.
11 *Per actorem et reum expeditur. Summa 'Elegantius'*, Part IV (3), pp. 2–3.
12 In ecclesiastical cases some are minor (that is, *pro materia*), and these are capable of being settled between the clerics themselves (*inter clericos tantum*), if there is agreement, though if there is not, a judge will be needed. The second sort of case involves persons (is *pro personis*). That needs a *iudex ecclesiasticus* to settle it. The problems about injustice with which we are chiefly concerned in this study have to do with persons and not property.
13 For example, Johannes Teutonicus touches on the debate over the right of the accused to elect to be tried in one or the other. *De Constitutionibus* I. 4, on *Cum accessissent 'vel aliunde'. Hec dictio, 'vel' non dat istis optionem eligendi sive de ecclesia sive extra. Set ordo verborum ostendit quod secundum illum ordinem procedere debeant ut, reprobatis personis capituli, tunc demum aliunde eligent.* Johannes Teutonicus, *Apparatus glossarum in compilationem tertium*, ed. K. Pennington (Vatican, 1981), II.4, p. 4. The Becket controversy of the twelfth century turned partly on the alleged abuse of the option for trial in an ecclesiastical court.
14 See J. W. Baldwin, 'A debate at Paris over Thomas Becket between Master Roger and Master Peter the Chanter', *Studia Gratiana*, XI, *Collectanea S. Kuttner*, 1 (Bologna, 1967), p. 126.
15 Anselm of Lucca, *Collectio canonum*, III. 47, ed. F. Thaner (Oeniponte, 1906), pp. 139–40.
16 *Frequenter enim interrogari oportet, ne aliquid pretermissum forte remaneat, quod adnecti conveniat.* Anselm of Lucca, *Collectio canonum*, III. 52, ed. F. Thaner (Oeniponte, 1906), p. 142.
17 *Quicumque vult actionem proponere.* Johannes Bassianus, *Summa 'Quicunque vult'*, *Quellen* (1925), IV. ii, p. 1.
18 Johannes Bassianus, *Summa 'Quicunque vult'*, *Quellen* (1925), IV. ii, p. 1.
19 *Huius officii summa est litem explodere iurgiumque sopire.*
20 *Summa 'Elegantius'*, VII (37), p. 175.
21 *Iudicis officium est citare ac compellere litigantes ac iudicium venire et his exhibitis allegationes eorum id est partium audire et postea singula cognoscere ac subtiliter examinare et partes sepius interrogare, quo facto pronuntiare debet.* Knut Wolfgang Nörr, '*Ordo iudiciorum* und *Ordo iudiciarius*', *Studia Gratiana*, XI, *Collectanea Kuttneriana*, 1 (Bologna, 1967), p. 331. *Summa Trecensis*, ed. H. Fitting, *Summa Codicis des Irnerius* (Berlin, 1894), p. 48. The likelihood of this text being Irnerius' own work is now uncertain.
22 Richard M. Fraher, 'Conviction according to conscience: the medieval jurists' debate concerning judicial discretion and the law of proof', *Law and History Review*, 7 (1989), p. 25.
23 As a further context for those discussed below, see Linda Fowler-Magerl's study which includes an edition of half a dozen short treatises of the eleventh to twelfth centuries. *Ordo iudiciorum vel ordo iudiciarius: Begriff und Litteraturgattung, Ius Commune: Repertorium zur Frühzeit der Gelehrten Rechte* (Frankfurt am Main, 1984), especially pp. 254 – 300. See, also, H. Kantorowicz, *Studies in the Glossators of the Roman Law* (Cambridge, 1938) and Fitting, *Juristische Schriften des früheren Mittelalters* (Halle, 1976), Richard M. Fraher, 'Ut nullus describatur reus prius quam convincatur. Presumption of innocence in medieval canon law?' *Proceedings of the Sixth International Congress, Monumenta Iuris Canonici*, Series C: *Subsidia*, 7 (Vatican, 1985), pp. 493–506.

24 *Si quis vult alicui movere quaestionem, debet iudici libellum porrigere, in quo signabit, quare conqueratur.* Magister Damasus, *Die Summa de ordine iudiciario, Quellen,* IV. iv, pp. 1–45.
25 Pillius, Tancredus, Grazia, *Libri de iudiciorum ordine* (reprinted Aalen, 1975), pp. 87–316.
26 William Durantis, *Speculum iudiciale* (Basel, 1574, reprinted Aalen, 1975).
27 *Select Cases from the Ecclesiastical Courts of the Province of Canterbury c.1200–1301,* ed. N. Adams and C. Donahue, Selden Society, 95 (1981), p. 37. The bibliographical note does not include the series of thirteenth-century procedural treatises discussed *passim* in the present volume.
28 *Ordo solitus est ut iudex prius de causa cognoscat quam pronuntiet, item ut prius reus citetur quam contumaciter condemnetur, item ut complectatnur in sententia allegationes hinc inde... item quod omnia precedere debent.*
29 Ricardus Anglicus, *Die Summa de ordine iudiciario, Quellen,* II.iii, Introduction.
30 *Select Cases of Procedure without Writ under Henry III,* ed. H. G. Richardson and G. O.Sayles, Selden Society, 60 (1941), p. xxi ff.
31 *Der Ordo 'Invocato Christi Nomine',* (I), p. 2.
32 Master Damasus, *Die 'Summa de ordine iudiciario'* (I) *Quellen* (1926), p. 1.
33 *Accusare volenti non satis est crimen coram iudice nudo verbo obicere set opus est per libellum quis quem de quo accuset exprimere ... iste libellus ... de substantia accusationis est ad remorandas accusationes inventus ut nullus ex precipitatione ad accusationes prosiliat set equo se id periculo facturum perpendat et ob id pigrius et consideratius hoc opus frequentet.* Summa 'Elegantius', II, Part V (106), p. 101. Cf. Jenny McEwan, *Evidence and the Adversarial Process* (Oxford, 1992), p. 10.
34 Ricardus Anglicus, *Die Summa de ordine iudiciario* (I), *Quellen,* II iii, pp. 1–2.
35 *Der Ordo 'Invocato Christi Nomine',* (III), p. 6.
36 *Der Ordo 'Invocato Christi Nomine'* (V), p. 15.
37 *Select Cases from the Ecclesiastical Courts of the Province of Canterbury c.1200–1301,* ed. N. Adams and C. Donahue, Selden Society, 95 (1981), p. 37.
38 The formal written accusation has rules, although these depend on the period and the circumstances. The *Summa 'Elegantius'* says that there is an appropriate form for the document of accusation. It has nine *articuli*. These include the name of the accuser, the nature of the offence, the time and exact place where it happened. *Summa 'Elegantius',* Part V (108), p. 103.
39 This period varies in the literature. The principle is that it should be adequate.
40 *Ne qua vel de hac re machinatio fiat.* Novels 53. 3. 1–2.
41 *Quae quisque actione agere volet, eam edere debet.* Digest, II. 13. 1. 1, pp. 58–9.
42 *Ut proinde sciat reus utrum cedere an contendere ultra debeat, et, si contendendum putat, venia instructus ad agendum cognita actione qua conveniatur.* Digest, II. 13. 1, pp. 58–9.
43 *Qui semel actionem proponit ... et adversario cognitio, necesse habebit usque in finem litem exercere.* Ricardus Anglicus, *Die Summa de ordine iudiciario* (XI), *Quellen,* II. iii, p. 8, *Der Ordo 'Invocato Christi Nomine', Quellen,* V. i, p. 3.
44 *Der Ordo 'Invocato Christi Nomine',* p. 3.
45 Lottin, V, p. 46.
46 *Trium personarum trinus actus: idest actoris ... rei. [et] judicis qui partibus medius esse debet Summa 'Elegantius',* Part I, (9), p. 3 and Part 1 (1), p. 1.
47 William de Drogheda explores a series of scenarios where various combinations of the parties are missing. William de Drogheda, lxxv, *Quellen,* p. 75ff.
48 *Summa 'Elegantius',* Part IV, (2), p. 2.

49 It is a complicating factor that in the later Middle Ages the business of the trial was often conducted by the 'professionals', the lawyers arguing it out before the judge, with the parties not necessarily present. Cf. Henry Ansgar Kelly, 'Inquisitorial due process and the status of secret crimes', *Proceedings of the Eighth International Congress on Medieval Canon Law, Monumenta Iuris Canonici*, 9 (1992), p. 409. Another set of elements puts weight on the solidity of the structure: the justice of the cause, the standing of the participants: *iustita cause, qualitas persone, auctoritas imperantis, ut videlicet publice potestates bello presideant, temporis aut loci opportunitas*, Summa *'Elegantius'*, III, (4), p. 216.
50 For example, *Digest*, 3. 3. 73; 4. 2. 9. 7. 1.
51 For example, *Digest*, 7. 6. 5. 6. 4.
52 Knut Wolfgang Nörr, 'Ordo iudiciorum und Ordo iudiciarius', *Studia Gratiana*, XI, *Collectanea Kuttneriana*, 1 (Bologna, 1967), p. 332.
53 *Ad actoris officium pertinet intendere et intenta probare, donec reus confessus sit vel iudicii fidem faciat.* Summa Trecensis, ed. H. Fitting, *Summa Codicis des Irnerius* (Berlin, 1894), p. 48. Knut Wolfgang Nörr, 'Ordo iudiciorum und Ordo iudiciarius', *Studia Gratiana*, XI, *Collectanea Kuttneriana*, 1 (Bologna, 1967), p. 331.
54 *Reus quoque vel negare debet vel confiteri et, si confiteatur, vel accipere debet et probare exceptionem quem ad modum actor probat intentionem, vel soluere. quod sit neutrum horum faciat, condemnabitur.* Summa Trecensis, ed. H. Fitting, *Summa Codicis des Irnerius* (Berlin, 1894), p. 48. Knut Wolfgang Nörr, 'Ordo iudiciorum und Ordo iudiciarius', *Studia Gratiana*, XI, *Collectanea Kuttneriana*, 1 (Bologna, 1967), p. 331.
55 *Der Ordo 'Invocato Christi Nomine'*, p. 3.
56 *Qualiter accusatio instituenda sit.* Summa *'Elegantius'*, II, Part V (106), p. 101.
57 *Tenetur autem iudex interrogationem facere a reo in omnibus articulis, in quibus actori incumbit onus probandi, quia si confessus fuerit reus, non habebit necesse actor probare; si vero negaverit, procurabit probationes.* Novels 53. 3. 1–2.
58 *Der Ordo 'Invocato Christi Nomine'* (X), *Quellen*, V. i, p. 24ff.
59 Master Damasus, *Die 'Summa de ordine iudiciario'*, (XIX) *Quellen*, III. ii, p. 16.
60 *Der Ordo 'Invocato Christi Nomine'* (XXV), *Quellen*, V. i, p. 49.
61 *Der Ordo 'Invocato Christi Nomine'* (XXV), *Quellen*, V. i, p. 50.
62 *Select Cases from ... Canterbury*, p. 322.
63 There is a distinct procedure which Tancred calls 'interrogatory'. These 'interrogatories' were questions each party asked the judge to put to the other party. Tancred, *Ordo*, 3.3, pp. 207–10.
64 *Select Cases from ... Canterbury*, p. 46.
65 *Select Cases from ... Canterbury*, pp. 269–70.
66 For example, *Select Cases from ... Canterbury*, B.3i, p. 71.
67 Tancred, *Ordo*, 3. 9. 2, p. 237.
68 *Select Cases from ... Canterbury*, pp. 278–9.
69 Tancred, *Ordo*, 3. 13, pp. 248–57.
70 *Select Cases from ... Canterbury*, B.3a, p. 64.
71 *Select Cases from ... Canterbury*, p. 346.
72 Master Damasus, *Die 'Summa de ordine iudiciario'*, (XXXII) *Quellen* (1926), p. 26.
73 Magerl, *Typologie*, p. 21.
74 Jenny McEwan, *Evidence and the Adversarial Process* (Oxford, 1992), p. 10.
75 See M. Horvat, 'Deux phases du procès romain', *Droits de l'antiquité et sociologie iuridique; Mélanges H. Lévy-Bruhl* (Paris, 1959), p. 164.

76 *Litis contestatio est negocii hicinde narratio apud iudicem.* Placentinus, *Summa codicis, C IIII*, ix, p. 100.
77 *Die Ehelehre des Magister Honorius*, ed. B. Grimm, *Studia Gratiana*, XXIV (Rome, 1989), pp. 316–17.
78 Jenny McEwan, *Evidence and the Adversarial Process* (Oxford, 1992), p. 169.
79 *Litis contestatio non fit nisi adversario praesente et competenter respondente, id est vel negando vel excipiendo, id est iudicium subeundo, non litem declinando.* Placentinus, *Summa codicis, C IIII*, ix, p. 100.
80 Peter Weimar, 'Argumenta Brocardica', *Studia Gratiana* XIV (Bologna, 1967), 91–123, and see p. 91.
81 H. Kantorowicz, 'The Quaestiones Disputatae of the Glossators', *La revue d'histoire du droit*, xvi.1 (1937/8), p. 17.
82 S. Kuttner, 'The revival of jurisprudence', *Studies in the History of Mediaeval Canon Law* (London, 1990), p. 310.
83 Peter Stein, *Regulae Iuris* (Edinburgh, 1966), p. 132.
84 S. Kuttner, 'The revival of jurisprudence', *Studies in the History of Mediaeval Canon Law* (London, 1990), p. 310.
85 See H. de Lubac, 'A propos de la formule: *diversi sed non adversi*', *Recherches de science religieuse*, 40 (1952), pp. 27–40.
86 *Brocardica Aurea* (Naples, 1568), *Corpus glossatorum iuris civilis*, IV (Turin, 1967).
87 See my *The Logic and Language of the Bible: the Earlier Middle Ages* (Cambridge, 1984).
88 See G. R. Evans, 'A Work of "Terminist Theology"? Peter the Chanter's *De Tropis Loquendi* and some Fallacies', *Vivarium* 20 (1982), 40–58, and "Ponendo Theologica Exempla'. Peter the Chanter's De Tropis Loquendi', *History of Universities* (1982), 1–14.
89 *Brocardica Aurea* (Naples, 1568), *Corpus glossatorum iuris civilis*, IV (Turin, 1967), p. 12.
90 *Brocardica Aurea* (Naples, 1568), *Corpus glossatorum iuris civilis*, IV (Turin, 1967), p. 21.
91 *Brocardica Aurea* (Naples, 1568), *Corpus glossatorum iuris civilis*, IV (Turin, 1967), p. 24.
92 *Quando iudices debent aliquem audire, sed non quemliber exaudire.*
93 *Male scriptum est. Brocardica Aurea* (Naples, 1568), *Corpus glossatorum iuris civilis*, IV (Turin, 1967), p. 124.
94 *Brocardica Aurea* (Naples, 1568), *Corpus glossatorum iuris civilis*, IV (Turin, 1967), p. 125.
95 *Hoc generale licet multas videatur recipere contrarietates, tamen si singula individua referantur ad suum genus, potius diversitates dicentur.* Azo, *Brocardica* (Basle, 1567), tit. 1, p. 5.
96 Quoted in Peter Weimar, 'Argumenta Brocardica', *Studia Gratiana* XIV (Bologna, 1967), 91–123, p. 95, from his *Materia pandectarum*. Robert C. Figuiera, 'Ricardus de Mores and his *Casus Decretalium*: the birth of a canonistic genre', *Proceedings of the Eighth International Congress of Mediaeval Canon Law, Monumenta iuris Canonici, Subsidia* 9 (1992), p. 170.
97 *Quod patet ex diffinitione, nam argumentum est ratio rei dubie faciens fidem.*
98 *Tractabo autem de argumentis dupliciter.*
99 *Convenit legistis pro proposito ostendendo.*
100 Baldus ad C 1.3.15 (Lyons 1545 and 1561), cited in Weimar, '*Argumenta Brocardica*', pp. 97–8.
101 Yet it is recognised that an adversarial battle may be a bad thing. Cinus comments that a public dispute does more harm than a private one and causes more damage by way of generating mistakes. A private argument: *est causa*

minoris erroris. Cinus, *Commentaria in codicem,* 1.1.4 (Frankfurt-am-Main, 1578), fol.3rb.
102 *Brocardicum in iure dicitur, quando ex utraque parte racionibus fortibus pro et contra argumentatur. Vocabularius Lipsiensis,* ed. E. Seckel, *Beiträge zur Geschichte beider Rechte im Mittelalter* (Tübingen, 1898), pp. 306–22.
103 Azo, *Lectura Codicis,* 4. 30. 13 (Paris, 1577).
104 *Illud est diligenter considerandum. utrum primum sit pro regula tenendum, an eius contrarium.*
105 *Hic enim, licet primum velut generale videatur assignari, tamen eius contrarium pro regula tenendum est.* Azo, *Brocardica* (Basle, 1567), Tit.1, p. 9.
106 *Collectio Canonum Remedio Curiensis Episcopo Perperam Ascripta,* ed. J. Herwig, *Monumenta Iuris Canonici,* Series B: *Corpus Collectionum* 2 (1976), Canon 20, p. 47.
107 And *Inter secretum conscientie et manifestas probationes perplexus est: utrum secundum allegationes an secundum veritatem, videlicet secundum merita cause an secundum merita persone pronuntiare deberet?*
108 *Summa 'Elegantius',* Part VII (5), p. 155.
109 *Judex ... non ante sententiam proferat finitivam, quam aut reus ipse confiteatur, aut per testes idoneos convincatur. Codex Theodosianus* 9. 40. 1.
110 *Nullum iudicium iudicetis suspicionis arbitrio, sed primum probate, et postea caritativam proferte sententiam.* Anselm of Lucca, *Collectio canonum,* I, 41 ed. F. Thaner (Oeniponte, 1906), p. 93, citing Ps.-Melchiades.
111 Ivo of Chartres, *Panormia,* II. cxix, *PL,* 161. 1208.
112 Burchard of Worms, *Decreta,* xvi. 30, *PL,* 140. 916. xvi.1, *PL,* 140. 909.
113 *Iudex criminosum discutiens non ante sententiam proferat capitalem quam aut reum se ipse confiteatur, aut per innocentes testes convincatur.* Gratian, *Decretum,* II. ii. q. 1. 2, citing Constantine, *PL,* 187. 582 and Friedberg, vol. I.
114 *Incerta nemo pontificum iudicare presumat. Quamvis enim vera sunt, credenda tamen non sunt nisi que certis iudiciis comprobantur, nisi que manifesto iudicio convincuntur, nisi que iudiciario ordine publicantur. Summa 'Elegantius',* II (2), p. 2.
115 *Quod ad plenam negotii cognitionem proficiat. Summa 'Elegantius in iure divino' seu Coloniensis,* ed. G. Fransen and S. Kuttner, *Monumenta Iuris Canonici, Corpus Glossatorum,* III, Part VII (2a), p. 153.
116 William de Drogheda, xlix, p. 48.
117 (Paris, 1559).
118 *Ordo si pervertitur, non valet sententia.* Knut Wolfgang Nörr, 'Ordo iudiciorum und Ordo iudiciarius', *Studia Gratiana,* XI, *Collectanea Kuttneriana,* 1 (Bologna, 1967), p. 336.
119 *Ceterum quia non iudiciario ordine quidam plerumque ab indoctis iudicibus condemnantur et a vulgaribus hominibus etiam ante cognitionem a propriis sedibus violenter deiiciuntur. Die Summa des Paucapalea über das Decretum Gratiani,* C. III, ed. J. F. von Schulte (Giessen, 1890), p. 63.
120 Knut Wolfgang Nörr, 'Ordo iudiciorum und Ordo iudiciarius'. *Studia Gratiania,* XI, *Collectanea Kuttneriana,* 1 (Bologna, 1967), p. 336.
121 Placentinus, *De actionum varietatibus, Quellen,* p. 1, Cf. J.IV.6.
122 Cicero, *De Inventione,* II. 19. 57.
123 *Select Cases in the court of the King's Bench under Edward I,* ed. G. O. Sayers, Selden Society, 57 (London, 1938), p. lxxxiv.
124 *Select Cases from ... Canterbury,* p. 267, pp. 232–4.
125 Gregory the Great MGH Epp. 2, p. 411, *CCSL,* 140A, Register Book XIII.46/47 Magerl, *Typologie,* pp. 20–1.
126 Gratian, *Decretum,* Part II, *Causa,* 2, q. 1. 7.

127 *Nullus est condempnandus, nisi iudicio ordinabiliter habito aut convincatur, aut reum se ipse confiteatur.* Gratian, *Decretum*, Part II, *Causa* 2, q. 1. 14.
128 Anselm of Lucca, *Collectio canonum*, III. 13, ed. F. Thaner (Oeniponte, 1906), p. 124.
129 Anselm of Lucca, *Collectio canonum*, III. 15, ed. F. Thaner (Oeniponte, 1906), p. 125.
130 *Sententia iudicis, quae absente accusato datur, irrita sit.* Anselm of Lucca, *Collectio canonum*, III. 28, ed. F. Thaner (Oeniponte, 1906), p. 130.
131 *Nemo sit condempnandus nisi legitime convictus aut … sponte confessus. Die Summa Decretorum des Magister Rufinus*, ed. H. Singer (Paderborn, 1902), *Causa*, II, p. 238.

15 Natural justice

1 Cf. Jenny McEwan, *Evidence and the Adversarial Process* (Oxford, 1992), p. 63.
2 Ronald Dworkin, quoted in A. J. Lisska, Aquinas' *Theory of Natural Law* (Oxford, 1966), pp. 34–8.
3 See R. Ombres, 'Giustizia ed equita' nel nuovo codice di diritto canonico latino: note introduttive', *Apollinaris*, lxi (1988), pp. 717–36, especially notes 1, 27, 28, 38, 43. I am grateful to Robert Ombres for commenting on an early draft of this chapter. The theme is also explored in Kuttner, 'A forgotten definition', as a theme embedded in the principle that justice ought to serve the common good, especially pp. 94 ff.
4 The 'Plato' in question is the Chalcidian commentary on the *Timaeus*, 5, ed. Waszink, pp. 59.3–8, but there is a tangled history, traced by Kuttner in 'A forgotten definition', and see S. Kuttner, 'Gratian and Platon' in *The History of Ideas and Doctrines of Canon Law in the Middle Ages* (reprinted Variorum), p. 1.
5 *Iustitia est secundum Platonem virtus que plurimum prodest his qui minimum possunt, nempe in personis miserabilibus evidentius clarescit iustitia.* Placentinus, *Summa Institionum*, (Mogunt, 1535), p. 1.
6 Cf. Jenny McEwan, *Evidence and the Adversarial Process* (Oxford, 1992), p. 62.
7 *In condemnatione personarum, quae in is quod facere possunt damnantur, non totum quod habent extorquendum est, sed et ipsarum ratio habenda est, ne egeant. Digest*, 50. 17, no.173.
8 'Legal rules are not to be applied to prejudice those who for some reason, for which they are not to blame, are incapable of safeguarding their own interests.' Peter Stein, *The Character and Influence of the Roman Civil Law* (London, 1988), p. 32.
9 *Nunc autem quod agit justitia in subveniendo miseriis.* Augustine, *De Trinitate*, XIV. 9. 12.
10 *Equitas suadet ne huic obsit simplicitas, illi autem prosit calliditas.* Baldus D.11.1.13, Norbert Horn, *Aequitas*, p. 98.
11 *Canonici autem non audientes rationabilem causam quare memoratum Iohannes a consortio suo deberent eicere, ebdomodarium ut curaverunt. Decretales ineditae saeculi xii*, 8, ed. W. Holzmann, S. Chodorow and C. Duggan. *Monumenta Iuris Canonici, Corpus collectionum* 4 (Rome, 1982), p. 15.
12 R. Helmholz, 'Standards of impartiality for papal judges delegate', *Canon Law and the Law of England* (London, 1987), p. 35.
13 *Difficile videtur naturam actionum in romane legis codicibus diffusarum agnoscere.* British Library, MS Royal II B XIV, ff,64r–66v, quoted by H. Kantorowicz, *Studies in the Glossators of the Roman Law* (Cambridge, 1938, repr 1969), pp. 224–5.

Notes 211

14 H. Kantorowicz, *Studies in the Glossators of the Roman Law* (Cambridge, 1938, repr 1969), pp. 224–5.
15 *Decretales Pseudo-Isidorianae et Capitula Angilramni*, ed. P. Hinschius (Leipzig, 1863), pp. 66–87.
16 *Decretales Pseudo-Isidorianae et Capitula Angilramni*, ed. P. Hinschius (Leipzig, 1863), pp. 94–102.
17 *Decretales Pseudo-Isidorianae et Capitula Angilramni*, ed. P. Hinschius (Leipzig, 1863), pp. 125–7.
18 *Decretales Pseudo-Isidorianae et Capitula Angilramni*, ed. P. Hinschius (Leipzig, 1863), pp. 137–43.
19 *Decretales Pseudo-Isidorianae et Capitula Angilramni*, ed. P. Hinschius (Leipzig, 1863), pp. 160–66.
20 *Decretales Pseudo-Isidorianae et Capitula Angilramni*, ed. P. Hinschius (Leipzig, 1863), pp. 1172–5.
21 *Decretales Pseudo-Isidorianae et Capitula Angilramni*, ed. P. Hinschius (Leipzig, 1863), pp. 183–9.
22 *Decretales Pseudo-Isidorianae et Capitula Angilramni*, ed. P. Hinschius (Leipzig, 1863), pp. 200–4.
23 *Decretales Pseudo-Isidorianae et Capitula Angilramni*, ed. P. Hinschius (Leipzig, 1863), pp. 502–8.
24 Hinschius gives the parallels in his footnotes, and explores the story of the collections in his introduction. For an important recent study, see Hubert Mordek, *Kirchenrecht und Reform im Frankenreich* (Berlin/New York, 1975).
25 *Ut episcopus nullius causam audiat absque praesentiam clericorum suorum, alioquin irrita erit sententia episcopi, nisi clericorum praesentia confirmetur.* Vetus Gallica, xxxvi, 1, Mordek, p. 476.
25 Cf. 'Natural justice may ... be used not as a standard for criticising the content of legal rules but to refer to the principles which must be followed in the application of rules, whatever their content, to particular cases.' Paul Jackson, *Natural Justice* (London, 1973).
27 C. Munier, *Les sources patristiques du droit de l'église du viiie au xiiie siècle* (Mulhouse, 1957), p. 32.
28 Gilchrist, p. cviii.
29 See, for example, R. Weigand, *Die Naturrechtslehre der Legisten und Dekretisten von Irnerius bis Accursius und von Gratian bis Johannes Teutonicus* (Munich, 1967).
30 *Sicut ex premissis necessariis non sequitur nisi conclusio necessaria, ita ex premissis que sunt iuste iustitia naturali sequitur conclusio iusta naturaliter.* Ms. Vat. lat. 832, s.xiiiex, from the Arts Faculty in Paris, O. Lottin, IV ii, p. 543.
31 Surviving in MS Erlangen 213.
32 *Deinde queritur utrum sit aliquod iustum naturale.* Lottin, IV ii, pp. 540–1.
33 *Day v. Savadge* (1614) Hob.85.
34 Lord Esher M.R., *Voinet v. Barrett* (1855) 55 L.J.Q.B. 39,41.
35 See on this theme, M. Villey, 'Le droit naturel chez Gratian', *Studia Gratiana*, III (Bologna, 1955), p. 85.
36 The question who may properly be an accuser is a good deal discussed in our texts.
37 *Nihil tamen accusatum absque legitimo et idoneo accusatore fiat. Nam et Dominus noster Iesus Christus Iudam furem esse sciebat, sed quia non est accusatus, ideo non est eiectus.* Ps-Eleutherus, Ep. 1,3 *Decretales Pseudo-Isidorianae et Capitula Angilramni*, ed. P. Hinschius (Leipzig, 1863), p. 126, *Diversorum patrum sententie sive Collectio in LXXIV titulos digesta*, ed. J. T. Gilchrist, *Monumenta Iuris Canonici: Series B: Corpus Collectionum*, 1 (Vatican, 1973), Titulus 5, (47), p. 45.

212 Notes

38 Johannes de Lignano, *Super Clementina 'Saepe'*, *Quellen*, IV, vi, p. 1, see p. 136.
39 See pp. 124, 126. Texts used in the treatises edited by Fowler-Magerl are I Timothy 5.24; Acts 5.3; Acts 8.20.
40 *Ego sum iudex et testis dicit Dominus*, Jeremiah 29.23.
41 Matthew 7.1.
42 Luke 12.14; John 13.14, cf. Acts 5.27, Matthew 19.28. Bernard, *De Consideratione*, I. vi. 7, *Opera Omnia*, vol. III.401.
43 Bernard, *De Consideratione*, I. vi. 7, *Opera Omnia*, vol. III. 402, and citing I Corinthians 6.2.
44 Grosseteste, Letter 72, *Epistolae*, pp. 206–7.
45 *Nemo, qui condemnare potest, absolvere non potest. Digest*, 50. 17, no.37.
46 Grosseteste, Letter 72, *Epistolae*, p. 209.
47 Grosseteste, Letter 72, *Epistolae*, p. 220.
48 Gratian, *Decretum*, II, *Causa* XXXIII q. iii, Dist. VI. c. 1.
49 *Sepe pastores ecclesie in solvendis ac ligandis subditis sue voluntatis motus non autem causarum merita sequuntur.*
50 *Sepe fit ut erga quemlibet proximum odio vel gratia moveatur pastor: iudicare autem digne de subiectis nqueunt qui in subditionem causis vel odia vel gratiam sequuntur.*
51 *Iniquum est aliquem suae rei iudicem fieri. Digest*, 5. 1. 17.
52 74 *Tituli*, ed. J. T. Gilchrist, *Monumenta Iuris Canonici, Corpus collectionum*, 1 (Vatican, 1973), 57, 74, 46, 13, 8, 5.
53 *Si iuste inquiiunt damnatur reus, non dampnat eum nisi qui sine peccato est Deus, quia etsi iudex dampnat, tamen non sibi set Deo. Summa 'Elegantius'*, VII (9), p. 158.
54 *Noli quaerere iudex fieri, nisi valeas virtute irrumpere iniquitates ... Noli esse pusillanimis in anima tua.* John of Salisbury, *Policraticus*, V. 11, p. 31.
55 *Et meo quidem tempore nichil miserabilius vidi quam iudices scientiae legis ignaros, bonae voluntatis inanes, quod convincit amor munerum et retributionum.* John of Salisbury, *Policraticus*, V.11, p. 331.
56 *Non solum cum subditis verum etiam cum praelatus excedit.* Fourth Lateran Council, Canon 8.
57 On the other hand, the Canon stresses that because senior prelates will inevitably make enemies, since they must *ex officio* condemn and discipline others, they are especially vulnerable as persons to the attacks of others; thus it is particularly important that they be afforded the protections of due process. Fourth Lateran Council, Canon 8.
58 *Summa 'Elegantius'*, Part VII (4), p. 155.
59 *Digest*, 4. 8. 9. 2. 1.
60 *Utrum iudex par in scelere scelera iudicare possit. Summa 'Elegantius'*, VII (7), p. 157.
61 *Pilii, Tancredi, Gratiae Libri de Iudiciorum Ordine*, ed. F. Bergmann (Göttingen, 1842), p. 321.
62 Master Roland, *Causa* III q. 7, p. 18.
63 *Summa 'Elegantius'*, Part VII (8), p. 157.
64 *Summa 'Elegantius'*, Part VII (8), p. 157.
65 *Summa,'Elegantius'*, Part VII (13), vol. 2, p. 159.
66 Hobbes, *Leviathan*, 15, Cf. Hobbes's '*Science of Natural Justice*', ed. C. Walton and P. J. Johnson (Dordrecht, 1987).
67 Hobbes, *Leviathan*, Chapter 15, laws 15 and 16.
68 *Priusquam interroges, ne vituperes quemquam; et cum interrogaveris, corripe iuste.*
69 *Antecessores nostri apostoli prohibuerunt.* Gratian, *Decretum*, II. iii. q. 5. 4, *PL*, 187. 677 and Friedberg, vol. I.

Notes 213

70 *Ne in sua causa quis iudicet* (II. ii).
71 Dari non potest iudex in causa sua, quoniam de ea non cognoscet neque pronunciabit. Pilii, Tancredi, Gratiae Libri de Iudiciorum Ordine, ed. F. Bergmann (Göttingen, 1842), p. 37.
72 See, too, Deuteronomy 1.17, Romans 2.11, James 2.9.
73 Quia munera excaecant oculos sapientium, et mutant verba iustorum, Burchard of Worms, Decreta, xvi.2, PL, 140.909.
74 Iustitiam ergo vendere iniquitas est. Policraticus, V. 11, ed. C. J. Webb, V.12 (Oxford, 1929) p. 332.
75 Iudices et accusatores tales esse debent qui omni careant suspicione et ex radice caritatis suam desiderent promere sententiam. Diversorum patrum sententie sive Collectio in LXXIV titulos digesta, ed. J. T. Gilchrist, Monumenta Iuris Canonici, 1 (Vatican, 1973), Titulus 12, (98), p. 70.
76 Sed nec iudicem terret auctorita ligatorum. Policraticus, V.11, p. 335.
77 Exuit persona iudicis quisquis amicum induit. Aequitas enim, cui iudex obsequium debet, odii sinistram aut amoris dexteram nescit; nam a veritate non licet in iudiciis declinare. John of Salisbury, Policraticus, ed. C. C. J. Webb, V.12 (Oxford, 1929), p. 334. Cicero actually says: ponit enim personam amici cum induit iudicis. De officiis, iii. 10. Cf. Policraticus, V.11, p. 338.
78 Iudices prius probare debent quo animo quisque accusat, quam accusationem suscipiunt. Ivo of Chartres, Panormia, IV. 30, PL, 161. 1189.
79 Inimici non possunt accusare. Ivo of Chartres, Panormia, IV. 62, PL, 161. 1196.
80 Nec accusatores vel testes supecti recipiantur quia propinquitatis et familiaritatis ac dominationis affectio veritatem impedire solet. Ps.-Calixtus, Ep. 2. 17, 18, Decretales Pseudo-Isidorianae et Capitula Angilramni, ed. P. Hinschius (Leipzig, 1863), 141; Diversorum patrum sententie sive Collectio in LXXIV titulos digesta, ed. J. T. Gilchrist, Monumenta Iuris Canonici, 1 (Vatican, 1973), Titulus V, (48), p. 46.
81 Dignum est ut vita innocentis non maculetur pernicie accusantium. Burchard of Worms, Decreta, xvi. 5, PL, 140. 910, Decretum of Pope Felix, Chapter 15.
82 Quod accusatores sacerdotum non debent audiri, nisi prius vita eorum et intentio discutiatur. Anselm of Lucca, Collectio canonum, III. 12, ed. F. Thaner (Oeniponte, 1906), p. 123, PL, 149. 494.
83 Anselm of Lucca, Collectio canonum, III.34, ed. F. Thaner (Oeniponte, 1906), p. 133, PL, 149. 495.
84 Suspecti, et inimici, et facile litigantes, et pravae conversationis, et qui non tenent ac docent rectam fidem, accusatores esse non possunt. Anselm of Lucca, Collectio canonum, III. 16, ed. F. Thaner (Oeniponte, 1906), p. 126, PL, 149. 494.
85 Nec falsi nec inimici nec suspecti suscipiantur in accusatione. Anselm of Lucca, Collectio canonum, III. 60, ed. F. Thaner (Oeniponte, 1906), p. 15, PL, 149. 496.
86 Gratian, Decretum, II, *Causa*, iii. q. 5. 2 and 3.
87 Convitiandi et maledicendi. Agant quod causa desiderat temperent se ab iniuria, Summa 'Elegantius', II, Part VI (52), p. 128.
88 Et calumpnia in omnem facient procul.
89 See p. 107.
90 Maximus of Tours, Collectio sermonum antiqua, Sermo 40.
91 Ipse voluit esse ipse advocatus tuus, ipse iurispertus tuus, ipse assessor patris, ipse iudex tuus. Augustine, Enarrationes in Psalmos, 54, xiv, CCSL, 39. Cf. Augustine, Sermones, 107, PL, 38.629, which simply has advocatus et iudex noster.
92 Augustine, Enarrationes in Psalmos, 66, vii, CCSL, 39.

214 *Notes*

93 *Sermones* 114, ed. *Revue Bénédictine*, 73, p. 27.
94 *Nullus umquam presumat accusator simul esse et iudex vel testis, quoniam in omni iudicio quattuor personas necesse est semper adesse, id est, iudices electos, accusatores idoneos, defensores congruos atque testes legitimos.* Ps.-Fabianus, Ep. 2.32, *Decretales Pseudo-Isidorianae et Capitula Angilramni*, ed. P. Hinschius (Leipzig, 1863), p. 165; *Diversorum patrum sententie sive Collectio in LXXIV titulos digesta*, ed. J. T. Gilchrist, *Monumenta Iuris Canonici*, 1 (Vatican, 1973), Titulus V, (50), p. 47.
95 Burchard of Worms, *Decreta*, xvi.15, *PL*, 140. 911, and Chapter 31, vol. 916.
96 *Nullus umquam presumat accusator simul esse et iudex vel testis quoniam in omni iudicio iiii personas esse necesse est: iudices electos, accusatores congruos, defensores ydoneos atque testes legitimos. Summa 'Elegantius'*, II, Part VII (5), p. 155.
97 *Nullus umquam presumat accusator simul esse et iudex vel testis quoniam in omni iudicio iiii personas esse necesse est: iudices electos, accusatores congruos, defensores ydoneos atque testes legitimos. Summa 'Elegantius'*, II, Part VII (3), p. 155.
98 See p. 113 following.
99 *Iudices debent uti equitate, testes veritate, accusatores intentione ad amplificandam causam, defensores extenuatione ad minuendam causam.* Ps.-Fabianus, Ep. 2. 32, *Decretales Pseudo-Isidorianae et Capitula Angilramni*, ed. P. Hinschius (Leipzig, 1863), p. 165; *Diversorum patrum sententie sive Collectio in LXXIV titulos digesta*, ed. J. T. Gilchrist, *Monumenta Iuris Canonici*, 1 (Vatican, 1973), Titulus V, (50), p. 47.
100 *Accusatores et iudices non idem sint, sed per se accusatores, per se iudices, per se testes, per se accusati unusquisque in suo ordinabiliter ordine.* Ps-Damasus, Ep. 3.16, *Decretales Pseudo-Isidorianae et Capitula Angilramni*, ed. P. Hinschius (Leipzig, 1863), p. 504, *Diversorum patrum sententie sive Collectio in LXXIV titulos digesta*, ed. J. T. Gilchrist, *Monumenta Iuris Canonici*, 1 (Vatican, 1973), Titulus 12, (101),p. 71. The same Ps.-Damasus text ruling that no one should be judge, accuser and witness: *Accusatores vero et iudices non idem sint sed per se accusatores, per se iudices, per se testes*, appears in shorter form in the *CLXXXIII tituli*, 77 (4), p. 127.
101 See further pp. 130–6.
102 *Non tanquam idem sit accusator et iudex, sed quasi denunciante fama vel deferente clamore officii sui debitum exsequatur.* Canon 8 of the Fourth Lateran Council, Benedict IX, *Decretals*, X. 5. 1. 24, and cf. Henry Ansgar Kelly, 'Inquisitorial due process and the status of secret crimes', *Proceedings of the Eighth International Congress on Medieval Canon Law, Monumenta Iuris Canonici*, 9 (1992), p. 409.
103 *Non ad praeiudicandum, sed potius ad ea quae Deo sunt placita prosequendum.* Gregory IX, *Decretales*, IX. 1. 31. 1.
104 *Select cases from ... Canterbury*, p. 42.
105 *Causam autem recusationis assigno quia estis vos domine cantor amicus sive familiaris abbati matine et conventui ligatoribus.* Transcript of a case of 1278, edited in R. Helmholz, 'Standards of impartiality for papal judges delegate', *Canon Law and the Law of England* (London, 1987), p. 38.
106 Magister Damasus, *Die Summa de ordine iudiciario*, XXVIII Quellen, III. ii, p. 22.
107 Magister Damasus, *Die Summa de ordine iudiciario*, XXIX Quellen, III. ii, p. 24 gives a list, and see R. Helmholz, 'Standards of impartiality for papal judges delegate', *Canon Law and the Law of England* (London, 1987), p. 21.
108 Magister Damasus, *Die Summa de ordine iudiciario*, XXIX Quellen, III. ii, p. 23.

Notes 215

109 R. Helmholz, 'Standards of impartiality for papal judges delegate', *Canon Law and the Law of England* (London, 1987), p. 28 and note 32.
110 R. Helmholz, 'Standards of impartiality for papal judges delegate', *Canon Law and the Law of England* (London, 1987), pp. 28–34.
111 R. Helmholz, 'Standards of impartiality for papal judges delegate', *Canon Law and the Law of England* (London, 1987), p. 27.
112 Magister Damasus, *Die Summa de ordine iudiciario*, XXIX *Quellen* (1926), p. 23.
113 *Impetratum, videlicet, ad postulationem adversarii tantum, ad cuius instancian solam curia romana non consuevit iudicem dare, nisi utraque pars in iudicem consentirent. Select Cases from ... Canterbury*, Selden Society 95, p. 380.
114 William of Drogheda, *Summa Aurea*, *Quellen*, II. ii, 2.2, 8.
115 R. Helmholz, 'Standards of impartiality for papal judges delegate', *Canon Law and the Law of England* (London, 1987), p. 21.
116 R. Helmholz, 'Standards of impartiality for papal judges delegate', *Canon Law and the Law of England* (London, 1987), p. 23.
117 R. Helmholz, 'Standards of impartiality for papal judges delegate', *Canon Law and the Law of England* (London, 1987), pp. 25–7.
118 *De recusatoris assensu*, *Glossa ordinaria* ad. X. 2. 28. 61,
119 William of Drogheda, *Summa Aurea*, 381–2, cited in R. Helmholz, 'Standards of impartiality for papal judges delegate', *Canon Law and the Law of England* (London, 1987), p. 25.
120 Anselm of Lucca, *Collectio canonum*, II. 10, ed. F. Thaner (Oeniponte, 1906). p. 80.
121 Demosthenes, *De Corona*, 1. Cf. Aristophanes, *The Wasps*, 725 and 919 and Euripides, *Heracleidae*, 180; *Andromache*, 957.
122 Seneca, *Medea*, 195.
123 *Digest* 5.1.17, *Code* 3.51. Article 10 of the Universal Declaration of Human Rights has it. It is the rule that arbitrators must not take into account evidence known to only one of the parties. 'I find the master minds of every century are consentaneous in holding it to be an indispensable requirement of justice that the party who has to decide shall hear both sides, giving each an opportunity of hearing what is urged against him.' Re Brook and Delcomyn (1864) 16 C.B. (N.S.) 403, 416, Erle C.J.
124 *Diversorum patrum sententie sive Collectio in LXXIV titulos digesta*, ed. J. T. Gilchrist, *Monumenta Iuris Canonici*, 1 (Vatican, 1973), p. 56ff. Cf. Ps-Anacletus, Ep. 2.20,21, *Decretales Pseudo-Isidorianae et Capitula Angilramni*, ed. P. Hinschius (Leipzig, 1863), 77, *Diversorum patrum sententie sive collectio in LXXIV titulos digesta*, ed. J. T. Gilchrist (Vatican, 1973), Titulus, VIII (70), p. 56.Cf. Ps-Sixtus II *Decretales Pseudo-Isidorianae et Capitula Angilramni*, ed. P. Hinschius (Leipzig, 1863), 72, *Diversorum patrum sententie sive collectio in LXXIV titulos digesta*, ed. J. T. Gilchrist (Vatican, 1973), Titulus, VIII (72), p. 57.
125 *Quae quisque actione agere volet, eam edere debet, ut proinde sciat reus utrum cedere an contendere ultra debeat. Digest*, II.13.1.
126 *Omnia ergo que adversus absentes in omni negotio aut loco aguntur aut iudicantur, omnino vacuentur.* Council of Chalcedon, *Acta*, 10, Mansi 7. 206.
127 *Omnia que adversus absentes in omni loco aguntur aut iudicantur omnino evacuentur, quoniam absentem nullus addicit nec ulla lex damnat.* Ps-Cornelius, Ep. 2.6, *Decretales Pseudo-Isidorianae et Capitula Angilramni*, ed. P. Hinschius (Leipzig, 1863), 174, *Diversorum patrum sententie sive Collectio in LXXIV titulos digesta*, ed. J. T. Gilchrist, *Monumenta Iuris Canonici*, 1 (Vatican, 1973), Titulus 13, (106), p. 72. Gratian, *Decretum*, II. iii. q. 9. 4 and 3, *PL*, 187. 697.

128 *Caveant iudices ecclesie ne absente eo cuius causa ventilatur sententiam proferant, quia irrita erit.* Ps.-Eleutherus, Ep. 1.5, *Decretales Pseudo-Isidorianae et Capitula Angilramni,* ed. P. Hinschius (Leipzig, 1863), p. 126; *Diversorum patrum sententie sive Collectio in LXXIV titulos digesta,* ed. J. T. Gilchrist, *Monumenta Iuris Canonici,* 1 (Vatican, 1973), Titulus 13, (103), p. 71, cf. *CLXXXIII tituli,* 76 (28), p. 125. Cf. Gratian, *Decretum,* II.iii.q.9.2, *PL,* 187.697 and Friedberg, vol. I, citing the same text. However, *rite* appears in Roman law too, where its loading must be rather different.Code 7.45.13, *quas non rite iudicatas.*
129 *Ut nemo absens dijudicetur: quia humanae et divinae hoc prohibent leges.* Burchard of Worms, *Decreta,* xvi. 13, *PL,* 140. 911, from Ps.-Zepherus.
130 Burchard of Worms, *Decreta,* xvi. 14, *PL,* 140. 911.
131 *Ea quae adversus absentes aguntur evacuentur.* Anselm of Lucca, *Collectio canonum,* III. 57, ed. F. Thaner (Oeniponte, 1906), p. 144. III. 57, *PL,* 149. 496.
132 *Accusatori omnino non credi decernimus, qui absente adversario causam suggerit, ante utriusque partis iustam discussionem.* Gratian, *Decretum,* II. iii. q. 9, *PL,* 187. 697 and Friedberg, vol. I.
133 *De libello infanie diximus, et quia absentem suggillat qui per libellum infamat, utrum quid in absentem vocem accusationis vel testimonii exhibere valeat disquiramus.* Summa 'Elegantius', Part VI (52), p. 128.
134 *Summa Codicis des Irnerius,* ed. H. Fitting (Berlin, 1894), IV.19, p. 91.
135 *Presens debeat esse ille contra quem fit inquisitio.* Vincent of Spain on Constitution 7. *Constitutiones Concilii Quarti Lateranensis una cum Commentariis Glossatorum,* ed. A. García y García, *Monumenta Iuris Canonici,* 2 (Rome, 1981), p. 299.
136 *Constitutiones Concilii Quarti Lateranensis una cum Commentariis glossatorum,* ed. A. García y García, *Monumenta Iuris Canonici, Corpus glossatorum,* 2 (Rome, 1981), p. 299.
137 *Debent autem esse presentes in inquisitione et se defendere Constitutiones Concilii Quarti Lateranensis una cum Commentariis glossatorum,* ed. A. García y García, *Monumenta Iuris Canonici, Corpus glossatorum,* 2 (Rome, 1981), p. 468.
138 *Constitutiones Concilii Quarti Lateranensis una cum Commentariis glossatorum,* ed. A. García y García, *Monumenta Iuris Canonici, Corpus glossatorum,* 2 (Rome, 1981), *Casus Fudenses.*
139 *Lite contestata sepe contingit reum abesse, et quidem quandoque contumatia, quandoque necessitate, quandoque ... negligentia vel voluntate. Distinctiones glossatorum,* Tübingen *Distinctiones,* ed. E. Seckel (Graz, 1956), p. 297. There are various ways in which this could be properly dealt with.
140 *Propria voce et presente eo quem accusare voluerit suam quisquis agat accusationem, nec absente eo quem accusare voluerit, quicumque accusator credatur.* Ps.-Calixtus, Ep. 2. 17, 78, *Decretales Pseudo-Isidorianae et Capitula Angilramni,* ed. P. Hinschius (Leipzig, 1863), p. 141; *Diversorum patrum sententie sive Collectio in LXXIV titulos digesta,* ed. J. T. Gilchrist, *Monumenta Iuris Canonici,* 1 (Vatican, 1973), Titulus V, (48), p. 46. Cf. CLXXXIII tituli, 81, pp. 132–3.
141 *Nec sententia absente parte alia a iudice dicta ullam obtinebit firmitatem, neque absens per alium accusare aut accusari potest ned adfinis testis admittatur.* Ps.-Felix 1, Ep. 2.13, *Decretales Pseudo-Isidorianae et Capitula Angilramni,* ed. P. Hinschius (Leipzig, 1863), p. 202; *Diversorum patrum sententie sive Collectio in LXXIV titulos digesta,* ed. J.T. Gilchrist, *Monumenta Iuris Canonici,* 1 (Vatican, 1973), Titulus V, (55), p. 49.

142 *Ut nullus iudicetur nisi legitimos habuerit accusatores praesentes.* Anselm of Lucca, *Collectio canonum*, III. 47, ed. F. Thaner (Oeniponte, 1906), p. 139, *PL*, 149. 496 and *Ut nihil contra quemlibet accusatum absque legitimo accusatore fiat.* Anselm of Lucca, *Collectio canonum*, III. 64, ed. F. Thaner (Oeniponte, 1906), p. 147, *PL*, 149. 497.
143 *Propria voce, si legitima et condigna accusatoris persona fuerit, presente videlicet eo quem accusare desiderat, quia nullus absente aut accusari potest aut accusare.* Ps.-Stephanus, Ep. 2.8, *Decretales Pseudo-Isidorianae et Capitula Angilramni*, ed. P. Hinschius (Leipzig, 1863), p. 185; *Diversorum patrum sententie sive Collectio in LXXIV titulos digesta*, ed. J. T. Gilchrist, *Monumenta Iuris Canonici*, 1 (Vatican, 1973), Titulus V, (52), p. 48. Cf. Ivo of Chartres, *Panormia*, IV.54, *PL*, 161. 1193.
144 Master Damasus, *Die 'Summa de ordine iudiciario'*, (XXXIII) *Quellen*, III. ii, p. 26.
145 *Select Cases from … Canterbury*, p. 39.
146 *Munimenta Academica*, ed. Anstey, Rolls Series, vol. II, p. 537.
147 Boniface VIII, *Statuta*, Sext. 5.2.20.
148 *Ei incumbit probatio qui dicit, non qui negat. Digest*, 22. 3. 2.
149 *Quia non statim qui accusatur reus est, sed qui convincitur criminosus.* Ps.-Jerome, *De Septem ordinibus Ecclesiae*, *PL*, 30. 154 and see R. Reynolds, 'The Pseudo-Hieronymian *De septem ordinibus ecclesiae*. Notes on its origins, abridgements, and use in early medieval canonical collections', *Revue Bénédictine* 80 (1970), pp. 238–43.
150 Richard M. Fraher, 'Ut nullus', p. 495.
151 The *Collectio in 183 titulos digesta*, ed. J. Motta, *Monumenta Iuris Canonici, Corpus Collectionum* 7 (Vatican, 1988), Tit. 76 (3), p. 12, from Ps. Felix (*Prius probare debet*).
152 Burchard of Worms, *Decreta*, xvi.18, *PL*, 140. 912.
153 *Ut nullus describatur reus, priusquam convincatur.* Burchard of Worms, *Decreta*, xvi.6, *PL*, 140. 910.
154 Gregory IX, *Decretals*, V. 1. 8.
155 *Sanctius est impunitum relinqui facinus nocentis quam innocentem damnare.* Bartolus on D. 48. 9, 5 no.2. W. Ullmann, 'Medieval principles of evidence', *Law Quarterly Review*, 62 (London 1946), p. 78.
156 *Quod si unius prae ceteris est fama hilarior, ex officio iudicantis prout poterit parti adversariae compensabitur.* John of Salisbury, *Policraticus*, V.13, ed. C. C. J. Webb (Oxford, 1929), p. 341.
157 Jenny McEwan, *Evidence and the Adversarial Process* (Oxford, 1992), p. 152.
158 'Legal rules are not to be applied so as to prejudice those who for some reason, for which they are not to blame, are incapable of safeguarding their own interests.' 'It can be argued that it is unjust to act on a probability to someone's disadvantage.' Cf. Jenny McEwan, *Evidence and the Adversarial Process* (Oxford, 1992), p. 38. Cf. J. J. Thompson, 'Probabilities as relevant facts' in (idem) *Rights, Restitution and Risk* (Cambridge, MA, 1986).
159 *Utrum liceat advocato eius qui impetitur linguam variare in ea excipere in qua potentior est queritur.*
160 *Iura ab origine dignitatis sue degenerant quotiens ab ore laico procedunt. Summa 'Elegantius'*, Part VI (69a), p. 135.
161 *Nec sine discussione admittere accusatores.*
162 *Ius suum consequi.*
163 *Apud eos probare crimina episcopi.*
164 To bring a defence is not implicitly to admit anything. Justinian, *Digest*, 44. 1. 9. *Agere etiam is videtur, qui exceptione utitur; nam reus in exceptione actor est.* Justinian, *Digest*, 44. 1. 1. Cf. *Neque pro inquisicione contra aliquem*

218 *Notes*

factam, nisi delatus in sui defensione daret testes pro quibus in sui defensione daret testes pro quibus recipiendi oporteret inquirentem extra locum exire. Valls Taberner, p. 330.
165 *Nemo prohibetur, pluribus exceptionibus uti, quamvis diversae sunt.* Justinian, *Digest*, 44. 1.8.

16 Notoriety

1. Luke 16.1ff.
2. The question of bearing false witness against one's neighbour, forbidden by the commandment, belongs to a different area, for the informer may very well be telling the truth. On the issue of propriety in a witness, and all the formal restrictions which attach to his acceptability in a court, the mediaeval texts have a great deal to say, but for reasons of space that must form the subject of a different study.
3. *Digest*, 50. 13. 5.
4. Edward Peters, 'Wounded names: the medieval doctrine of infamy', *Law in Mediaeval Life and Thought*, ed. Edward B. King and Susan J. Ridyard (Sewanee, 1990), p. 48.
5. For example, Ezekiel 16.36 and a number of references in the prophets and Wisdom literature, I Corinthians 11.4.
6. Isidore, *Etymologiae*, Book V. 27.
7. Edward Peters, 'Wounded names', pp. 48–50, citing Georg May, 'Die Anfänge der Infamie im kanonischen Recht', Zeitschrift der Savigny – Stiftung für Rechgeschichte', *Kanonistische Abteilung*, 78 (1961), pp. 76–94.
8. Edward Peters, 'Wounded names', p. 452.
9. E. Pólay, *Iniuria Types in Roman Law* (Budapest, 1986).
10. J. Balon, *Traité du Droit Salique, Ius Medii Aevi*, 3 (Namur, 1965), p. 375.
11. *Ignominium, eo quod desinat habere honestatis nomen is qui in aliquo crimine deprehenditur. Dictum est autem ignominium quasi sine nomine, sicut ignarus sine scientia, sicut ignobilis sine nobilitate. Hoc quoque et infamium, quasi sine bona fama (Etymologiae, V. 27).*
12. But loss of position or standing in mediaeval societies was a more complex matter, for arguably, even if everyone thought less well of him afterwards, the miscreant might remain – and mostly would remain – whoever he was before in terms of rank and possessions.
13. See Richard M. Fraher, 'Conviction according to conscience. The mediaeval jurists' debate concerning judicial discretion and the law of proof', *Law and History Review*, 7 (1989), p. 34.
14. For example, Tertullian *Ad nationes*, I. vii, p. 17.
15. Marius Victorinus, *De Definitionibus*, p. 10. Cf. Augustine, Letters 86, *CSEL*, 44. 2, p. 396.
16. *Apologeticum*, p. 7.
17. Chromatius of Aquilegia, *Tractatus*, 47, CCSL, 9A.
18. Augustine, *De moribus ecclesiae catholicae et Manichaeorum*, I, *PL*, 32. 1321.
19. *Summa 'Elegantius'*, Part V, p. 66.
20. For example, Theodosian Code 8.11. 4.
21. *Summa 'Elegantius'*, Part V, p. 51.
22. *Summa 'Elegantius'*, Part V, p. 67.
23. Cf. Augustine, *Enchiridion* 21, CCSL, 46.
24. *Et exspectavi, ut faceret iudicium, et ecce iniquitas, et iustitiam et ecce clamor* (Isaiah 5.7).

25 *Omnis amaritudo et ira et indignatio et clamore et blasphemia tollatur a vobis cum omni malitia.*
26 Augustine, *Sermo* 20, *CCSL*, 41, line 141.
27 Gregory the Great, *Regula pastoralis* III. 31, *PL*, 77. 113.
28 Theodosian Code 9. 34. 3, 320 AD.
29 Theodosian Code 9. 34. 9.
30 Theodosian Code 9. 34. 4, 328 AD.
31 Theodosian Code 9. 34. 1, 319 AD, cf. 9 3 4. 2 (313 AD).
32 Theodosian Code 9. 34. 6, 355 AD.
33 Theodosian Code 9. 16. 1.
34 Theodosian Code 9. 25. 3.
35 Theodosian Code 9. 39. 1 and 2 (383 and 385 AD).
36 Theodosian Code 9. 39. 3 (398 AD).
37 Theodosian Code,10. 10. 1.
38 Carlo Ghisalberti, 'La teoria del notorio nel diritto comune', *Annali di storia del diritto*, 1 (1957), 403–451. K. Pennington, *The Prince and the Law, 1200–1600* (Berkeley, 1993); C. Lefebvre, 'Les origines romaines de la procédure sommaire aux xii et xiiie siècles', *Ephemerides Iuris Canonici*, 12 (1956), 149–197. J. Franklin, 'The ancient legal sources of seventeenth-century probability', *The Uses of Antiquity*, ed. S. Gaukroger (Dordrecht, 1991), 23–88. R. Helmholz, 'Conviction according to conscience', *Law and History Review*, 7 (1989), 23–88. J. W. Baldwin, 'The intellectual preparation for the canon of 1215 against ordeals' *Speculum*, 36 (1961), 613–36.
39 *Digest*, 48. 16. 6. 4 (Paul). Cf. Code 9.2. 7.
40 Cf. *Causa*, 2.6.41 (titulus); *Causa*, 2. 1. 1.
41 By the early fourteenth century. It appears at the Council of Pisa in 1409. Lathan has it in 1280 (*Revised Medieval Latin Wordlist*).
42 Bernard of Clairvaux, *Sermo in Cantica Canticorum* 66.14, *Opera Omnia*, ed. J. Leclercq (Rome, 1957–78), II.187–8.
43 *Nullum damnare nisi comprobatum, nullum excommunicare nisi discussum. Nullus potest damnari, nisi prius canonice vocatus refutaveri reddere rationem. The Collectio in 183 titulos digesta*, ed. J. Motta, *Monumenta Iuris Canonici, Corpus Collectionum* Series B, 7 (Vatican, 1988), Tit. 85(1), p. 137, from 'Augustine'.
44 *Si per clamorem et famam ad aures superioris pervenerit. Decretal Inquisitionis negotium of 1212*, Gregory IX, *Decretals*, X. 5. 1. 21.
45 *Nec ad petitionem eorum qui libellum infamationis porrigunt in occulto procedendum est. Decretal Inquisitionis negotium of 1212*, Gregory IX, *Decretals*, X. 5. 1. 21.
46 *Crimen in publicam notitionem defertur. Summa 'Elegantius'*, vol. 2, Part 5, p. 55.
47 *Si servato ordine correptionis, odii magis amaritudine et sui ostensione quam zelo iustitie, crimen cuiuspiam publicatur. Summa 'Elegantius'*, vol. 2, Part 5, p. 55.
48 *Summa 'Elegantius'*, Part V, p. 62.
49 But the judge ought to distinguish between deliberate false accusation: *falsa crimina intendere* (*Digest* 48.16.1.1) and the making of a genuine mistake. Gregory IX, *Decretals*, V.2.1 and 2. *Summa 'Elegantius'*, vol. 2, p. 61. *bicunque potest dubitari, numquid actori ius competat ex probationibus factis, nec constat, ei ius non competere, nec in evidenti calumpnia invenitur, illic reus debeat condempnari.* Johannes Fagelli de Pisis, *Tractatus brevis de summariis cognitionibus.* ed. L. Wahrmund, *Quellen zur Geschichte des Römische-Kanonischen Prozesses im Mittelalter* (Innsbruck, 1928) IV. v, p. 24.

50 *Prevaricatores sunt qui vitia partis adverse attenuant et sua produnt et cum in causa iuvare simulent magis ledunt. Summa 'Elegantius'*, Part V, p. 63. The word can be used equivocally: *Equivocatur autem nomen ad falsum et fraudulentum advocatum et ad fictum accusatorem qui vera crimina non sincere prosequitur, contigentia omittens.*
51 *Summa 'Elegantius in iure divino'*, Part V (27), ed. G. Fransen and S. Kuttner, *Monumenta Iuris Canonici*, Series A: *Corpus glossatorum*, 1, vol. 2, p. 64.
52 Theodosian Code 9.38.3 (398 AD). This notion reappears in the twelfth century, for example in the *Summa 'Elegantius'*, where it is asked whether fresh allegations ought to be accepted after sentence has been pronounced, vol. 2, Part 7, 2a, pp. 153–4.
53 *De his criminibus de quibus absolutus est accusatus, refricari accusatio non potest*, Burchard of Worms, *Decreta*, xvi. 9, *PL*, 140. 911. See pp. 000.
54 Gregory IX, *Decretals*, V. 1. 6, ed. A. Friedberg, *Corpus Iuris Canonici* (Leipzig, 1881).
55 *Cum super excessibus suis quisquam fuerit infamatus ita, ut iam clamor ascendat, qui diutius sine scandalo dissimulari non possit, vel sine periculo tolerari* (Canon 8).
56 Richard M. Fraher, 'Conviction according to conscience: the medieval jurists' debate concerning judicial discretion and the law of proof', *Law and History Review*, 7 (1989), p. 33 ff.
57 Richard M. Fraher, 'Conviction according to conscience: the medieval jurists' debate concerning judicial discretion and the law of proof', *Law and History Review*, 7 (1989), p. 37.
58 Richard M. Fraher, 'Conviction according to conscience: the medieval jurists' debate concerning judicial discretion and the law of proof', *Law and History Review*, 7 (1989), p. 39.
59 Richard M. Fraher, 'Conviction according to conscience: the medieval jurists' debate concerning judicial discretion and the law of proof', *Law and History Review*, 7 (1989), p. 41.
60 *Justus non solum perpetrandi mali a se amputat levem occasionem, sed et radicem temerarii judicii, hoc est suspicionem.* Peter the Chanter, *Verbum abbreviatum*, 75, *PL*, 205. 220.
61 *Quia suspiciosi consueverunt esse rumorosi.* Peter the Chanter, *Verbum abbreviatum*, 76, *PL*, 205. 223.
62 *Et qui audiens at proferens illoto et turpi utitur sermone eius vita est inhonestior. Tales bibulas habent aures, linguasque prurientes, et sermonibus cognatis mores similes, rumorosi, rumusculosi et nugigeruli, qui, quod nesciunt, proferunt, cum viri sententia debeat esse certa animi et indubitata responsio.* Peter the Chanter, *Verbum abbreviatum*, 76, *PL*, 205. 224.
63 *Dubius testis non remanet impunitus, nec ergo dubius assertor alicuius rei.* Peter the Chanter, *Verbum abbreviatum*, 76, *PL*, 205.224.
64 *Magis periculosum est praecipitare sententiam, per quam laeditur fama alicujus et incrustatur, quam illam per quam minuitur, vel deperit recula ipsius.* Peter the Chanter, *Verbum abbreviatum*, 76, *PL*, 205.224.
65 *Hoc vitium rumorosorum comitatur inconstantia.* Peter the Chanter, *Verbum abbreviatum*, 77, *PL*, 205.225.
66 *Glossa ordinaria* to Gregory IX, *Decretals* X. 2. 27. 23 (*Cum te*), cited in *Select Cases on Defamation to 1600*, ed. R. Helmholz, Selden Society 101 (London, 1985), p. xix.
67 *Select Cases on Defamation to 1600*, ed. R. Helmholz, Selden Society 101 (London, 1985), p. xxi.
68 *Select Cases on Defamation to 1600*, ed. R. Helmholz, Selden Society 101 (London, 1985), pp. xxvi–xxvii.

69 *Select Cases on Defamation to 1600*, ed. R. Helmholz, Selden Society 101 (London, 1985), pp. xvi–xvii, and of course the Decretals of Gregory IX (1234) were not yet available.
70 *Select Cases on Defamation to 1600*, ed. R. Helmholz, Selden Society 101 (London, 1985), p. xiv.
71 *Select Cases on Defamation to 1600*, ed. R. Helmholz, Selden Society 101 (London, 1985), pp. xv–xviii.
72 *Select Cases from ... Canterbury*, D. 4, p. 378.

17 Shortening the process

1 *Select Cases from ... Canterbury*, p. 57.
2 *Sed crimen per officiales sufficit iudici denunciari*, Fowler-Magerl, Appendix IV, p. 292.
3 *In examinandis testibus officum judicis debet esse curiosum, id est, judex debet esse solicitus et ad curam judicis pertinet hoc, scilicet examinare, unde hoc non est in potestate partis*. Baldus on C. iv. 2. 19, no. 3, fol.53. W. Ullmann, 'Medieval principles of evidence', *Law Quarterly Review*, 62 (London 1946), p. 78.
4 *Iudex tamen potest ex officio suo testes producere ad inquirendam veritatem*. Bartolus, Lecture on C. ix. 42. 2, no.2, fol. 124. W. Ullmann, 'Medieval principles of evidence', *Law Quarterly Review*, 62 (London 1946), p. 79.
5 This takes the form of what was clearly a mnemonic:

> *Maior, sponte, sciens, contra se, ubi ius sit, et hostis*
> *Nec natura, rei favor aut lis iusve repugnet.*

Magister Damasus, *Die Summa de ordine iudiciario*, ed. L. Wahrmund, *Quellen*, IV. iv, pp. 1–45.
6 *Iudices prius probare debent quo animo quisque accusat, quam accusationem suscipiant*. Ivo of Chartres, *Panormia*, II. cx, PL, 161. 1205.
7 G. R. Evans, *Resolving Complaints and Grievances in Universities: The Way Forward*, Report No. 8, Council for Academic Freedom and Academic Standards (2000).
8 Richard M. Fraher, 'Conviction according to conscience: the medieval jurists' debate concerning judicial discretion and the law of proof', *Law and History Review*, 7 (1989), p. 25.
9 It is a normal requirement that those who are to accuse or bear witness must swear that they have no malicious motive: *Iurabit quidem actor, quod non animo calumpniandi petit vel quod non animo calumpniandi litem movit, sed quia existimat, se bonam causam habere secundum rationem aut secundum consuetudinem vel constitutum illius loci. Der Ordo Invocato Christi Nomine*, ed. Wahrmund, *Quellen*,Vi (Heidelberg, 1931), p. 69.
10 See pp. 162–3.
11 Jehan Dahyot-Dolivet, 'La procédure judiciaire d'office dans l'église jusqu'à l'avenement du pape Innocent III', *Apollinaris*, 41 (1968), 443–55. W. Trusen, 'Der Inquisitionsprozess: Seine historischen Grundlagen und frühen Formen', *Zeitschrift der Savigny – Stiftung für Rechtsgeschichte*, 74 (1988), pp. 168–230. Henry Ansgar Kelly, 'Inquisitorial due process and the status of secret crimes', *Proceedings of the Eighth International Congress on Medieval Canon Law, Monumenta Iuris Canonici*, Series C: *Subsidia*, 9 (Vatican, 1992), pp. 407–27.
12 *Prelati tunc procedant ad inquirendum cum clamor sine scandalo tolerari non possit. Constitutiones Concilii Quarti Lateranensis una cum Commentariis*

222   Notes

  glossatorum, ed. A. García y García, *Monumenta Iuris Canonici, Corpus glossatorum*, 2 (Rome, 1981), p. 142.
13 *Summa des Paucapalea über das Decretum Gratiani, Causa* II, q. 1. ed. J. F. von Schulte (Geissen, 1890), p. 57 and *Die Summa Decretorum des Magister Rufinus*, ed. H. Singer (Paderborn, 1902), p. 238.
14 *Sunt et crimina iudici et toti plebi notoria, in quibus minime iudiciarius ordo desideratur. Summa Magistri Rolandi nachmals Papstes Alexander III*, ed. F. Thaner (Innsbruck, 1874), *Causa* II, Q.1, p. 16.
15 *Summa 'Elegantius'*, Part V (4), p. 51.
16 *Summa 'Elegantius'*, Part V (8), p. 54.
17 *Super notorio procedit iudex nemine accusante*. Gregory IX, Decretals V.1, from 'Augustine on Genesis'.
18 Richard M. Fraher, '*Ut nullus describatur reus prius quam convincatur*.' 'Presumption of innocence in medieval canon law?' *Proceedings of the Sixth International Congress, Monumenta Iuris Canonici*, Series C: *Subsidia*, 7 (1985), p. 495. See also Bruno Paradisi, 'Il diritto Romano nell'alto medio evo, le epistole di Nicola I e un'ipotesi del conrat', *Studia Gratiana XI, Collectanea S. Kuttner*, I (Bologna, 1967), pp. 209–51.
19 *In manifestis enim calliditate accusantium non opprimitur reus, nec tergiversatione proprium crimen celatur quum culpa sua oculis omnium sponte se ingerat, qui ideo institutus est, ut nec innocentia insidiis pateret adversantium, nec culpa delinquentium sententiam effugeret justi examinis*. Gratian, *Decretum*, II, *Causa* 2 q. 1. 15 ff.
20 He comments: *Hoc autem servandum est quando reum publica fama non vexat. Tunc enim auctoritate eiusdem Gregorii propter scandalum removendum, famam suam reum purgare oportet*. Gratian, *Decretum*, II, *Causa* 6. v. 2.
21 *An in manifestis iudiciarius ordo sit requirendus. Causa*, II.q.1. i. Gratian explains in a rubric that a condemnation is not valid unless the accused has either been convicted or confessed: *Damnari non valet nisi aut convictus aut sponte confessus*. The rule applies, he thinks, only to matters where the guilt has to be proved because it is hidden (*Causa* II. q. 1).
22 *Summa 'Elegantius'*, Part V (7–8), p. 54. See, too, Fraher, p. 499.
23 Fraher, *Ut nullus*, p. 499, discusses this eventuality.
24 *Summa 'Elegantius'*, Part V (7), p. 54.
25 *Summa 'Elegantius'*, Part V (8), p. 54.
26 *Summa 'Elegantius'*, Part V (8), p. 54.
27 Which becomes X. 5. 1. 24 of Gregory IX's *Decretals*.
28 The Scott Inquiry into the 'arms for Iran' scandal in England in the early 1990s made this point, in connection with the need to protect those in prominent positions from unnecessary exposure of their mistakes or wrongdoings in an inquiry in which they are merely witnesses and not themselves charged.
29 On the acceleration of hearings, see R. H. Helmholz, 'Ethical standards for advocates and proctors in theory and pratice', *Proceedings of the Fourth International Congress of Mediaeval Canon Law, Monumenta Iuris Canonici*, Series C: *Subsidia*, 5 (Vatican, 1976), p. 291ff.
30 Johannes Fagelli de Pisis, *Tractatus brevis de summariis cognitionibus*, ed. L. Wahrmund, *Quellen*, IV. v, p. 1. (He is conscious that such a treatise is needed, because there is a lack of literature on the subject.)
31 Johannes Fagelli de Pisis, *Tractatus brevis de summariis cognitionibus*, ed. L. Wahrmund, *Quellen*, IV. v, p. 2.
32 Johannes Fagelli de Pisis, *Tractatus brevis de summariis cognitionibus*, ed. L. Wahrmund, *Quellen* (Innsbruck, 1928) IV. v, p. 25.

33 Johannes Fagelli de Pisis, *Tractatus brevis de summariis cognitionibus*, ed. L. Wahrmund, *Quellen* (Innsbruck, 1928) IV. v, p. 5.
34 Johannes Fagelli de Pisis, *Tractatus brevis de summariis cognitionibus*, ed. L. Wahrmund, *Quellen* (Innsbruck, 1928) IV. v, p. 7.
35 Johannes Fagelli de Pisis, *Tractatus brevis de summariis cognitionibus*, ed. L. Wahrmund, *Quellen* (Innsbruck, 1928) IV. v, p. 14.
36 *Inaudita causa neminem patitur aequitatis ratio condempnari.* Johannes Fagelli de Pisis, *Tractatus brevis de summariis cognitionibus*, ed. L. Wahrmund, *Quellen* (Innsbruck, 1928) IV. v, p. 2.
37 *Et ideo dicitur, quod debent esse luce meridiana clariores, C. de probationibus.* Johannes Fagelli de Pisis, *Tractatus*, IV. v, p. 3.
38 Johannes Fagelli de Pisis, *Tractatus*, IV. v, p. 4. where he cites Azo as authority.
39 *Summa 'Elegantius'*, vol. 2, Part 5, p. 51.
40 *Summa 'Elegantius'*, vol. 2, Part 5, p. 51.
41 *Debet igitur esse presens is contra quem facienda est inquisitio, nisi se per contumaciam absentaverit; et exponenda sunt ei capitula de quibus fuerit inquirendum, ut facultatem habeat defendendi se ipsum. Et non solum dicta, sed etiam nomina ipsa testium sunt ei, ut quid et a quo sit dictum appareat, publicanda, necnon exceptiones et replicationes legitime admittende, ne per suppressionem nominum infamandi, per exceptionum vero exclusiobem deponendi falsum audacia prebeatur.* Gregory IX, *Decretals*, X.5.1.24, *Qualiter et quando*.
42 Henry Ansgar Kelly, 'Inquisitorial due process and the status of secret crimes', *Proceedings of the Eighth International Congress on Medieval Canon Law, Monumenta Iuris Canonici*, Series C: *Subsidia*, 9 (Vatican, 1992), p. 411. Kelly suggests that the defendant's right to know his rights is first discussed as late as Philip Probus (= Philippe Lepreux), a jurisconsult of Bourges, in John Monk's *Glossa aurea* (1535). Here it is argued that a defendant who does not use a defence allowed to him loses it, but that that would apply only if he knew he had it.
43 *Ex suo mero procedit officio.* Johannes Fagelli de Pisis, *Tractatus*, IV. v, p. 10.
44 *Nam in omni causa civili et criminali actore non probante reus absolvitur.* Johannes Fagelli de Pisis, *Tractatus*, IV. v, p. 10.
45 *Quia quaedam dicuntur de plano cognosci, id est sine libello, ut quidem dixerunt.* Johannes Fagelli de Pisis, *Tractatus*, IV. v, p. 12.
46 Johannes Fagelli de Pisis, *Tractatus*, IV. v, p. 12.
47 Johannes Fagelli de Pisis, *Tractatus*, IV. v, p. 13.
48 *Cum iudex maxime niti debeat ad certam ferendam sententiam.* Johannes Fagelli de Pisis, *Tractatus*, IV. v, p. 20. *Mihi autem videtur sine praeiudicio sententiae melioris, quod in hiis et similibus, ubi reo potest maius praeiudicium generari, quam in actione ad exibendum et in aliis suprascriptis, quod semiplena probatio fiat non per sacramentum, sed saltim per unum testem, qui semiplenam inducit probationem.* Johannes Fagelli de Pisis, *Tractatus brevis de summariis cognitionibus*, ed. L. Wahrmund, *Quellen*, IV. v, p. 23.
49 Clement V, V. 11.2. Johanes de Lignano's text is edited by Wahrmund, *Quellen*, IV. vi.
50 Johanes de Lignano, *Super Clementina 'Saepe'*, ed. Wahrmund, *Quellen*, IV. vi, p. 1.
51 Johanes de Lignano, *Super Clementina 'Saepe'*, IV. vi, p. 1.
52 *Simpliciter et de plano, ac sine strepitu et figura iudicii procedi mandamus.* Johanes de Lignano, *Super Clementina 'Saepe'*, IV. vi, p. 9.
53 *De quorum significatione verborum a multis contenditur, et qualiter procedi debeat dubitatum.* Johanes de Lignano, *Super Clementina 'Saepe'*, IV. vi, p. 9.

224 Notes

54 *Citationem vero ac praestationem iuramenti de calumnia vel malitia, sive de veritate dicenda, ne veritas occultetur, per commissionem huiusmodi intelligimus non excludi.* Johanes de Lignano, *Super Clementina 'Saepe'*, IV. vi, p. 9.
55 *Non erit processus propter hoc irritus, nec etiam irritandus.* Johanes de Lignano, *Super Clementina 'Saepe'*, IV. vi, p. 9.
56 Johanes de Lignano, *Super Clementina 'Saepe'*, IV. vi, p. 9.
57 Johanes de Lignano, *Super Clementina 'Saepe'*, IV. vi, p. 9.

18 Divine judgement, human judgement

1 Agobard of Lyons, *De divinis sententiis contra iudicium Dei*, ed. L. van Acker, *CCCM*, 52 (1981), p. 31.
2 Gratian i. 18, 17.
3 C. R.Cheney, *English Synodalia of the Thirteenth Century* (Oxford, 1941, 2nd edn. 1968), p. 3.
4 C. Lefebvre, 'Juges et savants en Europe, xiiie–xvie siècle', *Ephemerides Iuris Canonici* 22 (1966), p. 87.
5 C. Lefebvre, 'Juges et savants en Europe, xiiie–xvie siècle', *Ephemerides Iuris Canonici* 22 (1966), p. 87.
6 V. 34. 4.
7 *Deficiente accusatore reus sit cogendus ad purgationem.*
8 *Tunc purgationis est adhibendum remedium. Summa Magistri Rolandi nachmals Papstes Alexander III*, ed. F. Thaner (Innsbruck, 1874), *Causa*, II, Q.V, p. 17.
9 Ambrose, *Expositio Psalmi* cxviii, Prologue, 2, p. 4.
10 *Purgatio est cum factum conceditur, culpa removetur.* Cicero, *De Inventione*, I.xi.15.
11 *Purgatio est per quam eius qui accusatur non factum ipsum, sed voluntas defenditur.* Cicero, *De Inventione*, I. xxxi. 94.
12 Augustine, *Sermones*, 22, *CCSL*, 41, line 182.
13 Cf. *omnis enim purgatio aut per aquam fit aut per ignem aut per aerem. Mythographi Vaticani*, 2, C.79, line 42.
14 J. W. Baldwin, 'The intellectual preparation for the Canon of 1215 against ordeals', *Speculum*, 36 (1961), p. 613. See, too, Ugonis Summula de Pugna, ed. J. Palmerio, *Scripta Anecdota Glossatorum* (Bologna, 1913), Proemium.
15 J. W. Baldwin, 'The intellectual preparation for the Canon of 1215 against ordeals', *Speculum*, 36 (1961), p. 617.
16 Gratian, *Decretum*, II, *Causa*, II. v. 7. *Absolutio, facta secundum purgationem vulgarem, non tenet*, V. 34. 8.
17 V. 34. 8.
18 *PL*, 205.227–8 and 544.
19 *Prohibitae, quia per eos multoties condemnatur absolvendus, et Deus tentari videtur.* V. 35. 1.
20 Richard M. Fraher, 'Conviction according to conscience: the mediaeval jurists' debate concerning judicial discretion and the law of proof', *Law and History Review*,7 (1989), p. 24.
21 Richard M. Fraher suggests as much, in 'Conviction according to conscience: the mediaeval jurists' debate concerning judicial discretion and the law of proof', *Law and History Review*, 7 (1989), p. 24.
22 *Sacerdos a populo accusatus iuramento innocentiam suam asserat.* Gratian, *Decretum*, C II. v. 5.
23 *Si legitimi accusatores crimina sacerdotis probare non potuerint, et ipse negaverit, tunc ipse cum septem sociis si ordinis (si valet) a crimine semetipsum*

expurget. Diaconus vero si eodem crimine accusatus fuerit, cum tribus semetipsum excuset. Gratian, *Decretum*, II, *Causa*, II. v. 12.
24 *Qui eum de homicidio convincere possint, ut cum septima aut quinta manu sui ordinis, sicut expedire cognoveris, per purgationem canonicam innocentiam suam ostendat, sibi iniungas; quam quum praestiterit, suspensionem sine mora et difficultate relaxes, et eum testimonii boni virum annuncians, ab infamia homicidii nullius contradictione vel appellatione obstante auctoritate nostra fretus absolvas. Is autem, qui infamatur, sese immunem a crimine homicidii praestito iuramento firmabit, et purgatores, quod eum credant verum iurasse, iurare debebant.* Gratian, *Decretum*, II, *Causa*, II. v. 12.
25 *Infamatus, contra quem crimen probari non potest, debet se purgare iuramento de veritate, compurgatores vero de credulitate,* V. 34. 5.
26 *Compurgatores debent esse honesti, et notum habere eum, quem purgant.*
27 *Nec debent a iudico vel alio impediri.*
28 *Et deficiens in purgatione punitur ut convictus,* V. 34. 7.
29 See pp. 96ff. and p. 150 for the division between these two kinds of testimony.
30 Harvard Law School, MS 162, fol.183v, quoted in John S. Beckerman, 'Procedural innovation and institutional change in mediaeval English manorial courts', *Law and History Review*, 10 (1992), p. 203.
31 On all this see John S. Beckerman, 'Procedural innovation and institutional change in mediaeval English manorial courts', *Law and History Review*, 10 (1992), p. 204.
32 *Infamatus fide dignus per iuramentum se purgat.*
33 V. 34. 1.
34 Richard M. Fraher, 'Conviction according to conscience: the mediaeval jurists' debate concerning judicial discretion and the law of proof', *Law and History Review*, 7 (1989), p. 27.
35 Richard M. Fraher, 'Conviction according to conscience: the mediaeval jurists' debate concerning judicial discretion and the law of proof', *Law and History Review* 7 (1989), p. 27.
36 Ronald G. G. Knox, 'The problem of academic language in Rufinus and Stephen,' *Papers of the Sixth International Congress*, ed. S. Kuttner and K. Pennington, *Monumenta Iuris Canonici*, Series C: *Subsidia*, 7 (Vatican, 1985), pp. 109–10.

19 Judicial discretion

1 *Fleta*, ed. and tr. H. G. Richardson and G. O. Sayles, Selden Society, 72, (London, 1955), II, p. 2.
2 *Videtur semiplena esse sententia; post dubitationem enim non est illata confirmatio.* Julian of Eclanum, *Exposition of Job*, 24, line 137.
3 *Probandum est iudici et ei fides est facienda et non adversario. Der Ordo 'Invocato Christi Nomine'* (XLII), p. 91.
4 But see Jean Philippe Lévy, 'Cicéron et la preuve judiciaire', *Droits de l'antiquité et sociologie iuridique: Mélanges H. Lévy-Bruhl* (Paris, 1959), p. 187, on Cicero's *Topica* XII. 51, where it is suggested that it may not be the law's task (*nihil ad ius*) to establish the facts.
5 *Ea res probanda est que in questione esse potest vel debet. Summa codicis des Irnerius*, ed. H. Fitting (Berlin, 1894), IV. 19, p. 90.
6 *'Certum' autem est quod ex ipsa pronuntiatione quid quale quantumve sit apparet. Summa codicis des Irnerius*, ed. H. Fitting (Berlin, 1894), IV. 2, p. 73.
7 *Res dubia non definiatur certa sententia.* Cf. Ivo of Chartres, *Panormia*, II. cxiii, *PL*, 161. 1206.

8 *Mendax precator habetur vel quia falsum asserit vel quia verum supprimit quod scisse iudici privilegium sibi concedentis interest.* Summa 'Elegantius' 1, Part 1 (105), p. 36.
9 Jenny McEwan, *Evidence and the Adversarial Process* (Oxford, 1992), p. 88.
10 *Sed cum principes et alii de iure tractantes circa equitatem et iustitiam intendunt constituere, hoc faciunt vel referendo se ad illam primam partem iustitie in qua iustitia, ratione naturali dictante, primum debuit officium suum exercere, ut Deum revereri, parentes liberos alere.*
11 *Aut referunt se ad illam secundam partem que, cum sit in se visa iniustitia tamen ex comparatione alterius iniustitie visa est iustitia.*
12 Rogerius, *Summa Codicis*, I, p. 50. This example is also used by Anselm of Canterbury.
13 *Quia hoc est in officio iustitie ne alium violes*, Rogerius, *Summa Codicis*, I, p. 50.
14 Richard M. Fraher, 'Conviction according to conscience: the medieval jurists' debate concerning judicial discretion and the law of proof', *Law and History Review*, 7 (1989), p. 24. See, too, K. W. Knörr, *Zur Stellung des Richters im gelehrten Prozess der Frühzeit: Iudex secundum allegata, non secundum conscientiam iudicat* (Munich, 1967).
15 Master Damasus, *Die 'Summa de ordine iudiciario'*, (LXII) *Quellen*, p. 45 (1926), p. 1.
16 Though not under the *ius commune* or canon law.
17 *Iudicium ergo dicitur multipliciter: animi scilicet discretio, iudicis quoque sententia. Iudicium vero, de quo intendimus, dicitur causa apud litis cognitorem ad examinandum deducta.* Procedural text edited in Linda Fowler-Magerl, *Ordo iudiciorum ver ordo iudiciarius* (Frankfurt, 1984), Appendix III, p. 273.
18 Richard M. Fraher, 'Conviction according to conscience: the medieval jurists' debate concerning judicial discretion and the law of proof', *Law and History Review*, 7 (1989), p. 28.
19 Richard M. Fraher, 'Conviction according to conscience: the medieval jurists' debate concerning judicial discretion and the law of proof', *Law and History Review*, 7 (1989), p. 60.
20 Discussed in Richard M. Fraher, 'Conviction according to conscience: the medieval jurists' debate concerning judicial discretion and the law of proof', *Law and History Review*, 7 (1989), for example, pp. 56 ff.
21 *A iudice tamen pendet cui potius credat.* Summa 'Elegantius', II, Part VI (98b), p. 149.
22 *Probatio quidem est rei dubie per argumenta iudici fidem faciens. Summa codicis des Irnerius*, ed. H. Fitting (Berlin, 1894), IV. 19, p. 90. There is ground for uncertainty as to whether this is actually Irnerius's work, but its period does not seem to be in doubt.
23 On aspects of this theme, see Gerhard Otte, *Dialektik und Jurisprudenz, Ius commune, Monographien* 1, (Frankfurt, 1971) and Alejandro Guzmán, Ratio Scripta, *Ius commune, Monographien* 14 (Frankfurt-am-Main, 1981).
24 *Summa 'Elegantius'*, Part VI (70), p. 135.
25 *Quia ergo, per accusationem ydoneum et irreprobabilem fundata accusatione, superest probationes inducere.* Summa 'Elegantius', Part VI (70), p. 135.
26 *Summa 'Elegantius'*, Part VI (70), p. 135.
27 *Instrumentum vero non omne quod instruit mentem nunc dicitur, sed id specialiter quod scriptura continetur.* They can be either public or private documents, *Summa 'Elegantius'*, Part VI (98a), p. 149, cf. *Summa codicis des Irnerius*, ed. H. Fitting (Berlin, 1894), IV.20, p. 91.

28 *Summa codicis des Irnerius*, ed. H. Fitting (Berlin, 1894), IV.20, p. 91. H. Kantorowicz, *Studies in the Glossators of the Roman Law* (Cambridge, 1938), discusses the attribution to Irnerius of the text published as his by Fitting, p. 33.
29 Magister Damasus, *Summa de ordine iudiciario*, ed. L. Wahrmund, *Quellen* (Innsbruck, 1926), IV i, p. 42.
30 Ricardus Anglicus, XXXIII, p. 59 and cf. Petri Blesensis, *De distinctionibus in canonum Interpretatione Adhibendi sive Speculum Iuris canonici*, XIV, ed. T. A. Reimarus (Berlin, 1837), p. 36. See, too Henry Bracton, *De Legibus et Consuetudinibus Angliae*, xxxix, ed. T. Twiss (Rolls Series, 1857), IV, p. 494, including the phrase *semiplena probatio*.
31 Master Damasus, *Die 'Summa de ordine iudiciario'*, (LIX) *Quellen* (1926), p 42.
32 Master Damasus, *Die 'Summa de ordine iudiciario'*, (LXIII) *Quellen* (1926), p. 46.
33 *Quia de salute hominis agitur, cautius est agendum*. Cynus in his lecture on C iv. 19. 23, no.1. W. Ullmann, 'Medieval principles of evidence', *Law Quarterly Review*, 62 (London 1946), p. 78.
34 *Criminalibus probationes debent esse luce clariores*. W. Ullmann, 'Medieval principles of evidence', *Law Quarterly Review*, 62 (London 1946), p. 78.
35 *Circa quam non potest intellectus errare, et ista est indubitata, quae nec elidi potest, sive loquimur in civile sive in criminali*. Baldus in his lecture on C. iv. 19. 25, no. 10, fol. 45, W. Ullmann, 'Medieval principles of evidence', *Law Quarterly Review*, 62 (London 1946), p. 77.
36 *Publica persona ... in medio posita*.
37 *Summa codicis des Irnerius*, ed. H. Fitting (Berlin, 1894), IV. 19, p. 91.
38 W. Ullmann, 'Medieval principles of evidence', *Law Quarterly Review*, 62 (London 1946), pp. 85–6.
39 Bartolus on D. 12. 2. 31, no. 25, fol. 33v. W. Ullmann, 'Medieval principles of evidence', *Law Quarterly Review*, 62 (London 1946), p. 85.

20 Evidence

1 *Select Cases from ... Canterbury*, p. 55.
2 *Summa 'Elegantius'*, Part VIII (41), pp. 186–7.
3 W. Ullmann, 'Medieval principles of evidence', *Law Quarterly Review*, 62 (London 1946), p. 85.
4 *Summa 'Elegantius'*, Part VI (77), p. 138. Cf. Baldus C. 1. 3. 8, no. 4, fol. 37 v. W. Ullmann, 'Medieval principles of evidence', *Law Quarterly Review*, 62 (London 1946), p. 85.
5 That is, take an oath.
6 *Summa 'Elegantius'*, Part V (99), p. 99. Schismatics can be called heretics. *Summa 'Elegantius'*, Part III (12), p. 118.
7 *Iurare autem in infinitum licet, sed an iudex modum iuriiurando statuere possit, ut intra certam quantitatem iuretur*. Digest, 12. 3. 4. 2. 1.
8 *Iuro dicere meram et puram veritatem pro utraque parte de his, super quibus sum productus et de quibus fuero interrogatus*. W. Ullmann, 'Medieval principles of evidence', *Law Quarterly Review*, 62 (London 1946), p. 85.
9 *Summa 'Elegantius'*, Part VIII (31ff.), p. 183ff.
10 *Summa 'Elegantius'*, Part VIII (48), p. 190.
11 *Summa 'Elegantius'* Part VIII (44), p. 190. on questions of intention to deceive, see here and Peter Lombard, *Sentences*, 3. 39. 2. 2, p. 219.
12 *Ut cum falsum quamquam ignoranter iuratur*. *Summa 'Elegantius'*, Part VIII (49), p. 191.
13 *Summa 'Elegantius'*, Part VIII (50), p. 191.

14 *Ea est natura cavillationis, ... ut ab evidenter veris per brevissimas mutationes disputatio ad eam quae evidenter falsa sunt, perducatur. Digest*, 50. 17, no. 65, *Digesta Iustiniani Augusti*, ed. T. Mommsen (Berlin, 1870), vol. 2.
15 *Etiam si in reum ante testimonium dixisti, denuo contra eum testari volens arcendus es, et si varia vel falsa testimonia dixisti, nequaquam admittendus es, aut si redemptus es, aut si utrique parti tuum prodidisti auxilium, aut si pecuniam ob dicendum vel non dicendum testimonium accepisti, Summa 'Elegantius'*, Part VI (73), p. 136.
16 Bernard of Clairvaux, Letter XIV, *Opera Omnia* 7, p. 63.12.
17 *Propter suspiciosam accusationem repudiantur et qui falsum testimonium subornati dixerunt, idest qui sub notabili verborum ornatu accusant ita ut compositum appareat quod asserunt, vel qui de falso testimonio convicti sunt. Summa 'Elegantius'*, II (12), p. 5.
18 *Calumnia est iurgium alienae litis, a calvendo, id est decipiendo dicta. Falsitas appellata a fando aliud quam verum est.* Isidore, *Etymologiae*, V. 26.
19 *Cum verbum oris non consonat verbo cordis, contra cor suum fit mendax falsis testis ... sub iudice quia falsus testis iudicem fallit et ipsum iudicium, licet forte non ex parte iudicantis, tamen ex parte eius cui iudicatum est, corruptum et iniquum effici. Et per hoc, cum finis iudiciorum sit pax hominum adinvicem, qui iudicem fallit et iudicium corrumpit quantum in se est pacis federa disrumpit iudices sint thronus Dei, in quibus Dominus sedens per eorum ora iudicia sua decernat.* Robert Grosseteste, *De Decem Mandatis*, ed. R. C. Dales, E. B. King, *Auctores Britannici Medii Aevi* (Oxford, 1987), Prologue, VIII. 1.
20 *Digest*, 22. 5. 3.
21 *Quedam iudiciorum preparativa explanaturi*, Fowler-Magerl *Ordo Iudiciorum*, pp. 82–3.
22 Cf. Jenny McEwan, *Evidence and the Adversarial Process* (Oxford, 1992), p. 82.
23 Gratian, *Decretum*, II. iv. qq. 2 and 3.
24 *Sit talis senectus vel infirmitas, quae induceret mentis exilium vel faceret memoriam turbare.* Baldus, on D 22.5.8, no. 1, fol. 184, W. Ullmann, 'Medieval principles of evidence', *Law Quarterly Review*, 62 (London 1946), p. 80.
25 W. Ullmann, 'Medieval principles of evidence', *Law Quarterly Review*, 62 (London 1946), p. 81.
26 *Non reputatur idoneus testis, quia gratia hominis moveretur ad dicendum.* Cynus on C. iv. 20. 5, no. 1, fol. 217. W. Ullmann, 'Medieval principles of evidence', *Law Quarterly Review*, 62 (London 1946), p. 81.
27 *Summa 'Elegantius'*, II, Part VI (73), p. 136.
28 *Contentio summopere est vitanda.* Anselm of Lucca, *Collectio canonum*, ed. F. Thaner (Oeniponte, 1906), III. 15, p. 125.
29 *Tota vis esse videtur in causa scientiae, quam testis in suo testimonio reddit, an sit sufficiens.* Lucas de Penna on C. xii. 35. 13, no. 18. W. Ullmann, 'Medieval principles of evidence', *Law Quarterly Review*, 62 (London 1946), p. 79.
30 *De illo sensu, per quem rei veritas comprehenditur.* Cynus, Commentaries on C. iv. 20. 18, no. 7. W. Ullmann, 'Medieval principles of evidence', *Law Quarterly Review*, 62 (London 1946), p. 80.
31 *Caveant etiam ut non ex opinione set ex cognitione, nec de his que ab aliis audierunt set que viderunt. Summa 'Elegantius'*, Part VI (74), p. 137.
32 *Testes ... presentes ex his que viderunt et noverunt veraciter testimonium dicant, nec de aliis causis vel negotiis testimonium dicant, nisi de his que sub presentia eorum acta esse noscuntur.* Ps.-Calixtus, Ep. 2. 17, 18, *Decretales Pseudo-Isidorianae et Capitula Angilramni*, ed. P. Hinschius (Leipzig, 1863), 141; *Diversorum patrum sententie sive Collectio in LXXIV titulos digesta*, ed. J. T. Gilchrist, *Monumenta Iuris Canonici*, 1 (Vatican, 1973), Titulus V, (48), p. 46.

33 *In rebus quae sunt artis seu scientiae alicuius et rationes et demonstrationes.* Bartolus on D. 12. 2. 31, no. 16, fol. 33. W. Ullmann, 'Medieval principles of evidence', *Law Quarterly Review*, 62 (London 1946), p. 87.
34 *In omni causa testis unus quasi nullus habeatur etiam si presidialis curie honore prefulgeat.* Summa 'Elegantius', Part VI (97), p. 147.
35 Summa 'Elegantius', Part VI (95), p. 147.
36 On the other hand, silence is consent: *Semper qui non prohibet pro se intervenire, mandare creditur. Sed et si quis ratum habuerit quod gestum est, obstringitur mandati actione.* Digest, 50. 17, 60.
37 *Qui tacet, non utique fatetur: sed tamen verum est eum non negare.* Digest, 50. 17. 142.
38 *Regulare est, quod in qualibet causa duo testes sufficiunt. Pilii, Tancredi, Gratiae Libri de Iudiciorum Ordine*, ed. F. Bergmann (Göttingen, 1842), p. 228 (Tancred).
39 *In testibus lege cavetur, quod ubi numerus testium non est diffinitus in iure, sufficiunt duo vel tres ad plenissimam fidem negotii faciendam*, ed. Wahrmund, Quellen, III. ii, p. 24.
40 *Summa Magistri Rolandi nachmals Papstes Alexander III*, ed. F. Thaner (Innsbruck, 1874), Causa II, Q. IV, p. 16. Cf. *Pilii, Tancredi, Gratiae Libri de Iudiciorum Ordine*, ed. F. Bergmann (Göttingen, 1842), p. 228 (Tancred).
41 *Der Ordo 'Invocato Christi Nomine'* (XLIII), p. 93.
42 *Non eadem est auctoritas presentium testium et testimoniorum que recitari solent.*
43 *Habet enim aliquid latentis energie viva vox testis que in aures iudicis transfusa fortius sonat.*
44 *Proinde et alia consideratio est contra testes atque alia contra depositas attestationes. Ibi dicentes, hic dicta examinantur; inde in personam agitur, hinc dicta refelluntur. Non ergo adimenta licentia est ex ipsis depositionibus testimonium arguere, set et si datione vel promissione pecuniarum corruptos esse testes liquidis probationibus ostenderit, et eam allegationem integram ei servari oportet.* Summa 'Elegantius', Part VI (98), p. 148.
45 *Nec per epistolam set per vive vocis energiam testimonium ferant.* Summa 'Elegantius', Part VI (74), p. 137.
46 *Per collationeum aliarum litterarum.*
47 Summa 'Elegantius', Part VI (99), p. 149.
48 Anselm of Lucca, *Collectio canonum*, ed. F. Thaner (Oeniponte, 1906), III. 53, p. 142.
49 Master Damasus, *Die 'Summa de ordine iudiciario'*, (LXVI) Quellen, III. ii, p. 47.
50 Master Damasus, *Die 'Summa de ordine iudiciario'*, (LXIII) Quellen, III. ii, p. 46.
51 Summa 'Elegantius', Part VI (77), p. 138.
52 Summa 'Elegantius', Part VI (93), p. 146.
53 Marcellus 510. 15.*Vocabularium Iurisprudentiae Romanae.*
54 *Quae cum ita sint, vestrum est consolari hominem, delinire tristitiam eius, excusatum me habere de tam rationabili causa. Postremo ipse quoque, ut scitis, in pendulo est, et saepe cogitavit relinquere domum suam.* Bernard of Clairvaux, Letter 293, *Opera Omnia*, VIII. 211. *Episcopo non licere alienam parrochiam, propria relicta, peruadere, licet cogatur a plurimis, nisi forte quis eum rationabili causa compellat, tamquam qui possit ibidem constitutis plus conferre, et in causa religionis aliquid proficere.* Collectio canonum in V libris (libri I–III) 1, c. 153. Consuetudines – Canonicorum regularium ord. Arroasiensis constitutiones, 199, line 22; *Horas canonicas sine certa et ratio-*

230 Notes

nabili causa nunquam negligat. Consuetudines – Liber ordinis S. Uictoris Parisiensis, 4, line 10.
55 Peter Stein, *The Character and Influence of the Roman Civil Law* (London, 1988), p. 34.
56 Gratian, *Concordia Discordantium Canonum*, Dist. VIII. 7.
57 The adverb *eleganter* is preferred to *elegantia*.
58 *Elegantius in iure divino vernantia comicato sermone adunare intendimus, ut cui prolixitas Gratiani au tediosa aut inexplicabilis extiterit hac nostra summa paucis ad multa iuvetur.* Summa 'Elegantius', Part I (1), p. 1.
59 Peter Stein, *Regulae Iuris* (Edinburgh, 1966), p. 65. The two final *tituli* of the *Digest* deal, respectively, with key words and with *regulae* or legal axioms. The *Digest* ends with two titles. 50.16 (*De verborum significatione*) contains 246 opinions of jurists on the meanings of key terms. 50.17 (*De diversis regulis iuris antiqui*) is made up of 211 fragments or extracts from the writings of jurists each containing a *regula* or *regulae*.
60 Peter Stein, *Regulae Iuris* (Edinburgh, 1966), p. 65.
61 *Regula est quae rem quae est breviter ennarrat*, Digest, 50. 17. 1.
62 Cf. 'A question or a distinction is elegant when it pinpoints in a dramatic or subtle way the exact limits of a rule, or when it shows by a nicely chosen example that a rule is not as tidy as it seems.' Peter Stein, *The Character and Influence of the Roman Civil Law* (London, 1988), p. 6.

21 Sentencing

1 See pp. 117–18.
2 *Non tamen iudici sunt credenda, nisi certis indiciis probentur.*
3 *Sed facile elicit misericordiam iudicantis non extorta confessio.* Victricius of Rouen, *De Laude Sanctorum*, XII CCSL, 64, p. 92.
4 Gratian, *Causa* 6.4.1 (*titulus*). Cf. *delicti declarati per sententiam, veluti cum iudex pronunciat*, Gratian, *Causa*, 3. 7. 2 (*titulus*); *sentencia dampnationis*, Gratian, *Causa*, 24. 1. 2 (*titulus*); *sentencia propria iudicare presumant*, Gratian, *Causa*, 23. 8. 30 (*titulus*).
5 Cicero *Fam*. 10. 12. 3. 10. Cf. *pronunciandi auctoritas perimatur*, Gratian, *Causa*, 24. 3. 38 (*titulus*). Cf. *arbitrium iudicis* (*Digest*, 4. 2. 14. 5. 9); *sine notione iudicis* (*Digest*, 4. 2. 23. 3. 2); *arbitrio iudicis* (*Digest*, 4. 3. 18. 1. 2 and 4. 2) – will/judgement; *arbitrio tamen bonae fidei iudicis etiam hoc congruit* (*Digest*, 12. 3. 4. 3. 1).
6 Pilii, Tancredi, *Gratiae Libri de Iudiciorum Ordine*, ed. F. Bergmann (Göttingen, 1842), p. 268 (Tancred).
7 *Utrum condicionem implicitam habere possit sentencia iudicialis, res iudicata dicitur quae finem controversiam pronuntiatione iudicis accipit.* Summa 'Elegantius', Part VII, p. 163 (19).
8 Justinian, *Digest*, 42. 1. 1.
9 *Quia non potest ex uno iudicio rei iudicata in partem valere, in partem non valere* (*Digest*, 10. 2. 27).
10 *Iudex posteaquam semel sententiam dixit, postea iudex esse desinit: et hoc iure utimur, ut iudex, ... qui ... semel condemnavit amplius corrigere sententiam suam non possit.* Justinian, *Digest*, 42. 1. 55.
11 Justinian, *Digest*, 44. 2. 3.
12 *Item quaeri consuevit multotiens, an confessio in uno iudicio facta prae iudicet in altero apud alium iudicem super eadem re et quaestione? Et potest respondere, quod sic.* Pilii, Tancredi, *Gratiae Libri de Iudiciorum Ordine*, ed. F. Bergmann (Göttingen, 1842), p. 33.

13 *Saepe constitutum est res inter alios iudicatas aliis non praeiudicare*, Justinian, *Digest*, 42. 1. 63.
14 Abelard, *Theologia Christiana*, II. 47, CCCM, 12, p. 151. 660.
15 Lottin, V, pp. 11–12, for example in MS Troyes 425 (*Liber Pancrisis*), f.95ra.
16 *Prose Salernitan Questions*, C 6, ed. B. Lawn (London, 1979), p. 326.
17 Anselm, *De Concordia, Anselmi Opera Omnia*, 2. 173. 9.
18 *In ecclesiasticis officiis plura sunt, in quibus Orientales ecclesiae et nostrae communi observatione sibi respondent. Sunt vero alia in quibus alias ab aliis cultu dispari, et varia observatione audivimus dissonare.*
19 *Sed nec pauca aut rara sunt, quae ab aliis necessario servanda, ab aliis non adea curanda aestimantur.*
20 *Nec tamen nos offendit observantiae diversitas, ubi fidei non scinditur unitas.* Fulbert of Chartres, Letters, *PL*, 141. 192.
21 Anselm, *De incarnatione verbi*, I. i, *Anselmi Opera Omnia*, 2. 5. 22.
22 Anselm, *De Processione Spiritus Sancti*, 12, *Anselmi Opera Omnia*, 2. 210. 30.
23 Peter Damian, *Sermones Sermo*, 5, 8, CCCM, 57, p. 30. 236. l.
24 Cf. Augustine, *De Civitate Dei*, 16. 9, after Cicero.
25 Anselm, *Cur Deus Homo, Anselmi Opera Omnia*, 2. 78. 12, cf. 79.26.
26 Anselm, *Cur Deus Homo*, 18, *Anselmi Opera Omnia*, 2. 82. 15.
27 *Attende etiam qualiter huic sententiae Veritas ipsa concordat.* Peter Damian, *Sermones, Sermo* 4, CCCM, 57, p. 17.45.
28 Peter Damian, *Sermones Sermo* 50, CCCM, 57, pp. 316–7.70.
29 Peter Damian, *Sermones Sermo* 28, CCCM 57, p. 162.28–9, referring to Ezekiel 18.20.
30 Cf. Peter Damian, *Sermones Sermo* 5,CCCM 57, p. 27. 122.
31 *Ergo sic historice oportet fidem tenere ut eam et moraliter debeamus interpretari et spiritualiter intelligere.* Lottin, V, p. 324.
32 *Qui omnes in tantum philosophorum doctrinis atque sententiis suos referserunt libros, ut nescias quid in illis primum admirari debeas, eruditionem an scientiam scripturarum. Theologia Christiana*, II. 3, CCCM12, p. 133.55, quoting from Jerome, *Letter* 70.
33 *Anselmi Opera Omnia*, 1. 149. 11.
34 *Vis itaque verborum tam in eisdem rebus quam in diversis diligenter est pensanda, ut sententiae veritas a veritate discerni queat.* Abelard, *Apologia contra Bernardum*, 13, CCCM 11, p. 365.208.
35 *Quod dicit EX FIDE – PER FIDEM diversitas est locutionis, non sententiae.* Abelard, *Commentary on Romans*, 2. 3, CCCM, 11, p. 122. 378.
36 *Sint que ipsa symbola ab invicem verbis diversa ac fortasse quibusdam sententiis, cum unum nonnumquam contineat quod alterum non habet.* Abelard, *Theologia Christiana*, 4.124, CCCM, 12, p. 327.1964.
37 *Cum autem de Deo vel Noy nasci sive creari sive fieri anima quandoque a philosophis dicitur abusio est verborum magis quam error sententiae.* Abelard, *Theologia Christiana*, I. 113, CCCM, 12, p. 119. 1486.
38 *Diversa autem definitione sunt qua eadem definitione sententiae terminari non possunt, hoc est quae talia sunt ut sese mutuo non exigant, licet eadem res sit utrumque, sicut est substantia et corpus, vel album et durum.* Abelard, *Theologia Christiana*, 3. 154, CCCM, 12, p. 252. 1875.
39 *Duplicem nam una pronuntiatio gerit sententiam, cum dicitur quia nihil fuit ante summam essentiam. Unus enim est eius sensus: quia priusquam summa essentia esset fuit, cum erat nihil; alter vero eius est intellectus; quia ante summam essentiam non fuit aliquid.* Anselm, *Monologion*, 19, *Anselmi Opera Omnia*, 1. p. 34.19.
40 *Nulla est sententiae controversia, sed verborum diversitas.* Abelard, *Theologia Christiana*, 4, 136, CCCM XII, p. 334.2178.

232 Notes

41 Tertullian, *De Carne Christi*, 18.
42 Cassiodorus *in Psalmos*, on Ps. 40.9, CCSL, 97.376.182.
43 Cassiodorus *in Psalmos*, on Ps. 48.14, CCSL, 97.436.218.
44 Salimbene de Adam, *Chronica*, CCCM, 125, p. 434. 10.
45 *De moribus ecclesiae catholicae et manichaeorum*, I, PL, 32.1322.
46 Bede, *In Marcam*, II. 7, CCSL, 120, p. 522. 1314.
47 *In Evangelium Sancti Johannis*, IV, p. 187; Bede, *In Johannem*, IV, CSEL, p. 187. 451.
48 *Si vis ergo in reum tuum districtae sententiae proferre vigorem, verbum examinetur, verbum iudicetur, verbum verberibus torqueatur.* Peter Damian, *Sermones Sermo32*, CCCM, 57, p. 186. 38.
49 *Sententia* 482, Lottin, V, p. 314.
50 Hildegard of Bingen, *Scivias*, Part 3, Visio 12. 215. CCCM, 43A.
51 Rupert of Deutz, *De Sancta Trinitate*, 16, CCCM, 22, p. 925.
52 Anselm, Oratio 13, *Anselmi Opera Omnia*, 3. 50. 11.
53 *Sententia eius semel prolata ... data sententia damnatum ad tormenta.* Anselm, Oratio, 13, *Anselmi Opera Omnia*, III. 50.24–6.
54 *Sententia* 140, Lottin, V, p. 109.
55 *Nam si nominatio sufficit, multi dampnandi sunt innocentes quia sepe false et iniquo examine nominantur.*
56 *Sed per iudicium auferendos esse malos ab ecclesie communione.*
57 *Nec Christus usquam legitur Iudam nominatim arguisse sed indeterminate: 'unus vestrum me traditurus est'. Sententia*, 476 bis, Lottin, V, p. 312.
58 *Sententia*, 126, Lottin, V, p. 101.
59 *Sententia*, 1 480, Lottin, V, p. 313.
60 Julian of Eclanum, *Expositio Libri Job*, 24, line 137, CCSL, 88.
61 *Digest*, 6.1.13, cf. *non ex rancore vel supicione set ex probata cognitione ferenda est. Summa 'Elegantius'*, Part VII, p. 180 (44).
62 *Si tamen condempnet certa debet esse condempnatio. Summa 'Elegantius'*, Part VII (14), p. 161.
63 *Summa 'Elegantius'*, Part VII, (19), p. 163.
64 *Summa 'Elegantius'*, Part VII (14), p. 160.
65 *Nocentem absolvere quam innocentem condemnare venialis est, leviusque misericordia quam crudelitate deviare.*

22 Appeal

1 *Ne innocens dampnetur et ne ecclesia detrimentum patiatur. Summa 'Elegantius'*, Part V (55), p. 79.
2 *Multos cognovimus pessimis machinationibus iniuste depositos*, Anselm of Lucca II. 27, p. 87.
3 *Der Ordo 'Invocato Christi Nomine'*, (LII), p. 128.
4 *Portamus enim onera hominum, qui gravantur.* Anselm of Lucca II. 27, p. 87.
5 *Summa 'Elegantius'*, Part V (48), p. 76.
6 *Porro de his qui aliena bona rapiunt et ad subsidium appellationis confugiunt, ut sic ecclesiasticam possint eludere disciplinam ... eius appellatio non debet admitti. Quod si hoc dubium fuerit, huiusmodi appellationi facte in iudicio apud ecclesiasticas personas debet deferri. Decretales ineditae saeculi xii*, 8, ed. W. Holzmann, S. Chodorow and C. Duggan. *Monumenta Iuris Canonici, Corpus collectionum* 4 (Rome, 1982), p. 21.
7 *Quos appellaturos in causis suius existimant, nulla penitus admonitione praemissa.*
8 *Summa 'Elegantius'*, Part V (57), p. 80.

9 *Summa 'Elegantius'*, Part V (57), p. 80.
10 *Summa 'Elegantius'*, Part V (46 and 47), p. 75.
11 *Constitutiones Concilii Quarti Lateranensis una cum Commentariis Glossatorum*, ed. A. García y García, Monumenta Iuris Canonici, 2 (Rome, 1981), pp. 296–7.
12 Anselm of Lucca II. 4, p. 77, Matthew 16.18.
13 Anselm of Lucca II. 5, p. 77.
14 *Ut eius uberibus nutriantur, auctoritate defendantur et a suis oppressionibus releventur, qui non potest nec debet mater oblivisci filium suum.* Anselm of Lucca II. 6, p. 77.
15 *Quod papa omnium ecclesiarum curam debet habere, et quod sedes sancti Petri sacerdotalis mater it dignitatis et magistra ecclesiasticae rationis.* Anselm of Lucca, *Collectio canonum*, I. 22, ed. F. Thaner (Oeniponte, 1906), p. 85. The key *mater et magistra* text is that of Lateran IV.
16 Anselm of Lucca, *Collectio canonum*, I, 36, ed. F. Thaner (Oeniponte, 1906), p. 91.
17 *183 Tituli*, ed. J. Motta, Tit.2.
18 *Potestatem habet solvendi iniuste damnatos, et damnandi quos oportuerit absque synodo.* Anselm of Lucca, *Collectio canonum*, II. 16, ed. F. Thaner (Oeniponte, 1906), p. 81.
19 Anselm of Lucca, *Collectio canonum*, I. 3, ed. F. Thaner (Oeniponte, 1906), p. 8.
20 *Quod de iudicio sedis apostolicae nullus debeat iudicare, ipsa vero de omnibus.* Anselm of Lucca, *Collectio canonum*, I, 56, ed. F. Thaner (Oeniponte, 1906), p. 101.
21 *Summa 'Elegantius'*, Part III (9), p. 117. Thus apostasy outweighs the rights of office because it effectually deprives him of that office. *Ut subditos vobis populos pleniter docere possitis, eique ad regna caelorum ducatum praebere domino annuente valeatis. Collectio Canonum Remedio Curiensis Episcopo Perperam Ascripta*, ed. J. Herwig, Monumenta Iuris Canonici, Series B: Corpus Collectionum 2 (1976), Canon 4, p. 140.
22 Yet in Gratian's Causa 25, it is argued that the Pope is in fact far from being unaccountable. He is not above the law. The Pope ought to observe the canons, even more than others ought to observe them (Gratian, *Decretum*, *Causa*, 25.1).The question whether the Pope is ever above the law arose with some urgency in the context of the Investiture Contest of the late eleventh and early twelfth centuries. In this emergency situation the Pope was responsible for extraordinary acts, which were in contradiction of legal norms. Papal privileges are private laws, and they thus provide a useful test-bed for the discussion of legislative power and its limits. See S. Chodorow, 'Ideology and canon law in the crisis of 111', *Proceedings of the Fourth International Congress on Mediaeval Canon Law* (1976), pp. 63–8.
23 Anselm of Lucca II. 3, p. 76.
24 *Ordo 'Invocato Christi Nomine'*, (LII, p. 128).
25 Anselm of Lucca II. 4, p. 76.
26 The denial of a right to appeal may logically be linked with the notion that some crimes demand instant condemnation without due procedure, or all the usual due procedure, being required. *Summa 'Elegantius'*, Part II, p. 89.
27 *Summa 'Elegantius'*, Part V (47a), p. 76.
28 *Summa 'Elegantius'*, Part V (46 and 47), p. 75.
29 *R. v. Cambridge University ex parte Bentley* (1723) 1 Stra 557 at 565, per Pratt, C.J.
30 See John Baker, *An Introduction to English Legal History* (Cambridge, 1971, 2nd edn, 1979), pp. 116–30.

23 Justice and mercy

1. *Inter misericordem patrem et iustum legislatorum.* Valerius Maximus Mem. 6.5. Cf. *On Mercy and justice of Alger of Liège*, ed. Robert Kretschman, *Quellen und Forschungen zum Recht im Mittelalter*, 2 (Sigmaringen, 1985), pp. 187–9.
2. *Decretales Pseudo-Isidorianae et Capitula Angilramni*, ed. P. Hinschius (Leipzig, 1863), pp. 66–87.
3. *Decretales Pseudo-Isidorianae et Capitula Angilramni*, ed. P. Hinschius (Leipzig, 1863), pp. 94–102.
4. *Denunciator ... ad correctionem tendit; accusator ... tendit ad poenam. Die Summa Decretorum des Magister Rufinus*, ed. H. Singer (Paderborn, 1902), *Causa* II, quaestio i, p. 241.
5. William de Drogheda, lxxv, lxxv p. 75.
6. *Select Cases in Manorial Courts 1250–1550*, ed. L. R. Poos and Lloyd Bonfied, Selden Society, (1998), p. xl.
7. R.Helmholz, 'Standards of impartiality for papal judges delegate', *Canon Law and the Law of England* (London, 1987), p. 36, citing Brentano, *The Two Churches*, p. 150.
8. There are glimpses, but no developed policy in line with modern moves to get the courts to encourage assisted settlement, for example, by using costs sanctions for unreasonable refusal to try alternative dispute resolution, or refusing to allocate a trial date until it has been attempted. *Journal of Alternative Dispute Resolution, Mediation and Negotiation*, 1 (2000), pp. 69–76.
9. *English Lawsuits, William I to Richard I*, ed. R. C. van Caenegem, Selden Society, 106 (1990), pp. 26–7.
10. *Select Cases in Manorial Courts 1250–1550*, ed. L. R. Poos and Lloyd Bonfied, Selden Society, (1998), p. xli.
11. *Novellae* 86. c. 2.
12. Justinian, *Digest*, 42. 1. 1.
13. *Ex pactione ipsorum liigatorum vel ex auctoritate iudicii deciduntur controversiae. Digest*, 12. 2. 1.
14. *Arbitrii vero debent partes vocare ad praesentiam suam et coram eis exceptione recusationis per ipsos vel per notariam.* Egidius de Fuscariis, *Ordo iudiciarius*, Wahrmund, IIIi (Innsbruck, 1916), p. 48.
15. *Non tamen recipiunt iurisdictionem a partibus, sed a iure.* Egidius de Fuscariis, *Ordo iudiciarius, Quellen*, III. i, p. 48.
16. *Digest*, 4.8. 13. 2, Linda Fowler-Magerl, 'Forms of arbitration', p. 134.
17. Linda Fowler-Magerl, 'Forms of arbitration', *Proceedings of the Fifth International Congress on Mediaeval Canon Law* (Rome, 1980), p. 134.
18. *Si se subiciant aliqui iurisdictioni et consentiant: inter consentientes cuiusvis iudicii, qui tribunali praeest vel aliam iurisdictionem habet. Digest*, 5. 1. 1.
19. Linda Fowler-Magerl, 'Forms of arbitration', pp. 135–7. Arbitrations have a likeness to judgements, says Irnerius, in that agreements are arrived at by judges in the same way as through an arbitrator: *Arbitria enim iuditii similitudinem habent: quemadmodum enim per iudices negotia expediuntur, eodem modo et per arbitros.* Fitting, Irnerius, *Tituli* II. 15. p. 43.
20. *Quid iuris de eo, qui recipit arbitrium, tamen malitiose recusat convenire cum altero ad diffiniendum articulum recusationis.* Egidius de Fuscariis, *Ordo iudiciarius*, Wahrmund, IIIi (Innsbruck, 1916), p. 46.
21. *English Lawsuits, William I to Richard I*, ed. R. C. van Caenegem, Selden Society, 106 (1990), p. 38.
22. *Casus Placitorum*, ed. W. Huse Dunham, Selden Society, 69 (1952), p. 63.

23 *Quod papa canonum decreta ita librare debet, ut quae necessitas temporum relaxanda exposcit temperet, quantum fieri potest.* Anselm of Lucca, *Collectio canonum*, I. 33, ed. F. Thaner (Oeniponte, 1906), p. 89.
24 *Canonici rigoris ab eo cuius interest pro ydonea causa facta relaxatio.* Summa 'Elegantius', I, Part 1 (82), p. 28.
25 *Pro loco, pro tempore, pro persona*, or for a *causa* of one sort or another: *pietatis, necessitatis, utilitatis, casualis eventus*. Summa 'Elegantius', I, Part 1 (83), p. 28.
26 Summa 'Elegantius', Part 1 (90), p. 30.
27 Summa 'Elegantius', Part 1 (90), p. 30.
28 *Ut si provinciam aliquem fame vel hostilitate ita coartari continget ut sacerdotibus careat, etiam in baptismali ecclesia licet monachorum amministrationem recipi.* Summa 'Elegantius', Part 1 (92), p. 31.
29 Summa 'Elegantius', Part 1 (93), p. 31.
30 *Ordo non solum pro culpa set et pro infamia et pro diminuta extrinseca vel intrinseca perfectionis prerogativa non ad tempus set perpetuo denegatur.* Summa 'Elegantius', Part 1 (89), p. 30.
31 See my *The Church and the Churches*.
32 *Praeter vis facilius facta toleramus quam talia facienda concedamus.* Summa 'Elegantius', Part 1 (88), pp. 29–30.
33 *Ubi autem dispensatio admittenda et ubi regula sequenda sit.* Summa 'Elegantius', Part 1 (89), p. 30.
34 Summa 'Elegantius', Part 1 (90), p. 30.
35 *Sciendum itaque quod prohibitiones ecclesiastice proprias habent causas quibus cessantibus cessant et ipse.*
36 *Ut enim laicus eligi prohiberentur, hec causa fuit qui vita laicalis ecclesiasticis non erudita disciplinis nescit de se exempla et documenta religionis prebere.*
37 *Si ergo laicus aliquis scientia vel vita insignis clericalem perfectionem transcendere cognoscitur, non immerito eius electio approbatur.* Summa 'Elegantius', Part 1 (95), p. 33.
38 *Nec canones resoluere nec per posteriora prioribus derogare valeat prima sedes.* Summa 'Elegantius', Part 1 (98), p. 33.
39 *Et canones abrogare eisque derogare et novos condere et privilegia dare dataque tollere plenam habent potestatem.*
40 *Dum tamen in his omnibus nichil contra fidem presumant vel in quo universalem ecclesiam offendant.* Summa 'Elegantius', Part 1 (99), pp. 34–5.
41 *Nulla iuris ratio aut aequitatis benignitas patitur ut quae salubriter pro utilitate hominum introducuntur, ea nos duriori interpretatione, contra ipsorum commodum, perducamus ad severitatem.* Digest, I. iii. 25, Modestinus.
42 Aquinas, *ST*, II i q. xcvi a. 6.
43 Aquinas, *ST*, II i q. xcvi a. 6.
44 Summa 'Elegantius', Part 1 (77), p. 26.
45 Summa 'Elegantius', Part 1 (78), p. 26.
46 Summa 'Elegantius', Part 1 (77), p. 26.
47 Summa 'Elegantius', Part 1 (79), p. 27.
48 *Quia nostram potius salutem cum omnium dampnatione quam salutem omnium cum perditione nostra alterutra condicione proposita eligere satius est.* Summa 'Elegantius', Part 1 (80), p. 27.
49 *Sed si qui originem cause inter Deum et diabolum vel inter Deum et hominem vel inter hominem et diabolum considerare voluerit, interveniet Deum iustissimum, diabolum vero iniustissimum.* Lottin, V, p. 46.
50 Isidore, *Etymologiae*, V. 27.

51 *Hoc enim et natura et lege est institutum, ut laedentem similis vindicta sequatur.* Isidore, *Etymologiae*, V. 27.
52 *Unde et illud est legis* (Matthew 5.38). *Oculum pro oculo, dentem pro dente.*
53 Burchard of Worms, *Decreta*, xvi. 18,PL, 140. 912.
54 *De his criminibus de quibus absolutus est accusatus, refricari accusatio non potest.* Burchard of Worms, *Decreta*, xvi.9, PL, 140. 911. Gregory IX has: *absolutus de certo crimine, de eodem iterum accusari non potest*, Gregory IX, *Decretals*, V.1.6, ed. A. Friedberg, *Corpus Iuris Canonici* (Leipzig, 1881).
55 Gratian, *Decretum*, II, *Causa*, II. q. 3.
56 See Ronald G. G. Knox, 'The problem of academic language in Rufinus and Stephen', *Proceedings of the Sixth International Congress of Mediaeval Canon Law* (Vatican, 1985), p. 113, from Vatican MS Vat. Borgh 287.

24 Conclusion

1 *Ego enim novi diversos qui juraverunt maximo iuramento se non esse nec fuisse reos in causa eis imposita, et tamen in privato foro fatebantur se veraciter reos esse, et sic nota, Cancellarie, quod in Oxonia ex purgationibus admissis indifferenter multiplicantur periuria, et hoc experientia plurium probavi.* Munimenta Academica, ed. H. Anstey, Rolls Series (1857), vol. 2, p. 536.
2 *Post rem iudicatam vel iureiurando decisam vel confessionem in iure facam nihil quaeritur post orationem divi Marci, quia in iure confessi pro iudicatis habentur.* Justinian, *Digest*, 42. 1. 56.
3 *Confessus pro iudicato est, qui quodammodo sua sententia damnatur.* Justinian, *Digest*, 42. 2.
4 Justinian,*Digest*, 42. 2. 8.
5 *Non omnimodo confessus condemnari debet rei nomine, quae, an in rerum natura esset, incertum sit.*
6 *Invocato Christi Nomine* (23), *Quellen*, II. iii, p. 46.
7 *Summa 'Elegantius'*, Part II (7), p. 43.
8 *In summa notandum est, quod confessus in iure iudici terreno habetur pro condempnato .... so quis confiteatur deo, id est sacerdoti per deum, quoniam hec confessio inducit absolutionem. Invocato Christi Nomine* (25), *Quellen*, II. iii, p. 49.
9 Hugh of St Victor, *De Sacramentis*, I. v.
10 Hugh of St Victor, *De Sacramentis*, I. v. Hugh of St Victor discusses Christ as Judge at some length. He stresses the swiftness of his judgement, Hugh of St Victor, *De Sacramentis*, II. xvii. 7–8.
11 Hugh of St Victor, *De Sacramentis*, I. xvii. 34.
12 There is a large mediaeval literature on the subject of the Last Judgement, which is of course the final and definitive 'sentence' on the individual.
13 B. Poschmann, *Penance and the Anointing of the Sick* (London, 1963) is still invaluable on the development of penitential theory and practice. See, too, L. Körntgen, *Studien zu den Quellen der frühmittelalterlichen Bussbüchern* (Sigmaringen, 1993); Allen J. Frantzen, *The Literature of Penance in Anglo-Saxon England* (New Jersey, 1983).
14 L. Körntgen, *Studien zu den Quellen der frühmittelalterlichen Bussbüchern* (Sigmaringen, 1993),p. 258 on the selection of suitable texts. Cf. B. Poschmann, *Penance and the Anointing of the Sick* (London, 1963), p. 146.
15 And one which remained largely unresolved in the Middle Ages and beyond.
16 B. Poschmann, *Penance and the Anointing of the Sick* (London, 1963), p. 159.
17 *Non quo sacerdotes leprosos faciant et immundos, sed quo habeant notitiam leprosi et non leprosi et possint discernere, qui mundus quive immundus sit.* B.

Poschmann, *Penance and the Anointing of the Sick* (London, 1963), p. 148 discusses this passage and the contrary opinions of authors who cite it.
18 Luke 17.12 ff.
19 *Conversio autem dicitur quasi cordis undique versio.*
20 *Si autem cor nostrum undique a malo ad Deum vertitur, mox suae conversionis fructum meretur, ut Deus ab ira sua ad misericordiam conversus peccati praestet indulgentiam, cuius primo praeparabat vindictam.* Gratian, *Decretum*, II, *Causa*, XXXIII q. iii, Dist. I, c. 24.
21 *Sacrificium ex lege offert, dum satisfactionem ecclesiae judicio sibi impositam factis exsequitur.* Gratian, *Decretum*, II, *Causa*, XXXIII q.iii, Dist. 1, c. 24.
22 *Satisfactio purgationis in voluntate consistit accusati, non in arbitrio iudicis.* Gratian, *Decretum*, II, *Causa*, II. v. 18.
23 *In praemissis autoritatibus subintelligitur, si reus se purgare voluerit, ut sacri canones modum, non necessitatem purgandi accusato imponant.* Gratian, *Decretum*, II, *Causa*, II. v. 17.
24 *Iniuste autem ligat, quisquis aliquem paratum satisfacere et audientiam implorantem.*
25 Beno, *Contra Gregorium VII et Urbanum Scripta*, ed. K. Francke, *MGH Libelli de Lite II* (Hanover, 1892), p. 373, para.1.
26 *Est penitentia vera que fit odio criminis et desiderio absolutionis, et est simulata que ex rubore et merore agitur vilitatis et spe vel ambitione honoris.* Summa 'Elegantius', Part III (89), p. 83.
27 *Summa 'Elegantius'*, Part III (11), p. 45.
28 *Ostendens in contritione cordis, quae in eiusdem scissione intelligitur, non in confessione oris, quae pars est exterioris satisfactionis, quam scissuram vestium nominavit, a parte totum intelligens, peccata dimitti.* Gratian, *Decretum*, II, *Causa*, XXXIII q. iii, Dist. I, c. 24.
29 *Ex his itaque apparet, quod sine confessione oris et satisfactione operis peccatum non remittitur. Nam si necesse est, ut iniquitates nostras dicamus, ut postea justificemur.*
30 *Qui promittit veniam occulte apud Deum non apud ecclesiam paenitentiam agenti, frustratur evangelium et claves datas ecclesiae.* Gratian, *Decretum*, II, *Causa*, XXXIII q. iii, Dist. I, c. 60.
31 *Cogitatio non meretur poenam lege civili, quum suius terminis contenta est. Discernuntur tamen a maleficiis ea, quae de iure effectum desiderant. In his enim non nisi animi judicium consideratur.* Gratian, *Decretum*, II, *Causa*, XXXIII q. iii, Dist. I, c. 20, cf. c.22.
32 *Quia manifesta peccata non sunt occulta correctione purganda.* Pierre Legendre, *Écrits juridiques du moyen âge occidental* (London, 1988), p. 592.
33 *Infamatus, tertio monitus se non corrigens, usque ad purgationem ab officio suspenditur*, say the *Decretals* of Gregory IX. V. 34. 2.
34 Augustine, *Enchiridion*, 25.
35 Augustine, *Enchiridion*, 27.
36 *Digest*, II. 3. 1.
37 *Is videtur ius dicenti non obtemperasse, qui quod extremum in iurisdictione est non fecit. Digest*, II. 3. 1.
38 *Summa 'Elegantius'* Part XV (89), p. 133.
39 *Summa 'Elegantius'*, Part XV (89a), p. 134.
40 Cf. Pierre Legendre, *Écrits juridiques du moyen âge occidental* (London, 1988), p. 577.
41 Augustine, *Enchiridion*, 71.
42 *PL*, 210. 279.
43 Four things are necessary to complete penance, says Peter the Chanter: the infusion of grace, contrition of heart, confession with the lips and suitable

238 Notes

satisfaction by deed: *Ad poenitentiam sufficientiam, perfectionem et integritatem, quatuor sunt necessaria, scilicet gratiae infusio, cordis contritio, oris confessio, operis digna satisfactio.* The last three are useless without the first. Petrus Cantor, *Verbum Abbreviatum*, PL, 205.

44 *Enchiridion*, 75.
45 B. Poschmann, *Penance and the Anointing of the Sick* (London, 1963), pp. 124–5 makes this point.
46 *Melius est hic in praesenti erubescere in conspectu unius hominis quam in futuro iudicio coram cunctis gentibus.*
47 From a Bavarian synod, this became a stock theme of the penitential literature. See B. Poschmann, *Penance and the Anointing of the Sick* (London, 1963), p. 141.
48 On this, see K. Müller, *Der Umschwung in der Lehre von der Busse während des 12 Jahr. in Festschrifte F. Weizsåacher* (1892), pp. 292 ff.
49 Jerome, *Letter*, 13.
50 *Iniuste autem ligat, quisquis aliquem paratum satisfacere et audientiam implorantem, neque convictum neque sponte confessum anathematizat, immo seipsum frustra maledicendo, quasi proprio iaculo in se retorto, maledicit et condempnat.* Beno, *Contra Gregorium VII et Urbanum Scripta*, ed. K. Francke, MGH *Libelli de Lite*, 2 (Hannover, 1892), p. 373, para.1.
51 With all due respect for the controversy about the power of the fallen will to act for good without the aid of grace.
52 L. Körntgen, *Studien zu den Quellen der frühmittelalterlichen Bussbücher* (Sigmaringen, 1993), p. 258.
53 Theodore of Canterbury, *Die Lateinischen Pönitentialbücher*, ed. F. Kunstmann (Mainz, 1844); *Canones Theodori Cantuariensis*, ed. W. Finsterwalder (Weimar, 1929).
54 *Summa 'Elegantius'*, Part IX (55), p. 74.
55 *Cur Deus Homo*, I. 7, S II. 57. 22–4.
56 *Enchiridion*, 75.
57 *Summa 'Elegantius'*, Part 1 (46), p. 13.

Bibliography

Primary sources

Accessus ad Auctores, ed. R.B.C. Huygens (Leiden, 1970).
Aegidius de Fuscarariis, *Der Ordo Iudiciarius*, ed. L. Wahrmund, *Quellen zur Geschichte des Römische-Kanonischen Prozesses im Mittelalter*, III i (1906) (reprinted 1962).
Aegidius, Magister, *Die Summa des Magister Aegidius*, ed. L. Wahrmund, *Quellen zur Geschichte des Römische-Kanonischen Prozesses im Mittelalter*, III ii (1906) (reprinted 1962).
Agobard of Lyons, *De divinis sententiis contra iudicium Dei*, ed. L. van Acker, CCCM, 52 (1981).
Ailred of Rievaulx, *De Spiritali amicitia*, Opera Omnia, CCCM, I.
Alger of Liège, *On mercy and justice*, in 'Preface', ed. Robert Kretschman, *Quellen und Forschungen zum Recht im Mittelalters*, 2 (Sigmaringen, 1985), pp. 187–9.
Allegationes Phalempinianae, Tijdschrift voor Rechsgeschiedenis, 49 (1981), pp.251–85.
Ambrose of Milan, *De Jacob et Vita Beata*, CSEL, 32ii.
Ambrose, *De apologia David ad Teodosium Augustum*, CSEL, 32ii.
—— *Expositio evangelii secundum Lucam*, CCSL, 14.
—— *Explanatio Psalmorum*, CSEL, 64.
Anonymous, 'La Summa Institutionum 'Iustiniani est in hoc opere', ed. P. Legendre, *Ius Commune*, Sonderhefte, 2 (1973).
—— *Diversorum patrum sententie sive Collectio in LXXIV titulos digesta*, ed. J. T. Gilchrist, Monumenta Iuris Canonici, 1 (Vatican, 1973).
—— *Liber Canonum diversorum sanctorum patrum sive Collectio in CLXXXIII Titulos digesta*, ed. J. Motta, Monumenta Iuris Canonici, Corpus Collectionum 7 (Vatican, 1988).
—— *Der 'Curialis'*, ed. L. Wahrmund, *Quellen zur Geschichte des Römische-Kanonischen Prozesses im Mittelalter*, IIIii (Innsbruck, 1905) (reprinted 1962).
—— *Der Ordo 'Invocato Christi nomini'*, ed. L. Wahrmund, *Quellen zur Geschichte des Römische-Kanonischen Prozesses im Mittelalter*, IIIii (Innsbruck, 1931) (reprinted 1962).
—— *Der Ordo Iudiciarius 'Scientiam'*, ed. L. Wahrmund, *Quellen zur Geschichte des Römische-Kanonischen Prozesses im Mittelalter*, II. i (Innsbruck, 1905–31) (reprinted 1962).
—— *Die Glossen zum Dekret Gratians*, ed. R. Weigand (Rome, 1991), 4 vols.

—— *Die Rhetorica ecclesiastica*, ed. L. Wahrmund, *Quellen zur Geschichte des Römische-Kanonischen Prozesses im Mittelalter* (Innsbruck) (reprinted 1962).
Anselm of Canterbury, *Anselmi Opera Omnia*, ed. F.S. Schmitt (Rome/Edinburgh, 1938–68), 6 vols.
Anselm of Laon, *et al.*, *Sententiae, Psychologie et morale au xiie et xiiie siècles*, ed. O. Lottin (Gembloux, 1942–59), 6 vols.
Anselm of Lucca, *Collectio canonum*, ed. F. Thaner (Oeniponte, 1906).
Aquinas, Thomas, *Summa Theologiae*, in *Opera Omnia* (Parma, 1852–73), 25 vols.
Arnulphus, Magister, *Die 'Summa Minorum' des Magister Arnulphus*, ed. L. Wahrmund, *Quellen zur Geschichte des Römische-Kanonischen Prozesses im Mittelalter*, III ii (Innsbruck, 1905) (reprinted 1962).
Augustine, *De Civitate Dei*, CCSL, 47–8.
—— *De consensu evangelistarum*, CSEL, 43.
—— *De Libero Arbitrio*, CCSL, 29.
—— *De moribus ecclesiae catholicae et manichaeorum*, PL, 32.
—— *De Trinitate*, CCSL, 50.
—— *Enchiridion*, CCSL, 46.
—— *Epistulae*, CSEL, 44.
—— *In Iohannis evangelium tractatus*, CCSL, 36.
—— *Sermones*, CCSL, 41.
Azo, *Apparatus*, ed. F.G.C. Beckhaus (Bonn, 1856).
—— *Brocardica* (Basle, 1567).
—— *Lectura Codicis* (Paris, 1577).
Baldus de Ubaldis, *Commentarius ad Digestum vetus* (Venice, 1616).
—— *L'Opera di Baldo*, ed. O. Scalvanti *et al.* (Perugia, 1909).
Bassianus, Joannes, *Materia ad Pandectum*, post Azo, *Summa* (Pavia, 1506, reprinted Turin, 1966).
—— *Die Summa 'Quicumque vult' des Johannes Bassianus*, ed. L. Wahrmund, *Quellen zur Geschichte des Römische-Kanonischen Prozesses im Mittelalter*, III ii (Innsbruck, 1925) (reprinted 1962).
Bede, *In Ezram et Neemiam*, CCSL, 119A.
—— *In prouerbia Salomonis*, CCSL, 119B.
Beno, *Contra Gregorium VII et Urbanum Scripta*, ed. K. Francke, MGH, *Libelli de Lite II*(Hanover, 1892).
—— *Gesta Romanae ecclesiae contra Hildebrandum*, ed. K. Francke, MGH, *Libelli de Lite* (Hanover, 1892).
Bernard of Clairvaux, *Opera Omnia*, ed. J. Leclercq (Rome 1957–), 8 vols.
Bernardus Dorna, *Die Summa libellorum des Bernardus Dorna*, ed. L. Wahrmund, *Quellen zur Geschichte des Römische-Kanonischen Prozesses im Mittelalter*, III ii (Innsbruck, 1905) (reprinted 1962).
Boethius, *De Consolatione Philosophiae*, CCSL, 94.
—— *Theological Tractates*, ed. H.F. Stewart, E.K. Rand and S.J. Tester (London, repr. 1973).
Bohier, Pietro, Bishop of Orvieto, *Liber Pontficalis Glossato*, III, ed. U. Prerovsky, *Studia Gratiana*, XXIII (Rome, 1978).
Bonizo, *Liber de Vita Christiana*, ed. E. Perels (Berlin, 1930).
Bracton, H., *De Legibus et Consuedutinibus Angliae*, V, ed. T. Twiss, Rolls Series (London, 1857), 3 vols.

Brevia Placitata, ed. G.J. Turner and Theodore F.T. Plucknett, Selden Society 66 (1951).
Brocardica Aurea (Naples, 1568), *Corpus glossatorum iuris civilis*, IV (Turnin, 1967)
Bulgarinus, *Excerpta legum edita a Bulgarino Causidico*, ed. L. Wahrmund, *Quellen zur Geschichte des Römische-Kanonischen Prozesses im Mittelalter*, III ii (Innsbruck, 1925) (reprinted 1962).
Burchard of Worms, *Decreta*, PL, 140.
Canones Theodori Cantuariensis, ed. W. Finsterwalder (Weimar, 1929).
Cassiodorus, *In Psalmos*, CCSL, 97.
Casus Placitorum, ed. W. Huse Dunham, Selden Society, 69 (1952).
Cicero, *De Inventione*, ed. G. Achard, Collection des universitaires de France, Serie Latine, 320 (Paris, 1994).
—— *De Officiis*, ed. M. Winterbottom (Oxford, 1994).
—— *De Re Publica*, ed. K. Zieglev (Leipzig, 1992).
—— *Topica*, ed. Georgius Di Maria (Palermo, 1994).
Cinus, *Commentaria in codicem* (Frankfurt-am-Main, 1578)
Collectio Canonum Remedio Curiensis Episcopo Perperam Ascripta, ed. J. Herwig, *Monumenta Iuris Canonici*, Series B, *Corpus Collectionum* 2 (1976).
Constitutiones Concilii Quarti Lateranensis una cum Commentariis glossatorum, ed. A. García y García, *Monumenta Iuirs Canonici, Corpus glossatorum*, 2 (Rome, 1981).
Corpus Iuris Canonici, ed. A.L. Richter and E. Friedberg (Leipzig, 1881).
Corpus Iuris Civilis, ed. Theodore Mommsen, Paul Kruger, Rudolf Chol and Wilhelm Kroll (Berlin, 1963–5), 3 vols.
Cyprian, *De opere et eleemosynis*, CCSL, 3.
Damasus, Magister, *Die 'Summa de ordine iudiciario' des Magister Damasus*, ed. L. Wahrmund, *Quellen zur Geschichte des Römische-Kanonischen Prozesses im Mittelalter*, III ii, IV iv (Innsbruck, 1926) (reprinted 1962).
Decretales ineditae saeculi xii, ed. W. Holzmann, S. Chodorow and C. Duggan, *Monumenta Iuris Canonici*, Series B, *Corpus Collectionum* 4 (Rome, 1982).
Decretales Pseudo-Isidorianae et Capitula Angilramni, ed. P. Hinschius (Leipzig, 1863).
Die Ehelehre des Magister Honorius, ed. B. Grimm, *Studia Gratiana*, XXIV (Rome, 1989), pp. 316–17.
Diversorum patrum sententie sive Collectio in LXXIV titulos digesta, ed. J.T. Gilchrist, *Monumenta Iuris Canonici*, 1 (Vatican, 1973).
The Earliest English Law Reports, ed. Paul A. Brand, Selden Society 111 (1996).
Egidius de Fuscariis, *Ordo iudiciarius*, ed. L. Wahrmund, *Quellen zur Geschichte des Römische-Kanonischen Prozesses im Mittelalter*, III i (Innsbruck, 1916).
Eibert von Bremen, *Ordo Judiciarius*, ed. L. Wahrmund, *Quellen zur Geschichte des Römische-Kanonischen Prozesses im Mittelalter*, (Innsbruck, 1906) (reprinted, 1962).
English Lawsuits, William I to Richard I, ed. R. C. van Caenegem, Selden Society, 106 (1990), pp. 26–7.
Extravagantes Johannes XXII, ed. J. Tarrant, *Monumenta iuris canonici*, Series B: *Corpus Collectionum*, 6 (Rome, 1983).
Fleta, ed. and tr. H.G. Richardson and G. Sayles, Selden Society, 72 (1955), 4 vols.
Fulgentius Ruspensis, *De Trinitate*, CCSL, 91A.

Gabriel le Bras, *Histoire du Droit et les Institutions de l'Église en Occident* (Paris, 1965), VII, p. 406ff.
Gilbert Crispin, *The Works of Gilbert Crispin*, ed. A. Abulafia and G.R. Evans (London, 1986).
Gratian, *Decretum, Corpus Iuris Canonici*, ed. A.L. Richter and E. Friedberg (Leipzig, 1879), Vol. 1.
—— *The treatise on laws (Decretum*, DD,1–20), tr. A. Thompson, *Studies in Mediaeval and Early Modern Canon Law*, 2, Catholic University of America Press, Washington, 1993.
Gregory IX, *Decretalium Collectiones, Corpus Iuris Canonici*, ed. A.L. Richter and E. Friedberg (Leipzig, 1881), Vol. 1.
Grosseteste, Robert, *De Decem Mandatis*, ed. R.C. Dales and E.B. King, *Auctores Britannici Medii Aevi* (Oxford, 1987).
—— *Epistolae*, ed. H.R. Luard, Rolls Series (London, 1861).
—— *Statutes of Lincoln*, in *Council and Synods, II (1205–1313)*, ed. F.M. Powicke and C.R. Cheney (Oxford, 1964).
Hactenus Magister, MS Bamberg St.B. Patr 18, f.240r–v.
Hildegard of Bingen, *Scivias*, CCCM, 43A.
Honorius, Magister, *Die Ehelehre des Magister Honorius*, ed. B. Grimm, *Studia Gratiana*, XXIV (Rome, 1989).
Hostiensis (Henricus de Segusio), *Summa Aurea* (Lyons, 1556).
Hugh of St Victor, *De Sacramentis*, tr. R.J. Defarrari (Washington, 1951).
Irnerius, *Summa Codicis des Irnerius*, ed. H. Fitting (Berlin, 1894).
Isidore, *Etymologiae*, ed. W.M. Lindsay (Oxford, 1911).
Iudicandi formam, MS London BM Royal 10BIV, f.33r–41r.
Iudicium est trinus personarum trium actus, MS London BM Royal 10B IV, f.59r–v.
Ivo of Chartres, *Panormia*, PL, 161.
—— *Prologue*, PL, 161.52.
—— *Prologue*, ed. J. Werchmeister, *Sources canoniques* (Paris, 1997).
—— *Correspondance* (1090–8), ed. J. Leclercq, 1 (Paris, 1949).
James of Ravenna, *Lectura super codice* (Bologna, 1959).
Jerome, *Epistulae*, ed. I. Hilberg, CSEL, 54, 55, 56, 88 (Vienna, 1910).
—— *The Letters of St. Jerome*, tr. C. C. Mierow and T. C. Lawlor, *Ancient Christian Writers* (London, 1963).
Johannes de Lignano, *Super Clementina 'Saepe'*, ed. L. Wahrmund, *Quellen zur Geschichte des Römische-Kanonischen Prozesses im Mittelalter*, IV vi (Innsbruck, 1928) (reprinted, 1962).
Johannes Fasolus, *Johannes Fasolus 'De summariis cognitionibus'*, ed. L. Wahrmund, *Quellen*, III ii (Innsbruck, 1928) (reprinted 1962).
Johannes Teutonicus, *Apparatus glossarum in compilationem tertium*, ed. K. Pennington (Vatican, 1981).
John of Salisbury, *Policraticus*, CCCM, 118 (Books I–V).
John of Salisbury, *Policraticus*, ed. C. C. J. Webb (Oxford, 1909), 2 vols.
Justinian, *Codex, Corpus Iuris civilis*, ed. P. Krueger (1954), vol. 2.
—— *Digesta Iustiniani Augusti*, ed. T. Mommsen (Berlin, 1870), 2 vols.
—— *Scritti teologici ed ecclesiastici di Giustiniano*, ed. M. Amelotti and L. M. Zingale, *Legum iustiniani imperatoris vocabularium, Subsidia* III (Milan, 1977).

—— *Justinians Edict über den Rechten Glauben*, ed. E. Schwartz, *In legum Iustiniani Imperatoris Vocabularium, Subsidia*, II (Milan, 1973).
Leo, *Epistulae*, ed. E. Schwarz, *Acts Conciliorum Oecumenicorum*, II. 4.
A List of English Law Officers. King's Counsel and Holders of Patents of Precedence, Selden Society, Supplementary Series, 7 (1987), (1932).
Marius Victorinus, *Explanationes in Ciceronis rhetoricam, Rhetores Antiqui Minores*, ed. C. Halm (Leipzig, 1867).
Marsilius of Padua, *Defensor Minor*, ed. Cary J. Nederman (Cambridge, 1993).
Martinus de Fano, *Das 'Formularium' des Martinus de Fano*, ed. L. Wahrmund, *Quellen zur Geschichte des Römische-Kanonischen Prozesses im Mittelalter*, III ii (1907) (reprinted 1962).
Maximus of Tours, *Collectio sermonum antiqua*, CCSL, 23.
Memorials of St. Anselm, ed. R. W. Southern and F. S. Schmitt (London, 1969).
Modus Componendi Brevia, ed. G. E. Woodbine, in *Four Thirteenth Century Law Tracts* (New Haven, 1910), pp.143–62.
Munimenta Academica, ed. H. Anstey, Rolls Series (1857), 2 vols.
Paucapalea, *Summa des Paucapalea über das Decretum Gratiani, Causa*, II, q.1. ed. J.F. von Schulte (Geissen, 1890).
Peter Abelard, *Commentary on Romans*, CCCM, 11.
—— *Ethics*, ed. D. Luscombe (Oxford, 1971).
—— *Theologia Christiana*, CCCM, 12.
Peter Damian, *Sermones*, CCCM, 57.
Peter Lombard, *Sententiae*, Grottaferrata (1971–81), 2 vols.
Peter of Blois, *De Distinctionibus in Canonum Interpretatione Adhibendis sive Speculum Iuris Canonici*, XVI, ed. T. A. Reimarus (Berlin, 1837).
Peter of Celle, *Commentaria in Ruth*, CCCM, 54.
Pietro Bohier, Bishop of Orvieto, *Liber Pontficalis Glossato*, III, ed. U. Prerovsky, *Studia Gratiana*, XXIII (Rome, 1978).
Pilii, Tancredi, Gratiae Libri de Iudiciorum Ordine, ed. F. Bergmann (Göttingen, 1842) (reprinted Aalen, 1975).
Placentinus, *Die Summa 'De actionum varietatibus'*, ed. L. Wahrmund, *Quellen zur Geschichte des Römische-Kanonischen Prozesses im Mittelalter*, IV iii (Innsbruck, 1925) (reprinted, 1962).
Prose Salernitan Questions, ed. B. Lawn (London, 1979).
Ps-Telesporus, Ep. 1, *Decretales, Pseudo-Isidorianaer Capitula Angilramni*, ed. P. Hinschius (Leipzig, 1863).
Ps.-Tertullian, *Adversus omnes haereses*, CCSL, 2.
Quellen zur Geschichte des Römische-Kanonischen Prozesses im Mittelalter, ed. L. Wahrmund (Innsbruck, 1905–31).
Rainerius Perusinus, *Ars Notarie*, L. Wahrmund, ed. *Quellen zur Geschichte des Römische-Kanonischen Prozesses im Mittelalter* IIIii (Innsbruck, 1917) (reprinted, 1962).
Readings and Moots at the Inns of Court in the Fifteenth Century, ed. S. E. Thorne and J.H. Baker, Selden Society, 105 (London, 1990).
Règles et pénitentiels monastiques de Saint Colomban, ed. A. de Vogüé (Bégrolles-en-Mauges, 1989).
Ricardus Anglicus, *Die Summa de Ordine Iudiciario*, ed. L. Wahrmund, *Quellen zur Geschichte des Römische-Kanonischen Prozesses im Mittelalter*, II iii (Innsbruck, 1915) (reprinted, 1962).

244 Bibliography

Roffredi Beneventani Libelli Iuris Civilis, Corpus Glossatorum Iuris Civilis (1968).
Rufinus, Master, *Die Summa Decretorum des Magister Rufinus*, ed. H. Singer (Paderborn, 1902).
Rupert of Deutz, *De Sancta Trinitate*, 16, CCCM, 22.
—— *In Sanctum Johannen*, CCCM, IX.
Salimbene de Adam, *Chronica*, CCCM, 125.
Select Cases in the Court of Kings Bench under Edward I, ed. G. O. Sales, Selden Society, 57 (1938).
Select Cases on Defamation to 1600, ed. R. Helmholz, Selden Society 101 (London, 1985).
Select Cases from the Ecclesiastical Courts of the Province of Canterbury c.1200–1301, ed. N. Adams and C. Donahue, Selden Society, 95 (1981).
Select Cases in Manorial Courts 1250–1550, ed. L. R. Poos and Lloyd Bonfied, Selden Society (1998).
Select Cases of Procedure without Writ under Henry III, ed. H. G. Richardson and G. O.Sayles, Selden Society, 60 (1941), p. xxi ff.
Stephen of Tournai, *Die Summa des Stephanus Tornacensis über das Decretum Gratiani*, ed. J. F. von Schulte (Geissen, 1891).
Summa 'Elegantius in iure divino' seu Coloniensis, ed. G. Fransen and S. Kuttner, Monumenta Iuris Canonici, Corpus Glossatorum, I (Vatican, 1969–90), 4 vols.
Summa Trecensis, ed. H. Fitting, *Summa Codicis des Irnerius* (Berlin, 1894).
Tacitus, *Dialogus de oratoribus*, ed. W. Peterson and M. Winterbottom (London, 1970).
Tertullian, *Opera*, CCSL, 1–2.
—— *Adversus Marcionem*, ed. E. Evans (Oxford, 1972), 2 vols.
—— *De carne Christi*, ed. E. Evans (London, 1956).
The Casus Placitorum and the Reports of Cases in the King's Courts 1272–1278, ed. William Huse Dunham, Selden Society, 69 (1952).
Theodore of Canterbury, *Die Lateinischen Pönitentialbücher*, ed. F. Kunstmann (Mainz, 1844).
Thomas of Chobham, *Sermons*, CCCM, 82A.
—— *Summa de arte praedicandi*, 5, CCCM, 82.
Tübingen Distinctiones, ed. E. Seckel (Graz, 1956).
Ugonis Summula de Pugna, Scripta Anecdota Glossatorum, ed. J. Palmerio, (Bologna, 1913).
Vacarius, *Liber Pauperum*, ed. F. de Zulueta, Selden Society, 44 (1927).
Victricius of Rouen, *De Laude Sanctorum*, XII CCSL, 64.
Vita Meinwerci, episcopi patherbunensis, ed. Pertz, MGHSS, XI (Hanover, 1854).
Vocabularius Lipsiensis, ed. E. Seckel, *Beiträge zur Geschichte beider Rechte im Mittelalter* (Tübingen, 1898).
Voinet v. Barrett (1855) 55 L.J.Q.B. 39.
Wilkins, J., *Concilia* (London, 1737), 4 vols.
William Durantis, *Speculum iudiciale* (Basel, 1574, reprinted Aalen, 1975).
William of Conches, *Moralium dogma philosophorum*, ed. J. Holmberg (Uppsala, 1929), p.12.
William of Drogheda, *Die Summa Aurea des Wilhelmus de Drokeda*, ed. L. Wahrmund, *Quellen zur Geschichte des Römische-Kanonischen Prozesses im Mittelalter*, IIIii (Innsbruck, 1914) (reprinted 1962).

Secondary sources

Allen, T.R.S., 'Justice and fairness in law's empire', *The Cambridge Law Journal*, 52 (1993), pp. 64–88.
Artonne, A., 'L'influence du décret de Gratien sur les statuts synodaux', *Studia Gratiana*, 4, 2 (1956).
Baker, J.H., *An Introduction to English Legal History* (2nd. edn, London, 1979).
—— *The Legal Profession and the Common Law* (London, 1986).
Baldwin, J.W., 'The intellectual preparation for the Canon of 1215 against ordeals', *Speculum*, 36 (1961), pp. 613–36.
—— 'A debate at Paris over Thomas Becket between Master Roger and Master Peter the Chanter', *Studia Gratiana*, XI, *Collectanea S. Kuttner*, 1 (Bologna, 1967).
Balon, Joseph, *Ius medii aevi, ii, Lex Jurisdictio* (Namur, 1960).
—— *Traité du Droit Salique, Ius Medii Aevi*, 3 (Namur, 1965).
—— *Grand dictionnaire de droit du moyen âge, Ius Medii Aevi*, 5 (Belgium, 1972).
Beckerman, J.S., 'Procedural innovation and institutional change in mediaeval English manorial courts', *Law and History Review*, 10 (1992), pp. 197–252.
Bellomo, M., *Aspetti dell'insegnamento giuridico nelle Università medievali, I, Le 'Quaestiones disputatae'* (Reggio Calabria, 1974).
—— *The Common Legal Past of Europe, 1000–1800*, tr. L. G. Cochrane (1988, tr. Washington, 1995).
Blumenkranz, B., 'Deux compilations canoniques de Florus de Lyon et l'Action Antijuive d'Agobard', *Revue historique de droit français et étranger*, 4, xxxiii (1955), pp. 227–54 and 560–82.
Boyer, G., 'La notion d'équité et son rôle dans la jurisprudence des Parlements', *Mélanges Maury*, II (Paris, 1960).
Boyle, L., 'The "Summa summarium": and some other English works of Canon Law', *Monumenta iuris canonici*, Ser. C,1 (1965), pp. 415–56.
Brand, P., 'Courtroom and schoolroom: the education of lawyers in England prior to 1400', *Bulletin of the Institute of Historical Research* (1987), pp. 147–65.
—— 'Learning English customary law: education in the London law school, 1250–1500', *Vocabulary of Teaching and Research between Middle Ages and Renaissance*, ed. O. Weijers (Turnhout, 1995), pp. 199–213.
Bras, Gabriel le, *Histoire du Droit et les Institutions de l'Église en Occident* (Paris, 1965).
Brundage, James A., 'A twelfth century Oxford disputation concerning the privileges of the Knights Hospitallers', *Medieval Studies*, 24 (1962), pp. 153–60.
—— 'Professional discipline in the mediaeval courts Christian: the Candlesby case', *Studia Gratiana*, xxvii (1996), pp. 41–8.
Bruno, Paradisi, 'Il diritto Romano nell'alto medio evo, le epistole di Nicola le un'ipotesti del conrat', *Studia Gratiana*, 11, *Collectanea Stephan Kuttner 1*, (Bologna, 1967), pp. 211–51.
Caron, P.G., '"Aequitas romana", "Misericordia patristica" et "epicheia" aristotelica nella doctrina dell "aequitas canonica"' (Milan, 1968).
—— 'Aequitas et interpretatio' dans la doctrine canonique aux xiiie et xive siècles', *Proceedings of the Third International Congress on Medieval Canon Law* (1971), pp. 131–41.

Cheney, C.R., *English Synodalia of the Thirteenth Century* (Oxford, 1941, 2nd edn 1968).
Cheney, M., 'Pope Alexander III and Roger, Bishop of Worcester, 1164–1179: the exchange of ideas', Fourth International Conference on Mediaeval Canon Law, *Monumenta Iuris Canonici Subsidia*, 5 (1976), pp. 207–27.
Chiappelli, *La glossa Pistoiese al Codice Giustinianeo* (Turin, 1885).
Chodorow, S., *Christian Political Theory and Church Politics in the Mid-Twelfth Century* (Berkeley and Los Angeles, 1971).
—— 'Ideology and canon law in the crisis of 1111', *Proceedings of the Fourth Congress on Mediaeval Canon Law* (1976), pp. 55–80.
Clarence Smith, J.A., *Medieval Law Teachers and Writers* (Ottawa, 1975).
Conklin, George, 'Stephen of Tournai and the development of *aequitas canonica*. The theory and practice of law after Gratian', *Proceedings of the Eighth International Congress on Medieval Canon Law* (1990), pp. 369–86.
D'Entrèves, A.P., *Natural Law* (London, 1970).
Dahyot-Dolivet, Jehan, 'La procédure judiciaire d'office dans l'Église jusqu'à l'avènement du pape Innocent III', *Apollinaris*, 41 (1968), pp. 443–55.
Dario Coposta, D., 'Il diritto naturale in Graziano', *Studia Gratiana*, 2 (1954), pp. 153–210.
Doe, Norman, *Fundamental Authority in Late Mediaeval English Law* (Cambridge, 1990).
Donahue, Charles, 'The monastic judge: social practice, formal rule and the mediaeval canon law of incest', *Studia Gratiana*, xxvii (1996), pp. 49–69.
Evans, G.R., *Old Arts and New Theology* (Oxford, 1980).
—— 'A work of "terminist theology"? Peter the Chanter's *De Tropis Loquendi* and some Fallacies', *Vivarium*, 20 (1982), pp. 40–58.
—— '"Ponendo Theologica Exempla". Peter the Chanter's De Tropis Loquendi', *History of Universities* (1982), pp. 1–14.
—— *Alan of Lille* (Cambridge, 1983).
—— *The Language and Logic of the Bible* (Cambridge, 1984–5), 2 vols.
—— *Problems of Authority in the Reformation Debates* (Cambridge, 1992).
—— *The Church and the Churches* (Cambridge, 1994).
Figueira, R.C., 'Papal reserved powers and the limitations on legatine authority', *Popes, Teachers and Canon Law in the Middle Ages*, ed. J. R. Sweeney and S. Chodorow (Ithaca, 1989), pp.191–211.
—— 'Ricardus de Mores and his *Casus Decretalium*: the birth of a canonistic genre', *Proceedings of the Eighth International Congress of Mediaeval Canon Law, Monumenta iuris Canonici, Subsidia* 9 (1992), pp. 169–87.
Fitting, H., *Juristische Schriften des früheren Mittelalters* (Halle, 1976).
Fournier, P., *Le premier manuel canonique de la reforme du xi siècle* (Rome, 1894).
—— *Une collection canonique italienne du commencement du xii siècle* (Grenoble, 1894).
—— *Les collections canoniques attribués à Yves de Chartres* (Paris, 1897), pp. 1–2.
—— *Yves de Chartres et le droit canonique* (Paris, 1898).
Fowler-Magerl, L., 'Forms of arbitration', *Proceedings of the Fourth International Congress of Mediaeval Canon Law, Monumenta Iuris Canonici*, Series C, *Subsidia*, 5 (Vatican, 1980), pp. 133–50.

—— *Ordo iudiciorum vel ordo iudiciarius: Begriff und Litteraturgattung, Ius Commune: Repertorium zur Frühzeit der Gelehrten Rechte* (Frankfurt am Main, 1984).
—— *Ordines iudiciarii et libelli de ordine iudiciorum, Typologie*, Fasc.63 (1994).
Fraher, R., 'The theoretical justification for the new criminal law of the High Middle Ages: *Rei publicae interest, ne crimina remaneant impunita*', *Illinois Law Review* (1984), pp. 577–95.
—— 'Ut nullus describatur reus prius quam convincatur. Presumption of innocence in medieval canon law,' *Proceedings of the Sixth International Congress, Monumenta iuris canonici*, Series C: *Subsidia*, 7 (Vatican, 1985), pp. 43–506.
—— 'Preventing crime in the High Middle Ages: the mediaeval lawyer's search for deterrence', *Popes, Teachers and Canon Law in the Middle Ages: Essays in Honour of Brian Tierney*, ed. S. Chodorow and J. Sweeney (Ithaca, 1989).
—— 'Conviction according to conscience: the medieval jurists' debate concerning judicial discretion and the law of proof', *Law and History Review*, 7 (1989), pp. 23–88.
Franklin, J., 'The ancient legal sources of seventeenth-century probability', *The Uses of Antiquity*, ed. S. Gaukroger (Dordrecht, 1991), pp. 23–88.
Fransen, G., 'Les "Quaestiones" des canonistes: Essai de dépouillement et de classement', (II) *Traditio*, 13 (1957).
—— *Colligite Fragmenta, Studia Gratiana*, 13 (1967), pp. 83–5.
—— *Les Décrétales et les collections de Décrétales, Les collections canoniques*, Fasc.2 *Typologie*, 10 (1972).
Fransen, G., et al., (eds), *Les questions disputées, Typologie*, Fasc.44–5 (1985).
Frantzen, A.J., *The Literature of Penance in Anglo-Saxon England* (New Jersey, 1983).
Frier, B.W., *The Rise of the Roman Jurists* (Princeton, 1985).
Gallagher, C., 'Canon law and the Christian community: the role of law in the Church according to the Summa Aurea of Cardinal Hostiensis', *Analecta Gregoriana* (Rome, 1978).
Genzmer, Erich, 'Gli apparati di azzone al digestum novum 50.17.1', *Annali di storia del diritto*, 1 (1957), pp. 7–11.
Ghisalberti, Carlo, 'La teoria del notorio nel diritto comune', *Annali di storia del diritto*, 1 (1957), pp. 403–51.
Godding, P., *Typologie des sources du moyen âge occidental*, fasc.6 (Turnhout, 1973).
Gouron, A., 'Canon law in Parisian circles before Stephen of Tournai's Summa', *Proceedings of the Eighth International Congress of Medieval Canon Law, Monumenta Iuris Canonici: Subsidia*, 9 (Vatican, 1992), pp. 497–503.
Green-Pedersen, N.J., *The Tradition of the Topics on the Middle Ages* (Vienna, 1984).
Greenawalt, K., *Conflicts of Law and Morality* (Oxford, 1987).
Grenidge, A.H.J., *Infamia: Its Place in Roman Public and Private Law* (Oxford, 1984).
Guzmán, A., 'Ratio Scripta', *Ius commune, Monographien* 14 (Frankfurt-am-Main, 1981).
Heintschel, D.E., *The Mediaeval Concept of an Ecclesiastical Office* (Washington, 1956).

Helmholz, R., 'Ethical standards for Advocates and Proctors in Theory and practice', *Proceedings of the Fourth International Congress of Mediaeval Canon Law*, Monumenta Iuris Canonici, Series C: *Subsidia*, 5 (Vatican, 1976).

—— 'Standards of impartiality for papal judges delegate', *Canon Law and the Law of England* (London, 1987).

—— 'Conviction according to conscience', *Law and History Review*, 7 (1989), pp. 23–88.

Hering, C.J., 'Die Aequitas bei Gratian', *Studia Gratiana*, 2 (1954).

Hobbes's *'Science of Natural Justice'*, ed. C. Walton and P.J. Johnson (Dordrecht, 1987).

Horn, N., *Aequitas in den Lehren des Baldus* (Graz, 1968).

Horvat, M. 'Deux phases du procès romain', *Droits de l'antiquité et sociologie iuridique; Mélanges H. Lévy-Bruhl* (Paris, 1959).

Issues in Contemporary Legal Philosophy, ed. R. Gavison (Oxford, 1987), pp. 127–8.

John Finnis, P., *Natural Law and Natural Rights* (Oxford, 1982).

Kalb, H., *Studien zur Summa Stephans von Tournai* (Innsbruck, 1983).

Kantorowicz, H., 'The *Quaestiones Disputatae* of the Glossators', *La revue d'histoire du droit*, xvi.1 (1937/8), pp. 1–67.

—— *Studies in the Glossators of the Roman Law* (Cambridge, 1938).

—— *The definition of law*, ed. A. H. Campbell (Cambridge, 1958).

Kelly, Ansgar, H. 'Inquisitorial due process and the status of secret crimes', *Proceedings of the Eighth International Congress on Medieval Canon Law*, Monumenta Iuris Canonici, 9 (1992), pp. 407–27.

Kelly, J.M., *A Short History of Western Legal Theory* (Oxford, 1992).

Knörr, K.W., *Zur Stellung des Richters im gelehrten Prozess der Frühzeit: Iudex secundum allegata, non secundum conscientiam iudicat* (Munich, 1967).

Knox, R.G.G., 'The problem of academic language in Rufinus and Stephen', *Proceedings of the Sixth International Congress of Mediaeval Canon Law*, Monumenta Iuris Canonici, Series C: *Subsidia*, 7 (Vatican, 1985), pp. 109–23.

Körntgen, L., *Studien zu den Quellen der frühmittelalterlichen Bussbücher* (Sigmaringen, 1993).

Kretzmann, N., Kenny, A. and Pinborg, J. (eds), *Cambridge History of Later Mediaeval Philosophy* (Cambridge, 1982).

Kuttner, S., 'New studies on Roman Law in Gratian's Decretum', *Seminar: an Annual Extraordinary Number of the Jurist*, 11 (Washington, 1953), pp. 12–50.

—— 'A forgotten definition of justice', reprinted in *The History of Ideas and the Doctrine of Canon Law in the Middle Ages* (Basingstoke, 1980, repr. 1992), pp. 75–6.

—— 'Urban II and the Doctrine of Interpretation: a turning point?', *Studia Gratiana*, 16 (Rome, 1972), pp. 55–85.

—— 'Gratian and Platon', *Church and Government in the Middle Ages, Essays Presented to C.R. Cheney*, ed. C. N. L. Brooke (Cambridge, 1976), pp. 93–118.

—— 'A forgotten definition of canon law', *Studia Gratiana*, 20 (1977), pp. 75–109.

—— 'Harmony from dissonance: an interpretation of mediaeval canon law', *The History of Ideas and Doctrines of Canon Law in the Middle Ages* (London, 1980).

—— 'Réflexions sur les Brocards des Glossateurs', *Mélanges Joseph de Ghellinck*, II (Gembloux, 1951), 767–92, reprinted in S. Kuttner, *Gratian and the Schools of Law* (London, 1983).

—— 'Zur Frage der theologischen Vorlagen Gratians', reprinted in S. Kuttner, *Gratian and the Schools of Law* (London, 1983), p. 245.
—— 'The revival of jurisprudence', *Studies in the History of Mediaeval Canon Law* (London, 1990), pp. 299–323.
Lefebvre, C., 'La doctrine de l'Hositensis sur la préférence à assurer en droit aux intérêts spirituels', *Ephemerides Iuris Canonici*, 8 (1952).
—— 'Les origines romaines de la procédure sommaire aux xii et xiiie siècles', *Ephemerides Iuris Canonici*, 12 (1956), pp. 149–97.
—— 'Natural equity and canonical equity', *Natural Law Forum*, 8 (1963), pp. 122–36.
—— 'Juges et savants en Europe, xiiie–xvie siècle', *Ephemerides Iuris Canonici* 22 (1966), pp. 76–203.
—— 'Hostiensis, maître de l'equité canonique', *Ephemerides Iuris Canonici* 28 (1972), pp. 11–21.
—— 'Récents développements des recherches sur l'équité canonique', *Proceedings of the Sixth International Congress of Medieval Canon Law*, ed. S. Kuttner and K. Pennington, *Monumenta Iuris Canonici*, Series 6: *Subsidia*, 7 (Vatican, 1985), pp. 369–87.
—— *Écrits juridiques du moyen âge occidental* (London, 1988).
Letters of F.W. Maitland, ed. N. N. R. Zutschi (London, 1995).
Lévy, J.P., 'Cicéron et la preuve judiciaire', *Droits de l'antiquité et sociologie iuridique: Mélanges H. Lévy-Bruhl*, (Paris, 1959), pp. 187–97.
Lisska, A.J., *Aquinas' Theory of Natural Law* (Oxford, 1966).
Logan, F.D., 'An early thirteenth century papal judge-delegate formulary of English origin', *Studia Gratiana*, XIV, *Collectanea S. Kuttner*, IV (Bologna, 1967), pp. 73–87.
Lottin, O., 'Le concept de justice chez les théologiens du moyen âge avant l'introduction d'Aristote', *Revue thomiste*, 44 (1938), pp. 511–21.
—— *Psychologie et morale aux xiie et xiiie siècles* (Gembloux, 1959).
Lubac, H. de, 'A propos de la formule: "diversi sed non adversi"', *Mélanges Lebreton, Recherches de science religieuse*, 39–40 (1951–2), II. pp. 27–40.
Maitland, F.W., *The Forms of Action at Common Law* (Cambridge, 1936).
Maritain, J., *Scholasticism and Politics*, ed. M. Adler (London, 1954).
May, G., 'Die Anfänge der Infamie im kanonischen Recht', *Zeitschrift der Savigny – Stiftung für Rechtgeschichte, Kanonistische Abteilung*, 78 (1961), pp. 76–94.
McEwan, J., *Evidence and the Adversarial Process* (Oxford, 1992).
McInerny, R., 'Natural Law and Natural Rights', in R. McInerny, *Aquinas in Human Action* (Washington, 1992).
McNabb,V., 'St. Thomas Aquinas and law', *Blackfriars* (1929), pp. 1047–67.
Metz, R., 'La contribution de la France à l'étude du décret de Gratien depuis le xvie siècle jusqu'à nos jours', *Studia Gratiana*, 2 (1956), pp. 496–518.
Mordek, H., *Kirchenrecht und Reform im Frankenreich* (Berlin/New York, 1975).
Morissey, T.E., '"More easily and more securely": legal procedure and due process at the Council of Constance', in *Popes, Teachers and Canon Law in the Middle Ages*, ed. J. R. Sweeney and S. Chodorow (Ithaca and London, 1989).
Morris, C., *The Discovery of the Individual* (London, 1972).
Müller, K., *Der Umschwung in der Lehre von der Busse während des 12 Jahr. in Festschrifte F. Weizsåacher* (Berlin, 1892).

Munier, C., 'Les sources patristiques du droit de l'Église du viii au xiiie siècle', *Revue du droit canonique*, 4 (Strasbourg, 1954).
Murphy, J.J., *A Bibliography of Mediaeval Rhetoric* (Toronto, 1971).
—— *Three Mediaeval Rhetorical Arts* (Berkeley, 1971).
Nicolini, U., *Pillii Medicinensis Quaestiones sabbatinae, Introduzione all'edizione critica* (Modena, 1933).
Nörr, K.W., 'Ordo iudiciorum und Ordo iudiciarius', *Studia Gratiana*, II, *Collectanea Kuttneriana*, 1 (Bologna, 1967), pp. 327–43.
Ombres, R., 'Giustizia ed equita' nel nuovo codice di diritto canonico latino: note introduttive', *Apollinaris*, lxi (1988), pp. 717–36.
Otte, G., *Dialektik und Jurisprudenz, Ius commune, Monographien* 1, (Frankfurt, 1971).
Patetta, F., *Studi sulle fonti giuridiche medievali* (Turin, 1967).
Pennington, K., *The Prince and the Law, 1200–1600* (Berkeley, 1993).
Peters, E., 'Wounded names: the medieval doctrine of infamy', *Law in Mediaeval Life and Thought*, ed. E. B. King and S. J. Ridyard (Sewanee, 1990), pp. 43–91.
Piano-Mortari, V., 'Il problema dell'interpretatio juris nei commentatori', *Annali di storia del diritto*, 2 (1958), pp. 29–110.
Pólay, E., *Iniuria Iypes in Roman Law* (Budapest, 1986).
Poschmann, B., *Penance and the Anointing of the Sick* (London, 1963).
Posthumus Meyjes, G.H.M., 'Exponents of sovereignty: canonists as seen by theologians in the late Middle Ages', *The Church and Sovereignty: Essays in Honour of Michael Wilks*, ed. D. Wood, *Studies in Church History, Subsidia*, 9 (Oxford, 1991), pp. 299–312.
Rathbone, E., 'Roman Law in the Anglo-Norman Realm', *Studia Gratiana XI, Collectanea S. Kuttner*, 1 (Bologna, 1967), pp. 253–71.
Reynolds, R., 'The Pseudo-Hieronymian *De septem ordinibus ecclesiae*. Notes on its origins, abridgements, and use in early medieval canonical collections', *Revue Bénédictine* 80 (1970), pp. 238–43.
Robertson, O.F., 'Public law and Justinian's Institutes', *Studies in Justinian's Institutes in Memory of J.A.C. Thomas*, ed. P. G. Stein and A. D. E. Lewis (London, 1983).
Rouco, A.C., *Le primat de l'Évêque de Rome* (Fribourg, 1990).
Rouse, R.H. and Rouse, M., 'Ennodius in the Middle Ages: Adonics, Pseudo-Isidore, Cistercians and the Schools', in *Popes, Teachers and Canon Law in the Middle Ages*, ed. J. R. Sweeney and S. Chodorow (Ithaca and London, 1989).
Shogimen, T., 'The relationship between theology and canon law: another context of political thought in the early fourteenth century', *Journal of the History of Ideas*, 60 (1999), pp. 417–31.
Smalley, B., *The Becket Conflict and the Schools: A Study of Intellectuals in Politics* (Oxford, 1973).
Somerville, R. and Brasington, B., *Prefaces to Canon Law Books in Katin Christianity: Selected Translations, 500–1245* (Yale, 1998).
Southern, R.W., *St. Anselm and his Biographer* (Cambridge, 1963).
—— *Mediaeval Humanism* (Oxford, 1970).
—— *St. Anselm* (Cambridge, 1990).
Stein, P., *Regulae Iuris* (Edinburgh, 1966).
—— *The Character and Influence of the Roman Civil Law* (London, 1988), p. 38.
Stump, E., *Boethius, De topicis differentiis* (Ithaca/London, 1978).

Sweeney, J.R. and Chodorow, S. (eds), *Popes, Teachers and Canon Law in the Middle Ages* (Ithaca, 1989).
Tarde, G., *La philosophie pénale* (Lyon/Paris, 1891).
Thomas, J.A.C., *Textbook of Roman Law* (New York, 1976).
Thompson, J.J., 'Probabilities as relevant facts' in J.J. Thompson, *Rights, Restitution and Risk* (Cambridge, MA, 1986).
Tierney, B., *Foundations of the Conciliar Theory* (Cambridge, 1955).
—— '"Sola scriptura" and the canonists', *Collectanea Stephan Kuttner* I, *Studia Gratiana*, XI (Bologna 1967), pp. 347–66.
Trusen, W., 'Der Inquisitionsprozess: Seine historischen Grundlagen und frühen Formen', *Zeitschrift der Savigny – Stiftung für Rechtsgeschichte*, 74 (1988), pp. 168–230.
Ullmann, W., 'Baldus's conception of law', *Law Quarterly Review*, lviii (London, 1942), pp. 386–99.
—— 'The influence of John of Salisbury on medieval Italian jurists', *English Historical Review*, 59 (1944), pp. 384–92.
—— 'Medieval principles of evidence', *Law Quarterly Review*, 62 (London 1946), pp. 77–87.
—— 'The defence of the accused in the medieval inquisition', *The Irish Ecclesiastical Record*, lxxiii (Dublin, 1950), pp. 481–9.
—— '*De Bartoli Sententia: Concilium Repraesentat Mentem Populi*', *Bartolo da Sassoferrato: Studi e Documenti per il vi centenario* (Milan, 1962), II. pp. 702–33.
—— *Mediaeval Foundations of Renaissance Humanism* (London, 1977).
Vetulani, A., *Sur Gratien et les Décrétales* (Aldershot, 1990).
Villey, M., 'Le droit naturel chez Gratian', *Studia Gratiana*, III (Bologna, 1955), pp. 83–99.
Vodola, E.F., 'Fides et Culpa: the use of Roman law in ecclesiastical ideology', *Authority and Power: Essays in Honour of Walter Ullmann*, ed. B. Tierney and P. Linehan (Cambridge, 1980).
—— *Excommunication in the Middle Ages* (Berkeley, 1986).
Walton, C. and Johnson, P.J. (eds), *Hobbes's 'Science of Natural Justice'*, (Dordrecht, 1987).
Weigand, R., *Die Naturrechtslehre der Legisten und Dekretisten von Irnerius bis Accursius und von Gratian bis Johannes Teutonicus* (Munich, 1967).
Weimar, P., 'Argumenta Brocardica', *Studia Gratiana* XIV (Bologna, 1967), pp. 91–123.

Index

Abbo of Fleury 52
abbots 43, 113, 139
Abelard, Peter 13, 16, 34, 57, 100, 143, 153, 155
Abraham 33
absenteeism 116
absolution 26, 140, 168
Acacian schism 20
academic law 31
accessus 52, 62
accusation 25, 115, 130, 131, 166
accusation, false 118
accused 64, 83, 91, 93, 94, 96, 100, 112, 117, 141, 146
accuser 83, 91, 93, 96, 103, 111, 130, 141, 146
Adam and Eve 7, 15, 30, 107, 136
adultery 11, 54, 117, 133, 135, 160, 170
advocacy 61, 62–4
advocates 61–8, 92, 96, 100
Aegidius de Fuscarariis 67, 163
aequitas canonica 29
Agatho, pope 79
Agobard of Lyons 139
Alan of Lille 172
Albertus Gandinus 93
Alexander III, pope 46, 74, 106
Alger of Liège 37, 57
alms 173, 174
alternative dispute resolution 162ff.
Ambrose 102, 140, 172
Ambrose of Milan 2, 33, 172
Anselm of Bec and Canterbury 7, 8, 9, 15, 34, 44, , 56, 63, 89, 153, 154, 155, 175
Anselm of Laon 44, 57, 88, 89, 103, 107, 111, 112, 115, 149, 151, 153, 157, 159, 160
apostasy 11, 20

Apostles 108
Apostolic authority 42
Apostolic See 44, 114, 160 and *passim*
appeal 46, 159–61
Aquinas, Thomas 11, 14, 24, 25, 33, 36, 37, 37, 78, 86, 165
arbitration 163
archdeacons 113
argumentatio 71, 72, 73, 74
argumentum 74, 100
Aristotle 22, 35, 36, 61, 147
Arnulphus 91
articuli 96
arts course 36
Athens 115
attorney 67
auctoritas 56, 111
audi alteram partem 115–19
Augustine of Hippo 2, 8, 22, 25, 33, 40, 62, 128, 156, 157, 171, 172
Augustine, Ps. 173
authority 44
authority, judicial 36
Azo 59, 75, 77, 86, 94, 101, 102

bailiff 64
Baldus de Ubaldis 7, 15, 22, 37, 76, 86, 93, 101, 105, 146, 151
baptism 23, 30, 164
Bardolo of Perugia 76, 146
barrister 51
Bartholomew of Beauvais 106
Bartholomew of Brescia 74
Bartolus of Saxaferrato 60, 118
Bassianus, Johannes 69, 71, 93, 101, 163
Becket, Thomas à 1
Bede 40
benchers 51

Index 253

Bernard of Clairvaux 13, 14, 40, 44, 62, 79, 108, 149, 125
Bernard of Pisa 94
Bertram of Metz 59
betrayal 157
bias 113–15; *see also* conflict of interest; *nemo iudex*
Bible 53–4, 69, 89, 101, 107, 112, 123, 126, 166, 171–2; *see also* Scripture
bigamy 73
bishop 17, 25, 44, 88, 89, 113, 139, 165
body politic vii
Boethius 29, 76, 77
Bologna 49, 50, 55, 57, 60, 73, 127
Boniface VIII, pope 58, 64, 117
Bracton 24, 42, 83, 94
bribery 25
Bride of Christ 17
brocards 75, 100, 101
Bulgarinus 100
Bulgarus 49
Burchard of Worms 56, 75, 102, 111, 112, 115, 118, 166
burden of proof 99, 117
Burgundio of Pisa 55

Caesar 25
calumny 126, 135, 149
Cambridge 65
Cambridge, John of 66
Candlesby, Hugh 65
canons 76
canon law 53, 85–6, 163, 175 and *passim*
canonists 128
canons, regular 49
Canterbury 50, 66, 94, 99, 114
captatio benevolentiae 71
Carthage, Council of (419) 123
Carthusians 13
cases 73
Cassiodorus 156
Celtic tradition 172
certiorari 161
Chalcedon 89, 151
change of heart 169
character 142
Christ 7, 21, 44, 56, 62, 63, 64, 56, 108, 123, 147, 157, 168, 173
Chromatius of Aquileia 124
Church vii, 1, 39, 40, 53, 56, 66, 103139, 159, 164, 173 and *passim*
Church of England 92, 197
churches 20, 153

Cicero 9, 12, 22, 29, 30, 34, 61, 86, 101, 147, 156, 171
citation 91, 94, 99
citizens 24
City of God 22, 26
civil cases 92, 94; civil law 52, 68
clamor 107, 113
clarity 131
Clement V, pope 136
clergy 42, 88, 96, 108–9, 113, 139, 164, 165, 172
Code (of Justinian) 20, 55, 59, 106, 115
collegiality 139
Common Bench 58
common good 23
compilation 57
compurgation 141
conciliation 163
confession 141, 162, 167–75; confessional 16; forensic 167; penitential 167; secrecy of 170
conflict of interest 113; *see also* bias; *nemo iudex*
conscience 142
consensus fidelium 21
consilia 72; *see also* opinions
constancy 34
Constantinople 381; Council of 118
Constitiones Clementinae 58
contempt of court 26
contradiction 2, 100
contumacy 66
convenientia 89
cooperativeness 25
Corbie 56
Corpus iuris canonici vii and *passim*
Council of Rheims 113
councils 3, 42, 139, 115, 139; councils, local 172
Counsel 29
counter-claim 99
Court of the Arches 50, 65, 66
courts 42–6, 69, 91ff., 123; ecclesiastical 92, 116; secular 92; standing 67
crimes, *crimina* 13, 97; *crimen ecclesiasticum* 119; criminal law 68; criminal trials 26
Curia 65
curriculum 50
custom 37, 38ff.
Cyprian 62

Damasus 74, 79, 145

254 Index

Damasus, Ps. 93
Dante 4
deacons 139, 142
deans 113
Decretals 128
Decretists 50
defamation 123, 126; see also infamia; notoriety
defectus 78
defence 64, 119
delator 113
delay 98–9, 160
demonstrative method 76–9
demotion 126
denunciation 130
deposition 103
deprivation 126
detractors 112
Devil 16, 95; see also Satan
Dicey, A.V. vii
Digest (of Justinian) 9, 15, 31, 34, 37, 39, 44, 46, 54, 60, 76, 79, 94, 105, 106, 108, 115, 118, 119, 147, 167, 171
dignitas 123
Dionysius Exiguus 52
disciplina, discipline 58, 127
disciplinary beating 15
discipline, academic 52–60
discretion 144–6
dishonesty 128
dispensation 164–5
disputations, academic 62
diversa 100
diversitas 2
divine judgment 139
doctors 50
documents 91, 150, 151
Dorna, Bernardus 9, 62
duel 141

Eden, Garden of 171
Edward I 2
Eibert von Bremen 83
Emperor 43, 125, 160
Empire 20
enemies 112, 113
equality 90; equal treatment 86; equality before the law 85, 90; equality of arms 105, 118
equity 29, 32, 85–90, 112
equivocation 156
ethics 12

Eucharist 171
Euclid 76, 77
Eugenius III, pope 46
evidence 118
evidence, documentary 79–80
evidence, rules of 127
ex officio powers 130
exceptions 99
exclusion 26
excommunication 1, 26, 74, 97, 105, 126, 159, 170–1
exemplum 73, 101
existimatio 123
Extravagantes 58
eye-witnesses 134

fairness 20, 29, 63, 85–90, 134
faith 20
false witness 147
fama 113, 124
Fathers 3, 33, 56, 154,
fees 63
feudalism 7
Fleta 4, 37, 42
Florus of Lyons 56
foreknowledge, divine 168
forgiven sinner 18, 19, 168, 169
forgiveness, declaration of 169
formularies 71, 91
fornication 105
Fortescue, Sir John 50
fraud 88
free will 9
freedom 9
Fulbert of Chartres 153–4

Gaius 35, 76
Genesis 124
Germany 41
Gilbert of Poitiers 143
Gilles d'Orléans 36
Glossators 65
glosses 49
God 13, 14, 33, 62, 83, 86, 88, 95, 107, 109, 112 , 139, 142, 143, 144, 154 and passim; God, nature of 7, 8
Godfrey of Cologne 59
good 32; good character 118; goodness 8
Gospel 107, 126, 142, 148
gossip 128
Grace 34
Gratian vii, 3, 12, 13, 16, 17, 18, 33, 34, 38, 43, 44, 45, 56, 57, 58, 59,

79, 92, 94, 103, 107, 110, 111, 112, 115, 116, 117, 124, 126, 128, 132, 133, 134, 139, 141, 145, 166, 169, 170 and *passim*
greed 62
Greek 76
Gregory I, pope 34, 39, 103, 108, 147
Gregory VII, pope 56
Gregory IX, pope 19, 57, 58, 113, 117, 118, 127, 131, 133, 141, 142
Grosseteste, Robert 16.108
guilt 117, 140, 142, 157, 171

habit 34
harassment, salutary 26
Harclay, Henry 117
healing 174
Heaven, Kingdom of 108
Henry II of England 1
Henry III of England 117
Henry of Rheims 106
heresy 73, 88; heresy, academic 43; heretics 20, 64
Hermannus 34
hierarchies of norms 15
hierarchy 23, 87–90
higher degrees 1
Hildegard of Bingen 156
hitting back 145
Hobbes 110–11
Holy Spirit 149, 154, 21, 45, 62, 63; *see also* Paraclete
homicide 160
Honorius, Master 70
Hospitallers 74
Hostiensis 45, 52, 59, 85–6, 113
Hugh of Lincoln 114
Hugh of St Victor 168
Huguccio of Pisa 59
human laws 37, 39, 115

iconoclasm 20
images 20
incest 567
infamia 26, 73, 123–9, 173; *see also* defamation; notoriety
iniuria 123
injustice 11, 22, 159
innocence 34, 140
Innocent III, pope 113, 131, 135
Innocent IV, pope 109
Inns of Court 50, 65
Inquisition 131–4

Institutes 59
intentio 16, 62
interrogation 97, 130
intimidation 98
Investiture 56
Irnerius 43, 49, 59, 145
Isidore 13, 33, 35, 37, 40, 64, 123
Isidore, Ps. 52, 56, 99, 106, 107, 112, 115, 116, 162, 171
iudicia peregrina 141
iurisperitu 31, 67–8
ius 32, 33, 35, 41; *ius divinum* 32 34; *ius gentium* 36; *ius positivum* 37; *see also* law; nature; right
iustitia 9, 32, 33–5
Ivo of Chartres 3, 18, 29, 31, 102

James 49
Jerome 9, 15, 124, 147, 154, 156, 172, 173
Jews 20, 23, 112, 147
Johannes Andreae 93
Johannes de Lignano 135, 136
Johannes Fagelli de Pisis 134
Johannes Galensis 60
Johannes Teutonicus 60
John of Salisbury 33, 109, 111, 112, 118
John XXII, pope 58
Judas 157
judge 44, 66, 69, 83, 96, 102, 103, 108–15, 130, 134, 135, 152, 163; judge, divine 143
judgement 100, 108–15, 168
Judgement, Day of 17
judges-delegate 45, 113, 114
judicial power 168
judiciary 10
Julian of Eclanum 144, 158
jurisdiction 43, 99
justice 7, 8, 9, 10, 29, 35, 105
Justinian 20, 21, 31, 32, 34, 52, 54–5, 59, 84, 92, 103, 106, 115; *see also* Code; *Digest*; *Novellae*

keys, power of the 108, 168
Kilwardby, Robert 66
kings 1, 2

laity 44, 88, 113, 164
Lanfranc 56, 162
Laon 152, 154
Lateran Council II (1139) 16, 49, 159
Lateran Council, IV (1215) 60, 109, 115, 123, 125, 129, 132, 134, 140, 141

Latin 118, 152
Laurentius Hispanus 60
law, *leges* 2; law, breach of 171–2; law, divine 33–9, 115; law, human 33–9; law, civil 86; *see also* nature, law of
law-giver 11
law schools 49–51
legislative power 29; legislator 44; legislature 10
Lent 74
Lèse-majesté 88
letter-writing 71
lex 33, 41
libellus 94
Liber Extra 46, 58
licentia docendi 51
life, eternal 8
litigation 9, 26
litis contestatio 61, 69, 70, 91, 98, 100–2, 113, 136
liturgy vii
local interests 37
loci communes 75
logic 31, 147; logicians 86
Lombard law-books 55
Lord's Prayer 174
love 14, 34
Lucius III, pope 141
lying 149
Lyndwood, William 129

Mâcon, Council of 583
magistrates 171
Maitland, Frederick William vii
Manichees 20
manifesta 133
manorial courts 64
manorial rolls 64
Marius Victorinus 33
marriage 31, 72
Marsilius of Padua 39
Martin Gosia 49
Martin of Braga 34, 53
massa peccatrix 15, 171
maxims 76–8, 86, 151, 153, 155–6; *see also regulae*
mediation 163
medicine 3
mercy 8, 9, 18, 29, 34, 61–5, 158
miracle 141
monks 49, 164
Monophysites 20
mooting 69–75

moral theology 15
motivation 16
murder 11, 54
music 83
mutuality 25

natural justice 105–20
nature, law of 110; *lex naturalis* 32, 37, 144; natural law 33–4, 35, 36, 37, 38–9, 105–20; *see also ius*; law
nemo iudex 107–15; *see also* bias; conflict of interest
Nestorians 20
New Testament 21, 33, 54, 111, 124
Nicaea, Council of (325) 21, 105
Nicholas I, pope 117, 133
notoriety 113, 123–9, 132; *notorii* 133, 134; *see also* defamation; *infamia*
Novellae (of Justinian) 55, 106

oaths 94, 141, 142, 147, 165
observantia 12
Odofredus 60
offences 26, 128
officer of the court 66–7
officium 110
Old Law 17
Old Testament 18, 38, 53–4, 83, 153
omnicompetence 11
opinion 67, 153–5, 156, 158
opinions, legal 72
ordeal 140, 141
orderliness 40
Ordination 88
Ordines 92
Ordo iudicialis 92
Ordo iudiciorum 92
Origen 20
orthodoxy 20
Oxford 50, 74, 117, 167
Oxford, Council of 129
Oxford, University of 43

pagans 20
Pallium 45
panegyric 61
Paraclete 62; *see also* Holy Spirit
Paris 12, 36
partiality 113
parties 93, 116
parts 24
pastoral care 17, 83
Paucapalea 34, 102, 132

Paul, jurisconsult 67, 76
Paul, St. 13, 14, 147
Pavia 55
peace 21, 22
penalties, temporal for forgiven sin 172
penalty 3, 168
penance 16, 19, 86, 140, 167; private 171; public 11, 26, 171
penances 18
penitentials 18, 168; penitential codes 17; penitential process 25; penitential system 16, 17, 169
Pentecost 74
perjury 97, 123
perseverance 16
persistence 34
Peter, St 21, 160
Peter Damian 154
Peter Lombard 34, 56, 57
Peter of Blois 2, 3, 75
Peter of Celle 13
Peter the Chanter 101, 128, 141
Petrine Office 160
Philip the Chancellor 34
philosophy 29, 53
physician 3
pietas 11, 24
Pillius 74, 94
punishments 167–75
Placentinus 29, 34, 96, 100, 102, 105
Plato 34, 105
plurality of office 112–13
poetry 71
Pomponius 76
poor 62
pope 44, 160, 165 and *passim*
positive law 85
potestas 44, 89
precept 29
preceptive manuals 92
prevarication 126
priests 17, 139
private law 24
privileges, papal 45
probable arguments 79
procedural manuals 59, 162
procedure 91ff.; *see also* summary procedure
proctors 65
proof, proving 61, 76–9, 79, 80, 141, 147
proof, *semiplena* 135
proof, standard of 136
property 58
proportionality 18

proprietas 89
provincial bishops 118
proving
public law 23, 24
punishment 142; purposes of 172–5
purgation 140, 142, 171
purgatio canonica 139

quaestiones disputatae 71
questions 69
Quodlibets 69

Rainerius Perusinus 84
Ralph Niger 65
rank 86
rape 160, 172
Raymond of Peñafort 19
reason 86
reasonableness 151, 166
reconciliation 131, 166, 174
recusatio 113–15
redress 174
reform 173
Reformation 139
Regnum 1
regulae 76–80, 151; *see also* maxims
religio 12
reparation 172, 173
repentance 170
reportatio 58
reputation 123, 124, 173
res publica 22, 23, 25
retaliation 174
retribution 18r
review 161
Rheims 43
Rheims, Council of 143
rhetoric 61, 62, 70–1
Ricardus Anglicus 94, 146
right 32, 35; *see also ius*
righteousness 30, 35
rigour 18
rites 39–40, 41, 72
Robert of Melun 46
Roffredus 74
Roger of Worcester, bishop 46
Rogerius 96, 144
Roland, Master 132, 140, 110
Roman Empire 49
Roman law 31, 76, 106, 110, 123, 124, 145, 151 and *passim*
Roman people 32
Roman society 124, 124

Rome 20, 21, 22, 23, 24, 25, 61, 62, 64, 94, 160 and *passim*
royal household 43
Rufinus 57, 103, 132
rules 76
Rupert of Deutz 33, 156, 157

sacerdotium 1
saints 147
Salic law 123
Salimbene de Adam 156
salvation 19, 45, 167–75
Samaritans 20
sanctuary 20
Satan 7; *see also* Devil
satisfaction 171–2, 173; vicarious 171
scandalum 127; *see also* stumbling-block
scientia 101
scribes 96
Scripture 2, 25, 147 and *passim*; *see also* Bible
sedition 160
self-evidency 76–9
semiplena 157
Sens 43
sentence 44, 103, 152; sentencing 105, 152–8; *sentential iudicialis* 153, 155
serious crime 160; *see also* crime
sermons 71, 91
servant 14
settlement 162–3
severity 34
Shakespeare 113
signs 173
silence 150
simony 88, 163
sin 2, 11, 15, 16, 18, 33, 171–2
sin, mortal 13
sinners 110
sky-worshippers 20
slave 14
social exclusion 26
Sodom 124
Soissons 43
soul 23, 33
sources 53–60
species probationis 145
spiritual law 68
standard of proof 142
Statutes 72
Stephen of Tournai 1, 3, 4, 85, 143, 166
steward 64; stewardship 127

students, 'graduate' 49
stumbling-block 164, 171; *see also scandalum*
substance and accident 80
suffering 30
summary procedure 130–6; *see also* procedure
supernatural 7
Supreme Being
suspicion 128
swearing 39, 147; *see also* oaths
syllogisms 72, 147
syncretism 20
synod 42, 45, 139; diocesan 139

Tacitus 61
talio 17, 126, 166
Tancred 59, 93, 98
teaching office 88
testimony 141, 147, 150; *see also* witnesses
Tertullian 2, 63, 172
Tertullian Ps. 62
Theodore of Canterbury 174
Theodosian Code 102, 111, 124, 125
Theodosius 54
theological controversies 72
Thomas de Nevill 97
Thomas de Piperata 127, 142
Thomas of Chobham 86
thought-crime 143
Toledo, Sixteenth Council 139
tolerance 165
topics 61, 71–5
torture 141
Tours, Council of 567
trial by ordeal 131
Trinity 14, 168
truth 86, 133, 144
Turncoats 126
Tynemouth, John of 74

Ugo of the Ravenna Gate 49
Ulpian 64, 67, 76
ultra vires 75
unity 20, 21
universitas civium 39
universities 72
utilitas 22, 53, 54

Vacarius, Master 50, 55, 83
Valerius Maximus 162
validity 86

venalia 13
veritas 12
vernacular 118
vested interests 111, 149
vice 16
victim 172
Victricius of Rouen 152
villeinage 64
Vincent of Spain 60, 159
vindicatio 12
virtue 12, 24
voiding 102,
Vulgate 33, 107, 123, 124, 153, 156

weak 105
whole and parts 78

William Durantis 93, 113, 142
William I King of England 162
William of Conches 23
William of Drogheda 64, 65, 66, 67, 69, 70, 102, 113, 114
William of Pagula 3
witnesses 79, 83, 96, 98, 130, 147–50, 151, 156, 166; *see also* testimony
women 149
Worcester, bishop of 2
writ 94
Wulfstan of Worcester 164

Yvo of Chartres 56